Elementary School Administration

Paul J. Misner, *Superintendent*
Glencoe, Illinois, Public Schools

Frederick W. Schneider
San Jose State College

Lowell G. Keith
San Jose State College

CHARLES E. MERRILL BOOKS, INC., COLUMBUS, OHIO

Library of Congress Catalog Card Number: 63-11457

PRINTED IN THE UNITED STATES OF AMERICA

PREFACE

Social and technological changes, international crises, an upsurge in public interest in education have combined to point up the importance of forward-looking leadership on the part of the elementary school principal. He and his associates indeed have an important responsibility as they set about to administer a school in which the finest possible education may be offered to pupils in their community.

The authors of *Elementary School Administration,* while recognizing the importance of the role of the principal, hold the viewpoint that effective administration of the elementary school also involves teachers, children, parents, other administrators, and noncertificated personnel. The writers recognize, respect, and, on several occasions in this book, emphasize the roles of all concerned as they seek to provide children with an education adequate to meet the challenges of the mid-Twentieth Century.

The authors also subscribe to the idea that a better school program results when educational administration theory and practice are brought close together. Therefore, they have expressed, or implied, an administrative philosophy, but, even more, have stressed a practical application of that philosophy by describing a number of the most promising practices currently underway in various elementary schools throughout the United States. It is hoped that present leaders of elementary schools, as well as those preparing for the principalship, may find help as they ponder programs which are, or have recently been, successful in actual school situations, and that they may adopt and adapt from these descriptions in order to improve administration and instructional programs in their own schools.

Finally, the authors believe that the only defensible reason for administration's very existence is that it contributes significantly to the teaching-learning situation. It is for this reason that the emphasis in this volume is on the principal's contributions to the teacher-learner relationship. The combined efforts of all may result in the most effective elementary school education possible for America's boys and girls.

This volume is organized into six major sections. Following Chapter One, which presents an introduction to, and overview of, the work to follow, Chapter Two and Three encompasses chapters on the evolving training programs for elementary administrators and teachers, and the rationale behind them. Administration's responsibilities toward, and descriptions of, some of the fine instructional programs in elementary schools in various areas of the nation are included in the five chapters which make up the third section. Chapters Nine and Ten deal with Special Education in the elementary schools, and include descriptions of effective programs and the administrator's role in them. The next section, including Chapters Eleven, Twelve, and Thirteen, describes programs and points up administration's part in pupil personnel services in elementary schools. The last section encompasses three chapters on an evolving and important aspect of elementary school administration, that of personnel administration, in addition to the final chapter which projects into the future of the elementary school and its leadership.

Following those chapters in which descriptions of programs are presented are included short case problems. The purpose of including these cases is to provide life-like situations related to the chapter topics so that college students or school practitioners may utilize problem-solving techniques in meeting administrative situations.

Some aspects of elementary school administration, such as the important area of public relations, have been treated as integral parts of the chapters which are included herein.

June, 1963
Glencoe, Illinois
San Jose, California

Paul J. Misner
Frederick W. Schneider
Lowell G. Keith

Contents

Chapter One

The People Look at Their Schools

In November, 1955, more than two thousand citizens representing fifty-three states and territories assembled in Washington, D.C. to participate in a White House Conference on Education. The conference had been called by President Eisenhower and was supported, in part, by funds appropriated by Congress. Prior to the convening of the national conference thousands of citizens throughout the nation had participated in local, regional, and state conferences where they made thoughtful appraisals of existing educational programs and formulated far-reaching proposals aimed at their improvement. Subsequently, the 2000 citizen representatives who participated in the Conference considered these recommendations and, following the national meeting, consolidated and included them in a report to the President.[1]

Never before in the history of public education had the system been so extensively appraised by so many lay citizens. The recommendations touched every phase of public school operation from kindergarten through the twelfth grade. The report refrained from carping criticism. It was written in a positive and affirmative spirit, and expressed appreciation for the many contributions that public schools

[1] *The Committee for The White House Conference on Education,* Bulletin of Superintendent of Documents, U.S. Government Printing Office, Washington 25, D.C., April, 1956.

had made to the national welfare in the past. It placed responsibility for current educational deficiencies mainly upon widespread apathy and indifference. Most important, the report recognized that in this technical age, the nation's schools are confronted with new opportunities and heightened responsibility, requiring significant improvement in the total educational establishment. The constructive and far-reaching nature of the White House Conference report is reflected in the following excerpts selected from the report itself:

> Nowadays equality of opportunity for adults means little without equality of educational opportunity for children. Ignorance is a greater obstacle to success of most kinds. The schools have become a major tool for creating a nation without rigid class barriers. It is primarily the schools which allow no man's failure to prevent the success of his son.
>
> The order given by the American people to the schools is grand in its simplicity: in addition to intellectual development, foster morality, happiness, and any useful ability. The talent of each child is to be sought out and developed to the fullest. Each weakness is to be studied and, so far as possible, corrected. This is truly a majestic ideal, and an astonishingly new one. Schools of that kind have never been provided for more than a small fraction of mankind.[2]

It is possible that the recommendations of the White House Conference for the improvement of education would have eventually received the approval of the nation's citizens. The population explosion with the attendant increase in school enrollments obviously placed new demands upon the schools. The continuing shortage of qualified teachers was becoming an increasingly critical problem for every community throughout the nation. Rapid technological change clearly required skills and competencies that had never before been required of the country's future citizens. When the Russians launched their first sputnik in the autumn of 1957 the recommendations of the White House Conference on Education assumed new and vastly increased meaning and significance. For a time, at least, the response to the Russian achievement assumed almost hysterical proportions. Any citizen who had access to the press, radio, television, or public platform hastened to present his pet proposal designed to cure all of public education's ills. Proposals were made to abandon compulsory education. A few distinguished individuals urged that we give up our efforts to educate all of the children of all of the people and focus our efforts upon an educational "elite." The evident need for the preparation of a larger number of scientists and engineers brought forth

---

[2] *Ibid.*, p. 9.

proposals that the arts and humanities be relegated to a place of secondary importance in the curriculum in favor of an increased emphasis upon mathematics and science.

As might have been expected, the hysterical response to Sputnik I soon subsided and thoughtful citizens and educators addressed themselves to the arduous task of designing educational programs and practices appropriate for a world in which cataclysmic change is the overriding reality. The publication of *The Pursuit of Excellence* by the Rockefeller Brothers Foundation in 1958[3] is representative of the efforts now being made to fashion a program of public education in the United States appropriate to the needs and aspirations of a people who are determined to remain free in a world threatened by slavery. The Rockefeller report, prepared by distinguished national leaders from various walks of life, makes its position abundantly clear on several major issues. The following excerpts from the report are illustrative:

> We do not wish to absolve our educators of the mistakes they have made. At the same time, we should not attempt to absolve ourselves. The fateful question is not whether we have done well, or whether we are doing better than we have done in the past, but whether we are meeting the stern demands and unparalleled opportunities of the times. And the answer is that we are not.[4]

> From time to time one still hears arguments over quantity versus quality education. Behind such arguments is the assumption that a society can choose to educate a few people exceedingly well or to educate a great number of people somewhat less well, but that it cannot do both. But a modern society such as ours cannot choose to do one or the other. It has no choice but to do both. Our kind of society calls for the maximum development of individual potentialities at all levels.[5]

It is against this background of public interest in and concern for education that *Elementary School Administration* was written and prepared for publication. In the preparation of the book the authors have made several basic assumptions. They are convinced that public interest in improved education will be maintained, and that changing world conditions will require continuous evaluation and improvement of educational programs and practices. It is for this reason that the book is oriented to the future rather than to the past. It is addressed to those readers who believe that education is a dynamic process and

---

[3] Rockefeller Brothers Foundation, *The Pursuit of Excellence* (Garden City, New York: Doubleday and Co., Inc., 1958).

[4] *Ibid.*, pp. 21–22.

[5] *Ibid.*, p. 22.

must always remain flexible enough to meet changing needs and conditions. Attention is called to promising innovations that are being introduced into the programs of many school systems throughout the country.

Chapter IV describes innovations in several school systems designed to improve conventional practices of grouping and promoting students. Illustrations of pioneering efforts to utilize educational television as a means of enriching classroom instruction are described. Team-teaching experiments in two school systems are included as suggested ways in which the competencies of teachers may be more effectively utilized. The possibilities of teaching machines and programmed instruction as a means of providing more effectively for individualized teaching and learning are given consideration.

In including extended descriptions of innovating practices, the authors have refrained from placing the Good Housekeeping stamp of approval on any of them. They are convinced that there is some merit in all of them. Perceptive and imaginative teachers and administrators will, from their investigation and study of these newer practices, be able to discover techniques and ideas that can be effectively utilized and adapted for the improvement of practices in their own schools.

During the decade of the fifties it was inevitable that the teaching profession should become the target of sharp and, at times, somewhat devastating criticism by prominent leaders of public opinion. In general, this public criticism produced salutary results. It focused attention upon the very great importance that the people attach to their public schools. It identified deficiencies for which the public and the profession were equally responsible. It stimulated constructive and far-reaching efforts on the part of the teaching profession to improve itself. The Cooperative Program in Educational Administration, initiated in 1950 with substantial financial support from the Kellogg Foundation, has resulted in significant improvements in the pre-service and in-service education of superintendents of schools. The nationwide efforts being made by general school administrators to improve the quality of educational leadership in the United States has been accompanied by similar efforts on the part of the Department of Elementary School Principals, the Department of Secondary School Principals, and the Association for Supervision and Curriculum Development. Recently a national committee composed of representatives of the foregoing organizations and the American Association of School Administrators was appointed for the purpose of co-ordinating the several programs and facilitating the effective cooperation of all groups in the improvement of school administration. The need for improvement in the preparation of classroom teachers is reflected in the action taken recently by the National Education Association recommending that a minimum of four years' preparation be required of all classroom teachers as the basis for professional certification.

In Chapters II and III, extended descriptions are included of programs newly designed to improve the quality of educational leadership and classroom teaching. They suggest clearly that teachers and administrators are fully aware of the increased responsibilities they must assume in these critical times, and that they are engaged in serious efforts to qualify themselves for these responsibilities.

Throughout the book the strategic role of the elementary school principal is stressed. The elementary school principal occupies one of the most important positions of educational leadership in the entire hierarchy of school administration. He is responsible for the education of young people during the most important period of their educational career. His elementary school district is a neighborhood, and provides him with unusual opportunities for the exercise of leadership in achieving effective school-community relations. Changing concepts of this role emphasize the responsibility of the principal to exercise instructional leadership rather than to remain cast only in the role of an administrative and managerial official. Current developments suggest clearly that the elementary principalship of the future will become a satisfying and rewarding career rather than a stepping stone to what in the past has been considered an administrative position of higher prestige.

In recent years leaders in school administration have made conscious and highly successful efforts to achieve a greater measure of democracy in the organization and operation of the schools. Provisions have been made for the active and responsible participation of teachers in the continuous evaluation and improvement of curricula and in the planning of policies and practices with which they are directly concerned. Increasingly, the efforts to practice democracy in school administration have been extended to include parents, other lay citizens, and students themselves. The central purpose of public education is the preparation of young people for the responsibilities of democratic citizenship. It is inconceivable that effective education for democratic citizenship can be achieved in an institution organized and administered on an autocratic and authoritarian basis.

The extent to which democracy is achieved in the day-by-day operations of the elementary school will depend greatly upon the leadership skill of the principal in the significant and highly sensitive area of human relations. Classroom teachers will respond to leadership if it is exercised in a spirit of mutual respect and confidence. They will accept the decisions that must inevitably be made if they have been permitted to participate in the decision-making process. They will engage enthusiastically in self-improvement activities if they are given reasonable freedom to participate in experimental programs that depart somewhat from the time-honored and conventional ways of doing things. Teachers who experience a sense of security and satisfaction in their work will accept readily the assistance and suggestions of specialists, supervisors, and administrators as they relate to enhancing the teachers' effectiveness.

It is evident that the evaluation and revision of school curricula will need increased attention in the future. The space age is characterized by dramatic explosions of new knowledge and an urgent need for greater skill and competency on the part of young people. Alert and responsible teachers and administrators will seek to meet the need for continuous curriculum improvement. A significant responsibility of the elementary school principal will be to lead the planning of in-service programs in which the entire school personnel can cooperate in curriculum revision and improvement.

The maintenance of a high level of morale among members of a school faculty will depend greatly upon the extent to which provisions have been made for effective communication. The principal who seeks to exercise democratic leadership will recognize a need to provide means for all school personnel to communicate readily with each other as an aid to the achievement of their common goals and purposes.

The achievement of desirable morale depends to a very great extent upon the consideration given to the personal welfare of people. The principal of an elementary school has a responsibility to actively seek appropriate salaries for his school personnel. He should be active in his advocacy and support of system-wide plans that seek to provide insurance protection, sick leave provisions, sabbaticals, and other fringe benefits for his associates. It is quite evident that no teacher, however dedicated he may be, can contribute his best efforts to teaching if he is continuously haunted by the fear of economic insecurity.

In Chapters VIII, XIV, and XVI are descriptions of practices which represent promising developments in democratic leadership and the improvement of human relations in the nation's schools.

The responsibility of the schools to identify the talents of every student and develop them to the fullest will require the most skillful planning of learning situations and the highest possible level of imaginative, creative teaching. The students who enroll in an elementary school present a wide range of abilities, interests, and experience. They live in a dangerous, rapidly changing and, to them, an exciting and adventurous world. They have ready access to radio, television, and science fiction. They are acutely aware of the continuing threat of atomic warfare and the disaster that would ensue from such a catastrophe. These young people will respond with little or no enthusiasm to a learning environment that is restricted solely to the acquisition of knowledges and skills, that, for them, have little relevance to the world in which they live.

The authors of *Elementary School Administration* contend that there is urgent need for more effective motivation of students at all educational levels. Countless students fail to develop their full potentialities in the nation's classrooms, and many of them leave school prematurely simply because they are uninterested and bored. In recent years new knowledge has come to light concerning the methods and techniques of motivation. Mass media of communication, business, and industry are making effective use of the improved methods of motivation. Certainly, schools have even greater need and responsibility to do the same. In Chapter V the subject of motivation is considered at some length, and in Chapter VI practices designed to provide meaningful and purposeful learning experiences for students are described.

The publication of the Rockefeller Brothers report stimulated widespread use of the concept of excellence as a condition of education much to be desired. From public platforms, television, radio, newspapers, and in both popular and professional publications, writers and speakers invariably expressed their commitment to the pursuit of excellence in education. A critical analysis of the many statements being made soon revealed that the term excellence was being used rather loosely and without precise definition. It appeared to mean different things to different people. To some observers it suggested that the quantity of work required of students be increased. They advocated a "get-tough" policy and contended that a greater expenditure of time and effort on the part of students would achieve a greater degree of excellence. To others excellence in education demanded a radical revision of the content of curriculum programs in which much greater emphasis would be given in the schools to the teaching of mathematics, science, and foreign languages. Some proponents of excellence insisted that the schools restrict their efforts almost exclusively to the intellectual development of students and delegate responsibility for character and citizenship development to the home and church.

Every effort should be made in the schools to improve the quality of student learning and achievement. Excellence, however, is a concept with many dimensions and implications. Excellence is not achieved simply by requiring more time and effort on the part of students. Quantity of work may be confused with quality. Unless the increased amount of work expected of students is accompanied by the development of the students' abilities to do independent, critical, and creative thinking, the results may be no more than mere memorization and verbalization. Under these conditions quality is being sacrificed for quantity.

What students are expected to learn is important. At a time when areas of knowledge have become so vast and so complicated it is the responsibility of the schools to determine and attach priority to those fields of knowledge that are of greatest significance both to students and to society. Recognizing that some fields of knowledge are of greater importance than others does not imply that all students should be expected to acquire the same knowledge without any consideration to individual interests, aptitudes, and abilities. To expect a student whose interests and aptitudes clearly suggest a successful career in the creative arts to acquire mastery of the same scientific subjects required of a potential research chemist is totally indefensible. Excellence in education can be achieved only to the extent that it is sought with reference to the individual student. What may be excellent achievement for one individual may be mediocre or dissipated achievement for another.

In recent years considerable progress has been made in the elementary schools in providing programs that are geared to the wide range of differences that exist among students. Research clearly indicates that individual students differ significantly in their readiness for learning, in the rate at which they learn, and in their potential capacity for achievement. Excellence in education will ultimately be determined by the extent to which schools succeed in providing learning experiences that result in the fullest possible development of every student.

Although significant beginnings have been made in many elementary schools throughout the country to provide more effectively for the individual needs of students, much more remains to be done. The growth and development of students is a complicated process which involves many and varied considerations. Innate intellectual endowment is one, but only one, factor to be considered in the growth of an individual student. Physical and mental health are important factors contributing to successful school achievement. The extent to which an individual is developing normally toward social and emotional maturity should be of concern to those responsible for his education.

It is evident that schools which seek to provide learning experiences geared most effectively to the needs, interests, and abilities of individual students need to give greater attention to guidance and evaluation activities than they have in the past. In Chapters VII, XI, and XII promising developments in the fields of guidance and evaluation are described. These fields of activity represent one of the greatest current challenges to elementary school leadership.

As efforts have been made in the schools to identify and to develop to the fullest possible extent the needs, interests, and abilities of each individual student, those individuals who present unusual or special needs and problems have, inevitably, needed extra consideration. The students included in this category range from highly gifted individuals to those students who are mentally, physically, and emotionally handicapped. Research and experience indicate quite clearly that the so-called average student is a myth and does not exist in reality. Schools enroll and are responsible for individuals who possess varied strengths, weaknesses, and abilities.

It is in the respect attached to the intrinsic worth and dignity of human personality that schools in a democracy differ most sharply and significantly from schools in a totalitarian society. Real effort is being made in schools throughout the nation to provide an appropriate education for all students irrespective of their native intellectual or physical endowments. The problem of providing an effective and appropriate education for students who present unusual or exceptional needs is admittedly difficult and complicated. As yet there is no essential agreement concerning how the schools should deal with gifted students. Some responsible observers contend that gifted students should be separated from their peers and be enrolled in special classes. Others look with disfavor upon such a procedure, insisting that it is an undemocratic and educationally unsound approach to the problem. A similar lack of agreement obtains with respect to the treatment of intellectually, physically, and emotionally handicapped students. Some individuals insist that these students should be segregated almost completely from their peers. Others are equally insistent that every possible effort should be made to provide many opportunities whereby these students participate with their peers in the regularly scheduled activities of the school system.

The problem of making appropriate provisions for exceptional students is further complicated by the necessity of determining the qualifications and competencies of teachers who can deal most effectively with them. With a continuing shortage of highly qualified teachers for all teaching assignments, the problem of identifying and recruiting teachers for exceptional children will require increased attention in the future.

In spite of the obvious problems involved, significant beginnings have been made throughout the country in meeting the needs of exceptional students. Descriptions of these developing programs are included in Chapters IX and X. They should be helpful to elementary school administrators concerned with this increasingly important administrative responsibility.

In the preparation of *Elementary School Administration,* the authors have stressed the dynamic nature of education and the responsibility of educational leadership for seeking the continuous improvement of educational programs and practices. They are firmly convinced that far-reaching changes will need to be made in the administration and operation of elementary schools as changing social needs and conditions impose new and increased educational responsibilities.

Effective change can be achieved only within the framework of clearly defined purposes and policies. The operation of an elementary school requires the most skillful planning of many routine operational procedures if conditions conducive to creative learning and teaching are to be achieved.

Modern elementary schools provide a variety of services that are essential to the welfare and well-being of students and teachers. Transportation must be provided for those students who are required to travel long distances to school. Food services must be provided for students who must remain in school during the entire day. The increasing importance being attached to health education demands that the schools provide a variety of services designed to promote healthful living.

In recent years increased importance has been given to the role of the library as an integral part of the total instructional program of the elementary school. One of the major responsibilities of the elementary school principal is to recognize the need of these many services and to organize and administer them with the greatest possible efficiency.

The elementary principal has a strong responsibility for the exercise of democratic leadership as it relates to the activities of his professional staff. Effective communication and the building of morale are essential conditions for such leadership. A high level of cooperative effort can be achieved among students, teachers, and administrators only to the extent that the responsibilities and relationships of all personnel have been clearly defined and translated into policy statements. Such policies should be cooperatively developed and made available to all concerned in well-edited written form. In Chapters XIII and XV promising practices that deal with the many details of school organization and operation are described.

In the preparation of this book the authors have sought to combine a defensible theory of school administration with an identification and description of emerging practices that seek to improve the quality of elementary school education. Throughout the book attention has been called to the results of research studies that should be considered in the continuing efforts that are made to improve educational programs and practices.

It is the hope of the authors that *Elementary School Administration* will stimulate widespread efforts that will result in better educational practices in the future than any yet conceived.

Chapter Two

Training Programs for Elementary Administrators

Elementary school administration is coming of age. Since the second decade of the twentieth century, elementary administration has been coming into its own from the standpoints of effectiveness, prestige, and remuneration. No longer in modern elementary schools is the principal simply the "head teacher" who is granted a little released time from his teaching duties to handle some of the administrative details involved in the successful operation of an attendance unit. He has become an educational statesman in his community, charged with responsibility for the improvement of instruction for the boys and girls in his school.

The changing and improved status of elementary school administrators has been accompanied by new requirements made by both state legislatures and colleges which train elementary administrators. State statutes have set forth more demanding licensing requisites, and the colleges and universities have become even more stringent in their requirements of candidates preparing for administrative credentials and positions. Today's programs of preparation for elementary school administration licenses include not only professional courses in educational administration and supervision, but also stress such disciplines as human growth and development, anthropology, psychology, sociology, oral and written English, and others. Modern administrators must not only know how to cope with problems in their attendance units, but also must be aware of, and know how to handle, problems of the society of which the school is a part. Pressures of an increasingly complex culture demand that persons in administrative and supervisory positions in today's elementary school be well prepared by wide study in many areas.

Elementary administration has gone and is going through what all professions must experience in order to reach maturity. A profession must encounter and satisfy certain developmental tasks as it progresses toward maturity, that maturity being marked by the assumption of responsibility for behavior and acceptance of the consequences of such behavior.

NEEDED: A FLEXNER REPORT IN EDUCATION

On September 21, 1959, Abraham Flexner died at the age of 92 years. His passing went relatively unnoticed by the general public, but medical educators, members of the Congress on Medical Education and Licensure, paid high tribute to the former elementary school teacher who, fifty years before his death, had conducted a two-year study of American medical schools financed by the Carnegie Foundation. Dr. Flexner's report, published in 1910, was largely responsible for the high-calibre training which medical doctors now receive and for the high professional status of the medical fraternity.

Flexner's report, known as *Bulletin Number Four,* described the shockingly bad situation that existed in medical schools at the turn of the century. The bulletin flatly asserted that many of the medical schools of the time enrolled scarcely literate boys and permitted them to graduate and practice medicine without adequate scientific training. Henry Pritchett, president of the Carnegie Foundation when Flexner's report was published, made the following statement in the report's introduction:

> The development which is here suggested for medical education is conditioned largely upon three factors: (1) the creation of a public which shall discriminate between the ill-trained and the rightly trained physician, and which will also insist upon the enactment of such laws as will require all practitioners of medicine . . . to ground themselves in the fundamentals upon which medical science rests; (2) upon the universities and their attitudes toward medical education standards and support; and (3) upon the attitude of the mem-

> bers of the medical profession toward standards of their own practice and upon their sense of honor with respect to their own profession.[1]

As a result of Flexner's work, based on his study of 155 medical colleges in this country, the medical profession took concerted action, and shortly thereafter the standards of preparation and performance required of physicians and surgeons were elevated to a point above those of other existing professions. A very real and ethical profession has passed through the stages of childhood and adolescence and is now enjoying the fruits of maturity.

Since administration is a part of the larger profession of teaching, it cannot be discussed as a separate entity; if the teaching profession needs to mature into responsible behavior, so does that part of the whole called elementary administration. The public must understand that this profession can provide for the proper education of all the children of all the people; that teachers can control entrance into the profession and see to it that those who do join the ranks will become well educated and will perform with excellence; and that educators have the ability to accept and carry out the responsibility which the public entrusts to them. Fagan, after his analysis of Flexner's *Bulletin Number Four,* stated:

> . . . at least five steps would seem advisable to bring teaching to a higher level of professionalization . . .
>
> 1. In-service training for unqualified personnel.
> 2. Drafting and implementing a Professional Practices Act.
> 3. Using the probationary period to eliminate unqualified teachers.
> 4. Evaluating the professional courses of teacher training institutions.
> 5. Increasing the number of males in the profession.[2]

Flexner's report insisted that the entire curriculum of medical schools be revised and that students who wished to enter such schools meet a drastic upgrading of admission and retention requirements. Is it less important that teacher education pre-service and in-service programs be evaluated, with special attention to selection and retention of students who wish to become teachers? A concept of what the profession of medicine ought to be and of what the public should expect of the medical profession has been determined. It is no less necessary that educators make the major decisions regarding their profession, set standards by which teaching practitioners enter the

---

[1] Henry Pritchett, "Introduction," to Abraham Flexner, *Medical Education in the United States* (New York: The Carnegie Foundation for the Advancement of Teaching, 1910), p. 13.

[2] E. R. Fagan, "Blueprinting a Profession," *American School Board Journal,* CXXXVII (July, 1958), pp. 9–12.

profession and receive their licenses, and set and enforce criteria which are to be met by teacher training institutions.

Perhaps education could well use a "Flexner report" to focus on the ingredients that make for professional status. In educational administration, the sponsorship by the Kellogg Foundation of the "Cooperative Project on the Superintendency of Schools" was "heralded to be potentially as important to school administration as the Flexner studies of earlier days had been to medicine."[3] Perhaps the Kellogg project is the first step in a needed program to upgrade the entire profession of education.

HUMAN RELATIONS AND SCHOOL ADMINISTRATION

Inherent in school administration's quest for professional status is the question of its appertenance to the area of human relations. The relationship is clearly revealed in the United States Supreme Court's definition of a profession: "A vocation involving relations to the affairs of others of such a nature as to require for its proper conduct an equipment of learning or skill, or both, and to warrant the community in making restrictions in respect to its exercise."[4]

A school administrator has contact with the public in many ways. He works with many people individually and in informal and formal groups, both within and without the school system. The elementary administrator, in his work with his staff, the school board, and with community organizations, needs to understand how and why people behave so that he may be in a better position to predict and, perhaps, control their behavior. Human relations top the list of problems reported by practicing administrators; a study made among administrators in the New England states revealed that the two major problem areas encountered were, first, personnel relations (90 per cent experienced critical occurrences here) and second, public relations (54 per cent).[5]

The elementary school principal has a special responsibility for the promotion of good interpersonal relations among members of his staff if the goals of the institution are to be reached. According to Thelen:

---

[3] *Professional Administrators for America's Schools,* 38th Yearbook of the American Association of School Administrators (Washington, D.C.: American Association of School Administrators, 1960), p. 5.

[4] John T. Wahlquist et al., *The Administration of Public Education* (New York: The Ronald Press Co., 1952), p. 559.

[5] H. B. Jestin, as reported in Hollis A. Moore, Jr., *Studies in School Administration* (Washington, D.C.: American Association of School Administrators, 1957), p. 35.

> Human relations problems in organizations are likely to be posed by the "top" people. The coldness of a department head, for example, presents the rest of the department with anxieties and inhibitions in the friendship relations. A dogmatic boss sets the stage for undercover revolt and a desire to out-maneuver him by his men. A hesitant or reluctant administrator engenders in workers much anxious conflict over their own roles in the organization. These phenomena are reactions by subordinates to the way their superiors relate to them. The existence of bad feelings within the superior is in itself evidence that he has false expectations about the relationship. False expectations by the top level present subordinates with a prediction of failure, and this strains the relationship further. The existence of false or inappropriate expectations indicates that false prophets have been used —i.e., wrong, inadequate, or inappropriate authority.
>
> The existence of confused expectations, in which nobody knows what to expect from himself or anybody else, is an even more serious problem, for it indicates a confusion of the relationships between power and authority. And without clarity in these matters there is no machinery for dealing with any other problem.[6]

The quality of staff relationships depends a great deal upon the administrator; his actions often speak louder than his words. The manner in which the administrator relates to others will demonstrate whether or not he has a sincere belief in the worth of the individual. The emphasis upon human relations in elementary school administration is a part of the new shift in concepts of administration in general. One of the greatest services the elementary school principal can offer is the encouragement of his staff members to be, spontaneously, *themselves,* so that relationships which are mutually satisfying and productive may be developed between the individual members. It is becoming more and more apparent that effective elementary school principals are those who show a sustaining interest in the creative work of their staff members, and who extend sincere appreciation for their contributions.

CURRENT PROGRAMS OF SELECTION AND TRAINING

With the current stress upon the human relations aspect of the principalship, a corresponding change in emphasis in the education of administrators has been from job-related knowledge to job-related behavior. In programs of selection and training, the effectiveness of

[6] Herbert A. Thelen, *Dynamics of Groups at Work* (Chicago: University of Chicago Press, 1954), p. 101. Copyright 1954 by the University of Chicago.

the candidates' social relationships is being emphasized. The elementary administrator of today must know how to relate his school's objectives to all of society.

While educators currently are greatly concerned with finding suitable selection criteria for future administrators, a relatively small amount of research in this area has been reported. Swenson conducted an interdisciplinary library study of criteria, methods and measures used for selecting prospective leaders in the armed forces, industry, government, and education and surveyed 127 school districts in the United States recommended by their chief state school officers as having noteworthy prospective principal selection programs.[7] Among his findings were these methods recommended by respondent school districts for the selection of prospective principals: (1) establishing an objective written testing program; (2) checking candidate's performance and training record; (3) identifying prospects early in their teaching career; (4) publicizing methods of selection; and (5) recruiting widely.

It is, of course, important that potential principals be identified and selected as early as possible. While self-identification has, to date, been the major locator of potential administrative talent, it is recognized that a planned program of identification and selection in which many persons are involved is a better technique.

Educational groups have for years been concerned with the problem of selection and training of potential leaders in administration. They have recognized that some type of program is needed which will better provide careful screening of possible school administrators and on-the-job training in which the successful candidates, just prior to the end of their formal education, are given the opportunity to put their theories into practice in as nearly actual situations as possible.

Currently, in many institutions preparing elementary school principals, aptitude tests such as the *Miller Analogies* and the *Graduate Record Examination* are used in selecting and screening persons who aspire to administrative positions. These institutions also recognize the importance of assessing the personality of trainees; and are using various standardized tests, interviews, observations, and field recommendations to this end. To date, no single type of personality seems to be closely linked to success or failure in educational administration, nor has any objective procedure been identified as valid or reliable in assessing the personality of trainees for selection purposes.

The few existing programs of selection of school administrators

---

[7] Leonard E. Swenson, "Selection of Prospective Elementary School Principals" (Abstract of Doctoral dissertation, University of Southern California, 1958), duplicated, p. 3.

include essentially the same factors found by Featherstone[8] in the state of Ohio, including: requirements pertaining to amount of prior teaching experience, recommendations from principal or supervisor, an examination of college credentials, some type of oral examination or interview, written examinations (in a few school systems), requirements relating to type of prior teaching experience, and final selection by the superintendent who recommends the candidates to the board of education.

Featherstone concluded that,

> The majority of the candidates for principalships in Ohio cities are selected on the subjective judgment of the superintendent, without consideration of the opinions of other professional persons . . . Actually, the majority of Ohio city superintendents seemed to consider the selection of candidates as a task which was expected of them.[9]

Featherstone did find, however, that the practice of using advisory committees, including assistant superintendents and other members of the administrative staff, was increasing.

In a research project by the Southern States Cooperative Program of Educational Administration at the University of Tennessee, a Rating Guide was constructed which proved to be a reliable instrument in recording characteristics of prospective educational administrators. It covered these categories: interpersonal relations, intelligent personal involvement in selection, condition of health (physical and emotional), ethical and moral strength, adequacy of communication, and operation as a citizen.[10] As a result of their study, the SSCPEA arrived at the following implications for a selection program:

> . . . First, we need to be keenly aware of the characteristics that people exhibit in defining and solving problems and in helping others to do the same. Second, we have come to believe that no professor or group of professors can determine adequately selection in any specific instances without the participation of the student under consideration. The student must be involved intelligently in his own selection. A part of the decision with regard to entrance in the program must be his. Unless this principle is followed, there is not an immediate involvement of the student in the process of understanding himself in relation to the job for which he intends to prepare. Third, we consider that selection is the beginning of the guidance process which must extend throughout the entire preparation period

---

[8] Richard L. Featherstone, "The Selection of Elementary-School Principals in Ohio Cities," *Educational Research Bulletin,* XXXIV (September, 1955), pp. 155–157.

[9] *Ibid.*

[10] Orin B. Graff and Ralph B. Kimbrough, "What We Have Learned About Selection," *Phi Delta Kappan,* XXXVII (April, 1956), pp. 294–296.

of the student, both pre-service and in-service. It is almost impossible to detect the dividing line between selection and guidance.[11]

Even though the preparatory institutions still have the greatest amount of information necessary for selection, there is a trend toward more and more participation on the part of the individual school districts in this activity. The school district is the final proving ground of all the selection techniques that have been employed previously.

PRE-SERVICE PROGRAMS FOR SELECTION AND TRAINING OF ELEMENTARY ADMINISTRATORS

Since the profession depends upon preparatory institutions to select and train elementary school administrators, what responsibilities should these universities and colleges assume in improving programs of selection and education? Nolte proposes the following:

> (1) Development of a state-wide plan of action for recruiting outstanding candidates to enter preparatory programs in school administration; (2) provision for a consultative staff to assist the other state-level organizations and agencies in the improvement of selection programs; (3) maintenance of a list of promising candidates for schools administration; (4) direction of research pertaining to best practices in selection; (5) development of evaluative instruments for better selection of persons to be admitted; (6) development of standards for persons entering preparatory programs; and (7) final determination of a candidate's acceptability for entry into the preparatory program.[12]

As seen by Nolte, these institutions have an additional responsibility to:

> provide consultative staff to assist the other state-level organizations and agencies in improving preparatory programs; develop standards for improving preparatory programs in school administration; and encourage experienced candidates to enter preparatory programs. The colleges should also provide scholarships for outstanding candidates in school administration; seek scholarships and grants from business and foundations; conduct research concerning best practices in preparation; conduct research concerning best practices in placement and follow-up. Preparatory institutions might do well to provide preparatory programs for school administrators which evolve

---

[11] *Ibid.*

[12] M. Chester Nolte, *Selection, Preparation, and In-Service Development of School Superintendents* (Unpublished Doctoral dissertation, University of Denver, 1958).

out of the needs of the position; provide preparatory programs for research specialists and instructors in educational administration as well as for practitioners; provide preparatory programs based on the needs of each individual; require a block of time equal to at least one year of uninterrupted study beyond the M.A. degree for school administrators; provide complete personnel services for graduate students in school administration; provide actual field experiences, such as internships, school surveys, and field studies in the preparatory program; provide periodic evaluation of each student's progress in the preparatory program; provide experimental laboratories and design displays for students; provide sufficient staff to supervise interns in the field; employ practicing administrators as instructors in educational administration; provide teaching staff members in the ratio of one staff member to each ten students in the preparatory program; and provide research opportunities as a cooperative venture involving both students and professors.[13]

THE TENOR OF CURRENT COLLEGE COURSES

The elementary school principalship calls for competence in professional and liberal education. Training programs in schools of education in the past have emphasized the managerial aspects of elementary school administration and have omitted the behavioral aspects of the position. Chandler and McSwain maintain that:

> . . . The typical preparation program in school administration still includes numerous courses which deal with the mechanics of school administration. It is a reasonable assumption that too many potential school administrators are well trained in the managerial facets of the job, most of which an efficient school executive does not do anyway; and too few administrators possess competencies which can be acquired only through graduate study in the historical, philosophical, sociological, and psychological foundations of education.[14]

There are a few indications that preparation programs for administrators are moving toward a balanced curriculum of courses in professional and liberal education, with an emphasis upon human relations. Such indications are evident in the core courses at Teachers College, Columbia University, the Career Program at Harvard, the Foundations in Educational Administration at the University of Texas, the interdepartmental seminars at Ohio State University, and the new administration program at Northwestern University.

---

[13] *Ibid.*, pp. 4–5.

[14] B. J. Chandler and E. T. McSwain, "Professional Programs for School Administrators," *Phi Delta Kappan*, XLI (November, 1959), p. 61.

Training in effective human relations was the objective of the Human Relations Training Seminars at Teachers College where learnings in psychology and sociology were drawn upon to assist students in developing skills in cooperative, democratic processes. Long-term changes in the training program for administrators at Teachers College resulted from the experimental courses which were conducted for several years in the early 1950s. In the Teachers College experiment,

> . . . Training methods included practice, through rotation, of the roles of leader, recorder, and observer; analysis through role-playing of a wide variety of interpersonal situations; practice of new skills; gathering of data in regard to the success of such practice, evaluation; and general discussion.[15]

The training program at Teachers College was designed to increase sensitivity to the dynamics of face-to-face groups; promote deeper understanding of the future administrator's role; gain more skillful collaborative operation in small groups; encourage internalization of democratic norms; develop greater self-understanding and acceptance; provide orientation to the Teachers College environment; aid the student's development as a professional administrator; achieve an increase in small-group skills; and encourage the student's development as a stable, mature person.

A changed approach to the introductory course resulted from discoveries made during the experiment. Prior to the experiment, the course served about 150 administration majors and non-majors, meeting for two hours on a week day. Departmental faculty members lectured on their specialties. There was no attempt to assess student perceptions, and marks were given after an objective test covering required readings. The present course, which was planned by a faculty committee after the experiment, serves about 110 administration majors and meets for four hours on Saturday so that the needs of more working teachers can be met. Large and small group meetings and seminars comprise the course's methodology. The major change which this comparison suggests is in the direction of increased concern with student needs, more willingness to experiment with ways of meeting them, and better long-term planning.[16]

The curriculum at Northwestern University emphasizes the balanced professional-liberal arts approach. At Northwestern, the student is *introduced* to the field of administration through the require-

[15] Teunison C. Clark and Matthew B. Miles, "Human Relations Training for School Administrators," *Journal of Social Issues,* X (1954), pp. 25–39.

[16] *Ibid.*

ments for the master's degree in administration which involve 36 quarter hours (24 semester hours) of graduate work in residence. Three courses are required of all students—Psychological Foundations of Education, Introduction to Research, and Historical and Cultural Foundations of American Education. All students enroll in Foundations of School Administration, but may elect either Administration —Principalship or Business Management. Each student must write a thesis, and enroll in not less than 12 quarter hours in cognate courses, such as anthropology, economics, geography, history, journalism, linguistics, philosophy, political science, psychology, sociology, and speech. The remaining six hours may be taken in professional education or cognate work, depending upon the student's background. For the Ph.D. or Ed.D. degrees, candidates pass both written and oral examinations in professional and cognate fields before being admitted to candidacy. The doctoral program requires three years for completion, three consecutive quarters of which must be spent in full-time residency. A minimum of 108 quarter hours above the baccalaureate degree is required to complete the doctoral program, 33 to 35 hours of which must be in cognate fields. The break-down of course requirements for the doctoral degree follows: master's degree or equivalent, 36 quarter hours; Statistical Method in Education; Seminar on Research for Doctoral Candidates, 3 hours; Organization and Administration of School Systems; Seminar in School Administration; Problems, Issues, and Practices in School Administration, 9 hours; cognate subjects, 21 hours; dissertation, 12 hours; electives (cognate or professional education), 24 hours.[17]

A new two-year program, which will prepare students for school principalships or other initial administrative posts, and which will award a degree of Master of School Administration, has been introduced by the graduate school of education at the University of Chicago. Students spend their first year in residence at the University and their second year chiefly in internship experiences. Candidates, university professors, and professional workers are brought together in seminars to evaluate the internship experience in relation to theoretical studies. Candidates for the Master of School Administration degree program are selected from applicants nominated by superintendents of cooperating school systems located in or near Chicago, but they may eventually be selected from all areas of the country. One major purpose of the program is to identify young teachers who show promise for administrative work.[18]

---

[17] Chandler and McSwain, *op. cit.*, p. 63.

[18] American Association of School Administrators, *The School Administrator*, XVII (May, 1960), p. 2.

The program of preparation for school administrators as proposed by the American Association of School Administrators in its 1960 Yearbook would include 15 semester units of foundation work in cognate fields; nine semester units of work in an "Admission Core" which would include a strong screening process plus a comprehensive study of a community, including historical background, geographical features, economic life, political life, recreation facilities, power structures, religious and ethical influences, formal and informal organizations, and provisions for education; 18 to 21 semester units of advanced studies which include, in the main, courses offered within the College of Education but taught by professors ordinarily assigned to other colleges or departments of the institution, such as economics, sociology, speech, and business management, and seminars offered jointly by professors from several departments including school administration, business administration, and public administration; six to nine semester units of preparation for specific positions wherein the prospective administrator *in general* begins to become *specifically* a superintendent, or a business manager, or an elementary school principal; and nine semester units of on-the-job learning in the field, consisting of either a full-time internship for one semester or a part-time apprenticeship for one school year.[19]

In current college and university classes in school administration, the traditional "read-and-recite" type of methodology is giving way to such newer methods as the use of internships, field work, case studies, role playing, individual and group reports of research, "in-basket" techniques, and others.

Rivzi found that the case method is widely used in training educational adminstrators in degree-granting institutions throughout the United States; 79 of the 149 institutions surveyed (53 per cent) reported use of cases, and 20 (13 per cent) indicated they planned to use cases in the near future.[20] The investigator found that the main objective in using cases is that of fostering in students the habit of logical thinking and illustrating the importance and complexity of human relations. Techniques employed in the case method include: discussion in small and large groups, forum, panel, symposium, role-playing, sociodrama, psychodrama, tape-recording, lecture, resource persons, class trip, written reports, and original case-writing. Special training is necessary in teaching by the case method, including practical ex-

---

19 *Professional Administrators for America's Schools,* 38th Yearbook of the American Association of School Administrators (Washington, D.C.: American Association of School Administrators, 1960), pp. 179–187.

20 Saiyed A. H. Rivzi, *The Case Method in Training Educational Administrators* (Unpublished Doctoral dissertation, University of Pennsylvania, 1959), duplicated, pp. 1–4.

perience in public school administration, thorough grounding in social sciences, skill in group dynamics, participation in seminars for professors, observation of teaching by case method, and visits to institutions using the case method of instruction.

"In-basket" techniques involve the making of decisions by the prospective administrators on specific problems in school systems. Studies of actual problems, recordings, films, and printed materials supply the background for the problems which the administrators-to-be attempt to resolve.

INTERNSHIP PROGRAMS

Many colleges and universities preparing school administrators now employ on-the-job training programs in which the prospective administrator serves an internship as a climax to his formal preparation program. In such programs, the intern generally assumes responsibility for completing one or more administrative duties in a school district during a full year, under the joint supervision of the district and the training institution.

At Stanford University the internship program has been "initiated to afford an opportunity for experienced administrators who already have demonstrated unusual effectiveness in instructional and community leadership in their beginning administrative positions to prepare for ultimate top-level posts."[21] Here an effort is made to place interns "in order to match the particular needs of each participating school system with the areas of competency of the interns."[22] Stanford's interns, who divide their time between their internship assignment and their courses on campus, are paid a salary of approximately $1500 to $3000 per year; half of which is financed by the cooperating districts, and the other half by a W. K. Kellogg Foundation grant. The interns at Stanford have the responsibility of developing a school district project and seeing it through from its inception to implementation in the district.

The emphasis in the University of Pittsburgh's internship program is not on the training of persons already in administrative positions, but rather on "those who aspire to administrative leadership from positions as teachers or other non-administrative employment."[23] Some of the projects at Pittsburgh have included developing public relations material, conducting tours of schools, preparing budgets,

[21] *Internship Program in School Administration* (Palo Alto, Calif.: Stanford School of Education, Stanford University, undated), p. 2.

[22] *Ibid.*

[23] *Activities and Evaluation of the Internship Program in School Administration* (Pittsburgh: University of Pittsburgh Press, undated), p. 4.

directing comparative studies of salary schedules, drawing up maintenance schedules for school plant facilities, and outlining suggested policy for promotion practices or sick leave plans.[24] Since prospective administrators in the Pittsburgh program have not had prior administrative experience, the program there strives to provide the intern with more breadth of experience and less depth.

At New York University, the program of experiences for the interns varies with each intern and is based upon the individual needs of each prospective administrator. Candidates with no administrative experience are placed with an elementary or secondary principal, and later given first-hand experiences with central-office and staff members. The program at New York is open to persons having three to five years of successful teaching experience. The local superintendent of schools and the school board recommend candidates for training, and the university accepts only those candidates who have completed appropriate basic training in educational administration and who have successfully completed several specialized courses.

As a prerequisite to internship in the Cooperative Program in Educational Administration at Harvard University's Graduate School of Education, the candidate must be accepted in the graduate school. He must be a resident student at Harvard for two semesters of full-time study in the Career Program. He must also take an examination in the special field of administration in which he is working. A minimum of two elective courses from other departments of the school is required. The internship program of the Harvard candidate involves an individual administrative responsibility equivalent to at least three-quarters of a semester's work and includes the defining, planning, developing, and carrying out of significant administrative tasks. The internship is usually completed in the school system in which the candidate is employed following his period of residency at Harvard. No provisions for financial aid are made, though a limited number of scholarships are available to men and women who have been accepted for the program.

The specific duties of an intern vary widely. He may make a community survey, he may help new members of the staff, and work for the improvement of staff welfare. He may be responsible for in-service education for staff members, and for studying teacher loads, class size, curriculum, and utilization of buildings. The intern may prepare a school budget; work with the P.T.A.; administer pupil attendance; prepare special school notices; report on special projects; study student activities; or provide leadership at staff meetings.

---

[24] *Ibid.*

Illustrative of a local district program for the training of administration and supervision interns is that in effect in the Campbell, California, school district. The growth of the Campbell Union district, which proceeds unabated as is true of so many other districts in California and other fast-growing states, shows the need for additional schools and, along with this, the need for additional administrators and supervisors. Cooperating with the district committee are Stanford University and San Jose State College.

Candidates for the program must have regular California teaching credentials covering current positions, and two years of successful teaching experience, one of which has been within the Campbell district. Candidates must be accepted by a college or university as a candidate for an advanced degree or credential in education, and must have completed a minimum of six semester units of work before application. Following a formal application, candidates are interviewed and appraised, then given the Stanford test battery. San Jose State College, after interviewing and screening procedures, accepts candidates from the school district, but requires they pass several specified courses before acceptance in the program. The Campbell Elementary School district releases the trainees for one-half day per week while a substitute teacher takes over the candidates' regular classroom activities.

Interns are assigned to principals who serve as advisors and help the candidates plan their programs of visitations. The principals also help plan experiences for the candidates, and evaluate the work of the administrators-to-be. During their released time, the candidates spend hours in visiting each school in the district, the superintendent, the assistant superintendent, and the business manager. Much time is spent by the trainees in teaching and curriculum work in areas with which they are least familiar, as well as in all other activities of the school community. Those who are closest associated with the interns in the Campbell program evaluate the trainee's work, making use of the *Appraisal and Interview Report on Administrative and Supervisory Applicants* (Figure 1).

Figure 1. CAMPBELL UNION SCHOOL DISTRICT APPRAISAL AND INTERVIEW REPORT ON ADMINISTRATIVE AND SUPERVISORY APPLICANTS

Name of Applicant ______________________ School ______________
Interested in Advancement to Administrative / Supervisory / Other Position
Date of Report ____________________ Reported by ______________

Instructions—Read Carefully

1. This appraisal and interview report is to be used to evaluate the potential capacities of members of the professional staff interested in

being considered for advancement into positions of administrative and supervisory responsibility. This report form may be used both as an appraisal form by those most closely associated with the staff member concerned and as an interview report form by those responsible for professionally interviewing prospective candidates.

2. This appraisal and interview report will be used as one kind of screening device in an attempt to evaluate staff members as potential candidates for advancement. The most objective approach possible should be applied in using this report form.
3. Blanks have been left for your comments. You are urged to make as many comments as you can.
4. Under *Personal Qualifications,* #2 and #5, you are requested to make comments about each factor.
5. Under *Professional Qualifications,* #1 and #4 and #7, you are requested to make comments about each factor.
6. If additional information seems desirable, it may be written on the back of these sheets.

A. PERSONAL QUALIFICATIONS

1. PHYSICAL HEALTH ______________________________

____

Consider such factors as:
- Physical Appearance
- Countenance
- Stamina
- Evident Physical Handicaps
- Susceptibility to illness or fatigue
- Mannerisms
- Other

2. MENTAL HEALTH

Consider such factors as:
- Irritability ______________________________
- Temperament ______________________________
- Reactions under pressure ______________________________
- Sensitivity to criticism ______________________________
- Judgment under stress ______________________________
- Rationality of behavior ______________________________
- Other ______________________________

3. VOICE ______________________________

____

Consider such factors as:
- Quality
- Pitch
- Enunciation
- Accent
- Defects
- Other

4. MORAL CONCEPTS ______________________________

____

Consider such factors as:

- Integrity
- Understanding of moral and spiritual values
- Conduct consistent with profession
- Concepts of individual and group morality
- Conformity to community mores
- Other

5. INDUSTRY AND ENTHUSIASM

Consider such factors as:

- Willingness to work ______
- Consistent efforts ______
- Dependability & responsibility ______
- Constancy of enthusiasm ______
- Originality ______

6. SENSE OF HUMOR ______

______

Consider such factors as:

- Cheerfulness
- Ability to laugh at oneself
- Ability to accept defeat graciously
- Recognition of feelings of others
- Sense of appropriateness

7. JUDGMENT AND COMMON SENSE ______

______

Consider such factors as:

- Personal relationships
- Personal tastes, clothing, etc.
- Business relationships
- Social relationships

8. SENSE OF FAIRNESS ______

______

Consider such factors as:

- Innate sense of fair play
- Willingness to share
- Ability to arbitrate disputes
- Open-mindedness
- Acceptance of other points of view

B. PROFESSIONAL QUALIFICATIONS

1. PROFESSIONAL EDUCATION ______

Consider such factors as:

- Level of professional training ______
- Current efforts in advanced training ______
- Evident understanding of educational psychology ______

  ______
- Broadness of scope of training ______
- Other ______

2. PROFESSIONAL ATTITUDES ______

______

Consider such factors as:

- Attitude toward role of public education
- Attitude toward co-workers
- Attitude toward our form of government
- Attitude toward criticism
- Professional loyalty
- Attitude toward our economic system
- Other

3. CAPACITY TO WORK WITH OTHERS ____________________

____

Consider such factors as:

- Acceptance of contribution of others
- Achievement of respect from others
- Cooperative spirit
- Willingness to do just share
- Acceptance of minor role
- Other

4. ACCEPTANCE OF RESPONSIBILITY ____________________

Consider such factors as:

- Ability as a leader ____________________
- Ability to carry through ____________________
- Willingness to accept assignments ____________________
- Ability as an organizer ____________________
- Acceptance by others of his leadership ____________________

5. UNDERSTANDING OF GOOD TEACHING TECHNIQUES ____________________

____

Consider such factors as:

- Ability to recognize good teaching
- Ability to analyze poor teaching
- Ability to discuss intelligently teaching techniques with others

6. UNDERSTANDING OF CHILDREN AND YOUTH ____________________

____

Consider such factors as:

- Concept of children as individuals
- Apparent knowledge of child psychology
- Liking for children and youth
- Impartial acceptance of all children regardless of race, creed, color or economic background

7. CAPACITY IN PUBLIC RELATIONS

Consider such factors as:

- Attitude toward parents, P.T.A., etc. ____________________
- Ability to represent public education ____________________
- Ability to speak on education ____________________
- Other ____________________

8. CAPACITY IN HUMAN RELATIONSHIPS ____________________

____

Consider such factors as:

Ability to deal with an unhappy child	Ability to sympathetically handle a problem situation
Ability to deal with a parent	Ability to communicate with children and adults

9. POTENTIALITY FOR SUCCESS ____________________

____

Consider such factors as:

Attitude toward self-improvement	Voluntary recognition by others
Evidence of personal and professional growth	Composite of all factors
	Others

The Lindenhurst, New York, intern training program for administrators selects the best of the 350 classroom teachers in the district and admits them into the corps of prospective school leaders. These teachers are relieved of all teaching duties for a period of six months, during which time they are systematically exposed to virtually all important administrative problems and experiences with which they will be confronted once they become principals.

FIELD WORK IN ADMINISTRATION

Some institutions preparing principals have another type of on-the-job training program involving a part-time apprenticeship in the field. The institutions arrange with several school systems in their service areas for special programs designed to train administrative candidates. After being assigned to principals or other administrators who have been carefully selected, the candidates work on administrative problems in their own school systems. Usually they are released from half of their teaching duties while they are pursuing the field work program. The schedule of field work activities is worked out by the district, and trainees in the usual program attend a bi-weekly seminar at which problems are discussed by regular principals, administrator-trainees, central office representatives, and consultants from the training institution. In some programs of this nature, the trainees work on problems assigned jointly by the school districts and the training institutions, and submit their solutions in written form.

In a study of field training experiences for elementary administrators, Bailey concluded that:

> Training should be based on a two-semester program. A two-semester field work requirement would enable the student to achieve a stronger over-all appreciation of the role of the elementary administrator than could be obtained during only one semester. Opinions of administrators in the field, research students and authorities in the literature indicate that the training program, in order to be effective, should cover a considerable period of time.[25]

CURRENT IN-SERVICE PROGRAMS

> To retain professional effectiveness, stature, and dignity, the school administrator must continue steadfastly to improve himself; to remain abreast of, often sharing in, innovations; to create for himself a disciplined program of in-service advancement.[26]

This assumption of the American Association of School Administrators points up the need for an in-service education program for the leaders of America's schools. No one would deny that one responsibility of a school administrator is to provide a program for the teachers through which they may improve their effectiveness and keep abreast of the latest techniques for teaching: who, then, would deny that such a program for administrators and supervisors is not just as necessary? It is a deplorable situation which finds teachers busy improving themselves under the direction of administrators who are not working in the same spirit.

Members of the medical profession do not end their training after eight years or more of formal education. In order to keep up with advances within their profession they attend schools and clinics and subscribe to journals and periodicals. Lawyers would hardly be able to follow the latest interpretations by the legal profession if they did not read the most recent journals and follow current decisions of courts of justice. Progress is made in bringing together theory and practice—or the science of knowledge and its application—only through a continuous program of growth in service. It is important that all school administrative, supervisory, and instructional personnel grow in service.

Responsibility for the growth of administrators rests with themselves. Principals grow as a result of what they are able to do for themselves and for others, as well as through what they may do cooperatively with others. The best growth takes place when principals

[25] Charles Weynard Bailey, *Effective Practices in Field Training Experience for Elementary Administrators in California* (Duplicated, no date), p. 7.

[26] *Professional Administrators for America's Schools,* 38th Yearbook of the American Association of School Administrators (Washington, D.C.: American Association of School Administrators, 1960), p. 87.

join as participants in initiating and planning the conditions that inspire growth, and then continue to participate in all its processes. This means that programs of real growth in service are developed by the people involved.

There are many resources to which principals can turn for help in improving their own effectiveness. Membership in professional organizations, such as the National Elementary School Principals Association, provide help through publications and local, regional, and national conventions. State departments of education make available specialists and consultants in a number of areas and provide opportunities for principals to serve on various state-wide committees. State and regional professional organizations often promote professional conferences and workshops. In some areas, school principals participate in small, informal, non-structured, semi-private group sessions which, in many cases, prove to be a most effective technique for motivating professional growth. Other media for the in-service growth of school principals include: action research on problems in their own school; public speaking; consulting with teachers and other administrators; participating in cultural activities; teaching in summer sessions and evening programs of colleges and universities; enrolling in college courses; and pursuing independent reading of professional materials.

According to a survey of Texas school administrators, sponsored by the Southwestern Cooperative Program of Educational Administration at the University of Texas, the five means of in-service education in order of frequency of use were: (1) reading in professional journals; (2) actively working in community service clubs; (3) participating in regional schoolmen's clubs; (4) attending short conferences sponsored by state departments of education; and (5) reading printed accounts of successful ways in which a problem has been met.[27] In contrast to these five means used for in-service improvement, the same superintendents indicated that the most valuable means of in-service growth were: (1) attending summer workshops on college campuses; (2) visiting other school systems; (3) forming self-study committees composed of local faculty members; (4) attending short conferences sponsored by state departments of education; (5) applying evaluative instruments in their own systems; (6) conducting research in their own systems; (7) participating in regional schoolmen's clubs; and (8) participating in clinics conducted by a school system around

---

27 Hollis A. Moore, Jr., "How Superintendents Grow Through In-service Opportunities." *The Nation's Schools* (May, 1953), pp. 56–59. With permission of The Modern Hospital Publishing Co., Inc., Chicago, owners of the copyright.

one particular problem.[28] From these two lists of in-service techniques, it is readily seen that the media which are considered to be of most value to administrators are not the ones that they commonly use. The results of this survey indicate that the most valuable experiences are those in which the administrators are brought into personal contact with each other.

The W. K. Kellogg-financed program at Teachers College, Columbia University, was aimed at aiding on-the-job administrators in keeping up to date. The project used a pattern of short-term clinics and seminars on topics of current interest. The program, staffed by persons from universities, associations, and the field—wherever unusual resources could be found—placed its emphasis, not upon degrees and credits, but rather upon current topics of interest and importance to school administrators.[29]

It becomes clear that the training given administrators in the past—that which presumed the school's administrative leaders were expert teachers who could tell others how to teach—is inadequate for the heads of today's elementary schools. These persons today must also be able to work cooperatively with all personnel in the school community, and must understand and hold real respect for the dignity of the individual.

CONCLUSION

Educational programs for the preparation of elementary school principals have assumed new and promising directions as the job has grown from a "head teacher" situation into a recognized school-community leadership position. Recognition of the importance of the principalship as a position of educational statesmanship has prompted a change in emphasis in preparatory programs from job-related knowledge to job-related behavior, since a large part of the principal's work is in the area of human relations. Great stress by colleges and public schools is currently and properly being placed on selection of likely candidates for administrative positions; the key to having good administrators in our schools lies in the proper selection of prospects. Once a dedicated aspirant is selected, the administrative education which is provided by the colleges and school district working cooperatively will more likely be effective.

A promising trend in the pre-education of elementary school principals and other administrators is the use, in professional courses, of

---

[28] *Ibid.*

[29] Daniel R. Davies, "The Impending Breakthrough," *Phi Delta Kappan,* XXXVII (April, 1956), pp. 275–281.

"life-like" techniques such as case studies, "in-basket" cases, role-playing, individual and group research techniques, and situations of all kinds in which scientific problem-solving methods are used. It seems a natural thing, then, for administrative candidates to move from these "life-like" situations in the classroom to *life* situations in the actual school community in such relatively new practices as field work and internship. In the latter two areas, the prospective principals and other administrative candidates have an opportunity to work, under close college and school district supervision, in real school administration situations and have an opportunity to engage in decision-making activities to implement the theory previously learned in the classroom.

In the light of an ever-changing culture and an ever-changing profession of school administration, the school principal's education does not—can not—end when he receives his license or degree. The research and experimentation currently underway have indicated new concepts and more effective techniques in elementary school administration. There are indications that as additional research and experimentation continue, still newer concepts and more effective techniques will emerge that will make the principalship a vastly more effective position for leadership in providing the best possible education for each child in America.

Principals need to be aware of the changing programs provided for the preparation of elementary school administrators. They need to keep abreast of all emerging practices which affect their profession. They must be particularly aware of the educational programs in which they themselves may be serving as teachers of future elementary school administrators. In order, too, for principals to be aware of the educational backgrounds of teachers who will be joining their staffs in the future, and to be able to provide valid in-service education for them, the administrators must know of the current and emerging programs for the education of teachers. This will be the consideration of the next chapter.

Short Case 1

Preparation for Administration?

The Education Department at Highview College became interested in developing a preparatory program for its administrative candidates, and worked in cooperation with nearby school districts for one year to determine requirements. Arrangements were made for seven outstanding candidates to function in part-time administrative capacities at a salary of $1300 for the ten-month school year. At the same time, the candidates would carry classes in administration at the college. This plan, when submitted to graduate students in the department, received enthusiastic response. But selection became difficult. The department set up a reviewing board consisting of six full professors within the department who would interview each applicant, study his records, and, finally, decide on the successful applicants.

Richard Torgering was happy to be chosen as one of the seven. He entered the program full of energy and dedication. He was placed in Bell Elementary School where he was assigned to what might be described as a vice-principal's position. At the end of October, Mr. Torgering asked his graduate adviser how he could be released from the assignment, stating that it was impossible for him to continue. He said that the principal refused to permit him to become a real part of the administration. He was permitted only to count cafeteria money, supervise the playground before school opened, supervise setting up chairs in the auditorium, run the film projector, fill teachers' supply requisitions, and collect the lounge coffee fund.

Problem: Was Mr. Torgering justified in his request to be released from his assignment? Why or why not? What are some of the responsibilities that a prospective school administrator who is involved in this type of training program might discharge?

Short Case 2

Course Work in Academic Areas

State College School of Education was attempting to create an elementary administration training program which would make its graduates second to none in effectiveness. The staff realized that, in addition to on-the-job experience, an important part of its program should be courses in inter-disciplinary areas especially related to the work a principal would be doing in his community.

As the staff considered the academic areas most needed by a prospective elementary administrator, an impasse was reached. Certainly, if he were expected to spend at least 50 per cent of his time in supervision, an administrator should have additional work in science, mathematics, English, art, music, foreign languages, and the social sciences, since he would be helping teachers with instruction in all of these areas in all grades of the elementary school. But, also, he would need to know how children grow, develop, learn, and differ, so he would have to enroll in classes in physiology, anthropology, psychology, and health. Since he would address various community and professional organizations, he could certainly use advanced courses in public speaking. An important part of his work would be understanding and dealing with the various forces within and without the school community which affect educational planning, so the administrator would have to take special courses in sociology and psychology. Because one of the administrator's most important tasks is that of providing for the adequate financing of the educational program and of accounting for school monies, he should have adequate training in certain fields offered in the School of Business. All of these in addition to professional courses in administration!

Currently, the reorganized administrative training program is stymied; the courses deemed necessary in a prospective administrator's program are so numerous that he could not possibly complete the work for his administrative certificate in less than two years.

Problem: How can the School of Education staff resolve its problem? Are there ways of determining which academic courses are more important or pertinent than others? Are there academic areas other than those mentioned in which an elementary school principal should be adept?

Short Case 3

The Self-Propelling Intern

Jules Lockhart, administrative intern, picked up his brief case and, looking at the retreating superintendent, made his way to the parking lot and his car. Settling into the homeward traffic, his mind raced over the current frustrations. What had he expected as an intern? Certainly not to be left alone. At the University, Dr. Collins had met with the superintendent of the district in which he would be placed as an intern. During the meeting they had outlined five major areas in which Lockhart would receive experience: coordination of the revision of the social studies curriculum for the seven elementary schools; development of an in-service program for all vice-principals on guidance; development of a new grade level in-service program in arithmetic; and development of an inter-school newspaper to facilitate awareness of activities of all the schools, including the central office. The fifth problem was to be one which Lockhart defined, solved and evaluated by himself. He was to have met regularly with Dr. Collins and the superintendent, but after the first two weeks, the superintendent had not been able to attend the meetings. Lockhart had had trouble pin-pointing appointments, and had been sidetracked when trying to find the superintendent outside his office. At home, Lockhart picked up the phone:

"Dr. Collins? If you are free tomorrow, we'd better discuss a new placement. It's not working out." At the other end of the line, Dr. Collins was smiling, "Well, I was wondering how long you would go without saying something. I asked our friend to meet us for an evaluation this Saturday morning. Be there at nine."

Problem: What is the basic problem in this case? What does Dr. Collins expect to accomplish at the Saturday meeting? What are some of the other problems that an administrative intern might face in his internship, and how can they be solved?

Chapter Three

New Programs for the Education of Teachers

Concern for the quality of teacher education in the United States has been the highest in history during the past few years. We cannot deny the vast responsibility placed upon the adults charged with the physical, mental, social, emotional, and spiritual development of the children in elementary schools throughout the country. There are many problems that must be resolved if elementary teachers are to be maximally prepared to fulfill their important role. The responsibility of the classroom teacher looms large as he attempts to help the world's people find answers to problems posed by nuclear energy, space exploration, automation, nearly incredible speeds, and increased leisure time.

THE CHALLENGE OF THE PAST

The past of the elementary school teacher is not one of which he can be completely proud, despite the fact that he had some outstandingly noteworthy predecessors in the persons of such men as Pestalozzi, Comenius, Cheever, and others. He must rise above a largely unfortunate heritage, and overcome the stereotyped image of the teacher which has been formed in the mind of the public.

Pedagogues in ancient Greece were slaves who escorted young male children to and from school in the gymnasia and palaestras of Athens. Under the Caesars in the Roman Empire, the term *pedagogue* came to be applied to all teachers, probably because their status was that of slaves.

Teachers were still "serfs" in England a thousand years after Rome fell, and the low regard for teachers came to America's shores with the early settlers during the seventeenth century. The threats of corporal punishment, insistence upon rote memorization, lack of attempts to meet children's needs and interests: all these practices of the early teachers helped keep the position in disrepute. No one believed that teaching in elementary school required a particular skill, or that teachers should be paid a respectable living wage.

No longer than thirty years ago, the House of Commons in England heard Macaulay define teachers as "The refuse of all other callings; discarded footmen, ruined pedlars, men who can't work a sum in the rule of three, men who don't know whether the earth is a sphere or a cube, and who don't know whether Jerusalem is in Asia or America."

The earliest teachers, being untrained, merely "kept" school by "rule of thumb" and did not have any specific methodology. According to DeYoung, teaching has undergone three not too well-marked stages of development which have been epitomized by the terms: (1) teacher *training;* (2) teacher *preparation;* and (3) teacher *education.*[1] It was not until the mid-1800's that teacher education became articulate through the words and deeds of such men as the Reverend Samuel R. Hall, Horace Mann, and the Reverend Cyrus Pierce. But the trustees of Franklin's Academy in Philadelphia revealed some awareness of the need for teacher education when they wrote this statement as one of the aims of the institution in the days before the republic was formed:

> That a number of students of the poorer Sort will be hereby qualified to act as Schoolmasters in the Country, to teach Children Reading, Writing, Arithmetic, and the Grammar of their Mother Tongue, and being of good morals and known character, may be recommended from the Academy to Country Schools for that purpose.[2]

Reverend Hall established a private academy for the education of teachers at Concord, Vermont, in 1823. Cyrus Pierce was the first principal of the first state-supported normal school in the United States,

[1] Chris A. DeYoung, *Introduction to American Public Education* (3rd ed.; New York: McGraw-Hill Book Co., 1955), p. 341.

[2] C. O. Williams, ed., *Schools for Democracy* (Chicago: National Congress of Parents and Teachers, 1939), p. 45.

established in 1839 at Lexington, Massachusetts, through the efforts of Horace Mann. Entrance examinations were required at this new normal school where, until 1860, the course of study was only one year in length.

Gradually, educational leaders began to realize that teachers had to be *educated* over a period of years rather than *trained* in an eleven-week term or a summer session or two. Quality as well as quantity of instruction was being recognized, and some educators saw that instead of equipping the prospective teachers with a "bag of tricks," it was necessary to prepare them for teaching and living with children. In 1860 the course of study at Lexington was doubled to two years, but it was soon evident that an institution with a higher rank than a two-year normal training school was needed.

Symbolic of this upward reach was the establishment in 1857 of Illinois State Normal University, which pioneered the participation of higher education in the preparation of teachers. There soon followed the creation of education departments in colleges and universities; the University of Iowa established the first part-time chair devoted to professional education in 1873; and the University of Michigan, in 1879, was the first to establish a permanent chair. Teachers College, established at Columbia University in New York City in 1887 by Nicholas Murray Butler, then professor of philosophy, has markedly affected teacher education in the United States and in foreign countries. Near the end of the nineteenth century, Colonel Francis Parker accepted the principalship of Chicago Institute, which later became the School of Education and is now the Department of Education at the University of Chicago.[3]

Despite the advances made, the status of preparation of most elementary teachers at the end of the nineteenth century was still very low. The amount of professional training possessed by most teachers was pitifully small, as is evidenced by the following:

> Certification requirements were low. As late as 1894 a teacher's examination in Iowa consisted of a few easy questions on the common branches. No knowledge of pedagogy was expected. As a speaker said at the Minneapolis meeting of the National Education Association in 1872, "The vast majority of teachers have not even the aid of an occasional swelter in an August vacation-school institute too often only an educational picnic."[4]

While the emphasis upon teacher *education* has no definite starting point chronologically, it is evident that it was latent in the minds of

---

[3] DeYoung, *op. cit.*, pp. 344–345.

[4] Ross L. Finney, *The American Public School* (New York: The Macmillan Co., 1921), p. 165.

early educators, although it did not actually provide much influence until about 1900.

THE PRESENT STATUS

The status of elementary school teachers is changing dynamically; the profession is progressing; it *is* rising above the past. The profession, however, still needs educational programs to help teachers become leaders in the search for answers to problems in a community not bounded by city limits, but extending throughout the world. It is important that elementary school administrators be aware of the programs for the education of teachers who either now are, or soon will be, under their leadership. The importance of adequate teacher education is indicated by Cottrell when he states:

> The fulfillment of the American dream of equal opportunity for all would not have been possible without the common school, but the common school cannot fulfill its mission unless it has a teacher equal to the task. By its nature and importance the task of teaching children requires general and professional education. Institutions for the purpose have evolved with the development of the common school in the United States.[5]

The general purpose of teacher education institutions is to prepare school personnel who will contribute to society's improvement as active citizens, as leaders in the community in the field of education, and as guides of children during their development into informed citizens. Society can ill afford teachers who act without thinking: a high calibre of scholarship in modern teachers is a necessity.

Stratemeyer states that those who are to be teachers must possess competence characterized by: (1) knowledge plus reflection upon the meaning and implication of that knowledge; (2) recognition of the relation of particular knowledge to other fields, and a usable acquaintance with sources of reliable information; (3) continued search for truth, for greater understanding and insight into new relationships, using methods appropriate to the disciplines involved; (4) courage to defend one's considered and independent judgment when facts and changing conditions suggest new and different conclusions; and (5) creativity in the translation of ideas and ideals into action in service to others.[6]

---

[5] Donald P. Cottrell, ed., *Teacher Education for a Free People* (Oneonta, N.Y.: The American Association of Colleges for Teacher Education, 1956), p. 18.

[6] Florence B. Stratemeyer, "Issues and Problems in Teacher Education," in Donald P. Cottrell, *op. cit.*, p. 57.

Most authorities break the areas of academic work for prospective elementary teachers into three or four divisions, such as general education, professional courses, professional laboratory experiences, and guided electives. Most teacher education institutions give some attention to each of the areas, though they differ considerably in the proportionate part of the total program devoted to each. There is still evidence in higher educational institutions of the most ancient of educational controversies: liberal or practical learning.

GENERAL EDUCATION

Authorities in the field of elementary education currently recommend for prospective elementary school teachers a general or liberal education as one phase of their preparation. That there is a trend toward more general or liberal courses for prospective teachers is indicated by Kyte who says that, because an elementary teacher needs a broad and rich educational background of usable information, the prospective teacher is being required to spend his first two years in a program of liberal education rather than in the old program of professional education.[7]

Yauch, Bartels, and Morris state that one-third to one-half of the course of study for a prospective teacher should fall into the following categories: (1) literature and the English language; (2) the social studies, including history, economics, sociology, political science; (3) the physical and biological sciences, including physics, chemistry, geology, geography, biology; (4) mathematics; (5) fine arts, including music, art, drama, dance; and (6) physical education and health.[8]

The Commission on Teacher Education, as long ago as the mid-1940's advocated:

> Teachers should receive the best possible general education, not only in order that they may share in what ought to be the birthright of all young Americans today, but also because to them is entrusted considerable responsibility for the general education of all young Americans tomorrow.[9]

Richey says:

> . . . (the prospective elementary teacher needs) a more thorough grounding in many areas of learning than does the secondary teacher. In addition to breadth of background, the elementary teacher must

---

[7] George C. Kyte, *The Elementary School Teacher at Work* (New York: Holt, Rinehart and Winston, Inc., 1957), p. 493.

[8] Wilbur A. Yauch, Martin H. Bartels, and Emmet Morris, *The Beginning Teacher* (New York: Holt, Rinehart and Winston, Inc., 1955), p. 27.

[9] American Council on Education, *The Improvement of Teacher Education* (Washington, D.C.: the Council, 1946), p. 82.

develop enough depth of understanding in each of the areas to guide children into increasingly rich and challenging learning experiences.[10]

PROFESSIONAL COURSES

Teacher education courses in the area of professional studies include elements which contribute directly to the teacher's understanding and skill in guiding the learning and development of boys and girls, and in working with lay people and colleagues in carrying out the role of the school in the culture. Methods courses, designed to educate teachers in sound techniques of teaching, are also on the programs of most colleges which educate prospective classroom personnel. Some institutions offer courses in the major curricular areas, such as the language arts, number experiences, social studies, sciences, and the fine arts, while others combine the specific areas into broader "method blocks" of a more general nature.

One of the most important of the professional courses offered in teacher education institutions is the one variously labeled as participation, observation, or teaching internship, in which the teaching candidate gains actual experience in dealing with boys and girls in classroom situations. Most institutions arrange for these experiences at various stages in the development of both the teacher candidates and the children. Authorities are in general agreement that teacher candidates should come into actual contact with children as early and as often in the program of preparation as possible.

PROFESSIONAL LABORATORY EXPERIENCES

Learning by doing is a concept to which most modern educators subscribe. They also believe that actual experience with children is one such avenue through which prospective teachers can learn. Because of this, laboratory experiences are found in the curricula of most colleges for teacher education. Hicks indicates that the experiences students have in such a program include graduated and differentiated visitation and observation in the classroom, participation in the routine of the classroom, and actual student teaching in which the prospective teacher is given individual responsibility for planning and carrying through learning experiences for children.[11]

Kyte is of the opinion that:

---

[10] Robert W. Richey, *Planning for Teaching* (New York: McGraw-Hill Book Co., 1958), p. 124.

[11] Hanne J. Hicks, *Administrative Leadership in the Elementary School* (New York: Ronald Press Co., 1956), p. 151.

> Considerable directed teaching is necessary if the student is to have practice in planning, using school and community resources, organizing the school day, attending to individual needs, grouping pupils, arranging the classroom environment, developing routines, using various teaching methods, and maintaining classroom control. The student teacher needs experience in performing routine duties, keeping school records, making out reports, preparing instruction materials, analyzing pupils' work, meeting parents, and attending various types of meetings. He should be supervised in the same ways that experienced teachers are when they, too, are aided in further development.[12]

GUIDED ELECTIVES

Some educators in the field of teacher education believe that the student who is preparing to be a teacher should elect a considerable portion of his program. This is justified on the grounds that differences exist among students preparing to become teachers, and they should not be required to conform to specific course programs. In order to help in alleviating specific weaknesses, or in order to satisfy certain interests, students may wish to elect courses in speech, art, music, folklore, public affairs, writing, crafts, or sociology.

Kyte would have the prospective teacher include various extracurricular and work activities in his college preparatory program, such as responsibilities in summer camps, scout troops, and work experiences in industry and business. These provide valuable experiences in leadership, cooperation, meeting responsibilities, developing resourcefulness, and working with other people.[13]

THE PROGRAM AT PENNSYLVANIA STATE UNIVERSITY

One of the most discussed programs in the literature is that which the faculty at Pennsylvania State University adapted to the needs of prospective elementary teachers in training at that institution. Park presents an overview of that program in a discussion of two of the several principles which serve as guideposts for the Pennsylvania State University.[14]

The first guiding principle which that author discusses is: *Human values and needs should be uppermost in all consideration and action.* In this regard, Park discusses the Pennsylvania State *Professional Semesters,* which he terms "our framework for action." Being the core

---

[12] Kyte, *op. cit.*, p. 495.

[13] *Ibid.*, p. 496.

[14] Lawrence Park, "Adventure for Teacher Education," *The National Elementary Principal,* XXXIV (May, 1955), pp. 14–16.

of the professional education program, they are scheduled as two 15-credit semesters, one in the junior year and one in the senior year. One-half of each semester is spent by students in a laboratory center made up of a community and its public school system; the other half is usually concerned with experiences centering about the campus and nearby school facilities.

The *Professional Semester* is a nearly self-contained unit for about twenty-five students under the leadership of a faculty coordinator. Besides its internal resources, the group draws additional help from a group of persons with specific professional skills. Considered of major import in the plan is the part each student plays in cooperative individual and group planning.

Human relations evolve within a group of people who live together for eighteen weeks; in this situation a whole matrix of interaction develops. Prospective teachers have experience in individual and group planning, seeing broad problem areas, using creative approaches to problems, examining consequences of planning, developing respect for other school personnel, working effectively with adults and children, and discovering human and material resources. In this way, the students may develop a professional and personal adequacy in human relations that reaches beyond self and children to include all of life about them. Nor does commencement day see the end of faculty contact with the prospective teacher, for graduates are visited by university staff members for two or three years following graduation.

A second guiding principle in the Pennsylvania State University program is: *Education cannot be in a vacuum, apart from the main stream of life.* Direct experiences are gained, half of the eighteen weeks centering on the campus, and the other half perhaps in a Pennsylvania community as far as 120 miles from campus. Away from the University, students face a first-year teacher's problems in becoming oriented to the job, securing housing, learning about community resources, discovering group mores, and generally fitting into the educational picture *in toto*. Prospective teachers learn to appreciate sets of values other than their own middle and upper-middle class standards as they work with children from different groups.

THE GEORGE PEABODY PROGRAM

Although there is no single truly "typical" program of teacher education among the many institutions in the United States, many institutions believe that their program is a typical one. Hill says that George Peabody College for Teachers, of which he is a past president,

> . . . offers a somewhat typical four-year undergraduate curriculum leading to a teaching career. The program consists of three or three

and one-half years of liberal arts or general education with about two quarters of professional education. About one-third of the candidates take practice teaching in the Peabody demonstration school, with a selected and limited enrollment of 500; another third in the Nashville city schools, with an enrollment of 30,000; and another third in the Davidson county schools, with an enrollment of 40,000. Thus, a wide range of opportunity for observations and practice is provided.[15]

A MYTHICAL "TYPICAL" PROGRAM

As has been stated, there is no typical program of curricular offerings for the prospective elementary school teacher in the college of teacher education. Divergence in practice seems to be the rule rather than the exception. However, Clark studied the curricula of sixty-eight state teachers colleges and arrived at a mean of the curricula studied and hesitatingly called it the "typical" program.[16]

In Clark's program, 51 per cent of the curriculum is devoted to required non-professional work, and 31.5 per cent to required professional courses. A total of 15-½ semester hours of non-professional work is in English, six hours of which are given to freshman English. Other requirements in the liberal arts area include: 18 hours in the social studies; 10.3 hours in the natural sciences; one course in general mathematics; 1.95 semester hours in psychology; 4.76 hours in art; 3.62 hours in music; and 3.6 hours in physical education activities, hygiene being required of all freshmen. No work in philosophy is required.

Of the total 128 semester hours required for graduation, 41.25 hours are in professional courses, according to Clark's study. Half of these professional hours are devoted to methods, materials, curriculum, and principles, including special methods courses in the teaching of art, music, and physical education. Twelve semester hours are given to student teaching, most often in a block in the senior year. Only 1.91 hours are spent in the social foundations of education, usually in history of education in the senior year. Students take 5.11 hours of professional courses in psychology, three of which are in child psychology during the sophomore or junior year.

Since the more recent trend away from professional courses in education and toward additional courses in the liberal arts, the "typical" program outlined above would probably show a larger percentage of

---

[15] Henry H. Hill, "Wanted: Professional Teachers," *The Atlantic Monthly,* CCV (May, 1960), pp. 37–40.

[16] Leonard H. Clark, "The Curriculum for Elementary Teachers in Sixty-eight State Teachers Colleges," *Journal of Teacher Education,* VI (June, 1955), pp. 114–117.

course work being taken in the liberal arts and less in the professional courses if such a study were made today. Teacher education institutions which face realistically the problem of educating future instructors will have their courses of study under constant evaluation, with resulting changes in emphases occurring as the program is continually reviewed.

BASIC AGREEMENTS IN TEACHER EDUCATION

It is obvious that colleges of teacher education do not have a standard curriculum for prospective teachers of elementary schools, and it is probably fortunate that such is the case. Despite this fact, there are basic principles upon which these institutions are in general agreement. Woodring phrases some of these principles as follows:

1. Every teacher, regardless of subject or age group he is to teach, ought to be liberally educated. His total liberal education should be not less than that represented by an A.B. degree from a good liberal arts college.
2. In the course of his college education, the teacher should come to see his own special field in its proper perspective.
3. In addition to his liberal education and his major field of specialization, every teacher should have some minimum of professional education. . . . We do not yet agree on the amount of this minimum in terms of semester hours, but perhaps we can agree on the following:
   a. The prospective teacher should have given careful thought to the meaning, purpose, and problems of universal public education—perhaps through a course in philosophy. This course should not consist of indoctrination in any one philosophy, but should introduce the student to different basic points of view in education.
   b. He should have a thorough knowledge of the learner and the learning process, and this will include a knowledge of the nature and extent of individual differences. He should learn to evaluate research in these fields and to draw proper conclusions from evidence.
   c. He should have some introduction to methods, materials, and curriculum organization, and this knowledge should be closely related to his understanding of educational philosophy and his knowledge of the psychology of learning. But his knowledge of methods and materials should be introductory rather than exhaustive, for much of this information will be gained on the job.
   d. He should have some minimum period of supervised practice teaching or cadet teaching, and during this period every effort should be made to see that the knowledge acquired in "a," "b," and "c" is applied in the actual teaching situation.
4. To achieve the above objectives it will be necessary for the teacher to

spend at least five years in preparation for his profession. He may, however, begin teaching at the end of four years of a properly planned program and complete his education through summer school attendance.

5. Though the college educational program may be broken by periods of teaching, it should be organized as a whole with the fifth year so planned as to avoid the duplications now all too common, particularly in the programs of those who choose to work toward a master's degree in education.
6. Even the best possible program of teacher education cannot produce beginning teachers who are fully competent in all aspects of their work. The public school system must accept a considerable amount of responsibility for on-the-job supervision and training of beginning teachers.[17]

THE CHALLENGE OF THE FUTURE

In the light of the tremendous responsibilities facing elementary teachers, leaders of teacher education are wrestling with the problem of what preparatory program should be offered. Some trends seem to be evolving.

The present orientation of the teacher education program is based upon an analysis of what is desirable in the future, while still respecting those things which have served well in the past and are cherished in the present. Systematic programs of teacher education in colleges are not enough for the elementary school teacher of tomorrow; also of importance is a complementary community situation in which the teacher is encouraged as a learner and as a student of the educational aspect of human affairs.

Hicks says there appears to be some agreement emerging as to the nature of a good program of teacher education for elementary school teachers, which includes the following aspects:

1. General education designed to broaden the prospective teacher's understanding of the historical, sociological, scientific, and aesthetic features of our culture.
2. Basic professional courses in philosophy and psychology of education and in human development.
3. Professional methods designed to develop proficiency in teaching techniques appropriate to various curricular areas and various age levels.

---

[17] Paul Woodring, "Basic Agreements in Teacher Education," *The Journal of Teacher Education,* VI (June, 1955), pp. 93–99.

4. Professional laboratory experiences with children in the classroom through observation, participation, and student teaching.
5. Elective pursuits through which dominant interests may be developed, weaknesses corrected, or skills improved.[18]

OFF-CAMPUS LABORATORY EXPERIENCES

There is a trend in teacher education programs toward having prospective teachers spend considerable time in actual teaching situations away from campus. Erickson says of the teacher education program at Michigan State University:

> It is hoped that all of our students will soon be involved in a full quarter of off-campus student teaching. They will live in the community and be under the supervision of a qualified person holding faculty status in the College of Education and a supervisory appointment in the school system. As a part of their term's work they will participate in community studies, teacher's meetings, classroom observation, and practice teaching. They will also meet regularly to discuss the problems of methods and procedures they will encounter in their experimental activities.[19]

Yauch describes the nine-week period of off-campus student teaching at his Northern Illinois State College.[20] The student lives in the community in which he is doing his work, and accepts all of the responsibilities and obligations of a full-fledged teacher, including attendance at meetings of professional organizations. The student teacher's supervisor, who is also the college instructor of the course which correlates with student teaching, visits the student several times during the nine weeks, and can help somewhat in guiding him into worthwhile professional activities, assuming that the local situation is such that this kind of experience will be rewarding. Local schools are encouraged to provide the student with all kinds of professional experiences in addition to regular classroom teaching.

In discussing the teacher education program at the University of Tennessee, Fitzgerald states that off-campus centers should preferably be 50 to 100 miles from the campus so that the students will not be

---

[18] Hicks, *op. cit.*, p. 149.

[19] C. E. Erickson, "Teacher Education as a Responsibility of the Entire Institution," *Teacher Education: the Decade Ahead* (Washington, D.C.: National Commission on Teacher Education and Professional Standards, DeKalb Conference Report, National Education Association, 1955), pp. 188–190.

[20] Wilbur A. Yauch, "Preparation for Professional Membership and Responsibilities," *Teacher Education: the Decade Ahead* (Washington, D.C.: National Commission on Teacher Education and Professional Standards, DeKalb Conference Report, National Education Association, 1955), pp. 122–126.

tempted to return often to the campus.[21] All student teachers should be required to stay in the community regularly for the entire quarter for full participation in community activities, including week-end recreation programs, Sunday School and church meetings, and other projects that provide opportunity to see not only the children, but other residents of the community in relationships away from the school.

THE FIFTH YEAR

In addition to the trend in teacher education toward off-campus laboratory experiences, there is also a trend toward requirement of a fifth year of training for prospective teachers. Educators believe that an effective fifth-year program will not only improve professional education of beginning elementary school teachers but will also improve the supply of teachers in making professional training available to college graduates who, while going through college, gave little consideration to teaching as a career, but who decided to prepare for teaching after college graduation.

Whether the program in the colleges and universities for the preparation of elementary school teachers is called a fifth-year program, an internship, or some other term, five years of preparation for prospective teachers should be considered the bare minimum. As the institutions of higher learning train those who will teach during the next forty years, it is imperative that they educate them to prepare children to face a changing world. In that world of tomorrow, these exist as realistic possibilities: the average work week will be from twenty-four to thirty-two hours, the average family income nearly $20,000, the average life span eighty years, distances will be measured in minutes, and the interaction of persons in various nations of the world will be almost as close as that between next-door neighbors. Preparation of teachers for the atomic age is quite a different procedure than was the preparation of instructors for the age of the horseless carriage, or even of the air age. Whether the year or less of total professional education is interspersed among academic courses during a five year college program, or whether the first four years of preparation are academic in nature, followed by one year of professional work, five years of preparation is an absolute minimum. Some authorities have even extended the prospective teachers' training program to include a total of seven years.

---

21 N. E. Fitzgerald, "Laboratory Experiences and Student Teaching at the University of Tennessee," *Teacher Education: the Decade Ahead* (Washington, D.C.: National Commission on Teacher Education and Professional Standards, DeKalb Conference Report, National Education Association, 1955), pp. 95–99.

LIBERAL EDUCATION

No professional educator would deny that a prospective elementary school teacher should have a broad educational background of usable information in the areas of English, speech, drama, philosophy, psychology, art, music, and natural and social sciences. Equipped with this type of background, the teacher on the job will be culturally ready to direct many discussions in the modern classroom and will be able to locate additional information as he needs it. There can be little question that the elementary teacher needs to understand the cultural context in which all education takes places.

Unruh conducted a study in which he solicited opinions from three groups of persons—deans of liberal arts, deans of education, and teachers and school administrators—as to what is needed in teacher education.[22] The deans of liberal arts were included since they supervise the general education and the subject matter specialization of teachers and administrators, and deans of education were included since they supervise the professional education of those persons.

Suggestions collected by Unruh, in their order of rank are:

Teachers and school administrators:

1. More and better teaching of the professional skills, methods, techniques, and management.
2. Teaching toward the improvement of professional attitudes.
3. Improved and more work in professional courses in background: history of education, theory of education, philosophy of education, methods of teaching, and knowledge of the public schools.
4. Better student teaching; including earlier contact with the classroom situation, longer contact, and teaching experiences in a variety of conditions, all under adequate supervision.
5. Improved general education with more education in the culture of the people, more knowledge, and correlation and interrelation of knowledge.
6. More professional education courses in terms of practical problems courses.

7.5 More work in the understanding of the community and of parents, also techniques of the parent interview.

9. More help in understanding the pupil and in working with him.
10. More cooperation between colleges of education and public schools.

Deans of education:

1. Improved and more work in professional courses in background: history of education, theory of education, philosophy of education, methods of teaching, and knowledge of public schools.

[22] Adolph Unruh, "What's Needed in Teacher Education," *Phi Delta Kappan*, XXXVII (March, 1956), pp. 258–261.

2. More and better cooperation between colleges of liberal arts and colleges of education.
3. Improved general education with more education in the culture of the people, more knowledge, and correlation and interrelation of knowledge.
4. Improved teaching in the professional courses which are sometimes taught by Ph.D. candidates not grounded in the principles of education or who have not had public school experience, or have no interest in or little understanding of the work.
5. Better student teaching; including earlier contact with the classroom situation, longer contact, and teaching experiences in a variety of conditions all under adequate supervision.
6. More professional education courses in terms of practical problems courses.
7. More work in the understanding of the community and of parents, also techniques of the parent interview.
9. More cooperation between colleges of education and the public schools.
9. More help in understanding the pupil and in working with him.
9. More follow-up of beginning teachers and help in making proper adjustments.

Liberal Arts deans:

1. Teachers need more knowledge and subject matter specialization.
2. Professional education courses should be reduced or eliminated.
3. Criticism of the high school.
4. More and better cooperation between colleges of liberal arts and colleges of education.
5. Better student teaching; including earlier contact with the classroom situation, longer contact, and teaching experiences in a variety of conditions, all under adequate supervision.
5. The professional courses in background: history of education, theory of education, philosophy of education, methods of teaching, and knowledge of the public schools should be both reduced and improved.
5. There should be better screening of candidates for teaching.
8. Teaching toward the improvement of professional attitudes.
9. Professional courses, e.g., methods and background, are not effective.
10. Improve college teaching (not necessarily related to courses in education).[23]

From these opinions, it can be seen that in many instances the future plans for teacher education include most of the needs as expressed by the teachers and administrators, liberal arts deans, and

[23] *Ibid.*

professional college deans. It is also apparent, however, that there is a very marked difference in the opinions of persons in professional education and those of deans of liberal arts. Additionally, it appears that if all the needs that are expressed above are met by colleges of teacher education, the fifth-year program will not only be desirable, but will be an actual necessity. The opinions of all show evidence of strong support for the liberal arts.

In newer programs of teacher education in such institutions as the Iowa State Teachers College, the George Peabody College for Teachers, the Colorado State College of Education, the University of Florida, the University of Minnesota, San Diego State College, and others, the belief is emerging that in the preparation of a good teacher, the prime requisite is the development of a liberally-educated person, with an understanding of present day problems, of the cultural heritage, and of the physical environment. The programs at such institutions include the development of the ability to understand the ideas of others and to express oneself effectively, to enjoy literature, art, music, and other cultural activities, and to maintain and improve one's health. Such programs also stress the development of moral, ethical, and spiritual qualities that are necessary for a happy and successful life. Chalmers advises that,

> . . . Our orators have reminded us since The Bomb that not engineering and weapons, but the establishment and spread of justice are our true defense. Without a widespread liberal study of the humanities—that is, poetry, history, religion, philosophy, and all literature—justice cannot live because it cannot be understood.[24]

THE "CRASH" PROGRAMS

During the mid-twentieth century shortage of qualified teachers for the nation's elementary schools, a number of programs evolved which were intended to aid in meeting the scarcity. These included such projects as recruiting former teachers, recruiting at high school and college levels, and establishing accelerated programs for the training of persons interested in entering the profession. Another reason in addition to shortage of teachers was advanced for some of the accelerated programs. It was asserted that these programs helped to break the impasse which allegedly existed between the liberal arts people and those in professional education. The former, it was

---

[24] Gordon K. Chalmers, "Liberal Education as Practical Education," *Ninth Yearbook* (Chicago: The American Association of Colleges for Teacher Education, 1956), p. 22.

claimed, protested that students were spending so much time on professional education courses that liberal arts programs were becoming emasculated, while professional educators "insisted that the amount of time allotted to professional courses and to practice teaching was so small as to make it impossible to provide prospective teachers with the professional preparation needed."[25] The programs that evolved, requiring a fifth-year for their completion, were deemed to include an appropriate amount of liberal arts and professional training.

INTERNSHIP PROGRAMS

Early in the 1950's some colleges and universities began accelerated fifth-year programs for the preparation of liberal arts graduates for the teaching profession. One of the first programs of this type and one of the most publicized was that at the University of Arkansas. The purpose of the project, which was underwritten by a grant from one of the national foundations, was to set up and sponsor a program of teacher education based upon a liberal arts program of four years, followed by a period of internship and professional educational study.

INTERNSHIP AT THE UNIVERSITY OF ARKANSAS

Two programs comprised the experiment at Little Rock; the Regular Program, which began in late 1952, and the Alternate Program, which evolved in mid-1955. The latter program grew out of the lessons learned in the Regular Program, since one of the purposes of the Regular Program had been to develop and evaluate a fifth-year program of professional teacher education for liberal arts college graduates. Participating liberal arts colleges screened and selected students for the Arkansas project; the students were given scholarships which amounted to $125 per month while they were in training. After four years of liberal arts training, the fifth year of professional education included twenty weeks of practice teaching with related professional seminars.

In the Alternate Program at Arkansas, which replaced the Regular Program, students were screened by colleges which participated in the program, and were then selected by representatives of the University's Education and Graduate Schools, and by the superintendent of schools in Little Rock. Candidates studied professional education courses in a twelve-week summer session; then were placed for an academic year in a full-time teaching situation, with weekly seminars,

---

[25] Paul Woodring, *New Directions in Teacher Education* (New York: Fund for the Advancement of Education, 1957), p. 30.

under close supervision of college representatives and the school principal. Following the year of teaching, the students spent a second summer session in professional education or academic courses. While no scholarships were offered the students, they did teach under a public school contract. At the end of the second summer, the students were awarded the Master of Education degree and the Arkansas Six-Year Teaching Certificate.[26]

HARVARD'S INTERNSHIP PROGRAM

The internship experiment at Harvard University, which began early in 1952 under national foundation grants, sought to increase the number and quality of graduates of liberal arts colleges entering teaching, and to provide a new program of paid internship training in actual teaching situations. Graduates of certain approved colleges were selected for the program. Students received scholarships ranging from $300 to $1200 per year, and internship stipends amounting to $1500. The training program began in summer sessions which included apprentice teaching. Half of the following year was spent in full-time graduate studies, and the other half was spent in teaching while carrying a minimum of course work at the university.

The interns at Harvard were assigned in pairs, and were employed to replace one beginning teacher, one intern teaching the first semester, the second intern teaching the last half of the school year. Interns were assigned all duties of a regular teacher, but received considerably more help in supervision from teachers, principals, supervisors, and Harvard staff members than did the usual beginning teacher. Successful candidates in elementary education received the Master of Education degree at the conclusion of their training.[27]

THE PROGRAM AT SAN DIEGO STATE

San Diego State College cooperates with the San Diego City Schools in the internship program in that southern California community. The college and the city cooperate in recruiting students for the program from the city and its environs through newspapers, educational newsletters, television, and talks in the community. Application for acceptance into the program is made by the student to the district and then to the college, and applications are screened by college and school district representatives through personal interviews and a series of tests. Assignments to schools are made by district officials.

During the spring semester prior to the intern year, the instruc-

---

[26] *Ibid.*, pp. 85–88.
[27] *Ibid.*, pp. 108–109.

tional program at San Diego provides for extension course work in which the candidate learns of the elementary curriculum and policies of the school district. During the first six weeks of that summer, the candidate attends a daily one-hour observation period at the grade level he will teach, as well as a college class which meets before and after the observation period. The class concentrates on the areas of social studies, language arts, reading, arithmetic, music, physical education, and art. In the last three weeks of the summer session, the student spends two weeks in college classes and one week in the classroom, where he prepares materials, practices skills, and spends much time with an advisory teacher in preparing the classroom for the opening of school.

During the intern's teaching year, he attends the district orientation meeting for all new teachers in the San Diego schools, and is assigned an advisory teacher who is available at all times for guidance and help. One advisory teacher is assigned for four interns. The intern is fully responsible for his class. One night a week during the spring semester, the candidate takes a college course in which he studies music, art, and physical education. Supervision is provided by the college director and teachers and administrators in the city system.

There is a large number of internship programs in existence at the present time, with the three described above being only illustrative. There is a feeling among some educators that intern training programs will become more prevalent, since the interns are generally more mature than many four-year or five-year graduates, and since they have had the advantage of contact with children prior to taking a number of their professional courses.

CONDENSED PROGRAMS IN TEACHER EDUCATION

Another example of accelerated "crash" programs of teacher education which seems to be meeting with more success than the internship type is a fifth-year experiment known generally as a "condensed" or post-baccalaureate program of teacher preparation. Several colleges and universities have inaugurated a project of this nature, in which liberal arts college graduates are encouraged to take a fifth year of professional preparation, including supervised teaching. Generally, candidates in these programs pursue a course of study which includes slightly more professional training than the state minimum requirements for a teaching certificate.

THE GRADUATE PROGRAM AT STANFORD

A new program, beginning in the summer session, 1960, at Stanford University's School of Education was opened for a limited and select group of graduate students desiring to prepare for elementary school teaching and leadership positions. The program provides a full year of elementary school teaching preparation for liberal arts graduates.

Stanford's accelerated program (for which scholarships are available) emphasizes the foundations of professional education, curriculum and instruction, and classroom observation and student teaching. In his first quarter in the program, the candidate enrolls in Social Foundations of Education, Psychological Foundations of Education, Philosophy of Education, and Guided Observation in the Campus Demonstration School. In the fall quarter, the student takes courses in Participation in Public Elementary Schools, Curriculum and Instruction in Elementary Schools (reading, language, and arithmetic), and Audio-Visual Laboratory. In the winter quarter, the candidate pursues courses in Curriculum and Instruction in Elementary Schools (science and social studies), Art in the Elementary School, Music in the Elementary Schools, and Physical Education in the Elementary School. The final quarter in the program provides for student participation in directed teaching. Upon the successful completion of the program, students are awarded both the Master of Arts degree and the California Elementary School Teaching Credential.

SAN JOSE STATE'S POST-BACCALAUREATE PROGRAM

A program three years older than the one at Stanford is found at nearby San Jose State College. That institution provides a program for students who are interested in securing California teaching credentials for the kindergarten-primary, or the general elementary area, as well as those interested in the secondary teaching area.

A full year's professional preparation course, the program at San Jose accepts applicants who have a liberal arts baccalaureate degree with high academic grade standing, and with other desirable qualifications of an elementary teacher. In his first semester in the program a student takes Curriculum and Observation, Audio-Visual Laboratory, Teaching of Reading, Teaching of Arithmetic, Child Growth and Development or Child Psychology, and Elementary School Penmanship. The second semester is spent in student teaching in the public schools of San Jose and environs, and in closely related group seminars on campus. Supervision is provided cooperatively by the college and the assigned schools' teachers and administrators. The appropriate credential is awarded students who successfully complete the two-semester program.

According to evaluative studies of the success of this program, as conducted by members of the San Jose State department of elementary education staff, candidates who complete the condensed program are not as effective or successful in the classroom after graduation as are the graduates of the regular four-year session in the department. Graduates of the condensed program tend to return to campus at their earliest opportunity to pursue some "how to teach" courses that they would have had had they completed the regular four-year program.

GEORGE PEABODY'S AND VANDERBILT UNIVERSITY'S GRADUATE PROGRAMS

An example of two colleges with different objectives cooperating in a graduate program to prepare teachers may be found in Nashville, Tennessee, at George Peabody College for Teachers and at Vanderbilt University. With the aid of a national foundation's funds, the two colleges provide fellowships to superior graduates of liberal arts programs for a full year of additional study leading to the Master of Arts in Teaching degree. Two of the four quarters of work are taken in subject matter areas at Vanderbilt, and the other two quarters of work are taken in professional education at Peabody. The entire program requires 60 quarter-hours, 30 of which are taken at one institution, 30 at the other. The course of study at Peabody includes 12 hours of practice teaching.[28]

In another program at George Peabody, selected graduates of liberal arts colleges participate in a full year of additional study if they are interested in entering the teaching profession. The liberal arts colleges recommend the graduates for the teacher education program, and the four quarters of work are tailored to suit the needs of the candidates. Half of this work is in professional education, and includes seminars each week in which students are encouraged to broaden their horizons and "expose their prejudices to free debate and discussion."[29]

IN-SERVICE EDUCATION OF TEACHERS

It is evident from the descriptions of programs of teacher education described above that school districts are playing an increasingly active role in the recruitment, screening, and education of their personnel. There is a trend for the districts to share more and more with the institutions of higher education in the training of teachers. Quali-

28 *Ibid.*
29 Henry Hill, *loc. cit.*

fied personnel in the colleges are being called upon increasingly to serve as resource persons to teacher groups.

Prospective teachers in colleges and universities are spending more time in the elementary schools during their training period, on the assumption that the more time students can spend with boys and girls in the actual classroom situation the better prepared they will be to assume their places in the elementary schools. Students are also afforded opportunities to be exposed to children earlier in their preparatory programs. During their training, students meet with school district supervisors and teachers and college instructors in seminar sessions to discuss their teaching experiences in relation to professional and other course work taken on campus. Many joint college-district activities carry on throughout the time students are enrolled in college classes, and into the time the students are beginning their professional careers.

In-service education is a type of continual expert guidance of teachers which encourages them to seek greater competence. The in-service education program should be concerned with local problems and applied to the larger community problems. An adequate program includes cooperative endeavors with other teachers and individual teacher effort. It is a program through which conscientious teachers may remain students of teaching problems, and represents an opportunity for continuing professional and personal growth. It is the responsibility of the elementary school principal to provide an environment in which teachers will find new understanding of the forces which impinge upon children and society; and in which they will develop new insights into the social significance of the elementary school program.

The concept of in-service education of professional personnel has been widely accepted among educators for a long while. But, as is true of so many other practices in education, that which is "accepted" and that which is "practiced" do not always coincide. In a survey of the in-service activities of secondary schools in Iowa, made in the early 1950's by one of the writers, it was found that most of the high schools in that state were concerned with in-service education of their personnel, but few actually instituted programs for that purpose. Those schools that did hold regular in-service sessions were principally those with large enrollments, and the same could be said for elementary schools throughout the nation in general. The survey also indicated that in-service education suffers as a result of the rapid turnover of school administrators, especially in smaller schools. Such turnover is not evident in larger schools, and that is undoubtedly one reason for the more active programs of in-service education.

Inadequacies in the institutional training of teachers, as well as the growing awareness of the complexity of teaching, make in-service education necessary in modern elementary schools. The privileges and rewards of creative teaching can be obtained only at the price of active and extended participation in in-service programs. Such programs in various schools emphasize locally-organized school-community activities, such as workshops, special study groups, work with consultants, work with parents, attendance at college or university, travel, and others. Programs in some communities are organized on a long-term schedule. Special themes or problems, such as cultivation of specific character traits, new orientations in education, directing pupil experience to the needs and capacities of children, and determining causes of pupil failure, characterize the programs of some schools. Results of in-service education programs include improved staff meetings, improved supervisor-teacher relationships, the formation of committees of teachers, pupils, and parents to work on school problems, and a rise in morale of administrators and teachers.

The most difficult obstacles in carrying out in-service programs are lack of time, heavy teaching loads, and heavy extra-curricular loads. Programs which are planned and carried out by faculty members themselves have proved most successful and profitable.

There are many teachers in the profession who would profit from an active, well-planned in-service education program. Sometimes school districts indirectly encourage individual teachers to improve themselves through a salary schedule which provides for professional growth increments or enables teachers to purchase books, go to summer school, or travel. In-service education may also be achieved through the occasional release of teachers to make classroom visitations, to work on curriculum committees, to attend conferences, and to participate in special workshops.

THE ROLE OF THE ADMINISTRATOR

Principals, superintendents, curriculum directors, and directors of instruction all have responsibilities in a system-wide program of in-service education. Their roles are determined in part by their concepts of the nature of in-service education, and in part by their understanding of the psychology of change and their attitudes toward group work. As an effective facilitator and coordinator of in-service education, an administrator must (1) provide inspiration; (2) encourage development of good organization of in-service education; (3) facilitate the work of groups; and (4) create a climate for growth. In order to do these things, Lewis believes an effective administrator needs the following knowledge:

1. An understanding of the psychology of change.
2. Knowledge of possible types of organization for in-service education.
3. Knowledge of how to use available resources for in-service education.
4. Understanding of the role of education in our society.

The effective administrator needs the following skills:

1. Ability to work cooperatively with the staff.
2. Expertness in group process.

The effective administrator needs the following attitudes:

1. Faith in teachers.
2. Respect for individual or human personality.
3. Recognition of the importance of working with groups.
4. Faith that a group can find reasonably sound solutions to problems.
5. Patience in working with groups.[30]

Simpson stresses the importance of the administrator's role:

> The administrator of an individual school is the key person in the in-service program; if he thinks in-service education activities are important and plans wisely for them, the teachers will usually reflect his attitude and interest. Unless the teacher catches the enthusiasm and interest of the principal, no actual changes will occur in instruction because, in the final analysis, improvement in the instructional program depends upon the teacher's appreciation of the social significance of teaching and upon his desire to use the most effective classroom procedures.
>
> Progress in improving the quality of education is made school-by-school. Although the principal may cooperate in over-all policy development and in-service education planning on a system-wide basis, the ultimate measure of progress must be determined by what happens to children and teachers in individual schools. The principal sets the stage, creates the atmosphere which facilitates progress or acts as a deterrent to progress.[31]

He further states that the administrator sets the stage in four ways:

1. The administrator works to create a common philosophy of education with teachers, parents, interested community leaders, and the children themselves.
2. The administrator works to make the physical environment for education as conducive as possible to the realization of the purposes of the modern school.

---

[30] Arthur Lewis et al, "The Role of the Administrator in Inservice Education," *Inservice Education,* 56th Yearbook of the National Society for the Study of Education (Chicago: University of Chicago Press, 1957), pp. 172–173.

[31] Roy E. Simpson, "The Principal's Role in Inservice Education," *California Journal of Elementary Education,* XXVI (May, 1958), p. 198.

3. The administrator works to make the intellectual environment of the school stimulating for children.
4. The administrator contributes significantly to the emotional climate of the school in which each person can be his best and do his best and in which good staff relations are fostered.[32]

In an address in 1958 before the American Council on Education, Dr. Virgil Hancher, president of the State University of Iowa, said:

> When in the eighteen seventies and eighties and nineties the learned doctors and professors of our universities and colleges felt it beneath their dignity to prepare teachers for the common schools, the need was met by the proliferation of normal schools and teachers colleges throughout the land . . . Nor should we expect the current need to be met by the transitory interest of the learned doctors and professors. It would be a glorious prospect if they could be expected to concern themselves in a long-range program for the improvement of schools. But they will not. Neither their professional interests nor their professional advancement, by the criteria which they themselves have set, lie in that quarter.
>
> Within five years most, if not all, of the present critics among them will have returned to Beowulf or Chaucer or the political policies of Sir Robert Walpole or the causes of the French Revolution or the peaceful uses of atomic power; and high school teachers of English and social studies and science will again find it necessary to turn to the professional educationists who are their only constant and true friends in time of need.[33]

To which the president of George Peabody College for Teachers adds:

> . . . The Teachers' Colleges will be few in number a decade hence, but if their successors retain a serious commitment of interest and money in teacher education, they may provide a broader cultural and social base, and perhaps attract abler persons to teaching. If, on the other hand, they become average and hum-drum arts colleges and lose their interest in teachers, another generation will have to start teachers' colleges all over again.[34]

CONCLUSION

When elementary school administrators respond to the challenge of leadership in the improvement of instruction, their role in the

[32] *Ibid.*, pp. 198–201.

[33] Virgil Hancher in an address to the American Council on Education, 1958, as quoted in Henry Hill, *loc. cit.*

[34] Hill, *loc. cit.*

pre-service and in-service education of teachers is vital. As principals assume increased responsibility in joint college-school teacher education programs, their suggestions for improving student teaching programs and methods and curriculum courses will increasingly be accepted on the grounds that these administrators understand what comprises good teaching.

Professional training, at both the pre-service and in-service levels, is becoming less book-bound and more concerned with enriching life and developing values which foster enduring satisfactions. With close cooperation between schools and colleges, principals can help prospective and beginning teachers apply what they have learned, and thus achieve increasing measures of competence and effectiveness.

There is no question that teacher education programs must include professional education courses and activities, as well as courses in the various subject-matter areas. The number of semester hours of college credit in education and in academic courses which are necessary for a well-grounded elementary school teacher will have to be decided by experts in the respective fields, and by public school personnel. It is important, however, that a proper balance of course work be achieved and maintained. Elementary school principals are in a key position to contribute their objective thinking with respect to what this balance should be; they are in the best position to take the leadership in initiating and coordinating activities that will lead to improvement of instruction.

While assisting in the determination of an adequate program of teacher education, elementary administrators must keep in mind the kinds of organizational situations in which new teachers may find themselves. Besides the more traditional schemes, a number of experimental programs of a more or less permanent nature are in existence. These will be discussed in Chapter IV.

Short Case 1

Motivating the Teacher

Mrs. Lyle had graduated from college twenty years ago and had been teaching the same grade in the Murray Elementary School since that time. She had made no attempt at self-improvement during those years, and as a result, her methodology was steeped in the traditional techniques advocated during her college career. When Mr. Young became principal of the school and attempted to introduce and demonstrate some of the newer methods being advocated in colleges and practiced by effective elementary teachers, Mrs. Lyle had little patience with either the new "upstart" or his "progressive schemes."

After Mr. Young had been at the school for four years, successfully helping the other teachers and occasionally aiding Mrs. Lyle to a slight extent, he left for another job; but he noticed that the year after he left Mrs. Lyle attended a workshop in the teaching of reading conducted by one of the nation's authorities in the field at a nearby state university.

Problem: What could Mr. Young have done to get Mrs. Lyle interested in self-improvement while he was principal at the school? Did he proceed properly? Why or why not? Does this case tell anything about the basic characteristics of most elementary school teachers?

Short Case 2

Ruth Edwards, Teaching Intern

Ruth Edwards sighed and tried again, "Ronnie, you just can't do that in the classroom. When you hit someone, they want to hit you back. Here we learn to think of each other."

Later she left a note on Principal Jack Fleeman's desk: "Mr. Fleeman: Ronnie Cushing has been disturbing the class and my teaching beyond reason. I have tried all I know to show him love and encouragement, but I honestly feel he needs more help than I can give him. Ruth Edwards, Fourth Grade Student Intern, Rm. 6."

Mr. Fleeman picked up the note when he returned from his luncheon meeting. Ronnie had been moved from pillar to post. No teacher would have him, and the mother refused to get outside help. Miss Edwards had provoked some good changes in Ronnie. She would probably follow up the note when classes were over. Mr. Fleeman sat looking at Ronnie's folder, thinking about the conversation coming up.

Problem: Try role playing the conversation between Mr. Fleeman and Ruth Edwards. Was there something missing in Miss Edwards' background or training that made her react as she did? What is necessary in an elementary teacher's training program besides course work in the academic area?

Short Case 3

A Student Teaching Problem

Joyce Adams, a senior at State University, was in her first week of directed teaching in a first grade classroom of a nearby public elementary school. Dr. Farr, her college supervisor, made an unannounced visit for the primary purpose of introducing himself to Mrs. Runyan, the resident teacher. Since student teachers generally did not take over any teaching duties that early in the term, he did not expect to see Joyce in the role of the teacher. To his astonishment, however, he found Miss Adams in the midst of a science lesson with the first grade youngsters and the topic was, of all things, electricity!

Following the lesson, Dr. Farr and Joyce Adams excused themselves from the classroom and went to the teachers' lounge to discuss the situation. Asked why she had taught the science lesson, Miss Adams told her supervisor that Mrs. Runyan had asked her that morning if she would take the science lesson while she checked some records in the office. Not wishing to displease the resident teacher, Miss Adams had agreed to the assignment.

"But why a lesson on electricity to first graders?" Dr. Farr inquired. "Well," said Joyce, "I found a lesson plan I had prepared in one of my science education methods classes in my notebook, so, in desperation, I used it." "I don't blame you, Miss Adams, I would have done the same thing."

Problem: What is the basic problem in this case? What suggestions might Dr. Farr have made to his student teacher so that she might better handle a similar situation should one occur? How was this case-situation a good experience for a student teacher?

Chapter Four

New Plans of Organization for Instruction

Elementary school instruction has felt the impact of criticism which befell American public education soon after Russia's Sputnik encircled the globe, and which still continues. Rightly or wrongly, critics have channeled a large share of their caustic comments toward the elementary school, and national foundations have allocated sizeable sums of money for experimentation in instruction at the elementary level. The allegation has been, of course, that the elementary schools have not taught children the fundamental rudiments; in effect, the cry has been for a "return to the three R's," a return to plans of instruction in vogue in an earlier day.

Those dedicated to the field of elementary education are not suggesting that the plan of organization for instruction in general use at this level for the past thirty years is perfect, or that it should continue to dominate elementary school instruction in the future. On the contrary, progressive administrators and teachers in the modern elementary school have been especially interested in experimenting, and in studying the experimentation of others, in the hope that such studies would point to more effective methods of providing a thorough education for the children in elementary school classrooms.

There has, then, been considerable experimentation in the elementary schools of America in recent years. This experimentation, it is hoped, will result in increased fundamental knowledge by the children, as well as an up-dating in methodology which will incorporate the vast amount of information secured through recent studies in child-training centers and clinics. Experimenters also hope that the new approaches to instruction will not negate the progress that has been made during recent years in public instruction in the more intangible areas, such as responsibility, integrity, friendliness, cooperativeness, understanding, fair play, self-discipline, and critical thinking, all of which are tantamount to effective democracy.

It is the purpose of this chapter to describe a few of the more promising plans of organization for instruction at the elementary level. These plans have been, or are in current use at the schools named.

CENTRALIZED VS. DECENTRALIZED SCHOOL ORGANIZATION

Before specific programs currently in use are described, it is appropriate to take a brief interpretative view of the problem: Should administration of the school district be centralized or decentralized? This problem will, ultimately, have an effect on the organizational plan for instruction which will be most effective in an individual school. Admittedly, the pattern of organization is secondary to program, but it is also true that an appropriate organization will facilitate the formulation and practice of a good program of instruction.

Line-and-staff organization, district-wise, has been the traditional scheme in America's schools. Under this design, in which planning and performance are almost completely separated, administrators in the central office make the plans and send their instructions down the line of authority to teachers and pupils. Such a plan is probably most effective in the small community with only one school. Centralized control under this plan is considered to be highly efficient in the prevention of friction and avoidance of waste which results from duplication of effort, since all schools in the district are usually controlled from one central point.

As a community grows and school units become a part of the larger district, the exclusive use of the line-and-staff organization becomes ineffective. The principal at the local level tends to view it as a faraway power with preconceived and unchangeable ideas. To counteract this feeling, some districts have placed a large degree of ultimate power in the hands of the local school principal, have set up official lay, or lay-teacher, bodies, and have given them responsibility for out-

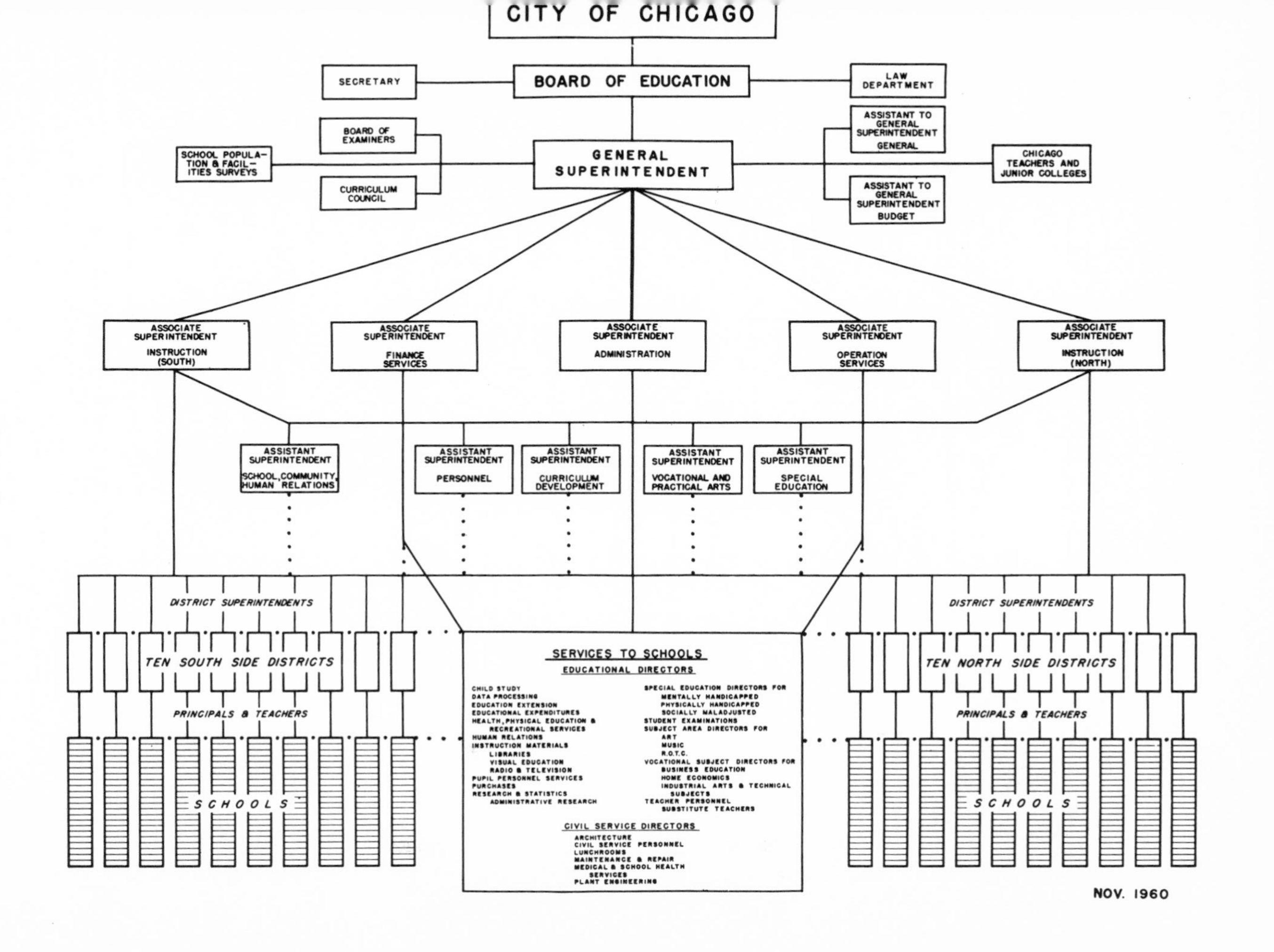
CITY OF CHICAGO
SECRETARY
BOARD OF EDUCATION
LAW DEPARTMENT
BOARD OF EXAMINERS
ASSISTANT TO GENERAL SUPERINTENDENT GENERAL
SCHOOL POPULATION & FACILITIES SURVEYS
GENERAL SUPERINTENDENT
CHICAGO TEACHERS AND JUNIOR COLLEGES
CURRICULUM COUNCIL
ASSISTANT TO GENERAL SUPERINTENDENT BUDGET
ASSOCIATE SUPERINTENDENT INSTRUCTION (SOUTH)
ASSOCIATE SUPERINTENDENT FINANCE SERVICES
ASSOCIATE SUPERINTENDENT ADMINISTRATION
ASSOCIATE SUPERINTENDENT OPERATION SERVICES
ASSOCIATE SUPERINTENDENT INSTRUCTION (NORTH)
ASSISTANT SUPERINTENDENT SCHOOL, COMMUNITY, HUMAN RELATIONS
ASSISTANT SUPERINTENDENT PERSONNEL
ASSISTANT SUPERINTENDENT CURRICULUM DEVELOPMENT
ASSISTANT SUPERINTENDENT VOCATIONAL AND PRACTICAL ARTS
ASSISTANT SUPERINTENDENT SPECIAL EDUCATION
DISTRICT SUPERINTENDENTS
TEN SOUTH SIDE DISTRICTS
PRINCIPALS & TEACHERS
SCHOOLS
SERVICES TO SCHOOLS
EDUCATIONAL DIRECTORS
CHILD STUDY
DATA PROCESSING
EDUCATION EXTENSION
EDUCATIONAL EXPENDITURES
HEALTH, PHYSICAL EDUCATION & RECREATIONAL SERVICES
HUMAN RELATIONS
INSTRUCTION MATERIALS
LIBRARIES
VISUAL EDUCATION
RADIO & TELEVISION
PUPIL PERSONNEL SERVICES
PURCHASES
RESEARCH & STATISTICS
ADMINISTRATIVE RESEARCH
SPECIAL EDUCATION DIRECTORS FOR
MENTALLY HANDICAPPED
PHYSICALLY HANDICAPPED
SOCIALLY MALADJUSTED
STUDENT EXAMINATIONS
SUBJECT AREA DIRECTORS FOR
ART
MUSIC
R.O.T.C.
VOCATIONAL SUBJECT DIRECTORS FOR
BUSINESS EDUCATION
HOME ECONOMICS
INDUSTRIAL ARTS & TECHNICAL SUBJECTS
TEACHER PERSONNEL
SUBSTITUTE TEACHERS
CIVIL SERVICE DIRECTORS
ARCHITECTURE
CIVIL SERVICE PERSONNEL
LUNCHROOMS
MAINTENANCE & REPAIR
MEDICAL & SCHOOL HEALTH SERVICES
PLANT ENGINEERING
DISTRICT SUPERINTENDENTS
TEN NORTH SIDE DISTRICTS
PRINCIPALS & TEACHERS
SCHOOLS
NOV. 1960

Figure 2

lining policy for local schools. Such decentralizing procedure tends to provide local checks and balances of such strength that control by the immediate community becomes more feasible and important.

A striking example of a large city organizational structure involving a decentralized line-and-staff distribution is that of Chicago, Illinois. Figure 2 shows the organization of the Chicago system. Each of the twenty district superintendents is responsible for the educational program in the elementary and high schools within a specific geographic area. The district superintendent is the instructional leader within the district. The district superintendents in turn are responsible to the Associate Superintendent in Charge of Instruction for the north or south section of the city, and the Associate Superintendent in Charge of Administration. The district superintendent works with Parent-Teacher Association representatives as well as representatives of community organizations within his area of responsibility. According to General Superintendent Benjamin C. Willis, each of the districts includes an enrollment of approximately 25,000 children.

There seems to be a trend at present toward decentralizing school administration. Houston examined the problem of decision-making in industry and related his findings to the problem of decision-making in centralized and decentralized school units.[1] He found that decentralized administration is identified with democratic administration and that professional people need the freedom and autonomy that accompanies decentralized administration. He concluded that decentralized administration within a school unit leads to the improvement of teachers, pupils, and administration, just as it leads to improvement of industrial decision-making, and subsequently to the improvement of the operation; that decentralized administration brings a decision closer to an actual need, and thereby betters the organization; and that the greater the individual differences influencing teacher professionalism among staff members, the greater the need for increased democratic administration.

The outstanding schools in this country and abroad, whether public or private, are those possessing a considerable degree of autonomy. Principals and teachers in these schools seem to experience an increased sense of unity in meeting needs and interests of boys and girls in the community. Some authorities are recommending that no decentralized unit exceed a maximum of fifty teachers.[2]

---

[1] Harry Herbert Houston, *An Inquiry into the Administrative Process as it Relates to Decision Making* (Unpublished Doctoral dissertation, Rutgers University, 1959).

[2] Francis S. Chase, "The Next Fifty Years in Public Education," *Problems and Opportunities in Financing Education* (Washington: Committee on Tax Education and School Finance, National Education Association, 1959), p. 16.

BACK TO THE UNGRADED SCHOOL

Before the Civil War, elementary schools in the United States were ungraded; that is, there was no grade one, grade two, grade three, and so on up the educational ladder. Each child proceeded at his own rate; when he completed one McGuffey's Reader, he began the next. Each child remained in school as long as he wished.

At about the time of the Civil War, our graded schools came into existence. This age-grade system of grouping children, which grew out of an expressed need for simplified methods of organizing and administering an elementary school, is still the most common method of grouping children today.

There is a recent tendency, however, for some elementary schools to drop the grade designation system in favor of a plan similar to that in vogue in colonial and early national periods of our country's history. This is especially true at the primary level grades one, two, and three, in the traditional arrangement. Each year more school systems experiment with the ungraded plan of administrative organization at the primary level: some are also extending the plan into the intermediate area of the traditional grades four, five, and six.

REASONS FOR THE UNGRADED SCHOOL

One purpose in designing the ungraded school is the provision for continuous growth and learning for each child through flexible groupings. Such flexibility aids teachers in dealing with individual differences among children, enabling them to give increased attention to each child's needs, interest, and abilities. It is a known fact that the range of ability of children in any given year of school is so great that it is virtually impossible to make them conform to specific grade levels. A typical second grade in the traditional graded school would include pupils achieving well above second grade level in reading and all other subject areas as well as pupils who are just beginning to read.

A second objective of the ungraded plan is the minimizing of grade lines. Under this organization, children generally are grouped according to achievement levels instead of grades. In the first three years of school following kindergarten, children usually progress through eight or ten levels. Corresponding to the traditional grade one would possibly be levels one and two, and perhaps part of level three; the traditional second grade would encompass levels three, four, and five; and the traditional third grade would, perhaps, involve levels six and seven. In some schools an eighth level of achievement would be an enrichment level for pupils who have completed the work of the traditional third grade, but who are not quite ready to enter the customary grade four.

The schools employing the ungraded primary unit normally define a level by the work to be mastered in it, and once a child achieves all of the objectives for a particular level he proceeds to the next higher level. Mastery of the basal reading series' pre-primer vocabulary, a knowledge of color and number words, the ability to write his name legibly in manuscript, the ability to form letters properly, the ability to get meaning from pictures, the beginning of the ability to recognize sounds, and the ability to count and understand numbers up to ten, all of this normally entitles the child to advance from level one to level two. A child does not need to wait until the semester's end to be advanced; he may advance at any time.

A third reason for the existence of the ungraded school is that promotion can be based upon the development of all aspects of a child's being, not just the intellectual aspect. In the ungraded school, physical, social, and emotional development can be considered. Statistics reveal that one in every five children who starts the traditional first grade faces the possibility of non-promotion during the next few years. For the child who gets off to a slow start, the ungraded plan offers a device other than non-promotion for regulating the child's progress. In a similar manner, a child who gets off to an unusually good start encounters many problems when the school resorts to "skip promotion," or "grade acceleration," as a device for moving him on to a more challenging level of work; the ungraded plan provides what seems to be a more satisfactory solution.

The ungraded plan of organization is consistent with recent psychological findings concerning growth, development, and learning in children. Schools utilizing this plan attempt to create a learning environment in which children can develop fully and normally, and in which children's individual needs and interests are given utmost attention. Subject matter content, designed in terms of the child's readiness and need for more functional learnings, is organized on the basis of individual maturation and growth patterns. The plan allows the pupil to advance step by step at his own rate, and at the same time reduces frustration due to failure at the end of each "grade" if his growth has been slow and certain academic standards have not been reached.

ADMINISTRATIVE PROBLEMS TO BE SOLVED

In adopting the ungraded primary unit plan of organization, there are certain administrative problems which must be solved by the personnel of the school. This, of course, holds true when any untried venture is attempted in any local attendance unit.

Staff orientation needed. Probably the first administrative problem which presents itself in the process of changing from a graded to an ungraded type of organization is that of staff orientation. Teachers, supervisors, and administrators must be thoroughly familiar with the philosophy and purposes of the ungraded unit, and with the bases and techniques of effective grouping of children. Too, they need a complete understanding of the learning and growth patterns of children from ages five through eight, as well as a thorough conception of the academic program of the elementary school grades kindergarten through three. Such orientation is obtainable only through careful and deliberate preparation in programs of action research, experimentation, and investigation of programs now in existence.

Once the ungraded plan is in operation in an elementary school, teachers generally react enthusiastically. If the ungraded plan cuts down the range of abilities of pupils with whom they work, the teachers' work will have been greatly simplified. Any teacher would prefer to work with three achievement levels instead of five! A second grade room with only second graders in it would be most inviting to any second grade teacher.

Parents' understanding needed. Before the ungraded primary program is begun, the school's parent group must be educated in regard to the philosophy, objectives, and operation of the program. Probably the best way to accomplish this is to call the parents in and talk with them individually and in groups, even though citizens' advisory groups may have helped plan the program. The new program should be explained in detail; the benefits to pupils in the school should be emphasized. When parents understand that a new procedure will do more for their children, that it will more readily provide for the needs of slow learners as well as more able learners, they will generally give it their support.

School people need to realize that the child's first teachers, his parents, are ready allies if they are but taken into confidence in any new endeavor which shows promise of facilitating the education of the children. Parents will attend school meetings if they are worth-while and planned to give them an opportunity to learn of a new procedure and to ask questions and receive rational answers. They will listen with special attentiveness to their children's teachers as they explain the new procedure in individual or group conferences.

Inaugurating the ungraded plan. The first year of the new ungraded organization presents some problems for the school's personnel to resolve. Probably the principal problem facing the staff is that of getting the program into operation; that is, assigning the pupils to the appropriate levels. Generally, this is accomplished in one or both of two ways: achievement tests, and teacher recommendation. Primary teachers know the achievement levels and IQ's of their pupils, so placement may be accomplished quite readily. New first graders or beginners in the school may be placed at level one and then proceed through the primary department. If an occasional beginner is not quite ready for level one, a junior-primary level may be inaugurated. In any case, as soon as a pupil completes the standards for one level, he proceeds immediately to the next.

Choosing level teachers. Which teachers should teach at which levels in the ungraded school? This may at first appear to be a critical question facing a staff about to launch into this new procedure; but actually teachers are assigned in the ungraded school in precisely the same manner in which they are assigned in the traditional graded elementary school. Those best prepared to teach at each level are assigned to those levels. Teachers who are particularly adept at experimentation and who are interested in using their ingenuity in challenging pupils should probably be considered for upper levels in the organization, or for classes of more able boys and girls. Others who may have a preference for working with slower achievers, who may have a more patient disposition, or who may like to work closely with individual problems, should probably be assigned to the lower levels or to groups of slow learners.

ORGANIZING THE UNGRADED SCHOOL

There is agreement between school personnel and parents alike that the grade level system used in the public schools is not an altogether valid system of determining at what point a child should be promoted to a higher level of learning. A classification system has long been desired which would place a child with a group doing school work at a level and standard of progress comparable to his. The ungraded plan of organization proposes to provide such a system of classification.

The ungraded elementary school is simply a plan by which children are grouped together with no grade level distinction. If the plan involves only the primary department, children in the traditional grades kindergarten, one, two, and three are affected; if the entire elementary school is ungraded, children in the traditional grades four, five, and six are also included. Under the ungraded plan the course of study at either departmental level becomes a very flexible program, and as a result there are fewer time limitations and crisis points where difficult decisions about promotions must be made. Normally, the average child progresses through the ungraded elementary school in much the same manner that he would move through a good graded school, while the bright child might complete the requirements for one of the departments in fewer than the usual number of years. While the average child is taking four years to progress through kindergarten and grades one, two, and three, the child of superior intelligence may be taking only three years, and the child with slow-learning ability is taking five years to complete the course. Possibly the only label on the classroom door is "primary" for the four, or three, or five years a pupil spends in classrooms in the primary department.

Pupils pursue the same lessons at approximately the same rate of speed that they would in the typical graded classrooms, with the difference that their "teacher has no grade level expectations against which to pace herself, and her only obligation is to keep youngsters moving along as fast as they are capable of moving. In June, when progress reports go home, no mention is made of grade level assignments for the ensuing year, and the parent is simply advised that the child will continue in primary and pick up in September where he has left off at this point in June."[3]

Recent research indicates that children do not learn more subject matter when they repeat a grade; rather, they achieve less growth in subject matter acquisition than when they are promoted. Because of this, the retention of children in an elementary school grade in order to assure mastery of subject matter is not often justified. The relationship of the child's normal development to educational goals, and the nature of anticipated learning experiences need to be carefully examined.

Data used in evaluating pupil progress in the ungraded school must come from a wide range of sources. The cumulative record may reveal the child's general pattern of progress in his previous school experience. The test data, which may include mental tests, diagnostic tests, personality tests and scales, and teacher-made tests, may give much insight into the child's status and progress. Inventories of interest and attitudes can be useful in reflecting inner feelings which may affect the child's progress. Valuable information may also be obtained through casual conversations and conferences with the individual. If this data is recorded, an intensive study of an individual over a period of time can reveal pertinent factors concerning physical problems. The sociometric techniques are frequently used by teachers to indicate the child's status with his peer group. Role playing, dramatic representa-

---

[3] Robert H. Anderson, "Ungraded Primary Classes," *The Education Digest,* XXI (November, 1955), pp. 47–50.

tions, projective techniques, and life space analyses are other means of learning more about children, their capacities, their growth, and their problems. By using as many of these devices as are available, school personnel can obtain a fairly reliable basis for evaluating the pupil's progress.

Following are some suggestions for the launching of an ungraded plan of organization as proposed by the schools in Green Bay, Wisconsin:

1. Develop understanding first on the part of teachers and parents.
2. Move toward ungrading a step at a time. Teachers may move from one grade to the next with pupils in preparation for an ungraded program to help overcome stereotypes.
3. Try to see an actual model early in the planning.
4. Once the step has been taken, go all the way. Removing grades in name only is not enough. Grade signs must be removed from doors and replaced with "Primary—Miss Smith," "Intermediate—Miss Brown." Progress must never be thought of as "promotion and non-promotion" or "skipping and repeating."
5. Rigorous record-keeping and careful, periodic testing are essential. *Continuous* progress does not mean *haphazard* progress.
6. Stick to the instructional methods previously assumed to be sound.
7. Experiment. Determine what happens when children are moved through a four-year primary unit beginning with kindergarten in three rather than four years. Determine the effects of remaining in such a unit for five rather than for four years. Seek to isolate the most significant factors determining satisfactory pupil placement. Find out what areas of instruction can be taken care of best through completely individualized methods, through small groups, and through total group techniques. Non-grading in itself is little more than door-opening. With the door open, look beyond to see what comes next in finding what we need to know and doing what we know to do.[4]

SELECTED EXAMPLES OF UNGRADED UNITS

Ungraded plans of elementary school organization are not the answer to all educational problems, but they do set up a structure within which more of our educational ideals may be realized. Each year finds additional systems in various parts of the United States adopting ungraded plans in an attempt to realize more of these ideals.

The Milwaukee plan. Among the earliest schools to adopt the ungraded plan was the Maryland Avenue School in Milwaukee, Wiscon-

[4] John I. Goodlad, Fred E. Brooks, Irene M. Larson, and Neal Neff, "Reading Levels Replace Grades in the Non-Graded Plan," *The Elementary School Journal,* LVII (February, 1957), pp. 253–256. Copyright 1957 by The University of Chicago.

sin, in the early 1940's. The schools in that city now utilize ungraded primary classes from grade one through grade three.

When children complete kindergarten in Milwaukee, they move into classrooms identified only by "Primary" and the teacher's name, and are placed with a group entitled P-1. As they progress through the primary unit they move from P-1 through P-8, regardless of grades or academic progress. Most children complete the primary school in six semesters, though some require as many as eight. Children are placed in classrooms on the bases of reading ability and other factors, and the "P" classification has no direct relationship to their placement in a particular classroom.

Progress in reading is recorded as a series of levels, broken down approximately as follows: level 1, pre-reading; level 2, chart reading; level 3, pre-primers; level 4, easy primers; level 5, hard primers; level 6, easy first readers; level 7, hard first readers; level 8, easy second readers; level 9, hard second readers; level 10, easy third readers; level 11, hard third readers; and level 12, independent reading. Every attempt is made to have three reading levels in each classroom. A wide variety of developmental reading books is used, and records are kept for each child, listing all the books he has read on each level. Textbooks in arithmetic and spelling are used by the children only in the last year of the primary unit.

In order to determine readiness for reading, children are given reading readiness tests in the kindergarten. Those whose test scores indicate they are ready for beginning reading are placed in P-1, but those who are not ready are retained in kindergarten for additional experiences to help them become ready for the primary school.

Immediately upon entering P-1, the child is placed in reading level 1 and remains there only so long as the teacher believes he needs to, after which time he is placed at level 2 and similar procedure is followed throughout the twelve reading levels. The shift from one level to another can occur at any time during the school year, and the teachers carefully record the date of the promotion to each ensuing level. If a child is moved to a new level just before the beginning of the summer vacation, he is not officially recorded as being at that level since a loss in reading ability often occurs during the summer vacation.

Placement of children into classes is determined not alone by reading ability; social growth, physical factors, and mental potentialities are also considered. It may be possible that a child is too socially immature to mix with others on the same reading level as he, so every attempt is made to place him in a class where his adjustment seems assured. No child in a room should be more than one year older or younger, chronologically, than the average in the room. In an attempt to eliminate the possibility of changing teachers at mid-semester, a child who is making rapid progress in reading at a special level would not be placed in a room where that level is the top reading group.[5]

The Park Forest, Illinois, program. One of the better-known ungraded primary units in the midwest is that of the Chicago suburb of Park Forest, Illinois. The ungraded plan was adopted by the board of education in Park Forest just one year after the school program was initiated in this new "model" community in the late 1940's. The program at Park Forest provides for continuous growth for each child, and does not allow him to skip or repeat any of the curricular areas or skills. Each child learns that which he is capable of learning, and is not expected to waste time waiting for children of lower learning ability. The children in this primary unit work with others at about the same level of academic, social, emotional, and physical development.

The grade level of a group of pupils is never referred to, officially. A card on the door indicates that the classroom is a primary unit, and displays the room teacher's name. Approximate homogeneous grouping is achieved on the bases of social and emotional maturity, social compatibility, and evidenced readiness for reading. One important factor in the progress of children through the primary unit is progress in reading. Each child resumes his work in September at the point where he left it the previous June, so that the sequence of learning experiences is continuous.

Pupils in each classroom are subdivided into learning levels, usually with three groups progressing at different rates. Movement from one reading level to another in the same room is made whenever there is an indication that a child's growth warrants such a change. When a child is considered ready to change to a new classroom, he visits the new room during the reading period for about two weeks. He is thus given a chance to become accustomed to the new group while still keeping social ties with his old classmates. When he finds experiences with the new group are more satisfying than those with his old group, he invariably desires to be moved permanently.

The average pupils complete the ungraded primary unit in Park Forest in the usual three years, and then go to the fourth grade. Some bright pupils are able to complete the unit in two years without skipping any lessons, though the percentage of these is very small. Less than six per cent of the pupils have required a fourth year in the Park Forest primary unit. School personnel in this system believe that the

---

[5] Alan T. Wilson, "The Ungraded Primary School," *The American Teacher,* XLIII (February, 1959), pp. 5–6.

children who require a fourth year are relatively unaware of their failure, and they and their parents are able to accept this arrangement with much less emotional upset than if they had failed in a typical graded school.

Aside from one thirty-minute period a week for music instruction by a special music teacher, instruction in the Park Forest schools is conducted by regular classroom teachers in a typical self-contained organization. Teachers in the unit are encouraged to work with a group for more than one year, and preferably for three.

An integral part of the total ungraded classroom structure is the program for recruitment of new teachers. The administration continually keeps in contact with teacher training institutions throughout the midwest, and frequently hires officials to visit these institutions and explain the ungraded school program to teachers in training. Primary teacher candidates are expected to observe the ungraded program in operation and, while they are visiting, the prospective candidates are interviewed by a group of veteran primary teachers who further explain the gradeless program. A one-week orientation workshop is conducted for new teachers prior to the opening of school in the fall, and all teachers attend grade level meetings, building meetings, and district meetings throughout the school year. Newly employed primary teachers are assigned a veteran ungraded primary teacher who acts as a "big sister" in professional and personal matters.

Complete parental cooperation and understanding are definite goals in the operation of the program. Parents are kept informed at all times of the status of their children. A meeting is held each spring for all parents of kindergarten children who will be entering the ungraded schools the next year. This meeting is sponsored by the local Parent-Teachers Association and school district professional staff. The P.T.A. takes charge of the publicity, invitations, and refreshments, and the school staff explains the program. Each school holds annual open house night, in which the meeting of the total group is followed by parents meeting with teachers in their classrooms. Each parent is given a handbook containing school district policies and a description of the ungraded primary school.[6]

The multigraded program in Torrance. Ungraded primary units appear to be coming into increasing use in elementary schools over the nation. In such communities as Burlington, Vermont; Hillsdale, Ore-

[6] Kent C. Austin, "The Ungraded Primary School," *Childhood Education,* February, 1957, Vol. 33, No. 6, reprinted by permission of the Association for Childhood Education International, 3615 Wisconsin Avenue, N.W., Washington 16, D.C. See also sections of John I. Goodlad and Robert H. Anderson, *The Nongraded Elementary School* (New York: Harcourt, Brace and Company, 1959).

gon; San Jose, California; University City, Missouri; Glencoe, Illinois; and Marblehead, Massachusetts, to name only a few, the ungraded primary plan of organization is already well established.

Another plan with a different approach, entitled "The Multigraded Program," in which eight grades of the typical elementary school are affected, is being employed at Torrance, California, a suburb of Los Angeles. In a challenge to the practice of grouping by age, school personnel at Torrance conducted the multigraded experiment in which the basis for grouping was wide differences of age and grade level.

The basic plan of organization in the original experiment, still currently in operation in the several schools in Torrance having multigrade classes, is that of arranging the primary multigrade so that the unit contains approximately equal numbers of first, second, and third grade pupils. The intermediate multigrade is arranged so that it contains approximately equal numbers of pupils of fourth, fifth, and sixth grade levels. Such grouping closely resembles a so-called regular classroom in which the teacher properly groups children so that provision is made for individual differences which exist between the pupils. Originators of the plan propose that the actual placing of children into a multigrade class recognizes the differences of pupils, and when the general spread of differences is increased, the learning situation in the classroom is enriched. No particular ability is a prerequisite for assignment to a multigrade class; assignment is based upon random selection.

Subject matter in the areas of reading, arithmetic, and social studies in the multigrade classes cuts across grade level lines and varies in each of the three curricular areas because of the wide variance in achievement among pupils in the room. School personnel using the multigrade plan believe that its primary advantage over the regular graded plan is that it forces a teacher to provide for differences in children, since there is such an obvious difference in the grade level and chronological age of children in the room. The spread of three grade-levels within one classroom provides an opportunity for children to learn something from one another in the room; younger ones learn from older as the latter carry out some activity in their learning experiences, and older pupils have a chance to review as the younger ones go through the learning activities which the older pupils have already encountered. Children are provided opportunities to develop in depth and breadth in all subject areas as they progress through the multigrade classroom. Multigrade classes point up the need for careful selection of materials used in instruction, so that individual differences may be more adequately satisfied.

Placement in the multigrade classroom is on a voluntary basis; only pupils whose parents requested their placement in such classrooms were assigned to those groups. Conventional graded classrooms are provided for pupils whose parents prefer this type of room assignment. It is not the intention of the Torrance district to organize the entire elementary system in accordance with the multigrade plan.

In the original study, a careful statistical analysis of the growth of children in both the regular grade and multigrade classes was made for the school year 1955–56. Comparisons were made not only on the basis of mean gain of the total classes, but also on the basis of the matched pair technique where matching was by sex, age, grade, IQ, and fall achievement score.

Rehwoldt and Hamilton, who made the study of the Torrance plan, concluded that there is considerable evidence to support a grouping pattern which would place children of three different grade levels in the same classroom. Their findings indicated that: (1) the academic achievement of pupils in most grade levels was favorably influenced by the fact that they were members of a multigrade (three grade) class; (2) membership in a multigrade class contributed to the greater personal adjustment of pupils; (3) the social adjustment of pupils was improved because of their membership in a multigrade class; (4) pupils in multigrade classes at five of the six grade levels made greater improvement in certain aspects of maturity, and (5) (that) the oldest pupils in each multigrade level made greater improvement in certain characteristics of behavior; (6) pupil attitudes toward school were better if they were members of a multigrade group; (7) parents of pupils in multigrade classes expressed strong support in favor of such grouping and evidenced better attitudes toward school than did the parents of regular grade pupils; (8) teachers and administrators of the multigrade classes expressed agreement with 13 of the 14 hypotheses formulated in support of multigrade grouping; and (9) pupil-pupil relationships within the multigrade classes were very similar to those existing in single grade classes, and there was considerable acceptance between pupils of different grades and ages within the multigrade classes.[7]

THE DUAL PROGRESS PLAN

A plan of elementary school organization for instruction which includes some of the elements of both the graded and the ungraded plans

[7] Walter Rehwoldt and Warren Hamilton, "An Analysis of Some of the Effects of Interage and Intergrade Grouping in an Elementary School" (Unpublished Doctoral dissertation, University of Southern California, 1957).

has been named the Dual Progress Plan. Aided by a sizeable grant from a national foundation, the school systems of Long Beach, New York, and Ossining, New York, set out to educate their third-through-sixth grade pupils under what has been termed the most revolutionary experiment the public schools have yet undertaken. The project was supervised by New York University, with George D. Stoddard, dean of the University's School of Education, in general charge.

Under the Dual Progress Plan, grades are retained in the language arts, social studies, and physical education, but grade levels are ignored in such other subjects as arithmetic, science, music, arts and crafts, recreation, and health. In describing this deviation from the customary self-contained classroom type of organization, Stoddard says:

> A (home-room) teacher would be responsible for registration and counseling; she would then teach reading and the social studies. The other half day would be assigned to special teachers who would teach mathematics and science, music, arts and crafts, recreation and health, and, beginning with grade five, an optional sequence in a foreign language. The special teachers in each subject or cluster of subjects would offer the work on a longitudinal basis straight through the elementary grades; and in a combined school, throughout the twelve grades. Thus the special teachers, as a team, would be in a good position to judge the quality of special aptitudes and their course of growth throughout the child's school life. Test scores, profiles, ratings, and sample items would furnish a continuous comprehensive record. All special teachers would encourage pupils to form social clubs that would cut across the grades and be based on content interest.
>
> Generally a pupil's grade standing, which is an all-around maturity concept, would be determined by his home teacher, but he would be free to pursue avidly a specialty according to his aptitude. Thus, a fifth-grade pupil might play in the high school band or orchestra, and a pupil gifted in mathematics or science would be brigaded with like-minded students in more advanced grades.[8]

REASONS FOR THE DUAL PROGRESS PLAN

The Dual Progress Plan is based upon the idea that every person in our culture should have a knowledge of the basic tools of everyday living—language arts and the social studies. As a result, it is in these areas that arbitrary standards are set up. Supporters of the plan hold that no such universal obligation exists in subjects like arithmetic, music, art, and science, so children progress only as rapidly as their abilities permit. Reading, writing, speaking, listening, deciding, and

[8] G. D. Stoddard, in C. W. Hunnicutt, ed., *Education 2000 AD* (Syracuse: Syracuse University Press, 1956), p. 149.

appreciating are tools which everyone uses, proponents of the Dual Progress Plan hold; but comparatively few persons excel in performing. Performance by above average children in the special subjects is noted and encouraged by teachers in the Dual Progress Plan of organization.

A mathematical genius or gifted artist might be only "average" in social studies and the language arts under the Dual Progress Plan; in the traditional classroom arrangement, such talent may never be discovered and the pupil may be labelled "average" in all subject areas. Unfortunately, in too many traditional situations, children who have the ability to do arithmetic a level or two above their grade never have the opportunity to do so.

ADMINISTRATIVE PROBLEMS TO BE SOLVED

The Dual Progress Plan is very simple in its organizational design. It is basically a semi-departmentalized plan, with schedules built so that

BLOCK 1 (Morning or Afternoon) "Home-room" teacher Specialist in Language Arts and Social Studies (Also teaches physical education and provides for guidance services)
BLOCK 2 Specialists in: Science—40 minutes daily Arithmetic—40 minutes daily Arts and Crafts—40 minutes every other day Music—40 minutes every other day Grouped by ability

Figure 3. CHART SHOWING ORGANIZATIONAL STRUCTURE OF THE DUAL PROGRESS PLAN

the children spend a half day in language arts, social studies, and physical education with one teacher, and the other half day in forty minute sessions of arithmetic, science, music or arts with individual specialized teachers. Half of the pupils have the core subjects in the morning while the others are attending the specialized courses; in the afternoon the schedules of the two groups of children are reversed.

Under the Dual Progress Plan, it is desirable for teaching teams to stay with classes from grade three through all intermediate grade levels, and possibly through the junior high school work. This calls for special attention on the part of those making the teacher assignments to assure that instructors placed with those classes can work effectively with children on four to seven different grade levels in all academic areas. If the current trend requiring teachers in the public schools to have academic majors and minors in their preparation persists, the placement of teachers as suggested above should pose no problem from the standpoint of subject matter proficiency. Some other aspects, however, such as personality conflicts, need to be watched: occasionally, changing a few pupils to other teachers' classes will be necessary. Age and grade are not the determinants of a pupil's assignment to a particular specialized class or teacher; the determining factors are, rather, the pupil's special aptitudes, interests, and achievements.

Another problem connected with the operation of the Dual Progress Plan may arise because the home-room, or core, teacher must also be responsible for registration and counseling. In addition to being capable of teaching the language arts and social studies, this person must also be well-versed in procedures of pupil accounting and guidance. If core teachers are not adept in these areas, they may need to take college courses or participate in an in-service education program.

Provision needs to be made in the courses of language arts and social studies for individual differences between children in the same classroom, just as such provision should be made by the teacher of the self-contained grade. Of course it is reasonable to expect that, all things being equal, children will make some progress in the basic courses; but the fundamental laws of growth, development and learning will obtain, and must be considered if effective teaching-learning experiences are to be carried on in the classrooms.

The problems of staff orientation, parental understanding, and inauguration of the plan occur in the Dual Progress Plan, just as they do in the ungraded plan described previously. Considerable preparation of staff is necessary for this plan, particularly since most elementary school teachers are orientated toward the self-contained plan and feel they can teach their pupils more effectively in this traditional plan where they work with the same students all day. Also, at present, most elementary teachers have not had the academic preparation necessary to meet the dual progress objectives.

The Long Beach and Ossining plans of organization. More than 100 teachers and 2,700 pupils are involved in the identical Dual Progress Plans in Long Beach and Ossining, New York. Schedules for the two cities' elementary schools provide a half-day for social studies, language arts, and physical education; followed, or preceded by, daily periods of forty minutes each in science, arithmetic, and arts and crafts or music.

The original experiment in the two New York schools was scheduled to run for a period of three years under the grant of the national foundation. As boys and girls advanced in the program into the seventh, eighth, and ninth grade levels, the school systems planned to make special reports of the students' progress, and also to study closely the reorganization of the Ossining and Long Beach high schools. Pros and cons of the plan were to be thoroughly evaluated, along with a coordinate plan for studying the implications for the education of prospective teachers.

Probably the one important difference between the Dual Progress Plan and other plans of teaching is that of departmentalization of a part of the pupils' program; but sponsors of the plan have wisely omitted such departmentalization in kindergarten, first, and second grades. Actually, one of the plan's strongest points is its adaptability to a large number of different types of situations in different types of buildings. Ideally, of course, it is desirable for a plant to have facilities adaptable to the broad curriculum which the Plan makes possible, as well as for a wide variety of activities and laboratory experiments.

The Dual Progress Plan provides an administrative device which helps to solve the problem of crowded classroom conditions. The plan is very similar to that started in the early 1900's which came to be known as the platoon school. This organizational plan was essentially a clever administrative device which enabled school buildings to accommodate larger numbers of children, thus cutting the per capita cost of the building. The platoon schools, while popular in the 1920's, died out in the following decade because they were not considered conducive to good teaching and learning. One objection raised to platoon schools was that fundamental knowledge and skills were neglected because so much time was spent on other activities, although evidence indicated that children in the platoon schools did about as well as children in other types of schools in subject-matter achievement. A second objection to departmentalized teaching was that pupils lacked integrated educational experiences. There was little objective evidence to support these claims, however, so perhaps the Ossining and Long Beach experiments will produce results which will definitely indicate the superiority, or inferiority, of the Dual Progress Plan of organization.

An adaptation of the Dual Progress Plan is used in many of the so-called "seventh and eighth grade schools," or "intermediate schools," which have become a popular type of organization in many fast-growing areas in states like California. This administrative plan serves well in the two-graded "transition" schools where boys and girls remain a part of the self-contained organization, while becoming oriented to departmentalization characteristic of public secondary schools.

THE TEAM TEACHING PLAN

Elementary schools and secondary schools alike have been experimenting in recent years with a plan of organization for instruction which has been designated as team teaching. In this case, again, national foundations have granted large sums of money in an effort to ascertain through experimentation the advantages and disadvantages of another departure from the self-contained classroom situation.

REASONS FOR THE TEAM TEACHING PLAN

In recent years, particularly during the two decades following World War II when schools grew by leaps and bounds, many educators have begun to question the traditionally favored class-size of 25 to 35 pupils. These educators have wondered about the validity of *all* classes in *all* subject areas being of this approximate size; in short, they have been questioning the validity of the relatively small self-contained classroom in the elementary school.

Another facet of elementary school organization under suspicion is the idea, inherent in the self-contained situation, of the teacher being the super-human master of all professional skill and knowledge. They point to the fact that in the medical profession, for example, physicians long ago found it virtually impossible for one of their number to master all the skills and knowledge of a very complex field, and specialization resulted in the practice of medicine. Some educators hold that the business of educating all the children of all the people has become so complex that specialists are needed in the elementary school just as they are used in most secondary school situations.

The team teaching plan resulted from these questions concerning the relatively small self-contained classrooms, the inordinate demands made upon elementary school teachers in both knowledge and skills, plus the growing numbers of increasingly heterogeneous groups of students. Proponents of the plan hold that such a plan in a school system might attract greater numbers of superior teachers because, under this plan, the teacher gains both satisfaction and prestige.

ADMINISTRATIVE PROBLEMS TO BE SOLVED

Inauguration of the team teaching plan would involve rather radical changes in administration and supervision. If an elementary school contemplated a change to team teaching, careful attention by the school's personnel to the administration and supervision of the plan would obviously be necessary.

Activities of the staff. As a member of a team, in contrast to being *the* teacher of *a* classroom, each teacher must re-orient himself to his basic responsibilities to boys and girls in the school. He needs to realize that he has been assigned to a class on the basis of being a specialist, not a "generalist," and that he may be assigned as a specialist for large group instruction or, in other circumstances, as a specialist with a smaller group. All of this points up one problem of the administrators in charge of hiring staff: in the team teaching plan of organization, specialists will be employed in subject areas as well as in such other areas as evaluation, guidance, and services to exceptional children; and an adequate "balance" of specialists on the staff must be maintained. At the same time, employing officials must also obtain other members of the team, some of whom are instruction assistants, clerks, general aides, and community consultants.

While teaching teams utilize subject-matter specialists as teachers, they do contain so-called "teacher specialists" and "general teachers." The former members of the team have considerable experience, and hold at least a master's degree. While having the responsibility for supervising all instruction in a given subject-matter area, they themselves also teach in that area, usually to large groups of pupils. They are in general charge of evaluation of pupil achievement. Commensurate with their background of training and experience, teacher specialists are the highest paid members of the team.

Since more time for preparation and planning is necessary for the professional specialist teacher who works with large groups, he spends fewer hours in actual teaching in the classrooms. A teacher who, in the self-contained classroom situation, spends from twenty-six to thirty hours a week with his pupils would, under the team plan, spend possibly only eighteen to twenty hours before the class if he were a specialist teacher. Approximately half of the eighteen to twenty hours spent by professional specialist teachers are with small groups which average fifteen or fewer pupils.

General teachers, while fully certified, have less training and experience than the teacher specialists and, correspondingly, are usually paid less. Their principal responsibility is that of serving as consultants and observers in discussion groups, and a smaller portion of their time is required for preparation and planning. There is no appreciable difference in amount of time spent with pupils between the general teachers and the teachers in the self-contained classroom. General teachers work with and assist the teacher specialists so that coordination of all phases of school work may be effected.

Instruction assistants are aides to the teaching specialists and general teachers; they grade some types of pupil work, serve as laboratory, library, and materials center assistants, and may, if sufficiently competent, instruct on occasion. Clerks perform routine tasks such as grading objective tests, keeping records, copying materials on the typewriter, operating duplicators, and handling supplies. General aides supervise students on playgrounds and in cafeterias, corridors, auditoriums and large meeting rooms, and also help at school performances. Community consultants are those persons in the community with special qualifications—physicians, ministers, business men, and others—who are used in carrying out specific assignments. Their services are usually voluntary.[9]

Costs of team teaching. There are those who say that the team teaching plan costs no more than does the self-contained or departmentalized type of organization. There are others, however, who perhaps take a more realistic view and maintain that the team teaching plan is more costly, in terms of dollars, than a more traditional structure. It seems highly improbable that a team teaching plan in the elementary school could operate for approximately the same amount of money as would the self-contained type of organization; costs would probably be substantially greater, but this is a moot point. If educational outcomes would be greater per capita under a more expensive program, which type of organization would ultimately be the most "economical?"

Proponents of team teaching propose that teacher specialists' salaries should range from $10,000 to $15,000 per annum. Salaries of others on the team—instruction assistants, clerks, and general aides—would also add to the cost of the program. However, the fact that the efficiency of professional teachers is seriously impaired by routine, time-consuming tasks is widely acknowledged by both educators and lay persons. Education should train persons for uncertificated and technical roles as assistants to the master teachers. The philosophy determining salary under the team teaching plan is "professional salaries for professional services," based upon consideration of the teachers' back-

---

[9] For a more detailed analysis of positions, see J. Lloyd Trump, *Images of the Future* (Washington: National Association of Secondary-School Principals, National Education Association, 1959), pp. 15–18.

ground of training and experience, assignment, quality of service, and hours worked.

Additional costs in the team plan involve the purchase of instructional materials and capital outlay for buildings and other accommodations. All manner of media for instruction are used under this plan: textbooks, television, radio, recordings on discs and tapes, and teaching machines. Not only must libraries, shops, cafeterias, gymnasiums, and various special study-resource rooms be provided, but classrooms for groups of ten, twenty, fifty, one hundred, or perhaps more pupils must also be made available.

Scheduling. Flexibility is the by-word of the team teaching organization. In today's typical elementary school, the problem of scheduling is of minor importance since the teacher, if he teaches through unifying experiences, will determine with his pupils the various phases of the program for his grade and the amount of time for each phase; if he teaches in the traditional "compartmentalized" program, he determines the order of subjects and the time to be spent on each. Schedule makers under the team plan utilize varied schemes in working out the day's program: homogeneous groups are scheduled for one activity, heterogeneous groups for another; large classes are scheduled for certain subject-matter areas, small classes for certain other areas; satisfying experiences for pupils of moderate or below average ability, challenging activities for pupils of high achievement capacity. The time and place for independent study varies with needs and abilities of pupils. Electronic devices utilize the recommendations of adult school personnel in the scheduling of individual programs.

ORGANIZING THE TEAM TEACHING PLAN

Basically, the team teaching plan operates in this manner: instead of each teacher having charge of a class of 30 or 35 pupils, two or more teachers who are specialists in a subject-matter field bring their pupils together for part of each week in a large classroom, and one of the team presents a series of lessons in his field of specialty. While this is taking place, the other teachers on the team prepare lessons, audio-visual aids, bibliographies, study guides, and other material, and begin study for the next sequence. At certain scheduled intervals, small groups of twelve to twenty pupils meet for discussion; at other scheduled or unscheduled times, pupils engage in individual research or study. The assisting members of the team, the instructional aide, clerk, and others, take care of most of the details of the class.

In this way, some highly qualified teachers are assigned to classes of from 75 to 100 or more pupils; this, paradoxically, provides more opportunities for pupils to explore ideas in small groups and on an individual basis; since, according to the advocates of team teaching, the elementary school which is organized under this plan can then make use of both large and small classes as well as individual study.

Master teachers, who have had time for preparation, and who have the best in teaching materials and equipment at their disposal, are in charge of the large classes. Pupils are in large classes about 40 to 50 per cent of the time, depending somewhat upon the subject being studied, the stage within the subject at which a large group finds itself, and the student interest and maturity manifested within the class.

Some activities which the master teachers are undertaking before the large classes are:

1. Introduction. New topics, units, and concepts are introduced and placed in relation to other knowledge. Purposes are presented. Preparation for learning is developed.
2. Motivation. Reasons for study are understood. Interest is stimulated. Students are assisted in self-analysis of present knowledge.
3. Explanation. Understanding of terms and concepts is further developed. Questions by students and teachers are raised and answered.
4. Exploration. Identification of the range of possible learning activities is provided. Interests are amplified. Problems to be solved by students are considered.
5. Planning. Decisions are made regarding learning activities. Methods of study are planned.
6. Group Study. What has been learned is shared by use of buzz-sessions, panels, and other group techniques. Drill, memorization, problem solving, and organization devices are practiced.
7. Enrichment. Content not readily available to students is introduced.
8. Generalization. Understandings and appreciations are developed. Concepts that can be transferred to other situations are summarized.
9. Evaluation. Knowledge, appreciations, skills, and generalizations are measured prior to study, during study, and at the conclusions of the activity. A variety of evaluation techniques is utilized.[10]

Twenty to 30 per cent of the pupil's time is spent in small classes of 12 to 15 members, where understanding is enhanced through such activities as problem solving, examining concepts and terminology, and reaching agreement or disagreement. Social amenties are also developed through the small group activities. The teacher serves, in this situation, in the capacity of a consultant.

The remaining 20 to 40 per cent of the pupil's time is spent in indi-

[10] *Ibid.*, p. 8.

vidual study or research with a minimum amount of supervision, done by teachers who act in the capacity of consultants. All resources of the school and community are made available to pupils as they read, write, listen to records and tapes, experiment, question, analyze, think, create, memorize, make, self-appraise, and participate in other types of individual activities.

SELECTED EXAMPLES OF TEAM TEACHING

Several elementary schools in recent years have been experimenting with the team teaching plan. Perhaps such experimentation will result in positive guidelines for team teaching enterprises in the years to come.

The Lexington plan. One of the most elaborate team teaching projects is that which is being conducted at the Franklin School in Lexington, Massachusetts. Here, eighteen classroom teachers have been operating within a team structure in a building which is of standard design, and which is inadequate for this type of organization. Four teachers work with 100 or more first grade pupils, using large-group lessons and intra-team deployment of youngsters. Officials at the school maintain that these six-year-olds enjoy and profit from working with different teachers and with large "families" of fellow pupils in a variety of first-grade activities. Team Alpha, as the initial grade group of teachers is called, has one teacher specialist, or "team leader," and three general teachers, or "regular teachers."

Team Beta, consisting of six teachers of second and third grades, is the second team; here there is a teacher specialist, a "senior teacher," and four general teachers. The senior teacher is subordinate to the teacher specialist in title and salary, the latter carrying the major responsibility for directing the work of the team.

The third team, Omega, consists of eight teachers of grades four, five, and six, with the teacher specialist being assisted by two senior teachers and five general teachers.

At Franklin School about 20 to 25 per cent of the daily schedule involves pupils in large class activities. One of the objectives of the experiment at this school is to ascertain which subjects and which types of lessons may be taught as well or better to large groups of children as to small groups. Science material and other types of information which lend themselves especially to demonstration and lecture-type presentations have been found particularly suited for large classes, according to early findings of the experiment.

While large classes are being conducted by one of the team, most often the teacher specialist, others on the team engage in such activities as helping with the large-class lesson, working with smaller groups of children in remedial lessons, engaging in lesson planning, and participating in parent-teacher conferences. Each team has clerical assistance; Team Omega receives about thirty-five hours of service weekly, Team Beta about twenty-seven hours of service, and Team Alpha about eighteen hours of service each week.[11]

Small classes consist of some typical self-contained groups, as well as subgroups from the large classes, divided among the various teachers. Small groups may be established on the basis of achievement in some of the academic subject areas, such as reading and arithmetic, or they may be established on the basis of interests in such subjects areas as science and the social studies.

Anderson says that there are certain presumed advantages and disadvantages of the team teaching plan for children.[12] First, it has been hypothesized that instruction may be more stimulating when each lesson is taught by the team members whose greater relative strength is in that subject. It is also believed that the frequent regrouping of children, to meet specific needs and interests in all areas, will be to the child's advantage. The opportunity to know and work with a greater number and variety of teachers and fellow pupils is also believed to have potential intellectual and social values for the children.

On the negative side, it was originally suspected that some children might get "lost" in the large social groups, that some would find it difficult to tolerate the frequent changing of class groups and classrooms, and that some might forfeit the "security" that is alleged to result from the typical 1:25 pupil-teacher ratio in the self-contained classroom. None of these suspicions, however, has so far been substantiated in actual experience. While there are a few children who do express or manifest such feelings, their proportion is very much smaller than had been expected. Furthermore, the overwhelming weight of opinion as expressed both by children and their parents to date is enthusiastic, the typical comment being that the larger number of friends, the interesting changes in activities and locations, and the opportunity to study under many different adult personalities are the good things about the program.

The Norwalk plan. Some seven or more elementary schools in the Norwalk, Connecticut, school system are using the team teaching plan of instruction in their organizational structure. This system, too, is experimenting with the plan, backed by funds from a national foundation.

---

[11] Robert H. Anderson, *Team-Teaching—Backgrounds and Issues* (duplicated explanation), p. 6.

[12] *Ibid.*, pp. 5–6.

The plan in Norwalk is similar to others in operation: 65 to 75 pupils on the same grade level are grouped with a teaching team which consists of a leader who is considered to be an exceptional teacher and who receives a bonus in salary, a regular or general teacher, and a clerical worker who takes over records and clerical details. Classes work together in group activities such as music, but they are divided into sections according to ability for curricular offerings such as reading, arithmetic, social studies, and geography. The scheme in use at Norwalk is being used in random classes from the second to the sixth grades.

Pupils taking part in the plan are tested at the end of each school year, and the results are evaluated by school personnel during the summer months.

Members of the board of education and parents in Norwalk seem to be satisfied with results of the program. Parents questioned the innovation when it was first introduced, but as the plan progressed, they reported excellent progress on the part of their children.

Other school districts experimenting with the team teaching plan at the elementary level include Flint, Michigan, where the plan is used at the primary level, Englewood, Florida, and Fort Wayne, Indiana.

USE OF TELEVISION AT THE ELEMENTARY LEVEL

The plans of organization for instruction which have been presented in the earlier sections of this chapter have had as one of their objectives the partial solution of the problem of increased enrollments in the elementary schools of the nation. Just as educators were searching for an answer to this problem following World War II, a new medium for the dissemination of information, as well as for entertainment, appeared on the national scene. Television, utilizing both sound and sight in the transmission of pictures of events, often at the precise moment of happening, is a mighty means of communication. The ultimate potential of television in educating boys and girls, in presenting more information of a complicated and difficult nature, and in meeting the continued shortage of teachers and building space has not been even minutely realized.

A NEW MEDIUM ON THE HORIZON—FRIEND OR FOE?

Television is here to stay! Within a dozen years after its introduction following World War II, television sets were firmly entrenched in

American homes, and were considered an almost necessary piece of furniture in the living room or family room. The sets held a magnetic attraction for all members of the family, from grandparents to very young children. Children, whose lives were vitally affected in a number of ways by the electronic device, were watching television programs for as many hours a day as they were spending in school. Older persons' lives were enriched; illness was made more durable; loneliness was greatly alleviated—all because television came within the means of most of the people. There has probably been no other medium or technique that has done more to advance common learnings among people since the introduction of movable type.

Despite evidence which shows that television can definitely aid in alleviating the crises of increased enrollments, increased amounts of complicated learnings, and continuing shortages of able teachers and adequate buildings, there are some well-intentioned educators who resist its application to education. They present objections based on practical considerations of *how* television can be used in schools, as well as objections based on prejudice, lack of knowledge, and differences of opinion. As someone once said, "It takes fifty years for a good idea in education to catch on," and perhaps this will be true of educational television. This is not, however, necessarily bad; educators are wise in being slow to try new gadgets and new ideas on this nation's greatest natural resource—its boys and girls! Centuries ago, educators were very unenthusiastic about printed textbooks, since for years formal learning had been handed down primarily on parchment made by writers who took pride in the beauty and artistic form of their books, which printers were unable to match. But just as teachers have accepted printed textbooks, and ultimately chalkboards, film strips, tape recorders, movie films, and numbers of projectors of various kinds, it is probable that they will do the same with television.

Some educators predict that television may change learning from purposeful, meaningful activity into the passive experience of sitting before a television screen, an exercise of merely watching and listening. But can education ever outlaw a medium that shows the promise that television shows in the real function of the school: the education of boys and girls? Some educators believe that television is a fine entertainment medium, but question its introduction into the sober business of education where there are so many serious problems with which to wrestle. But there is a possibility that television may help solve these very problems.

In almost every meeting where television is discussed as a potent medium in the education of children, some have wondered if the use of television on a wide-spread basis in the schools will create a shortage of jobs for teachers. In answer to this query, theorists, backed by the early results of experimentation, indicate that effective teachers will continue to be needed as badly as ever. In fact, television properly used will relieve teachers of part of their job, with the result that they can do better work in research and in individual pupil-teacher contacts. The indications are that teachers' positions may be enhanced. In any event, in the face of the present 1:30 teacher-pupil ratio, some kind of plan must be devised to meet the teacher shortage, regardless of how and what teaching is done. Television may help solve the problem by getting a larger job done with fewer people than would otherwise be needed in the future. Regardless of what that future brings, teachers will still be needed to direct and supervise activity programs, group discussions, drills, testing, and for remedial teaching; teachers will continue to be essential in the development of pupils' ability to evaluate, to exercise critical judgment, to do problem solving, and in the establishment of desirable habits and worthy ideals.[13]

There has been considerable apprehension among educators with respect to the cost of television in school systems. Since the medium is established in the culture, and since it is recognized as a potential giant in the dissemination of information, its inclusion in budgets will become, eventually, a virtual necessity. Its savings may in time even offset its costs by making necessary fewer buildings and personnel than will be needed if present programs in schools are continued. H. J. Skornia of the National Association of Educational Broadcasters has estimated that

> . . . full-sized educational television stations could be built on every one of the more than 250 channels now reserved for education, and could be operated for five years at a cost approximately *two per cent* of the sum estimated as needed for *additional* school rooms and buildings alone, to meet the building requirements of the next five years.[14]

From several hundred research studies that have been made on educational television, several of which are discussed later in this chapter, comes one outstanding conclusion: instruction by television is, in general, as effective as instruction presented in the conventional manner. This persistent conclusion appears to be effective from primary grades through higher education, and for a variety of subject areas taught under various instructional conditions. There is reason to believe, then, that the teaching-learning situation can be made more

---

[13] Alexander J. Stoddard, *Schools for Tomorrow: An Educator's Blueprint* (New York: Fund for the Advancement of Education, 1957), p. 30.

[14] *Ibid.*, p. 32.

effective through use of both machine and human beings: the machine imparting facts and helping to develop skills, and the teacher developing depths of understanding and comprehension, and promoting such concomitant learnings as proper attitudes and appreciations. This is not too radical a departure from what we have done with other audio-visual aids. Like the author of a textbook, the television teacher is cast in the role of an expert who carefully arranges and presents material so that it is readily understandable and useful to the learner.

Educational television is, then, a means to an end, not an end in itself. The art of teaching boys and girls cannot be turned over to an untrained technician. But the acceptance of television as an ally can help teachers meet the professional responsibility of providing a high quality of education.

ADMINISTRATIVE PROBLEMS TO BE SOLVED

Administrative problems connected with educational television resemble those presented in team teaching, since the organizational structure (to be discussed next) is very similar for the two programs. Before an educational television program is initiated, there are, of course, the necessary steps to be taken by the school's administrative personnel in gaining acceptance of the program by the faculty and people of the community. In areas where this important task has not been completed effectively, strong antagonisms have arisen between faculty, administration, and patrons.

There is general agreement that television as a teaching tool will be used increasingly and more effectively. Administrative action needs to be guided by the measure of effectiveness of television-taught lessons. This effectiveness must be measured for pupil achievement through standardized tests and other techniques so that comparisons may be made with similar groups taught in conventional ways.

The problems pointed up under "Activities of the Staff" and "Scheduling" in the section of this chapter entitled *The Team Teaching Plan* would also be applicable in a situation where television was in widespread use in the school, since the organizational plan for instruction would be essentially a team teaching plan. Imagination and flexibility are necessary in television teaching, since personnel in the school have to be adaptable to changing conditions, and able to anticipate and provide for them in the system. Personnel in the school also would need to become familiar with equipment used in open and closed circuit television and language laboratories. Television teaching first necessitates elimination of resistance on the part of school personnel toward any of the methods of mechanized instruction which are destined to have a growing acceptance and influence in the school systems of this nation.

Reference has been made above to the problem of the cost of television and the inevitability of its inclusion in the school budget. Since this item is relatively new, it will undoubtedly meet the usual opposition accorded any item which appears in the budget for the first time. Adequate closed circuit television equipment can, nonetheless, be installed in school buildings for less money than is often expended for shops, laboratories, cafeterias, libraries, gymnasiums, and some specially-equipped classrooms. More than 250 channels have been reserved for educational use; some school systems participate in owning or operating educational channels, or have them directly available for their use; and more will do so in the future. An example of costs incurred at the higher education level at Pennsylvania State College will illustrate possible savings when utilizing television teaching:

Course	*Educational Television*	*Classroom*
Psychology	$14,680	$23,825
Accounting	7,520	8,000
Sociology	7,527	10,274
Air Science	22,557	50,000
	$52,284	$92,099

Savings: $39,815, or 43 per cent of classroom cost.[15]

The problem of buildings. One of the greatest problems posed by the increased use of television is that of buildings. Most of the buildings housing classrooms are inadequate for team teaching with television; they were built for another type of instruction and are not sufficient for requirements of television teaching. Stoddard submits that no new elementary school should be built without the following: (1) two or three large rooms planned to seat comfortably from 100 to 300 pupils each, equipped with television receiving apparatus, properly sound-proofed, and equipped with all the other aids to large-group instruction available today; (2) a large pupils' auditorium to seat about 100–200 pupils, with a small stage and an activities space in the front of the room; (3) play facilities, preferably a covered space outdoors, where from 100–200 pupils can play at any time of day without interfering with other school or classroom activities; and (4) a television studio and closed circuit apparatus and connections for telecasting to all parts of the building and play spaces.[16] For a more

[15] Leon C. Fletcher, "How Much Does Educational Television Cost?", *The American School Board Journal* CXXXIX (September, 1959), pp. 38–39.
[16] Stoddard, *op. cit.*, p. 52.

detailed analysis of the requirements for maximum television use of new buildings and buildings now in use, and for television origination rooms and receiving rooms, the reader is referred to pages 53–56 of *Schools for Tomorrow, An Educator's Blueprint,* by Stoddard.

ORGANIZING FOR TELEVISION TEACHING

The organizational structure for teaching via television is, in most situations where the new medium is being used, identical with that used for team teaching, described previously. This can easily be seen in the following plan which has been proposed by Stoddard as one possible administrative pattern at the elementary level:

1. For part of the school day place half of the children with regular teachers, in smaller than normal-sized classes and assign these teachers responsibility for performing the usual instruction in the usual manner or method, involving subject matter best adapted for the usual teacher-class procedures.
   To begin with, until more is known about what kind of teaching best fits what kind of learning experiences, such subjects as English, reading, writing, arithmetic, social studies, the drill and technique sides of art and music might be assigned to this regular teacher.
   Give these teachers some clerical or other assistance to relieve them of some of the chores and other non-teaching duties that someone else other than the teacher could perform as well or better, and thus free them to concentrate on the essential phases of teaching.
2. The other half of the children would be participating in class experiences (a) in a "Resources Room," utilizing television programs and any or all other aids to instruction, (b) in the auditorium, library, music room, little theatre or activities related to or growing out of these rooms, or (c) on the playground or in the indoor playroom or gymnasium.
4. After lunch, the two schedules would be reversed, the same teachers doing for the second half of the day what they had done in the first half.[17]

As an example, Stoddard would have 300 children in a 600-pupil elementary school divided up into twelve traditional 25-pupil classes with one teacher each in such subjects as English, arithmetic, and social studies, for the entire morning.[18] During the same morning hour, the other 300 children would be scheduled approximately as follows:

From 9 to 9:45 A.M., 150 pupils would be in the resources room

[17] *Ibid.,* p. 44.
[18] *Ibid.,* p. 45.

with one teacher and one aide, while 75 pupils with one teacher and one aide would be in the auditorium, and the other 75 pupils with one teacher and one aide would be on the playground. From 9:45 to 10:30 A.M., the 150 pupils from the resource room would split, with 75 pupils going to the auditorium and the rest going to the playground; meanwhile, the 75 each from the playground and auditorium would go to the resources room for instruction. From 10:30 to 11:15, the 150 pupils from the resources room would go back to the playground and auditorium, reversing the schedule they had in those locations during the first period; the boys and girls who had spent this period in the auditorium and on the playground would assemble again in the resources room. From 11:15 to 12:00, the 150 children from the resources room would again split ranks and move back to the auditorium and playground, but reversing their classes they attended during the second period; meanwhile, the two groups of about 75 pupils from the auditorium and playground would again combine into another 150-pupil class in the resources room. For the afternoon, the programs followed in the morning would be reversed.

Such a program would require twelve regular teachers, three special teachers, four aides (one for resources room, one for auditorium, one for playground, and one general aide), one curriculum coordinator, and perhaps a half-time music teacher and a half-time secretary. The plan reduces the number of subjects which are usually required to be mastered by the elementary school teacher, and, as a result, lessens the possibility of confusion and affords teachers the opportunity to give attention to individual needs. Under this plan, specialists in subject-matter fields teach in the area of their specialization. It is entirely possible that a core of specialists may provide a more effective teaching staff than the "generalists" who have comprised the elementary school faculty in the self-contained situation; time and experimentation will tell.

SELECTED EXAMPLES OF TELEVISION TEACHING

It is agreed that television is not a cure-all for the ills of education, but under existing circumstances it certainly deserves a chance to prove its effectiveness in elementary schools. Some schools are already experimenting with the medium as a regular part of their instructional programs.

The Hagerstown project. The Washington County (Maryland) Closed Circuit Educational Television Project, often referred to as the Hagerstown project, is one of the largest and most publicized instructional television projects in the nation. Undertaken as a five-year study, it was begun in the 1956–57 school year as a joint effort of the

Washington County Schools, the Radio-Electronics-Television Manufacturers Association, a national foundation, and the Potomac and Chesapeake Telephone Company of Maryland, which supplied the wire for the telephonic transmission of the programs from studios to schools. At the end of the third year of operation, the closed circuit television system reached 16,500 of the 18,000 pupils in the county, and the plans called for the inclusion of the remaining 1500 pupils in the potential television audience at the end of the fourth year of operation.[19] Courses in various subject areas are being taught through television to students in grades one through twelve.

Intensive evaluation of the project is under way. Some preliminary surveys have been completed. The attitudes of pupils in the classrooms toward television instruction as determined by the answers given on an anonymous questionnaire by 32 per cent of the pupils involved are:

1. Students in Washington County are accepting educational television as a standard method of teaching.
2. The changed conditions under which questions may be asked and answered during a television lesson do not seem to be a problem to the student. Only 5 per cent of the total sample indicated that they never had their questions answered.
3. The period of discussion, or the follow-up session which comes after the telecasts, seems to be of great benefit to the students. Eighty-seven per cent of these indicated this.
4. Fifty-eight per cent of the students indicated that they thought they learn more in a classroom with television than in a classroom without television. Sixty-six per cent thought "this subject would be more interesting," and 68 per cent said that "you would have to pay closer attention" in a television classroom.
5. Students reported that television in the schools had caused a change in a variety of their activities.
   60 per cent of the students reported they studied more.
   52 per cent indicated that their learning about different ways of making a living increased.
   53 per cent mentioned that they talked more frequently with their parents about school and school work.
   50 per cent reported reading a greater number of library books.
   50 per cent said that their participation in class discussions increased.[20]

In addition, 520 families living in the area covered by the closed circuit television system were interviewed by telephone or in person to determine community attitudes toward the project. The survey

[19] The Board of Education, *Closed-Circuit Television-Teaching in Washington County, 1958–59* (Hagerstown: The Board of Education, 1959), p. 2.
[20] *Ibid.*, pp. 17–18.

showed that a majority of the families questioned approved of the schools and the children taking part in the project, felt that the children would receive a better education through the use of television, preferred that their children receive television instruction, and felt that they were better informed about the schools since the inception of the television project.[21]

The attitudes of classroom teachers toward the television project were also surveyed through an anonymous questionnaire, to which 90 per cent of the instructors in the television schools responded. Over 80 per cent of the teachers felt that the aid of television was a stimulating adventure in education, preferred the aid of television, felt that television could improve the quality of instruction, and felt that just the right amount of time was being devoted to television instruction.[22] (The time devoted to ITV in most cases was less than one hour a day for any one student except in grades seven and eight which received eighty minutes daily.)

Preliminary results of achievement tests in various subject areas show that students receiving television instruction achieved more than those receiving conventional instruction. It should be noted, however, that the most pronounced growth occurred in the first year of television instruction, and that such growth may have been in part the result of such secondary factors as the novelty and glamour of television as a new tool, and an unconscious emphasis on televised subjects by the classroom teacher.[23]

The St. Louis television study. During the school year 1956–57, the St. Louis, Missouri, Educational Television Commission conducted a study of the effectiveness of direct teaching by television over its community-owned and operated VHF station, KETC-TV. Instruction was offered in ninth-grade general science and English composition, and in second-grade spelling. Large groups of pupils, up to 150 in number, received instruction by means of television alone, without supplementary teaching of the receiving groups. Instruction in two of the subject areas continued for a full semester; general science and English instruction were presented for thirty minutes each day. In spelling, instruction continued for a full year of twenty minute sessions each day. Two St. Louis High schools and three elementary schools in the public school system participated in the experiment.[24]

Questions the experiment attempted to answer were: (1) Is it possible for a competent television teacher to teach large groups of

---

21 *Ibid.*, pp. 19–20.

22 *Ibid.*, pp. 20–21.

23 *Ibid.*, pp. 24–31.

24 Earl G. Herminghaus, *An Investigation of Television Teaching* (St. Louis, Missouri: Educational Television Commission, St. Louis Public Schools, 1956), p. 2.

children effectively without supplementary activities? (2) Is it possible that the traditional pattern of classroom instruction can be modified so that an entirely new concept of teaching personnel, numerically and functionally, may be developed? And (3), what is the reaction of pupils and teachers to large-group direct television teaching?[25]

A coordinator of school programs and station relations directed the general organization of the project. Personnel in teaching roles included three television teachers who devoted full time to the preparation and presentation of lessons and seven teacher assistants who aided seven supervising classroom teachers in the performance of such routine tasks as taking attendance, marking papers, and preparing reports.

The experimental study was designed so that achievement between the large television classes and control classes of like numbers of pupils could be compared. Television teachers, all with long records of successful teaching experience in the St. Louis system, were selected after a series of auditions. Scope of the material to be covered was agreed upon by teachers of the experimental and control groups prior to the experiment. Pupils were equated on bases of intelligence quotient, age, and father's occupation as an indication of socio-economic status.

The lessons were telecast daily, Monday through Friday, from February 8 through June 6, 1956, for a total of seventy-nine lessons.[26] In an attempt to compensate for the lack of pupil-teacher interaction, a recognized weakness in television teaching, every effort was made to stimulate pupil involvement in lessons. In addition, there was a daily report from each supervising teacher in the receiving classrooms to the coordinator and the television teachers.[27]

Physical conditions of the receiving classrooms, although the best that could be provided under the circumstances, were far from ideal. Experts recommended the use of 24-inch, rather than 27-inch, screens because of ease of maintenance, clarity of image, and cost of replacement parts.[28]

During the term, several lessons were kinescoped and telecast in order that teachers might have opportunity to visit the receiving classrooms and view actual reception and utilization of their lessons.

Results of the study, as measured by the testing instruments employed, indicated that students in large group television classes in ninth grade English composition and ninth grade general science

---

[25] *Ibid.*
[26] *Ibid.*, p. 6.
[27] *Ibid.*, p. 7.
[28] *Ibid.*, p. 9.

showed a degree of achievement at least equal to that of the control classes taught in the conventional manner. It was recognized that this was only a partial answer, for effective teaching involves intangibles which are not capable of measurement by objective tests.[29]

The study did not furnish any conclusive evidence in answer to the second question of whether it is possible for the traditional pattern of instruction to be modified so that a new concept of teaching personnel may be developed. Although pupil achievement was satisfactory, more experimentation under a variety of conditions is necessary to warrant a positive answer to the question. While the teacher assistants in spelling did a satisfactory job, the teacher assistants in the high school classes were inadequate, according to reports from television and supervising teachers. The burden of duties was great, and their background and training did not equip them to exercise the judgment necessary for valid marking of papers and successful contacts with pupils. It was evident that the function of the teacher assistant was more than that of a clerk.[30]

In respect to the reaction of students and teachers to large-group television teaching, the pupils, on the whole, did not react favorably to the program, while the teachers had mixed reactions. More than half of the students thought that they would have learned more in the regular classroom than they did in the television course. They found television classes less interesting than regular classroom lessons. The chief disadvantages as seen by the teachers concerned the difficulty of meeting the needs of pupils of varying abilities, plus the inherent unsatisfactory physical conditions in the large-group nature of the classes.

The Pittsburgh television experiment. Pittsburgh, Pennsylvania, is experimenting with television in its public school classrooms. The first in-school television lessons there were designed to bring supplementary material into the classroom, but later lessons evolved into a minimum of five series each week, with each series presenting one new lesson per week. The lessons are kinescoped; and each one is shown at five different broadcast times each week, at a different hour on each day of the week. This enables the teacher to choose the most convenient time to fit the lesson into his schedule. Each series is presented in an eight-, sixteen-, or thirty-two-week sequence. The television teaching was started in Pittsburg in September, 1955, and during the series almost every subject taught in the schools has been telecast. The first lessons over WQED were in reading, arithmetic, and French, all at the fifth grade level, and all beamed to 20 classrooms in two counties. In 1958, the Pittsburgh programs were beamed to 1,060

[29] *Ibid.*, p. 44.
[30] *Ibid.*, p. 45.

classrooms and to 60 school districts within the wave-length of WQED. At present, lessons in English, reading, general science, physics, beginning and intermediate French, and others are included in the Pittsburgh program.

Advantages of television teaching as advanced by Pittsburgh school personnel are: (1) television can offer certain courses which the school does not offer; (2) it seems that television stimulates students to study more and, in general, to be more active academically; and (3) instruction by experts in particular fields can be given to several students in different areas at once.[31]

The San Diego television study. In the early 1950's, the San Diego, California, city schools, after having watched educational television develop in several communities in the United States, ventured an experimental educational television program jointly sponsored by the schools and station KFMB-TV. The board of education granted permission for the full-time release of teachers who were responsible for the development and production of a six-week, eighteen-program series of educational TV telecasts. On the basis of reports from other systems, a program incorporating typical classroom situations was decided upon as the type to be used in the San Diego series.[32]

Based upon the commonly accepted educational philosophy of the San Diego City schools, the six-week, eighteen-program series was arranged, and definite scheduled dates were assigned for programs. Seven programs were planned for the elementary level, nine for the secondary level, and two represented service departments of th system. At the primary elementary level, three programs were presented by third grade teachers and their pupils. The first lesson, "From Printing to Cursive Writing," was given in the handwriting area; the second, "Demonstration of String Class Methods," in the music area; and the third, "The Phonetic Approach to Spelling," in the language arts.[33] At the intermediate elementary level, two lessons were presented by sixth grade teachers and pupils, and one was given by a teacher and his combined fifth and sixth grade group. One lesson, "The Western Movement and Modern California," was in the social studies area; another lesson, "Improper Fractions and Denominate Numbers," was in the arithmetic area; another lesson, "Demonstration of Elementary School Chorus," was in music; and a final lesson,

---

[31] *The Superintendent's Viewpoint on Educational Television* (Champaign, Illinois: Region I Conference of the National Association of Educational Broadcasters, Thomas Alva Edison Foundation, 1958), p. 14.

[32] Stanley Degraff, *A Summary Report and Evaluation of San Diego City Schools–KFMB-TV Channel 8 Educational Television Experiment* (San Diego: San Diego City Schools, June, 1952), p. 4.

[33] *Ibid.*, p. 8.

"Atomic Energy and Its Potential Applications," was in the science area.[34] The music lesson in this series was the one presented by the combined fifth and sixth grade class. The junior high school programs, numbering five, were on the following topics: "How to Find Pi" (arithmetic); "Circulation, Digestion, and Osmosis" (science); "Review of American History from Colonial Times to the Civil War" (American history); "Baby Sitting" (Homemaking); and "Drawing from Life" (art).[35]

Twenty 20-inch television sets were loaned to the San Diego schools for the experiment, and were equipped so that only station KFMB could be tuned in. For purposes of evaluation in the experiment, it was important that the programs witnessed by student viewers be controlled.

The San Diego City Schools were interested in evaluating television as an educational, audio-visual medium for in-school and at-home viewing, and its value to pupils and parents for educational purposes. When direct instruction was considered to mean the substitution of television for regular classroom instruction, the evaluations expressed disapproval; but when educational values of the new medium were considered from the standpoint of an instructional aid which motivated further classroom discussion, the evaluations expressed decided approval.

The following statements were compiled from evaluation sheets and from observations made by various members of the Advisory Committee of Educational Television in San Diego:

> The value of television as a public relations medium seems clearly established.
>
> Too little experience has been gained as yet to properly evaluate television.
>
> Demonstration lessons such as were developed in science seem to have a D. I. quotient higher than most other types of programs.
>
> Study guides would greatly increase the educational value of television direct instruction.
>
> Television's potential faculty of bringing specialists into the classroom has real value (untried in this experiment).
>
> Community resources can be brought to large groups of students at one time via television.
>
> A definite inservice training potential exists by using television as an observing-learning process for the in-service training of teachers.

---

[34] *Ibid.*
[35] *Ibid.*, p. 9.

Seeing others of one's own age doing a good job can motivate thinking and inspire good work.

A summary of the week's most significant news, aided by the use of charts and graphs and "beamed" at pupils in language they can comprehend was suggested.

Because of television's multi-sensory stimulation, television can more effectively portray the immediate than any other mass media.

Television inspires children to look for further information.

Television's potential for showing the minute to large groups is tremendous . . . the surgical amphitheater now is a thing of the past.

"Television field trips" will help more students see more, be safe, and cost the taxpayer less.

The expense of costly, only-occasionally-used demonstrations can be reduced by the use of television.

More demonstration aids can be "brought into the class" via television without requiring the usual amount of moving and setting up of equipment on the part of the teacher . . . this can include the use of films and the presently required need to move a projector into the classroom.[36]

OTHER EMERGING PRACTICES IN THE ELEMENTARY SCHOOL

The programs in elementary schools described in the preceding sections of this chapter indicate a number of experiments in organization for instruction which are being tried out in various school systems over the nation. But there are other innovations which deserve some attention before leaving this general topic.

THE EXTENDED SCHOOL YEAR

During the past several years the idea of an extended school year has been considered by many, adopted temporarily by some, rejected by others; but, nevertheless, the idea is continually being reviewed. Historically, the idea of the year-around-school may be traced back to 1866 when such a school was established by the Church of Boston; New York City's board of education opened a number of year around schools in 1897; and in 1916 the United States Office of Education reported summer elementary schools in 211 cities, with terms rang-

[36] *Ibid.*, pp. 36–37.

ing from four to eleven weeks.[37] Glencoe, Illinois, and Rochester, Minnesota, have enrichment summer programs which have been in continuous operation since they were initiated in 1946.

Three general plans for an extended school year exist currently: one provides for summer sessions with optional attendance; another provides for regular classes all year with students attending three of the four quarters; and another provides for a longer school year of ten and one-half or eleven months.

Administrators of many local school districts recognize that the historical necessity for summer vacation is outdated and are currently offering summer school programs or are actively considering starting such programs. These districts are more effectively utilizing their school plants, establishing better public relations, giving students an opportunity to take electives they could not normally include in lock-step programs leading to college entrance, meeting the needs of some youngsters who require remedial work, and are enabling some teachers to increase their income.

The staggered four-quarter plan provides for a year divided into four quarters, with each student attending three. The four-quarter plan, not staggered, provides more days in a school year for pupils, but they would complete a year's work in three quarters. The quarter plans have not been successful.

A school year of eleven months is proposed by many educators and lay-persons who feel it is time to provide educational opportunities for our children in line with a realistic view of the demands of our present society.

TEACHING MACHINES

In recent years education has been criticized for not providing individualized instruction, teaching for mediocrity, spending too much time and energy on slow learners, and for not taking care of the needs of the superior pupils. As a result, one of the most discussed innovations in the education field in recent years is the teaching machine. Of course, in a strict sense, the devices such as television sets, radios, motion picture projectors, slide projectors, tape recorders, opaque projectors and many other media, even textbooks, which teachers have been using for years to *help* in their job of teaching youngsters, can technically be classified as "teaching machines." However, the media referred to in this paragraph are the automated and electronic pieces of equipment which certain industries are now producing and which are called simply "teaching machines," or "elec-

---

[37] C. L. Ogden, "Four Quarter Plan: How Practical an Idea?" *American School Board Journal,* CXXXIII (July, 1956), p. 19.

tronic tutors." These are machines designed to free teachers to work with children, and thus provide genuinely individualized instruction.

A characteristic common to the teaching machines is the automatic "feedback" of information to the pupil. This feedback is important in teaching, and normally is attained by examining pupils in one way or another, through tests of various kinds, class discussion, and other techniques. The teacher adjusts his instruction by objectively interpreting the feedback. It has been found that, even under the best of conditions, the rate of instruction may be too slow for the fast learners or too fast for the slower learners. The new teaching machines are intended to automatically correct this situation by enabling each pupil to proceed at his own pace, and so reduce total training time per pupil.

Experimentation in the psychology of learning points up the fact that more learning takes place when mistakes made by pupils are made known immediately. One of the basic characteristics of the teaching machine is "knowledge-of-results" immediately; the machine discovers errors in understanding and corrects them before they can impede the progress of a pupil.

Some of the newer automated teaching devices examine the pupil almost continuously, automatically adapting teaching materials to his needs, and preserving a complete record of the pupil's progress in the course. These machines provide a continuous feedback, allowing the pupil to know how he is progressing and, in case he errs, the machines tell the pupil why he is wrong. A number of the machines are basically automatic, random-access, recording microfilm-motion picture projectors, designed so that the material is presented to the pupil, followed by an examination in which the pupil is required to show understanding before the next point is taken up.

According to Fry, machines allow for more complete individualization of teaching. He asks:

> Why shouldn't a good student be learning the multiplication tables up to the twenty-fives while the average student is struggling to get up to the twelves? Or a bright student can be learning German vocabulary while waiting for the duller class members to finish their regular work.[38]

Experiments, using machines in the teaching of elementary school arithmetic and spelling, have been carried out with satisfactory results; and thought is now being given to the programming of material

---

[38] Edward Fry, "Teaching Machines: The Coming Automation," *Phi Delta Kappan,* XLI (October, 1959), pp. 28–31.

in other subjects such as science, foreign language, grammar, and the social studies.[39]

Teaching machines give promise of solving some of education's most pressing problems, and also give some indication that they may improve the learning process itself.

> The role of the teacher may well be changed, for machine instruction will affect several traditional practices. Students may continue to be grouped in "grades" or "classes," but it will be possible for each to proceed at his own level, advancing as rapidly as he can. The other kind of "grade" will also change its meaning. In traditional practice a C means that a student has a smattering of a whole course. But if machine instruction assures mastery at every stage, a grade will be useful only in showing *how far* a student has gone. C might mean that he is halfway through a course. Given enough time, he will be able to get an A; and since A is no longer a motivating device, this is fair enough.[40]

CONCLUSION

Several exciting innovations in elementary school organizational structure have emerged in recent years. In the face of greater numbers of pupils in attendance in the public schools, and of the ideological conflict between the world's two leading nations, public school personnel have shown considerable initiative and courage in launching new organizational plans and teaching techniques so that children in America may receive an education second to none in the world. In many of these innovations, they have had the encouragement and backing of parents and lay persons. The experimentation and research already done in such areas as ungraded, dual progress, and team teaching plans, and in the use of television and teaching machines and longer school years is commendable and should be continued.

The school principal and other personnel must, however, view these innovations and the parts they play in terms of the entire school program. Many of the innovations show promise in meeting current and future educational needs. On the other hand, the assumptions held by some persons, that any one of the innovations is the answer to our educational problems, are not supported by the results of experimentation at the present time. Research currently indicates that if educational innovations are to be successful, they must involve

[39] Eugene Galanter, ed., *Automatic Teaching: The State of the Art* (New York: John Wiley and Sons, Inc., 1959), pp. 83–90.

[40] B. F. Skinner, "Teaching Machines," *Science*, CXXVIII (October 24, 1958), p. 976.

appropriate adaptations in methods used by teachers. It is important that the thoughts and actions of the teachers themselves be directed toward the basic problems which prompt the trial of such innovations. The key to success may well lie in the ability of the principal and other administrators to provide leadership toward this goal.

Short Case 1

Beginning a New System in the Primary School

The teaching staff of the Northgate Elementary School, sparked by an enthusiastic principal, decided to experiment with a new system of organization in the first through third grades. Several plans were considered, but the one accepted for trial was that in which the first, second, and third grade children would be mixed into eight classrooms. Factors to be considered in the placement would include individual friendships, reading achievement, balance of ages, sexes, and abilities, and parental preferences when expressed. The average child would spend three years in the primary school. In each room each year a group of older children would move on, a group of younger ones would enter, and a sizeable group would remain from the previous year, thus giving stability to the program. If a child were ready to move out of the primary program earlier than the stated period, he would be moved along with older friends in his group; or if he needed longer than the three years, he would be kept on with his younger friends, with whom he was already associating.

Permission was secured from the board, and a series of P.T.A. meetings were scheduled to introduce and explain the idea to the parents. The general reaction was one of cautious acceptance. There were, however, several parents who did not attend the meetings. At the beginning of the school year, when the system was put into effect, some of these parents complained bitterly that they had not been properly informed and consulted. Several of them applied for their children's transfer to other schools in the district.

Problem: Compare advantages and disadvantages of the suggested plan. What other possibilities might have been considered? In what ways could public relations have been handled? How should the requests for transfer be handled?

Short Case 2

An Upper-Grade Dual Progress Plan

For several years the fifth and sixth grades of the Jefferson School had operated on a standard six-period day. Language arts, social studies, arithmetic, science, and physical education took five periods, and the sixth, an activity period, was divided in the fifth grade between art and music, and in the sixth grade used to fulfill a requirement of homemaking for the girls and manual arts for the boys. There recently had developed considerable opposition to this traditional program after the staff and parents had learned of some experiments being conducted in other schools.

Finally, a principal-appointed faculty study committee recommended a plan whereby the student body would be divided into two sections. Each morning one group would be instructed in the core program, consisting of one period each of language arts, social studies, and physical education (required by law). The other group would have science and mathematics at varying levels according to interest and ability. The remainder of the second group's morning would be divided in the fifth grade to allow both art and music and a choice of craft or foreign language, and at the sixth grade level to allow for the requirement of home-making and manual arts, and two of the four extra activities. In the afternoon the scheduling would be reversed, with the core being given for the second group and the enrichment courses for the first group.

With certain reservations, the faculty adopted the plan; the board voted three to two to allow it to be carried out. The two dissenters felt that too much attention was being given to the "frills," not enough to science and mathematics; also they were concerned for fear the best hours were not being given to intellectual activities.

Problem: What is your opinion of the committee's recommendation? What other plans might be tried in scheduling these two grades? How could the two dissenters on the school board be answered?

Short Case 3

An Administrator Decides on Team Teaching

For two years the Grasshill Elementary School faculty curriculum development committee worked cooperatively with the district curriculum consultant to revise the programs at the fifth- and sixth-grade levels. The experimental plan called for a team of four teachers, two with special competencies in the language arts and two with special abilities in science and mathematics; the teachers would work together with a flexible schedule so that teaching might be accomplished in large groups, small groups, laboratory groups, and supervised study groups. Attempts would be made to permit integration of all subject matter areas when valuable and feasible. The teachers were to be given the use of the cafetorium for one morning and one afternoon hour whenever needed during the week for the purpose of large group instruction. They were also to have the use of two general classrooms, one social studies resource classroom and one classroom equipped with science laboratory equipment. Any interested teachers were eligible to participate.

The superintendent was highly interested and approved the committee's plans, with one exception. He felt that participating teachers should have equal training, experience, and merit ratings by supervisors, and that selection for participation in the experiment should be reserved as a function of the supervisory staff.

The committee presented several arguments against the superintendent's ideas. He listened carefully, but remained adamant, and the committee was forced to accept his decision if they wished to initiate the experiment.

Problem: What, essentially, is the problem in this case? What may have been the arguments of the committee? What situations may arise to cause problems? How should teachers be selected for experimental programs? What other ideas should the committee have included in their presentation? Try role playing the interview with the superintendent. What would you, as a supervisor, do to try to initiate team teaching?

Chapter Five

Motivation: A Creative Approach

John Amos Comenius, the Moravian bishop and outstanding European educator of the seventeenth century, wrote in *The Great Didactic:* "Let the main object of this, our didactic, be as follows: To seek and to find a method of instruction by which teachers may teach less, but learners may learn more."[1] The importance of motivation in the instructional processes is implied in this statement by the far-sighted philosopher-educator.

Even though Comenius and others of his time recognized the value of motivation in instruction, the study of motivation is still considered to be in its infancy. Before 1920, psychologists and educators scarcely recognized motivation as a psychological phenomenon. The literature in psychology and education clearly demonstrates the need for valid and reliable research in the area.

Motives were once regarded by psychologists and educators as stemming largely from drives or needs, such needs being inherent and possibly in conflict with each other. New concepts point up the inadequacies of this explanation, however, and suggest that selection may involve preferred motives and stem from many sources. Some authorities aver that man, being a physical, social, emotional, sexual,

[1] M. W. Keatings, *The Great Didactic of John Amos Comenius* (London: Adam and Charles Black, 1896), pp. 156–157.

and spiritual being, responds at all times to all situations with his whole being; others tend to emphasize only one of these factors, as, for example, the social factor, and hold that man's social environment conditions him to select and maintain certain motives above all others.

Maslow, a Brandeis University psychologist and authority on the subject of motivation, views the individual as an integrated organized whole—a concept which makes possible a plausible theory of motivation, and which integrates factors of growth and development with those of needs and drives.[2] This theory holds that the whole person is motivated, not just part of him.

Theories and problems in motivation are invariably complex and, at times, contradictory; however, behavior is never simple, and the unknown may bring profound questioning of well-conceived theories.

MOTIVATION DEFINED

A simple definition of motivation might be *that which impells or incites*. Hilgard states that motivation is "referring to the regulation of need-satisfying and goal-seeking behavior, including the avoidance of dangerous or unpleasant situations."[3] In discussing motivation in education, Good defines the term as "the practical art of applying incentives and arousing interest for the purpose of causing a pupil to perform in a desired way."[4] March believes that motivation is "something which produces an incentive, inducement, or motive,"[5] and Pressey classifies motivation as being either intrinsic or extrinsic when he declares:

> Intrinsic motivation is defined as a state in which an individual wants to do or learn something for its own sake. It presents values which are directly satisfying. . . . Extrinsic motivation is defined as a state in which an individual does or learns something, not for its own sake, but as a means of obtaining some wished-for or desirable goal which is artificially or arbitrarily related to the activity.[6]

[2] A. H. Maslow, *Motivation and Personality* (New York: Harper and Brothers, 1954), p. 63.

[3] Ernest R. Hilgard, *Introduction to Psychology* (New York: Harcourt, Brace and Company, 1957), p. 106.

[4] Carter V. Good (ed.), *Dictionary of Education* (New York: McGraw-Hill Company, Inc., 1959), p. 354.

[5] Leland S. March, "Motivation, the Key to Good Teaching," *Education Digest,* XXV (January, 1960), p. 24.

[6] Sidney L. Pressey et al., *Psychology in Education* (New York: Harper and Brothers, 1959), p. 211.

While these definitions present the picture of motivation in slightly different hues, they all contain the implication that before a child will learn he must want to learn, and that he will want to learn only those things which he believes will satisfy his needs. The pupil's personality, his family background, his social status, and his physical composition are all factors which will affect *how* and *when* the individual can be motivated.

PSYCHOLOGICAL ASPECTS OF MOTIVATION

The question of motivation is a question of what makes us do the things we do. Psychologists generally agree that actions and thoughts of human beings center on meeting their needs, which arise from within themselves or from their environment. Though students of psychology are not quite sure how and to what extent motives facilitate learning, they are certain that in some way or another motivation exerts a powerful force in the process of learning. It is evident that attention to basic physiological and physical needs, such as the needs for food, warmth, and affection, results in action on the parts of human beings; but the fact is that these more primitive motives are seldom directly involved in the activities of the elementary school classroom. Before children in school can gain skills and knowledge which will enable them to meet their needs in society, they must want to learn, and they will learn only those things which they believe will help them satisfy their needs. The teacher's job is to identify the drives of his pupils and to formulate techniques which will help the pupils satisfy these needs in an acceptable manner.

INTENTION TO LEARN

It seems trite to state that a person who has the intention to learn will learn more effectively than one without that intention. The acquisition of knowledge, the quest for the meaning of life, the attempts to regulate and govern life are characteristic of man, and the need to know and to understand is an observable feature of human behavior. While it seems self-evident that teachers can motivate children by pointing out what they are expected to learn, it is also evident that boys and girls often do learn when no effort has been expended in this direction, and when they do not intend to learn. Children, having intended to learn the alphabet forward and having achieved this objective, often find they can repeat all or part of the alphabet backward without effort; thus, "backward association" comes into play. At present a good many experiments are being conducted concerning subliminal learning and learning while one is asleep; the varying results of these could indicate a good deal of learning without intention. Children learn many attitudes, such as liking dogs or hating them, without intention.

Regardless of the fact that many persons learn material which they do not intend to learn, it is still true that deliberate intention to learn is a real aid to learning. Effort alone is not as effective as effort with intent to learn.

Waetjen, in similar vein, has written,

> Some people dispute the fact that all human beings desire to learn. They are quick to point out that an individual known to them has no desire to learn despite all teaching efforts. So the statement must be modified to read that all individuals not only have the capacity but the desire to learn that which is significant to them. Things which have a significant meaning to people motivate them to learn and have the greatest impact on behavior. In self-directed situations people are free to learn and grow, and rarely, if ever, do they need to be threatened or promised rewards. Learning that which is significant to people is reward in itself.[7]

EGO-INVOLVEMENT

When a pupil feels and accepts a certain challenge, it is said that his ego is involved. If he fails in an assigned chore he suffers an impairment of the ego, some loss of self respect, or a reduction in his sense of worth, according to Stephens.[8] The same writer continues,

> There is no question that a moderate amount of ego-involvement is a powerful aid to learning. Students will perform better and acquire more skill when they are made to feel that success in the assigned task is important to them, that in some way it is a measure of their real worth as persons.[9]

It is now almost axiomatic in education that every child needs to experience some degree of success and social approval. Good mental health depends upon an individual finding success in some area or areas. While some authorities still argue that happiness depends upon satisfaction of the hunger drive, the sex drive, or the several other biological drives, it is becoming apparent that the ego also needs to be satisfied.

---

[7] Walter B. Waetjen, "Learning—Now and in the Future," *Educational Leadership,* XIV (February, 1957), p. 269.

[8] J. M. Stephens, *Educational Psychology* (New York: Holt-Winston-Rinehart, Inc., 1958), p. 299.

[9] *Ibid.,* p. 300.

FREQUENT TESTS

Teachers sometimes use tests as motivators, believing that if pupils know they will be examined at the end of a certain lesson they will study harder and acquire more knowledge. This is a questionable technique, especially at the elementary level. Results of some studies indicate that less frequent tests are more valuable than more frequent ones, and that more learning takes place when tests are announced in advance than when they are given without notice.

KNOWLEDGE OF RESULTS

A pupil's knowledge of the results of his work is an important factor in motivation. The experiments dealing with this factor in general reveal that knowledge of one's performance rating builds up a favorable attitude toward improvement, whereas continuous work with only partial knowledge of results may lead to a sense of failure and depression. It is to be noted here that knowledge of results tends to promote more vigorous practice, but it is not as yet possible to determine whether or not more actual learning takes place. While there is some indication that improvement in learning accompanies knowledge of results, there needs be more intensive research in this area before conclusions can be formed.

OTHER PSYCHOLOGICAL ASPECTS OF MOTIVATION

Psychologists list other factors which affect learning or performance, such as the prospect of failure or success, social facility, scrutiny by others, and competition. The value of these aspects in the real learning situation is subject to suspicion, though it is generally agreed that they may increase speed and volume of output on the part of pupils.

MOTIVATION OF LEARNING AT THE ELEMENTARY LEVEL

Since factors involved in the motivation of human behavior are extremely complex, experimentation in this area is generally of an exploratory nature. The major portion of educational research concerning motivation has dealt with social incentives, regarded as environmental factors, acting as positive and negative forces on behavior.

Experimental studies have been conducted which have attempted to measure the influence of social approval or disapproval, or "praise and reproof." In one such study, Hurlock required school children to take a series of addition tests under different incentive conditions.[10] On the first day all children were given a preliminary addition test which provided the basis of forming four groups. One of the groups was praised for its work, another reproved, and a third ignored. A control group was taken to another room where it worked under ordinary classroom motivation. No comments were made to this group except that the numbers were to be added. After a careful analysis of the results, Hurlock concluded that consistent praise is superior to consistent reproof as an incentive for school work of this type. Both praise and reproof were found to be superior to being ignored.

After reviewing several studies in the area of blame and praise, Stephens concludes that if the results from school situations suggest anything, it is that blame may be more likely to induce greater effort, but the advantage, if any, is slight and in no way dependable.[11] He adds:

> Some studies suggest that failure or blame will boost the performance of extroverts but not of introverts. Other studies produce results in the opposite direction. Some work on anxiety may be promising in this respect. It suggests that failure or blame may be especially bad for people who are very tense to begin with, but may help people who show little anxiety.[12]

It would seem then that there is no conclusive evidence supporting either praise or blame as being the more effective in stimulating learning. In one teacher-pupil relationship, praise may be more effective, but in another relationship, blame may have the edge. Marx states that "praise is regarded as superior to reproof in schools."[13] This is in accord with the generally accepted positive approach in the philosophy of teaching.

The effect of frustration upon motivation was the subject of a study made by McDonough.[14] The purpose of the study was to investigate possible age and sex differences in strength of reaction to frustration as related to the motivational level. It involved 100 children from the ages of three to nine and one-half years of age. Some were arbitrarily frustrated in their attempt to fill a board with marbles and hit a plunger to signify completion. It was found that some of the subjects increased their performances following frustration while

---

[10] Elizabeth B. Hurlock, *Child Development* (New York: McGraw-Hill Book Company, Inc., 1950), p. 311.

[11] Stephens, *op. cit.*, p. 303.

[12] *Ibid.*

[13] Melvin H. Marx, *Encyclopedia of Educational Research* (Third Edition; New York: The Macmillan Company, 1960), pp. 888–889.

[14] Leah Brooks McDonough, "A Developmental Study of Motivation and Reactions to Frustration," *Dissertation Abstracts* (January, 1960), p. 2892.

the efforts of others diminished, and some showed no effect at all. As a conclusion to this study, it was suggested that frustration seemed to exert a general inhibitory effect. The advisability of its use in general teaching practices is discussed by Symonds; he summarizes by stating that its use is dependent upon the effect produced.[15] If increased effort is achieved, he maintains that frustration is actually conducive to good mental hygiene, but, if it produces anxiety or hostility, it should be eliminated.

OTHER RESEARCH STUDIES IN MOTIVATION

An experiment concerning the level of aspiration or goal-getting which deals directly with "success and failure" was reported by Child and Whiting.[16] It was concerned with the analysis of incidents in the lives of fifteen men who were undergraduates in an eastern university. Each student, as a project in his psychology course, was required to write a description of three incidents in his life; the first one involving complete frustration in which he never reached his goal, one in which a period of frustration was finally followed by attainment of his goal, and one of simple attainment of a goal without any appreciable frustration. The generalizations perceived in this study were that success generally leads to a raising of the level of aspiration, and failure leads to a lowering of this level. Also, shifts in the level of aspiration are in part a function of changes in the subject's confidence in his ability to attain his goals.

In appraising results it is important to consider that the effects of success and failure are relative in one's level of self-evaluation and self-concepts. At the Monterey County Schools in California, Lumpkin engaged in a study designed to examine relationships that might exist between the self-concepts of a group of elementary school children and their achievement in reading.[17] Twenty-four over-achievers and twenty-five under-achievers were matched on the bases of chronological age, sex, and home background. Comparisons were made on the bases of responses to a variety of psychological instruments designed to explore the dimensions of self-concept, as well as teacher perception of the child, and peer status. Statistical analyses were made and the

---

[15] Percival M. Symonds, "Is Frustration Compatible with Good Mental Hygiene?" *Progressive Education,* XXX (1953), pp. 107–110.

[16] Irvin L. Child and John W. M. Whiting, "Determinants of Level of Aspiration: Evidence from Everyday Life," *Journal of Abnormal Social Psychology,* XLIV (1949), pp. 303–314.

[17] Donavon D. Lumpkin, "The Relationship of Self-Concept to Achievement in Reading," *Dissertation Abstracts* (September, 1959), p. 205.

findings coupled with case profiles of children in each achievement group. Findings through this study indicated a variety of significant relationships between pupils' self-concepts and achievement in reading. The over-achievers not only demonstrated superior performance in reading and other subjects, but revealed more positive self-concepts, higher levels of adjustment, and saw themselves as liking reading. They were also viewed positively by peers and teachers. In the under-achiever group lower scores on measures of achievement were formed. A negative perception of self was predominantly manifested, as well as a desire to be different from the way they saw themselves. Expressed feelings of conflict were also found more frequently in this group. "It can be stated with confidence that in the group studied, the concept of self which the individual accepts influences his behavior qualitatively and may determine the direction and degree of his expression in academic work as well as in his social relationships."[18] One of the recommendations made in this study suggests that schools engage in practices which would provide increased understanding of the child who expresses aggressive, withdrawing, and non-achieving behavior as a result of his concept of himself.

SELF-MOTIVATION VS. GROUP MOTIVATION

Early studies by Maller in "cooperation and competition" contrasted working for personal gain, or self-motivation, with working for the advantage of one's group, or group motivation.[19] In general, it was found that the performance was consistently higher under self-motivation than under group-motivation. Even when conditions were arranged to provide free choice between the two forms of motivation, self-motivation was preferred in close to three-fourths of the trials.

It would appear that the more closely a motive is related to self-interest, the greater its effectiveness. Recent investigations have, however, shown results contrary to this conclusion. In a study in 1953, fifty volunteers from a course in introductory psychology were divided into ten groups of five members each.[20] These groups worked on two types of tasks, one consisting of puzzle problems, and the other problems in human relations. The groups met for a three-hour period once each week for six weeks. Competitive orientation was created for half the groups. In this section it was arranged that the student who contributed the most to the group solution of the problem would be exempt from having to submit a term paper and would be granted an "A" grade for the paper. The other half of the groups were told that

[18] *Ibid.*

[19] Reported in Glenn Myers Blair, et al. *Educational Psychology* (New York: The Macmillan Company, 1956), pp. 180–181.

[20] Hilgard, *op cit.*, p. 502.

the group making the best showing would all be excused from a term paper and be granted an "A." The results indicated that the group effort was superior in that there was a better quality of work submitted, more effective communication, more attentiveness to suggestions of other members, and more coordination of effort. This case shows that cooperative effort may produce more efficient behavior than individual reward. The structure of the groups involved, the previous experiences and personalities of the individuals, and the nature of the task involved are factors which must also be taken into account as influencing the effect of competition and the performance of either individuals or groups. Under the expert guidance of a good teacher, however, the technique of group motivation could be a rewarding experience to all concerned.

In a dissertation presented by Zimny to the psychology department at the University of Minnesota, the author discussed his findings in a study on the effects of various motivational techniques upon learning and performance tasks.[21] In the first part of his study, the author determined to measure the effects of the various motivating techniques under constant conditions. Four groups, each consisting of twenty-five college men, were asked to learn a practice list of twelve nonsense syllables. Then, three of the groups were urged to learn another set of nonsense syllables, for one of the following reasons: (1) the incentive that group members would be excused from a regular classroom assignment; (2) the threat of electric shock; and (3) to prove the statement that this learning activity was a measure of intelligence. The fourth group served as the control; members were assigned to the task for "additional practice." Determination of the results of this verbal experiment was based on both absolute (one-trial practice result), and relative (comparative experiment results) measurements. Evaluation of data led Zimny to report that "the three techniques had no discernible effect on mean performance or variability of performance in the verbal learning task, when both absolute and relative measures were employed."

The second part of Zimny's study attempted to measure the effect of a single motivating technique when applied to a different type of activity, namely a motor activity. To complete this experiment, the experimenter used two groups, each composed of twenty college men. The experimental group was motivated by incentive (release from a class assignment) to sort ten decks of forty cards. The control group was not motivated, but assigned to the identical task. Procedures

---

[21] George H. Zimny, "The Effect of Various Motivational Techniques Upon Learning and Performance Tasks," *Journal of Experimental Psychology*, LII (April, 1956), pp. 251–257.

parallel to those used in the first part of the study were followed; practice assignments preceded the actual experiment, and both absolute and relative measures were used to score results of the two groups. The incentive technique had no discernible effects upon mean performance or variability of performance in the motor tasks when absolute measures were employed. In addition, the author reported that in the case where relative measurement was utilized, motivation by incentive method failed to cause any effect on the variability of the motor activity. However, test results indicated that relative measurement did produce a significant facilitating effect upon mean performance during the first half of the task. Zimny concluded that the nature of assignments employed in the study of the influence of motivation becomes an important variable, depending upon the techniques of measurement applied to a study.

While the results of experimentation point up various advantages and disadvantages of different motivational techniques, all imply that interest and participation are enhanced when the activities of children are personal, meaningful, and purposeful. There can be little question but that children will assimilate a great deal more if the subject matter is related directly to their real and unique needs. This presents a sizeable challenge to a teacher of twenty-five to thirty-five youngsters in a classroom situation. Insofar as possible, teachers must abolish the practice of presenting artificial, often meaningless, problems to their pupils if they expect the children to learn the deeper meanings of the subject matter being presented.

MOTIVATION OF TEACHERS BY THE ADMINISTRATOR

It is generally established that it is important for elementary school teachers to motivate boys and girls if they are to become interested in acquiring suitable attitudes, knowledge, and skills. It is no less important that administrators and supervisors, as teachers of teachers, spend as much time and effort in motivating teachers—not only in their roles in the teaching-learning situation, but also in the extra-class activities with which all instructors are confronted.

Of a total work week of about forty-seven to forty-eight hours, the elementary teacher spends 59 per cent, or about twenty-eight hours and fifteen minutes, in class instruction. If the premise is true that the responsibility of the teacher lies in arranging the environment and motivating pupils, then a large amount of the teacher's time should be spent in motivating children in the classroom. The elementary school principal, along with whatever supervisory personnel is available, should then spend a considerable portion of his time in assisting teachers with the problems of instruction, especially in an area which is generally neglected, that of motivation. Suggestions which principals might present to aid teachers in motivating children are indicated in the latter half of this chapter.

But how does the elementary teacher spend the remaining portion of his work week? According to the research division of the National Education Association, 25 per cent, or eleven hours and fifty-two minutes, is spent in out-of-class duties, including preparing materials, correcting papers, personal preparation, individual help, and parent contacts.[22] Sixteen per cent, or seven hours and forty-three minutes, of the teacher's time is spent in miscellaneous duties, including monitorial duties, records and report cards, and official meetings. The question is, do elementary principals spend time and effort in motivating teachers to participate in the out-of-class instructional activities and in those classified as miscellaneous? Should not administrators inspire teachers to participate willingly in these extra-class activities which, while not as paramount as the instructional activities, are still part of the teaching-learning phenomenon?

Of course, teachers are motivated extrinsically to discharge all their duties in order to receive their paycheck at the end of the month, or to please their "superiors." But should they not also experience an intrinsic motivation—an inner feeling of satisfaction—values that are directly satisfying—just as they endeavor to have pupils gain from their school work in ways other than "earning" a grade or in satisfying the teacher?

Principals need to understand that the same psychological aspects of motivation that apply to children in their learning also apply to teachers in gaining understanding of their work in class instruction, in out-of-class instructional duties, and in miscellaneous activities. Intention to learn, ego-involvement, frequent tests, knowledge of results, failure versus success, social facility, scrutiny by others, and wholesome competition are aspects of motivation which should be considered in moving teachers (and administrators) to do what should be done, just as they should be in moving children toward this end. When a staff is motivated intrinsically, much progress is achieved; an intrinsically motivated staff is a powerful staff in terms of attainment possibilities.

Job satisfaction on the part of teachers is important in their class instruction, and this is also true in their out-of-class instructional and miscellaneous activities. Chapter XVI of this book discusses in considerable detail matters pertaining to teacher morale, but it is well to point up here the importance of job satisfaction as it relates to

[22] *Teacher Load in 1950,* Research Bulletin of the National Education Association. (Washington, D.C.: The Association, Vol. 29, February, 1951), p. 17.

instructional competency. Five components of job satisfaction are (1) self-respect; (2) recognition; (3) satiation of wants; (4) pleasure; and (5) affection.[23] Griffiths discusses these components as they fall quite naturally within the framework of the aspects of motivation cited above.[24]

Self-respect, says Griffiths, is treated as the extent to which a person lives up to moral norms, or levels of aspiration, which he has built into his own personality structure. By aiding faculty members to develop a realistic level of aspiration and providing means by which they can attain this level, a principal contributes toward the building of self-respect in the staff.

It would be rather difficult, according to Griffiths, for a person to have self-respect if he did not gain *recognition,* the second component listed above. One of the causes of low morale among staff members which tends to permeate the school is lack of recognition. The principal can best show recognition by keeping abreast of what each teacher is doing in his work, and letting him know this. Some principals write the teacher a note when some outstanding feat is accomplished; some arrange for publicity for a teacher whose particular accomplishment is outstanding. However recognition is provided, it is paramount that the principal know what is going on and acknowledge the fact.

Satiation of wants implies doing a good job "for what we can get out of it," states Griffiths. Some of the "getting" involves extrinsic motives, such as salary or recognition, but in all cases a person needs to get some satisfaction out of doing a job, or he will not do it at all.

Pleasure, according to Griffiths, should not be the sole end toward which a person strives, but rather should be construed as "a function of the total personal equilibrium of the individual." One should enjoy his work and should derive from it the same type of pleasure that he does from playing games or taking part in other forms of recreation. The provision by a principal of those things which make teaching a pleasure will act as a powerful incentive.

Having to do directly with the establishment of rapport between the principal and his faculty is the element of *affection,* according to Griffiths. Friendship between members of the staff is an important incentive; this friendship can be directed toward teamwork necessary for a successful educational organization. If negative relationships are allowed to develop, low morale, bickering, back-biting, and low production are the inevitable results.

---

[23] Talcott Parsons, "Motivation of Economic Activities," *Canadian Journal of Economics and Political Science,* Vol. VI (1940), pp. 187–202.

[24] Daniel E. Griffiths, *Human Relations in School Administration* (New York: Appleton-Century-Crofts, Inc., 1956), pp. 36–38.

Griffiths continues by pointing up that a good *atmosphere,* as well as job-satisfaction, is important to good school management and motivation of teachers. Creative activity springs up in schools where there is an atmosphere of freedom—a permissive atmosphere. This permissive atmosphere is necessary if teachers are to be relieved of their timidities and if they are to function up to their capacity.

CREATING LEARNING SITUATIONS THAT COMPARE WITH THE WORLD OUTSIDE THE CLASSROOM

Let us now turn to the importance of motivation in the instructional activities in the classroom which comprise almost 60 per cent of the teacher's time. The teacher's need for the principal's or supervisor's help in motivating boys and girls to learn cannot be overemphasized.

In a sense, teachers do not *teach* children at all; they merely arrange the environment and motivate children so that they *learn.* This accomplishment, if it is achieved, is no mean task to be gained with any "bag of tricks" technique. As elementary principals work with teachers in improving the instructional program for students, what they are really doing is creating situations and planning activities in which the child may learn more thoroughly by himself.

It is possible that the great majority of teachers spend more time and energy in attempting to *teach* their knowledge to children than they do in planning activities which will stimulate the boys and girls in their charge to learn for themselves. The wise principal or supervisor will spark in teachers a concern for motivating youngsters so that the classroom will be just as interesting and inspiring as the "great big wonderful world" outside the classroom.

The final section of this chapter will present some of the many successful teaching methods which have been used to motivate children in actual classroom situations, and which elementary school principals might present to teachers for use in their own classes.

LEARNING TO READ

Since reading is basic to all curricular areas, and since there are many kinds of reading in a school situation, it is given first emphasis here. Primary children are concerned principally with learning to read; intermediate grade children read to learn; all pupils, at times, read just for fun. The first set of motivational techniques concerns learning to read.

1. Let each child choose a character or a narrator when re-reading

a story. This can be expanded into creative dramatics, and the story can be acted out in the children's own words. Simple costumes made in the classroom add to the enjoyment, and a background can be drawn on the blackboard, or the children can make one in art class. Other rooms can be invited to share in the experience, or several simple stories can be dramatized for an assembly.

2. Children enjoy memory games with new words. Write the words on the chalkboard, and then erase them one or two at a time to see if the children can remember them. This also can be done with endings or prefixes.

3. Children can illustrate by crayon drawings or paintings the story they like best when they have finished with a reading book. Or they might illustrate one story with a series of drawings.

4. From free reading or library books, have children tell the most exciting part of a story to interest other children in the book. This builds skills of retention and attention to details.

5. Word wheels can be made for word recognition and for blends. Two cardboard circles (one 8 inches in diameter, the other 7½ inches) can be put together with a brad. Words or groups of letters can be written on the smaller top wheel. By rotating the top wheel new words and letter combinations can be formed.

6. Vowel or consonant Bingo is a good game. The teacher can make as many cards and markers as are needed. Key words are read by the teacher and the child covers the word on his card which begins with the same sound.

sun	mother	horse	baby
pig	fish	cat	wagon
goat	rabbit	nest	doll
jump	leaves	table	luck

7. Children enjoy matching words. Mimeograph two sheets of words per child with the words in a different order on the two sheets. Have the child cut out the words on one sheet and match them with the words on the other.

8. Most children have fun with crossword puzzles using basic words or spelling words. These can be mimeographed for the room by the teacher.

9. A good word game is called "Playing Opposite." This can be played as a group game. Cards with certain words are given to half of the group while the other half receives cards with words opposite in meaning to the first set. Children can then find their opposites as the cards are read. The same learning can be accomplished through the use of a worksheet like the one discussed in No. 7 above.

10. A variation of the familiar card game, "Fish," can be made with sets of cards built around familiar vowel sounds. The player

asks for a word with a particular vowel sound. If another player has a card with such a word on it, he says the word and gives up the card. If not, he tells the player who is "IT" to "fish" for a card from the pile. Four words of each vowel make a book.

Learning to read, of course, does not end at the primary level, but extends into upper grade levels. Intermediate grade teachers have used the following motivational techniques at that level.

1. This technique is a booster for children who have trouble reading in thought units. Even fourth graders may be taught that some ideas can be conveyed with one word, while at other times a group of words may give a better picture, e.g., John sat *there,* and John sat *on a rickety old fence.* Thus, children may be taught that a phrase is a group of related words that may take the place of one word and that such phrases may tell:

a. *how*—I played hard. I played unusually hard.
b. *when*—He came today. He came early in the day.
c. *what*—I ate the pie. I ate the pie on the paper plate.
d. *how much*—He bought a little food. He bought more than he needed.
e. *how far*—He jumped far. He jumped farther than any other boy.

Later, the children should practice finding such phrases in their reading material, explaining what each phrase tells.

2. The recognition of short and long vowels is very essential in "breaking down" new words when reading to learn. It is equally important in developing independence in spelling. To arouse interest in reviewing such sounds, it is useful to employ a game called "Hear Me." Make 100 cards with one-syllable words containing long and short *a's.* These are dealt five to each player. The remaining ones are turned face down in the center of the table, except the top one, which is turned face up beside the stack. Each player groups his cards into long and short *a's.* Taking turns in a clockwise order, a player may take the one card facing up, or he may take the chance of getting what he needs from the large stack. When he succeeds in getting four long *a's* or four short *a's,* he stops the game by saying, "Hear Me." He then pronounces the words from the cards, and if they are correct, he has a trick which he puts face down in front of him. If he is wrong, other players tell him so, and he must wait another turn to finish his book or trick. After securing a book, he draws three more cards. The child getting the most tricks wins the game. When the *a's* are mastered, new sets are used with other short and long vowels until all have been used. Then all sets may be shuffled and a general review enjoyed.

3. The game "Tan Tan" provides learning in both word recognition and the ability to see relationships. Prepare twelve or fifteen sets

of cards, four cards to a set. A set of cotton cards might be "gin," "chopping," "linter," "bales," or "bolls." Another set of related cards might be "hatchery," "incubator," "fowls," "capon," or "breed." One card from each set is put aside for the player's pool. The remaining words are kept by the leader for his pack. Players sit at a table facing the leader. Each player draws one card. The leader then shuffles the cards in his pack and flashes them one at a time before the players. The player whose card belongs to the same set as the flashed card calls, "Tan Tan," and also calls the flashed card. Unclaimed cards go back into the pack to be flashed again. As soon as a player has completed a book of four cards, he lays them on the table and draws another card to start another book. The player with the largest number of books is the winner.

4. Children may be stimulated to master homonyms by using this technique: on one set of cards write or print homonyms; on another set, place meanings. During spare time, a child may take a turn at matching homonyms with the proper meanings. When children have mastered one set and can prove it by using them correctly in sentences or filling in blanks with them, new sets may be supplied.

5. The following technique not only develops vocabulary, but it is an aid to independent spelling as well. Early in the year a simple letter combination may be placed on the board, such as "at." Using this as a base, the children are asked to build new words by adding a prefix, a suffix, or both. This affords a good opportunity for teaching when and when not to double the final consonant.

at				
bat	batter	batted		
fat	fatter	fatten	fattened	
hat	hatter	shatter	shattered	shattering
mat	matter	smatter	smattering	
pat	patter	pattering	pattern	
spat	spatter	spattering	spattered	

6. While many word meanings should be secured through context clues, children should become skillful in using the dictionary. We drill on one dictionary skill at a time until the children seem to have several skills well in hand. Then we stop for a time test. Those who do not finish in the given time must complete it after time has been called. This is a sample of a test to be done in twenty minutes:

1. The phonetic spelling for disobey. ____________.
2. Plurals for the noun "fish" are ____________ and ____________.
3. Two meanings for *dispel* are ____________ and ____________.
4. As a numeral or figure, *M* stands for ____________.
5. *M* or *MM* are abbreviations for ____________.

6. The small *m* is an abbreviation for __________ or __________.
7. "Apricot" may be pronounced ____________ or ____________.
8. The syllabication for "reverberate" is ________________.
9. A good definition for the noun *retort* is ____________________.
10. The accented syllable of "chalet" would rhyme with (play, pet, crochet).

7. Before introducing a poem that is to be read chorally, it is helpful to practice some catchy tongue twister, such as "Betty Botter bought some butter." This not only helps the children to realize how essential proper enunciation and pronunciation are to understanding, but it slows the faster readers down enough to give the slower ones a chance to feel and sense the pace needed for clarity and expression. It also draws in the timid or shy child who fears individual performance.

8. Much new vocabulary may be built through antonyms, homonyms, and synonyms. Make sets of antonyms (twenty in a set) on oak tag. During leisure time, a child matches the antonyms in a set and then gets permission to use the key for that particular set to check his own errors. He mixes or shuffles the cards, leaving them to be sorted and arranged properly by another child, who has some leisure time. When this set has been mastered a new set of twenty antonyms is put out for the children to learn. The same scheme may be used with sets of synonyms, using only five words in a set.

9. To help the slow learning child to read more comprehensively, it is possible to make a game consisting of fifty-four cards. On eighteen of these write subject phrases; on another eighteen, action phrases; and on the other eighteen, phrases which show when, where, how, how much, how far, or why. Here are the rules for a game using these cards:

1. The cards are placed in three piles, each with eighteen cards in it.
2. Put all subject phrases in the first pile.
3. Put all action phrases in the second pile.
4. Put other phrases in the third pile.
5. Shuffle the cards and deal.
6. Lay cards out in front.
7. The first player who finds that he can make a sentence reads it.
8. The next player may need another card to complete his sentence. He may then ask another player to trade a card with him unseen.
9. If he receives a card he can use, he reads his sentence and puts it down. Otherwise he has to pass.
10. The child who completes the most sentences wins the game.

10. Here is an interesting game called "Vocabulary Baseball":

1. Arrange review words in groups of nine.
2. Each time a player makes a "home run," a point is credited to his team.

3. To make a "home run," it is necessary for the player to:
    a. Pronounce a word from a card.
    b. Tell what it means.
    c. Use it correctly in a sentence of his own.

READING TO LEARN

Children learn to read, not as an end in itself, but as a means to an end; they learn to read so they may get meaning from printed symbols. This reason for learning to read extends into all of the other subject areas in the elementary school classroom, so instruction to this end must be employed in the elementary grades, and it must be motivated. Some of the techniques employed by an actual faculty in teaching children to read for information include:

1. In science or social studies, clip pictures from magazines to create a desire in children to read topics that will answer questions suggested by the picture. Questions may be formulated to accompany the pictures and direct the children's attention toward certain channels of thinking.

2. Giving children a list of questions for which they are to find answers encourages and trains them to read with a definite purpose. These same questions may serve as hooks upon which new ideas may be fastened.

3. A useful scheme in encouraging children to read difficult assignments is to create a "mind-set" for it. This may be done by:

    a. Talking about pictures and illustrations connected with the material;
    b. Recalling something similar that has been previously read;
    c. Working out new vocabulary that may be encountered in the selection so they will not "bog down" or get lost in unfamiliar words and phrases;
    d. Clarifying new concepts with which children may not be familiar.

4. Pictures that can be enlarged on an opaque projector never fail to motivate children to read the poems and classics depicted. This is a good way to interest children in the classics, and help them to a well-balanced reading background.

5. Painting a background for a poem or a piece of classical literature is a good scheme for stimulating the children's interest in reading the selection.

6. Children entering the fourth grade are often bewildered as they move into new and longer assignments in which they read to learn. They, therefore, need a great deal of guided or directed reading, and help in learning how to select:

a. new vocabulary (through context clues);
b. causes and effects;
c. points that prove a certain statement;
d. summarizing points.

Since textbooks are not their property, teachers find that weekly newspapers are especially valuable in encouraging careful, accurate, and specific reading drill for students. Direction by the teacher in guided reading develops good study habits for social studies and science without too much writing on the part of children, for different marks may be placed on the paper, grading factual content independent of spelling and grammar. Each child's weakness is easily determined, and necessary remedial work may follow.

7. Giving children a well-organized outline stimulates them to read with a purpose, as well as to organize their findings in such a way that the facts they read become their own. This is especially helpful in the acquisition of science and social studies data. After ample experience with filling in outlines in the intermediate grades, most children will be able to efficiently make their own outlines in the upper grades.

8. After the children have read titles and headings for science and social studies materials, allowing them to make questions which they hope will be answered in the reading helps them to proceed with their reading in a purposeful way.

9. A teacher can also devise reading work sheets with blank spaces for the children to fill in from the reading. For younger and less experienced readers, the questions should follow the sequence of the reading, with other clues such as chapter titles and section headings. Older children who are more skillful readers should be expected to dig deeper for the information and to draw some conclusions of their own.

10. An excellent technique to help a child collect data on an independent study project is to provide him with file cards or slips of paper. At the top of each card he writes the facet of his subject with which the information on that card will deal. Then, using various sources, he can fill out his cards. One card may deal with important industries in a given country, while others may deal with population, colonization, and the like. By arranging these cards in a logical sequence, the child is able then to give an oral or written report on the material he has collected from a number of different sources.

READING JUST FOR FUN

A great deal of the reading we do as children and as adults is for the sheer enjoyment that it provides. But children must *learn* to read for fun and, again, they must be motivated. The following techniques have been used by successful teachers in motivating children to learn to read for pleasure.

1. The use of pictures from magazines and book covers, and enlargements made with the opaque projector from book illustrations, goes far to set an atmosphere conducive to reading. They develop curiosity and build interest, especially when the books they represent are displayed nearby.

2. The teacher-created "favorite book contest" or book of the month contest puts children's desire for competition to work without divorcing the goal from the means. Trophies and plaques bearing miniature replicas of the books are especially appropriate as prizes, though they require extra work on the part of the teacher, whose ingenuity is already taxed providing rules and materials for the games.

3. Dramatization of stories and oral interpretation of certain passages go far to make the story a real life experience for the child. If the teacher is handy with photography, it is an especially effective technique to record on film the sequence of the story with the children themselves interpreting the characters and incidents.

4. Within the school system there probably are a number of fine recordings of children's classics, folk tales, or Landmark books, which can be used to great advantage in connection with the reading program.

5. For a child who has not developed an interest in reading, the library can be a forbidding place with its multitude of books, so many of which are not "right" for him. A small classroom library with select books that fit the interest and reading levels of the children can go far to meet this problem.

6. It adds immeasurably to the enjoyment of a classic for it to be read and shared as a group. The school system probably has a number of copies of *Tom Sawyer,* adapted for fifth and sixth grade reading. This makes an ideal book for group reading, discussion, interpretation and dramatization. If enough teachers feel the need for other classics in several copies for group reading, they should be provided.

7. If space allows, it would be effective to have a leisure reading corner where books could be displayed in an inviting and interesting fashion, and where furniture could be arranged in a casual manner.

8. Children should not be expected to write a lengthy report on every book they read, but it is helpful to have a brief record of the books that they have finished and their reactions to them. This can be used by the teacher to help other children with similar reading and interest levels find books they would enjoy. If this information

is recorded on file cards or mimeographed forms, it can be filed away in a place where the children themselves can make use of it.

9. Group reading should be combined with listening, discussion, interpretation and dramatization. The regular reader and workbook should be supplemented with many other group reading experiences.

10. Children are often more likely to find books which they will enjoy through an informal sharing of "good ones" which goes on between children than through formal oral or written reports.

LANGUAGE MECHANICS

A certain amount of formal language instruction is carried out in the elementary schools, particularly in the intermediate and upper grades. Due to the difficult concepts involved in formal grammar and composition for children of these ages, a great deal of motivation is necessary if the material is to be presented in an interesting manner. Following are techniques which have been used:

1. To improve punctuation, it is helpful to select sentences from the children's own work where meaning has been lost because of improper punctuation. Searching for errors in sentences written by a child's unknown peers usually motivates children to look hard for mistakes.

2. Sometimes it motivates children to use care in constructing sentences if they know that samples from their work are to be taken for class correction, especially those in which the thought is lost through poor structure.

3. Dividing a class into two groups or teams with a captain for each is a good method of identifying subjects and predicates in sentences. The captain helps the teacher keep score for his team. The game is operated like a spelling bee, with each team taking turns.

4. To help children see the importance of correct spelling, sentences in which the words from the spelling unit are used can be dictated. The children listen with pencils on desks and then give the sentence back in unison. Next, they write and punctuate it. To proofread, they read their sentences in unison, pointing to each word as they read it. If a child discovers that he has written a wrong word, inserted one, or omitted one, he holds up his hand and is given time to make corrections. Sometimes it is possible to use several of the words from the unit in one sentence.

5. In addition to enlarging their speaking and writing vocabularies, children find great interest and fun in acting out different substitutes for overworked verbs such as "walked." Each child acts out his choice of a substitute while others try to guess what it is. One child should be chosen as recorder to list the words to be kept for future reference

and use in story writing. Examples: Some substitutes for "walked" are: stalked, stamped, strutted, ambled, tramped, staggered, wandered, roamed, strolled, sauntered, loitered, limped, and trudged.

6. Children find it difficult to punctuate sentences containing a quotation. On strips of wrapping paper, the teacher can write such sentences without any punctuation marks. Instead of writing in punctuation marks, he can make them on oak tag and color them. These can be stuck on with pins and then removed for future drill. It not only motivates the children because it resembles pinning on the donkey's tail, but it saves the teacher time in making drill sentences every few days. By using two similar groups of sentences, races may be held between boys and girls. Remembering one basic sentence properly punctuated helps the child to attack new and unfamiliar sentences. This is especially true of the slow learner.

7. It is a good technique to give sentences containing a misused word and have the children find the incorrect word and provide the correct substitute.

8. Children usually enjoy making posters to illustrate the proper use of pairs or sets of homonyms. By associating the word with the picture on the poster, the children are able to keep the homonyms straight in their minds.

9. Children find writing business letters more meaningful and purposeful when they actually write for free materials for themselves or their classroom. They may be encouraged to do their best writing, their most careful punctuation and sentence structure.

10. The correct form for a friendly letter can be taught by asking children to write personal notes of welcome to their parents to be left in their folders on the "Back to School" night or upon similar occasions during the year. They can also be asked to write thank you notes for gifts, as well as bread and butter letters that are actually to be mailed.

CREATIVE WRITING

A vital part of the intellectual growth of boys and girls, creative writing involves pupils' real or imaginative experiences composed in a "free" style, in the sense that pupils have chosen their own material and are seeking their own most adequate form of expression. Following are techniques which teachers have used to promote creativity in elementary school children's writing activities:

1. The teacher must accept the child's writing with sympathetic interest. Criticism or rejection of something a child has written is just as inappropriate as criticism of a personal gift would be.

2. The teacher must place stress on content, not mechanics. The

important thing in creative writing is getting ideas down on paper. Anything which hinders the child in so doing must be discarded in the interest of better content. When primary emphasis is placed upon mechanics, the content can only be mediocre.

3. The teacher should respect a child's privacy. He must read the child's creative writing and share it with the rest of the class only upon the child's request, or with his approval. Some children may not wish to share everything that they write. This is their privilege.

4. Children find material for stories from within their experience. That is why any activity which broadens their experience and stimulates their imagination is conducive to good creative expression. Trips with the family, field trips with the class, interesting motion pictures—these are all possibilities.

5. A teacher may clip pictures from magazines which suggest ideas for stories. This method often provides the boost for the child who can't think of anything to write.

6. Children enjoy seeing things they have written in print. The teacher might find time to type some of the stories written by his group. Children particularly enjoy having their best stories put together in creative writing booklets from time to time. They may wish to illustrate their own stories with drawings. Small local newspapers are often interested in printing some of the best examples of writing done by children in the community. Children are highly motivated by seeing something they have written in a newspaper.

7. It is both helpful and challenging at times to provide children with titles around which to build a story. These titles should not be limiting but instead broad or ambiguous. Examples might be: "Me," "Suddenly," "The Most Exciting Day of My Life," "The Lion, the Rose, and the Star," "If I Had Three Wishes," "I Wish I had Been There When," "1984," "If I Could Be Someone Else," "The Thing-a-ma-bob," "The Twelve Loveliest Things I Know."

8. Creative writing films are available. These (usually without words) present a story which leaves much to the imagination of the viewer. After seeing them, children develop stories from what they have seen. *Encyclopedia Britannica Films* has produced some entitled: "The Hunter and the Forest," "The Tale of the Baby Foxes," and "The Tale of the Fiords," which are particularly good.

9. Give children ample opportunity to share what they have written *if they wish to do so.* Have story sharing times, or a story bulletin board. The creative writing booklet mentioned above is another method. It is most interesting for children if the teacher will try his hand at some creative writing from time to time and share the results with them.

10. Different visual and auditory stimuli often provide a boost for children in creative writing. The teacher might play classical music or sound effects, and have the children write. Or they may look at an abstract picture or certain combinations of colors and try to translate their feelings about these into stories. A look from the window or a walk in the park may provide stimulus for stories.

ARITHMETIC

Since the emphasis in arithmetic has, for the past several years, been upon the meaningful approach to its teaching, the subject no longer holds the adverse effect on children that it did in an earlier age. Nonetheless, teachers must still keep their guard up to prevent this potentially thrilling subject from becoming purely an abstract symbol. Superior pupils, too, are quick to become bored if the numerical manipulations become repetitious and tedious; they need challenging work, not "more of the same." Motivational techniques which teachers have used for arithmetic are:

1. Whenever possible, arithmetic should be built around real or hypothetical situations involving the children themselves. Young children like story problems in which their own names are used. Running a play store, keeping the class treasury, building a scale model or baking a cake—these all involve very real work with numbers. The learner must see how that which he learns is useful to him. Counting money, measuring and weighing things, making calendars, and other such activities bring home to children the functional importance of arithmetic.

2. There are innumerable number games available, ranging from number lotto or bingo, through magic squares, to all kinds of interesting number tricks and calculations. These are available in most libraries or curriculum centers. Number booklets containing games for all ages are available. Teachers can make number puzzles which work like crossword puzzles, and any number of other games which meet the needs and requirements of their own group.

3. Older children gain great pleasure from different number oddities or unusual methods of calculation. In addition to holding interest, these methods provide practice in some of the basic calculations. To list them all would fill volumes. Interested persons can find them readily available in libraries or from teachers who specialize in mathematics.

4. Rapid calculations and mental arithmetic provide a much needed challenge for many youngsters. They also develop important mathematical thought processes which speed up the rate of calculation.

5. Relays, games of lotto, bingo, flash card speed tests, and other such methods provide interesting ways for children to learn the basic combinations that are so important to all mathematical processes.

6. Visual devices, such as filmstrips, charts, and solids make arithmetic more interesting and meaningful to most children.

7. Children can carry mathematics into the shop by making mathematics aid boards, geometric solids, scale models, movable angles, and other such projects. Decimal peg boards with 100 holes, fraction circles cut into different fractional parts, and charts showing the different formulae for area and perimeter are other suggestions.

8. To help young children develop number concepts, many teachers use bulletin board displays, worksheets, or toys which can be counted or arranged in different-sized groups.

9. Many children enjoy chalkboard races where individuals or teams race to see who can be first to complete certain calculations. This method can be unpleasant for the slow child, and should be used with discretion.

10. For a child who is having special trouble with arithmetic, individual and private help from the teacher or another child is most helpful. The child may even be given a head start on the rest by having a new process introduced to him first before the others have a chance to learn it. Thus, through repeated teachings, he is more able to hold his own with the group, and needn't suffer the embarrassment that sometimes comes with slow learning.

SCIENCE

Since there is in the normal child an innate curiosity about the "great big wonderful world" all about him, science is the easiest area toward which to motivate him. Knowledge of astronomy, geology, botany, zoology, physics, and chemistry can be gained without leaving the school yard. All too often, however, elementary school children have been introduced to the wonders of the living and physical world through the eyes of someone else who has recorded them in dusty volumes. It behooves teachers to continually stimulate children's innate curiosity by using some such techniques as these:

1. A science curriculum should involve many experiments and demonstrations which children may observe, and in which they may participate.

2. If an experiment cannot be reproduced in the classroom, it can usually be shown by some other visual means, such as a drawing, a chart, a filmstrip, a motion picture.

3. Science can make ample use of reality. Living plants and animals,

machines, magnets, rocks, sea shells, and leaves are only a few of the many things which can be brought into the classroom. Substitutes, such as pictures or motion pictures, should be used only when the real article is not readily available.

4. Field trips are a must in the area of science. A study of plants leads quite naturally to the woods. Likewise, astronomy suggests a trip to a planetarium or an observatory. Rock quarries, museums, aquariums, zoos, lake fronts, and factories are other suggestions.

5. A science classroom or laboratory should be supplied with certain basic materials with which large numbers of experiments can be performed. Much of the needed material can be supplied from science kits. Others can be obtained quite inexpensively from drug and hardware stores or science supply houses. But one of the best sources of materials needed in science is the children themselves. They can bring from home innumerable items which have outlived their usefulness there, but which will add greatly to the school science supplies. Science textbooks and teachers' manuals suggest much such equipment.

6. Well-planned, attractive bulletin boards are a must in science. In addition to being "pretty," they should contain vital information or, perhaps, questions which provoke thought and make the children "want to find out."

7. The children themselves should have many opportunities to conduct experiments, give demonstrations, and present written or oral reports to the group.

8. Arts and crafts can very well be correlated with the science program. The possibilities of charts, graphs, and models which children might make to correlate with the science program are limitless.

9. Children should be given a number of challenging assignments which raise questions in their minds and develop a desire to know. They should then be helped to discover the means by which they can find out these answers for themselves.

10. The child should have available to him many different kinds of books which contain information about the area he is studying. These should include textbooks, reference books, and library books, in addition to pamphlets and newspaper and magazine articles.

SOCIAL STUDIES

The social studies, often the springboard for experience units at the elementary school level, offer almost limitless possibilities for a creative teacher to provide stimulating learning experiences for children. Here again, many pupils need to be motivated in certain areas of the social studies; following are techniques which have been used in elementary classrooms:

1. A teacher may have a discussion with his group to determine their backgrounds, interests, as well as their information or lack of information about a forthcoming unit. This gives an excellent idea of where to start, and it also arouses curiosity and motivates the youngsters to move ahead.

2. The use of real objects related to a unit that is to be introduced, or to one in progress, may motivate the group. Often the children have items of real interest, and may be encouraged to share them with the group.

3. Pictures displayed in an attractive, unique way will often motivate children to seek knowledge about items of interest depicted. An attractive bulletin board is a must in the area of the social studies. It can be used to provide information, raise questions, or stimulate interest. In addition to the pictures, three dimensional objects add considerably to most bulletin board displays.

4. There are often persons in the community or on the faculty who have traveled and had experiences pertinent to the unit. They may have taken slides or collected souvenirs which can be shared with the youngsters. Calling upon these people to visit the group can help motivate the children and can contribute greatly to their work, as well as improve public relations for the school.

5. Trips to points of interest in the community or in neighboring communities can be an effective means of motivation. Factories, museums, fire departments, police departments, and historic sights suggest only a few of the possibilities.

6. Children love to make slides, a filmstrip, or a motion picture to show information gained or any activity related to the unit. They might also make a series of pictures which can be put together into a "movie roll" of the unit. Other possibilities are puppet plays, shadow plays, or similar activities.

7. Audio-visual devices, such as moving pictures, film strips, records, tape recordings, pictures viewed via the opaque projector, slides, charts, and blackboard drawings are very good media for motivation.

8. Dramatic plays or productions are valuable ways of developing interest and motivating children in all areas of social studies. These may range from simple, informal skits to large-scale productions involving costumes, stage settings, and make-up.

9. Children usually enjoy making maps by any number of interesting methods. They can enlarge maps by using the opaque projector. Other possibilities include: filling in desk size outline maps and making three dimensional relief maps with papier mâché or wheat paste and sawdust. It is an excellent group project to make large bulletin

board maps to show political features, physical land features, distribution of rainfall and vegetation, land elevations, or products. Murals showing historical events are also effective.

10. Compiling a class book or individual books for each child as a unit progresses will continue to motivate children throughout the duration of the unit. These might consist of stories, articles, charts, graphs, and pictures.

PHYSICAL EDUCATION

While most children have an innate interest in most physical education activities, there are still times when teachers must use certain motivational techniques in order to interest all children in the proceedings. Some techniques which may be helpful to teachers in stimulating student interest in this area include:

1. Introduce challenging games and sports. Provide many new games or new variations of old games. Try out new techniques and new equipment. This means constant search for new things, both in books and magazines. Also helpful is a change in the rules of existing games, or allowing the children to make variations of their own.

2. Try to create a desire in children to learn games and techniques not only for enjoyment, but also to improve their coordination and general health. Make them aware of the effect that different types of activities have upon their developing bodies.

3. Games for physical education are seasonal. Soccer or similar games are played in the fall. Dancing, tumbling, basketball or badminton are winter games. Baseball comes with spring. Many simple games for primary children can be played outside in spring or fall.

4. Developmental organization and skills required should be low in the primary grades, and high at the intermediate level. The teacher can defeat his purpose if highly skilled games are taught too soon. Furthermore, young children should not be burdened with bulky sets of rules.

5. Competition can be used to good advantage, especially in the intermediate grades. The desire to excell is strong at that age, and can be guided to develop good sportsmanship and team spirit.

6. Visual aids, especially in developing skills, are effective at the intermediate level. Also helpful are demonstrations of skills by the teacher, or by other youngsters who are proficient.

7. The teacher can often motivate by entering into games or dances when children have learned the skills. Most children enjoy experiences which the teacher shares.

8. Individual tests above the third grade level are excellent for showing where improvement is needed. Most children enjoy compet-

ing against themselves to see how they can develop their own potentials. The teacher must be careful of the feelings of the totally unproficient child lest he be embarrassed or hurt by comparison with more able youngsters.

9. By example, the teacher can create a desire for health and cleanliness. Careful check of children as to neatness of appearance and cleanliness is needed to call attention to their importance.

10. It is often effective to tie in certain physical education activities with activities in the classroom. Certain exercises apply to a study of muscle development in a science unit on human anatomy and physiology. Certain folk dances can be taught in relation to a social studies unit on a particular country.

ARTS AND CRAFTS

There are a number of motivational techniques which administrators may suggest to teachers in the area of arts and crafts. Individual children may need to satisfy any of a number of desires or needs, such as a desire for the end product, to use tools or machine tools, to create or design new projects, to work in a new medium, or to participate for pleasure. Some of the methods of motivation are:

1. A field trip to collect art materials is a good technique. A hike to a beach or to the woods provides all kinds of different and unusual materials, such as attractive stones, pieces of driftwood, or leaves, which can be developed into interesting art projects.

2. Art activities which tie in with room activities are usually most successful. The classroom science or social studies program provides ample opportunities for correlation with art.

3. With young children it is effective to use activities that catch and hold interest, such as crayon magic. Art counsellors can provide many suggestions for such activities.

4. Intermediate children are more interested in learning new skills and working with new media.

5. Primary children respond to working informally in a casual setting, such as on the rug or in the play corner.

6. The classroom teacher should not bring the group totally unprepared to an art counsellor. He should begin to stimulate interest in the activity before turning youngsters over to a special teacher. Furthermore, by showing continued interest as the activity progresses, the classroom teacher builds pupil interest as well.

MUSIC

Whether or not the teacher is a musician of some ability is not the essential factor in teaching elementary school music; what is more important is interest and willingness on the teacher's part to integrate musical activities with other classroom projects as the occasions arise. Some motivational devices which have been successful in actual classroom situations are:

1. The names of the lines and spaces of the staff can be taught by having the children spell words by placing notes on the scale. Teams can be chosen and the teacher can spell words by placing whole notes on the staff. The teams can then take turns reading the words that have thus been written.

2. Write a scale for each key, one at a time, and then practice reading the scale using figures first, then letter names, and, lastly, syllables—do, re, me, and so on.

3. Little sentences or phrases help children remember the order of lines and spaces on the staff as well as the names of the sharps and flats, as

lines on the staff—(E)very (G)ood (B)oy (D)oes (F)ine
spaces on the staff—F A C E
Sharps—(G)o (D)ick (A)nd (E)at (B)read
Flats—(F)at (B)oys (E)at (A)pple (D)umplings (G)reedily

4. Writing a simple song in 4/4, 3/4, or 6/8 time, using various values of notes, is an excellent scheme for motivating children to learn both the value and placement of notes.

5. The incorporation of popular music and songs of a folk or ballad nature adds interest to the singing program for intermediate children.

6. It is effective if the classroom teacher plays the piano. If not, a record player and records can be made available, and children can bring records from home.

7. Children enjoy writing group or individual poems and then setting them down to music.

8. Older children get a lot of enjoyment out of producing a little play or operetta built around familiar music.

9. The music program can well be correlated with science or social studies activities. Folk music is especially appropriate, as are songs about weather, seasons, and animals.

10. Children should have a good listening program with a wide variety of kinds of music: classical, folk, ballad, popular, and show tunes.

CONCLUSION

While the purpose of this book is not one of methodology, considerable space has been given to techniques of motivation that have been used successfully in the elementary school classrooms in Glencoe, Illinois, and other systems throughout the nation. The authors subscribe to the idea that administrators and supervisors exist in the school for one purpose only: to assist teachers in their important work of guiding the learning of children. They also subscribe to the proposition of the National Elementary School Principals that an administrator in an elementary school should spend *at least* one-half of his time in improving the program of instruction. In order to meet the challenges presented by either or both of these objectives, the principal, as an integral part of his job, must know methodology; how better could the administrator help meet these challenges than to be able to present functional, time-proved techniques to members of his staff, particularly in the important area of motivation? It is hoped that the practical suggestions presented here will help principals in this aspect of their work.

Short Case 1

Children Make Cards

Miss Kipp was teacher of the fourth grade in Oakview School, situated in a lower socio-economic area of the city. In her class there were many children who had never known the security of a home with the love of a father and mother. Miss Kipp found it difficult to interest these children in a project of making Mother's Day cards in art class; after all, how could they display their affection for their mothers, when their past experiences had imprinted on their hearts a lack of mother's love? There existed no real purpose in making such a card.

The teacher at last encouraged these particular children to make a card for their grandmothers, aunts, or whoever took care of them. Miss Kipp made it clear to these boys and girls that these people were the ones who loved and cared for them, and explained to them the reasons they should be grateful.

Problem: How did Miss Kipp promote permissiveness in her classroom, and help her children accept and examine difference? How was this a desirable learning experience? Explain why Miss Kipp's motivational technique was real and purposeful.

Short Case 2

All Heads Face Teacher

Fruitvale School was located in an average rural community. Miss Faye, in her first grade classroom, became weary and disappointed with the results of attempting to gain attention of her pupils by using the time-worn statements,

"Let's all look up here while I tell you about something new and exciting," and "Johnny, put down your pencil; Susan, turn around."

Miss Faye struck upon the idea of softly saying to her group, "I see Johnny's lovely blue eyes," and "I see Susan's pretty brown eyes and Mary's big, hazel eyes." Before she knew it, the teacher had all heads facing her. There was not a sound in the room, and all attention was focused upon her.

Problem: Describe the reasons for the psychological reaction of the children to the teacher's resorting to the ego-involvement technique. What are some other methods of getting children's attention? How are they better, or worse, than the one used here? In what other ways could Miss Faye just as effectively have motivated the children in the introduction of some new material?

Short Case 3

A Sudden Change

John Handler couldn't remember when morale had been so high during his six years as principal of Yelton School as it was this spring. At long last, after 10 years of sharing space at Turner School, the Yelton faculty and pupils next fall were to occupy their own new building. Teachers fairly beamed with elation; excitement ran high!

One morning three weeks before school was to dismiss for the summer, Mr. Handler interrupted the talk of the move in the teachers' room by announcing, "Next week's faculty meeting will be held on Wednesday instead of Tuesday." Objections were overruled by, "Sorry, that's the way it has to be." Two teachers attempted to detain him, but the principal explained that he was already late for a meeting at the superintendent's office. The next morning John Handler posted a district notice on the faculty bulletin board, which explained that the following year Yelton School would adopt a semi-departmentalized organizational plan. Next to the notice were the subject area assignments for each teacher. Three days later, Bill Dacker, Sy Jackson, and Belle Hodson, sixth, fifth, and third grade teachers, respectively, submitted their resignations.

Problem: What administrative philosophy seemed to guide the educational program in this district? What important aspects of planning a new program and motivating teachers for their parts in it have been ignored? How did the principal fail to accept responsibility? For what possible reasons did the faculty object to a change in the faculty meeting schedule? What would the teachers' reaction be to the notice posted on the bulletin board? Why did the teachers submit their resignations?

Chapter Six

Pupil Activities in the Elementary School

Everything that goes on in an elementary school building should be a learning activity. No enterprise can justifiably be undertaken that does not have as its purpose the furtherance of learning on the part of children or adults. On the other hand, many of the pursuits which critics of the schools are prone to label "fads and frills" are, in reality, perfectly legitimate activities which contribute toward the civic-moral-social aim, in its broadest conception.

Some pupil activities, even though not accepted as part of the regular curriculum, are intermingled with instructional activity to the point that they are sometimes not distinguishable from it. These activities are called, variously, extra-class, extra-curricular, or co-curricular activities. They have an important part in the elementary school program which strives to attain the commonly accepted goals of education. Such activities play an important role in the development of children because they afford types of experiences which often are difficult or impossible to provide through the regular curricular offerings of the school. These experiences help to develop a child's feeling of security; as he assumes responsibility for group participation he promotes within himself a feeling of unity with the group or a feeling of being needed. In reality, there is a very fine line of distinction, if any exists at all, between the curricular and the extra-curricular; each activity should be closely evaluated to determine its part in the development of children, and then assigned to a proper place in the overall, well-balanced school program.

While it is true that extra-class activities affect how children will feel, think, and act in the future, it is important that an elementary school policy not "go overboard" in trying to justify the experiences educationally. As Spain, Drummond, and Goodlad point out, "the *best* activity is not necessarily the one that *best* fulfills a single goal. It follows, then, that school activities must be justified on the basis neither of simultaneous attainment of all objectives nor attainment of a single, traditional objective, but rather on the fulfillment of the particular objective or objectives for which it is appropriate."[1]

Pupil activities in an elementary school cover a wide field indeed. Scouting clubs, hobby clubs, Junior Red Cross, parties, picnics, school and class assemblies and programs, and school newspapers are some of the activities in which elementary school boys and girls have an opportunity to participate. A few of these will be discussed in detail in this chapter.

THE PRINCIPAL'S ROLE IN PUPIL-PLANNED ACTIVITIES

Whenever any phase of an elementary school program is considered, the principal and his role in that program come to the fore. If the community, through the board of education, places the principal in a position of responsibility for the individual attendance unit and its program, then it is necessary that he be aware of all that transpires within his building, and he must assume the authority consistent with that responsibility. In this respect, the principal should keep in central focus the welfare of the children in his school, and be certain that teachers employ proper instructional procedures and principles in carrying out their responsibilities as sponsors of the pupil-planned activities.

The public relations aspect of extra-class activities is an important one, and an alert principal will see that it is handled appropriately and positively. Parents and other lay persons who do not understand what the school is trying to accomplish, and why, are justly inclined to be critical; they feel that Mary and Johnny should do more "learning" and less "playing." Parents who participate in planning for their children's school's activities are much better informed as to the objec-

[1] Charles R. Spain, Harold D. Drummond, and John I. Goodlad, *Educational Leadership and the Elementary School Principal* (New York: Holt, Rinehart and Winston, Inc., 1956), p. 235.

tives of those activities, and are more favorably inclined toward helping them be successful. Understanding on the part of lay persons brings cooperation and support!

Creativity in pupils' activities may blossom if the principal's attitude is such that free and natural functioning is encouraged. If the activity is to be truly child-centered, the child must be free from pressure to perform and conform. Because the principal's attitude permeates throughout the building to teachers, parents, pupils, custodians, and all others concerned, he determines to a large degree the amount and kind of creative activity pupils are encouraged to undertake.

THE ELEMENTARY SCHOOL STUDENT COUNCIL

There has, in recent years, been a considerable surge of interest among elementary school educators in student government geared to the maturity level of children in the six-to-eleven age-group. There is little information in the literature on this relatively recent innovation at the elementary level, but studies indicate that there are, in fact, a considerable number of student councils in existence in the fifty states. Most of the councils have come into existence only since the turn of the mid-century, however.

Although McKown holds that the student council should logically arise from an expressed need, and that the principal's decree that a student council shall be formed hardly expresses such a need,[2] Gaynor's study reveals the fact that administrators cite a desire to give pupils an opportunity for greater participation in school activities and in helping plan school affairs as being the primary purpose for organizing a student council.[3] In this activity, pupils develop democratic participation and habits of good citizenship. Some of the more basic principles underlying student councils have been stated by McKown, as follows:

1. There should be a continuous need for the council.
2. Participation should be introduced gradually.
3. A study of objectives should precede an attempt at organization.
4. The council should represent the school as a whole.
5. The average student should feel he is represented.
6. Both students and faculty should be represented.
7. The council should not be too large.
8. The council should have definite powers and duties.

---

[2] Harry C. McKown, *Extracurricular Activities* (New York: The Macmillan Company, 1952), p. 89.

[3] Alta I. Gaynor, "A Survey of Student Councils," *The National Elementary Principal,* XXXVI (October, 1956), pp. 24–25.

9. The council should not be a dumping ground for disagreeable tasks.
10. The head of the school should retain the veto power.
11. There should be continuous evaluation.[4]

Wide pupil participation in student government is an aim of most elementary schools fostering student councils. This is achieved by involving a large number of pupils in special council-sponsored positions and activities, and by rotating council officers after short terms. Often children serving on the council are awarded certificates, letters, arm bands, badges, and other symbols of recognition. Gaynor's study revealed that the specific values of student councils are: (1) they permit pupils to assume responsibilities and have experience in democratic participation; (2) they develop a closer relationship between pupils and faculty; (3) they build school spirit and pride; and (4) they develop pupil self-improvement in citizenship and leadership.[5]

Gaynor found that a number of schools provide for specific leadership training through special classes and meetings for student council members.[6] In some schools the leadership classes are conducted for *all* pupils. Unfortunately, however, the study showed that generally pupils are not permitted to participate in the organization and administration of council activities; it indicated that principals are the prime promoters of the student councils.

Typically, elementary school student councils become involved with pupil problems found on the playgrounds, in assemblies, in corridors, and in committee work, as well as problems of safety procedures at school. At times the council is called upon to provide ushers and receptionists for special school occasions, to maintain a pupil bulletin board, to assist in various school offices, and to cooperate with parent organizations.

Nelson lists the following guides for those whose responsibility it is to organize and conduct the activities of a student council:

A. Selection of representatives
   1. Representatives are selected only after a period of orientation designed to acquaint all pupils with the functions, duties, and qualifications needed.
   2. Representation in the council is school-wide.
   3. No restrictions other than enrollment in the school are placed on candidacy for the Student Council.
   4. Pupils may nominate more than one pupil as their candidate.

[4] McKown, *op. cit.*, pp. 89–94.
[5] Gaynor, *loc. cit.*
[6] *Ibid.*

5. A representative is elected by the group of which he is a member.
6. The voting is by ballot when the maturity of the voters warrants this procedure.

B. Involvement in the real problems of the school
1. In the council meetings there is an atmosphere of permissiveness in the discussion of school problems.
2. The student council deliberates on those problems which are of interest and concern to groups in the school.
3. All groups have opportunity to present problems for consideration by the student council.
4. When there are problems beyond the reasonable authority and maturity of the council, limiting factors are explained frankly by the sponsor.

C. Communication of Ideas
1. Every pupil in the school has opportunity to be heard.
2. Student council members report to the groups they represent.
3. There is opportunity for groups to discuss and decide upon questions to be presented to the student council.
4. There is opportunity for groups to discuss questions which have been or are being discussed by the council so that the student council member may effectively represent his group.

D. Skills to be developed
1. Teachers and sponsors provide opportunities to improve discussion techniques.
2. Teachers and sponsors acquaint pupils with problem-solving techniques.
3. Student council members practice problem-solving skills.
4. Student council representatives are helped to communicate ideas effectively from the council to the groups they represent.
5. Student council representatives are helped to gain competency in handling the minimum skills of parliamentary procedure.

E. Attitudes and behaviors
1. The council and its activities should be fully recognized and given a place of prestige in a school's program.
2. The faculty should exhibit interest in the welfare of the student council.
3. Membership in the student council should contribute to the acceptance of greater responsibility for the welfare of the school on the part of student council members.
4. Duties and responsibilities of leadership in the student council should be emphasized, as well as the rights and privileges of leaders.
5. Student council members should, as a result of their group experiences, exhibit a feeling of group loyalty to the school.
6. Membership in the student council should improve pupil dis-

> cernment between democratic and undemocratic situations and increase commitment to democratic action.[7]

In general, local needs of the council should determine its organization, which may vary from the simplest to the most complex. In small schools, the class officers may be the entire council functioning as a single committee; in larger schools, each grade or class may elect members who may, in turn, select from among themselves persons to perform a specialized function. Most councils elect their own corps of officers which, again, may be as simple as a single officer to conduct the meetings, or as complex as a complete set of officers, standing committees, and liaison officers. Meetings of the group should not be held except in the presence of a faculty member, but the faculty member should not conduct the meeting.

Each recognized group in the elementary school should be represented on the council. Since there are few organized activities in a typical elementary school, representation on the council will be chiefly from the various classrooms, usually one pupil from each room.

A COUNCIL IN LEVITTOWN, PENNSYLVANIA

The council at Thomas Jefferson School in Levittown, Pennsylvania, is comprised of two representatives from each classroom in the school, both of whom are elected, under teacher guidance, by the pupils in grades 1 through 6. Members of the council from grades 3 through 6 may then run for one of the four offices of the organization: sixth grade council members may run for president; fifth grade members for vice-president; fourth grade members for secretary; and third grade members for assistant secretary. The entire student body of the school, not just the council, then elects the officers of the council; thus, the interest of all of the pupils is further stimulated, and the original high interest is maintained over a longer period of time.

An interesting activity of student government at Thomas Jefferson School is the assembly for campaigning candidates. After the nominating speeches are given by pupils, the school principal calls up those running for the four offices and has them re-tell their names. In a few days printed ballots are distributed to each of the 18 classrooms in the school; here the voting takes place. Results are forwarded to the council sponsor's classroom, and she and her class tabulate the final results. Then, at the end of the day, the school secretary announces on the inter-communications system the names of the new officers.

The council at Jefferson considers general school problems that arise. The group has undertaken projects to make the playgrounds

---

[7] Esther Nelson, "Student Government in Grades Seven and Eight," *California Journal of Elementary Education,* XXVIII (February, 1960), pp. 180–182.

safer and cleaner, to make recess periods "more fun for more people," to urge fellow pupils to learn new games for use in outside play periods. The council works to keep the playground free of paper, and wages a continuous campaign to instill pride for the school as a whole.

Meetings of the Jefferson council are held once a week and last from fifteen to thirty minutes. They are conducted with decorum; children like the feeling of importance an orderly meeting gives, and they practice some of the basic parliamentary rules of order. Still, the atmosphere is kept permissive, insurging ample opportunities for exchanging ideas.

The sponsor of the Jefferson council sees that discussions are eventually channeled to a conclusion, with suggestions either discarded or accepted by the group. Prolonged disussions with no decisive action are avoided. To avoid "never getting anything done," teachers and the principal cooperate to help translate any suggestion into action. Pupils want to have the satisfaction of accomplishing something worthwhile.[8]

THE ELEMENTARY SCHOOL NEWSPAPER

Many elementary school educators feel that it is never too early to motivate children to do creative writing. A school newspaper provides the young writer with a medium in which his material may appear in print. In addition, the activities of organization and publication of the newspaper provide opportunities for other educational sound benefits to elementary boys and girls.

While educational benefits are derived primarily by pupils involved in the production of the school newspaper, the publication should provide useful and beneficial services to the remainder of the school community. General objectives of an elementary school newspaper are:

1. To integrate thinking, reading, listening, speaking, and writing skills with proper attitudes and ideals, and to channel them into constructive activities.
2. To motivate growth in the responsibilities of democratic citizenship.
3. To stimulate growth of pupil leadership.
4. To encourage cooperative endeavor and the values of working together in a worthwhile activity.
5. To provide an opportunity for pupils to be active in serving their school-community.
6. To develop an understanding of the newspaper and its purpose in a democratic culture.

---

[8] See Albert J. Crispell and Hope Mountford, "Our Student Council at Thomas Jefferson School," *School Activities,* XXI (May, 1960), pp. 263–264.

The elementary principal has a definite role to play if his school anticipates the publishing of a newspaper. The first important step he must take is that of choosing an advisor for the paper. It is well if the teacher has some knowledge of journalism, but it is more important that he have a real interest in sponsoring the newspaper. A principal would do well to provide a prospective sponsor with books and materials on the fundamentals of journalism, which can be found in any high school or college library.

Since most elementary school newspapers are duplicated, the expense is not exhorbitant, and is usually included in the budget item providing for instructional materials.

Generally, the first question facing the sponsor and staff concerns the content of the newspaper. Of course, the publication should contain news concerning past school activities, and announce coming events, but the elementary school newspaper should also contain more than that. Here is an excellent medium in which children's fiction, poems, jokes, riddles, art pieces, cartoons, and columns might be circulated among their peers and among parents and other lay persons in the community. Classroom teachers should be kept alert for pupil contributions which might be appropriate for publication in the newspaper.

With so many opportunities for the newspaper to glean creative selections and art work for its columns, there is little excuse for hackneyed, time-worn jokes and expressions, stale riddles, and dull and uninteresting items, and these should certainly be discouraged.

THE PASHLEY PARTY-LINE

The masthead of the paper in Burnt Hills-Ballston Lake, New York's Pashley Elementary School carries the name, *The Pashley Party-Line,* and represents one of the school newspaper staff's earliest creative activities in relation to publication of their paper, that of selecting its name. The project at Pashley School developed from the activity of one of the classes in the school, which conceived the idea and invited a newspaper photographer-reporter from the community to come to the classroom and tell about the basic planning and creative thinking that goes into every newspaper.

The first act of the class in preparing to publish their newspaper was the election of an editor and an associate editor, whose duties were to write editorials about pertinent subjects related to the school, to be in charge of assembling the paper, to enforce observance of deadlines, and to arrange for the distribution of any notices that had to be sent to classrooms concerning the newspaper. Ten reporters from the various classrooms were elected, and they contacted teachers, observed certain especially interesting classroom activities, and wrote them up for the newspaper. The class also elected ten interviewers, pupils who were, or became, adept at asking the right types of questions, at knowing how to conduct and to conclude an interview, and how to write up the information they had gained. The interviewers, of course, had to learn how to make appointments with their interviewees. Classroom teachers were alerted to be on the lookout for good poems or stories written by pupils; any pupil could contribute puzzles and cartoons.

The class set and observed deadlines for materials. Copy from the various classrooms was edited and re-edited by pupils for errors in punctuation and spelling, for effective sentence arrangement, and for factual accuracy. A dummy paper was made by copying each individual's contribution onto plain paper to produce a facsimile of typewritten articles. This was cut out and pasted onto dummy sheets so that exact arrangements could be completed. The school secretary typed the duplicate stencils from the dummy.

The actual publication of the newspaper was done by the children on a duplicating machine; a total of 200 copies was printed, enough to supply five copies per classroom. The children then arranged a long double row of desks and placed the fifteen pages individually on each desk in assembly-line fashion. The pages passed down the line to a child who checked them to see that all sheets were intact, and finally to the child who stapled the newspaper together. Finally, the newspapers were distributed to each classroom. The group planned to publish the *Party-Line* every six weeks.

The newspaper's sponsor indicates that the newspaper project has helped the children improve in many ways: they have shown growth in cooperative group planning; they have become aware of a need for accuracy in the written word; they are developing ability to transmit conversation and observation onto paper; and they have seen the necessity for improvement and development of mannerly and conversational rapport in unnatural situations.[9]

CLUB ACTIVITIES IN THE ELEMENTARY SCHOOL

Clubs in the elementary school often provide opportunities for experiences and expression which are not normally found in the classroom itself. While the classrooms do provide some opportunity for freedom of expression, it is not to the same extent or degree as in a

[9] Esther Holt Bennett, "Elementary Pupils Successfully Publish School Newspaper," *New York State Education,* XLVI (February, 1959), pp. 352–353.

more "informal" club activity. In the classroom the pupil is often under the influence of restrictions imposed by the teacher or the subject matter, while in the club the method of dealing with a problem may be of his own choice.

The elementary school principal should encourage pupils to participate in the school's clubs, and should motivate teachers to sponsor those in which they have special interests or ability. The club is an activity which may stimulate pupil participation and initiative in learning; it provides an atmosphere where the teacher is no longer a person who is evaluating with the purpose of grading. The teacher-sponsor may be a consultant able to provide special information when called upon; he may be an authority able to resolve a special issue; he may be a resource for providing information in special areas; or he may be a leader to guide the club when it needs stabilizing, but only until a pupil leader emerges from the group.

While clubs provide a framework in which pupils may develop skills in exercising judgment, at the same time they should reflect a permissive atmosphere in which pupils may learn independence. Permissiveness with no restrictions would result in chaos; clubs cannot function with a complete lack of restriction. Clubs, like our democratic culture, must encompass restrictions and limitations which are imposed for the good of the majority. Many of the restrictions on clubs are imposed by the administration; others are of the members' choice; and still others are of the clubs' sponsors.

Offering many opportunities for the development of interests boys and girls currently have, and providing for the initiation of new ones, are such organizations as these: Junior Red Cross, boys and girls scouting clubs, bands, art clubs, Boys' Club, Audubon Junior Club, science clubs, 4-H clubs, language clubs, social studies clubs, and others. Among the objectives of such organizations are the preservation of human values and the development of a deeper appreciation of each individual's worth.

A PRIMARY SCIENCE CLUB

An interesting example of a club activity in the lower grades of an elementary school is that of a first grade group in Lordsburg, New Mexico. Motivation for this club was effected through the teacher's reading of a children's book about the Desert Rat Club, a fictitious account of the activities of some small boys who formed a club. The result was a demand for a similar club in the teacher-reader's classroom.

The activities of the Lordsburg primary club can be adapted to fit in any grade situation in any kind of school in any community. In the

New Mexico school the group voted on a name for the club, from among such names as the Desert Rat Club, the Coyotes, the Cactus Wrens, and others. Purposes and values of the club are: to awaken an interest in the deserts and mountains of the Great Southwest; to appreciate the beauty of deserts and western mountains; to learn about trees, shrubs, flowers, insects, animals, and rocks of the desert; and to further develop and maintain this interest as the pupil advances in school. The Lordsburg club meets from 2 to 2:30 o'clock once a week in the classroom. Officers, who hold office for one semester, include a president, vice-president, secretary, and treasurer; and there are standing committees appointed for program and bulletin boards, as well as special committees when needs arise.

Each member of the Lordsburg club makes a trip to the desert, and later tells about it to his classmates. Each member is encouraged to feed and care for an animal or an insect. In the fall, the children in the club study animals and insects; in the winter, they study animals through use of pictures, stories, and other vicarious techniques; and in the spring they study flowers and birds of the desert, and start a cactus garden. The club maintains a bulletin board and a science corner, and on the last-day-of-school program there is a special bulletin board depicting activities of the primary science club. The club also has animal and insect exhibits, and displays a cactus garden. Another activity of the club is an occasional field trip to see specific things of the natural world.[10]

CAMPING PROGRAMS IN THE ELEMENTARY SCHOOL

An activity of growing proportion in American elementary schools, and one which can in only a very limited sense of the word be considered an "extra"-curricular activity, is that of school camping. The school camp affords unique opportunities for all who attend to have beneficial experiences. As children participate in the activities, they are exploring nature; learning about fire prevention, erosion control, tree culture, stars, weather and rocks; learning nature crafts; acquiring good forest manners; and developing valuable understandings and appreciations. Further, they acquire skills and desirable attitudes concerning the conservation of natural and human resources. Children in camping situations are afforded rich opportunities to make meaningful use of the democratic processes through participation in activities which require group planning, decision-making, and evaluation.

[10] Lucy Bugg, "A Science Club in the Primary Grades," *School Activities,* XXXII (September, 1960), pp. 6–7.

Through dining hall activities, such as setting the tables, serving food, cleaning up, and using good table manners, and through activities which necessitate being responsible for one's own belongings and for cabin clean-up, boys and girls are aided in developing desirable individual and group work habits, and in gaining understanding and appreciation of health and safety practices.

An activity of humanity as old as civilization itself, camping is still the major way of life for some people in the United States. In Alaska, for example, the Indians in the interior of the state have two camps that they use during the year: a fish camp, used in the spring in order to obtain enough fish for an average family of eight and their dogs, and a trapping camp, upon which many families depend as a means of support.

Early attempts at initiating school camps in the 1920's, '30's, and '40's were chiefly confined to vacation periods or to a school outing for a day. Several efforts in the 1930's provided camping facilities and personnel so that groups of school children could live, work, and play in the wilderness for a week or more at a time during the year, and these early attempts at organized camping programs for children proved so promising that school personnel from many parts of the United States subsequently tried similar activities.

The financial support and encouragement of the W. K. Kellogg Foundation was instrumental in the early successes in the development of the school camping program. That Foundation inaugurated an experimental community school camp in 1940 in Michigan, and provided personnel for other similar projects that followed. The Kellogg Foundation, along with the American Camping Association, also provided a number of workshops for the pooling of intelligence and experience. About 50,000 pupils were in public school camps in the United States in the 1959–60 school year.

There are several school camps in existence in the United States at the present time. Among the better known ones are Camp Tappan, operated by the Tappan Junior High School of Ann Arbor, Michigan; Camp Cuyamaca, under the auspices of the San Diego, California City-County Camp Commission; Clear Lake Camp, sponsored by the public schools of Battle Creek, Michigan; Lindlof Camp, for New York City children; Camp Tyler, near Tyler, Texas; and Camp Redwood Glen, the campsite for the children of Santa Clara, Santa Cruz, and Monterey counties in California who, prior to the 1960–61 school year when the combined camp was established near San Jose, attended individual school camps in each of the three counties. Except for minor differences, due principally to locale, the school camps are similar in philosophy and operation, and all uphold the thesis that children learn best and quickest through direct experiences and contacts with native materials and life situations.

THE UNIVERSITY OF WYOMING LABORATORY SCHOOL CAMPING PROGRAM

One of the better school camping programs of the nation is the one for fourth, fifth, sixth, and eighth grade pupils at the University of Wyoming Laboratory School in Laramie. The following somewhat detailed description of this camp, with its special emphasis upon the initiation of the project, is primarily for the benefit of those principals in school systems which are considering the establishment of an outdoor curriculum situation of this type.

The careful investigation of camping programs currently in existence in other school systems was the first undertaking of the university staff when it decided to consider a program for the Wyoming school. When this investigation by a special committee was completed, the school's administrators and teachers were favorably impressed with the advantages of such a program, and decided that the next step was the education of parents with respect to the camping project. Public relations media and techniques of all kinds were employed to inform parents of the program. A final parents' meeting which gave the school the whole-hearted support of the lay-group featured a film built around the San Diego school camp which had already been in existence for almost a decade.

The University's Recreation Camp previously had been made available to the elementary school, so the problem of camp site did not exist in this situation. The next step was to provide a staff of qualified camp counselors, since a competent group of counselors is the most important single element in a successful camping venture. The camp director was chosen on the basis of his thirteen years of experience with camps for boys and girls; he was considered the best qualified of all the university's personnel for this important position. Then came the selection of an assistant director, program specialists, health staff, dietary and dining room staff, all of whom were assisted by classroom teachers and student teachers who served as supervisors and program aides when necessary. Classroom and student teachers attended a weekly conference with the director for six weeks prior to the opening of the camp.

When the pupils were told of the camp, teachers helped them discuss the purposes of the activity. The children understood that, from the beginning, they would share responsibility for the camping activities and that they would have a major part of the work to do in the operation of the camp. Under careful guidance, the children planned the camp. After the first group of fifth and sixth grade children, those initially involved in the University's camping program, had determined the things that needed to be accomplished, committees were formed to work on specific areas of the camping project. The camp director was invited to talk to the children, and he answered many of their questions about procedures and equipment. The classroom teachers spent about three months in planning with their children for the camping experience. The project was, in fact, an activity unit, culminating in the actual stay at the camp.

The camping project led to a successful study of community health. Local health authorities and other interested persons came to the classroom to talk about the city's water supply and other phases of community health. The pupils were given a physical examination prior to their departure for camp.

Material available to schools on proper diet and good foods was studied with interest. The children then planned meals for camp, and the person in charge of purchasing camp supplies assured the pupils that the menus would be followed. The children checked carefully to see that the foods were nutritious and that all the meals for one day comprised a balanced diet.

A representative form of government was carried out at the camp as the pupils chose their own representatives who, in turn, accepted leadership responsibilities and delegated duties and activities to group members. The classes discussed group living, planned the camp together, and decided on standards of camp courtesy.

One thing with which the children were particularly concerned was the selection of individuals for the groups, each of which would be comprised of eight children living together in a unit. It was decided that, insofar as possible, children who wished to be together would be placed in the same group. Teacher-made sociograms were used to mix the fifth and sixth grade pupils. Each boy was asked to write the names of two sixth-grade boys and two fifth-grade boys with whom he would like to be grouped. The girls were asked to do the same. It was possible to keep the proper ratio of fifth and sixth grades, and also of children who were leaders in each group. In the final grouping, every child except one had at least two friends in his group, and many had more.

Arithmetic was adapted to the camp experience in many interesting ways. Mileages were checked; distances between historic and hiking places were computed. Food costs and other maintenance costs were discovered and analyzed, and problems were solved involving transportation and food costs per meal per person. The children also planned the camp store and bank. It was decided that no one would be allowed to spend more than fifty cents while at camp for candy and fruit at the store. The store handled no cash; each child deposited his money in the bank and then wrote checks at the store for his purchases. In this manner, the pupils learned to write deposit slips and checks, to keep the check stubs, and to read bank statements.

In the language arts area, the children presented book reports and recommended books to others to take to camp for reading in spare time. The children decided to take a number of books to camp and to open a camp library. The library committee went with a teacher to the school library and checked out books on animals, insects, rocks, birds, flowers, weather, and other topics that might be used to advantage during the stay at camp. Letter writing was also a pre-camp emphasis, and one of the projects was to write to the United States Forest Ranger near the camp to invite him to appear on one evening program during the camp session. The pupils decided that a post office would be needed at the camp, so a post office staff was selected. A unit on the United States Post Office Department evolved from this activity. The children also dramatized stories in class and worked out original ideas for skits on conservation topics and camp life for presentation at the evening programs.

In the area of recreation, the pupils reviewed for use at camp familiar songs, folk dances, games, and crafts, and learned new tracking and nature games. New crafts, such as spatter painting, plaster of Paris casting, and map making were also part of the preparation.

In the areas of the social studies and sciences, the boys and girls studied the geographical story of the region, interesting highlights of local history, and folk tales of the community. In connection with this study, the pupils made maps and received instruction in map reading. The use of the compass was part of the pre-camp training program. A study of weather included observance of temperature changes, the use of the barometer, graphing, and trips to the weather bureau in the community; and the pupils erected their own weather station. In connection with a conservation topic, the interdependence of the plant and animal kingdoms and the importance of plant growth to soil were stressed. The camp's own power plant was the central point of attention in a study of electricity.

The camp program was planned around the pupils' interests, and included such activities as: exploratory hikes, nature hikes, arranging nature displays, planning cook-outs, square dancing, preparing for stunt nights, learning new songs, and studying erosion, animal life and conservation.[11] In a letter to the authors, the camp director further explains the camping activity:

> Our School Camp has been in continuous operation since 1950. This will be our eleventh year and it has become a well-established and accepted part of our curriculum. Since 1950 we have established a three-day School Day Camp for our fourth grade and a week of residence camp for eighth grade. We have set up skills and competencies for these grades according to needs, interest, and advancement. Every student doing student teaching in our fourth, fifth, and sixth grade spring semester is required to take the School Camping Education course. This is an accredited 2–3 hour course. In addition to student teachers, who are spring semester Juniors or Seniors in Elementary Education, we often have as many as ten physical education majors or graduate students in the course. Every person who takes the course is required to go to camp in order to gain the practical experience. Not all are able to get classroom pre-camping experience, since those who are student teachers must do this, but each person has an opportunity to do some work with the group to which he will be assigned.
>
> Basically, our program has not changed although our evaluations indicate to us that we are bettering the content each year. The required course helps considerably. My book, *School Camping and Outdoor Education,* is my textbook and is used as a basis for this course. We use a great deal of supplementary material in each program area.[12]

CONCLUSION

The elementary school activities program has, in recent years, assumed an increasingly important role in fulfilling a well-rounded educational program in America's public schools. These include activities which afford educational experiences not normally provided in the regular curriculum, but which are necessary in the mental, emotional, and social development of children.

The principal's role with respect to the activities program is an important one; the various tasks of administration become obvious as problems of curriculum, finance, public relations, pupil personnel, physical facilities, and organizational structure come to the front. The activities program demands tremendous insight on the part of the school's administrative leader as he provides for the programming of

---

11 Dorothy Lou MacMillan and Lawrence Walker, *School Camping* (Laramie, Wyoming: University of Wyoming Press, 1951), pp. 12–58.

12 From a letter by Dr. MacMillan to the authors, dated December 14, 1960. Dr. MacMillan directs the School Camp and teaches the course in School Camping at Wyoming.

each activity; stimulates interest and participation by pupils and faculty; coordinates the efforts of all persons concerned; and provides leadership in a comprehensive, continuous, and cooperative process of evaluating the various aspects of the program.

Direct and concomittant learnings result from the various activities in the school's program. In too many school situations, it is only in the program of extra-curricular activities that school becomes as exciting and as valuable as the activities of the world outside the classroom. School principals, then, should take the lead in seeing that their schools initiate and maintain an educationally defensible program of pupil activities.

Short Case 1
A Student Council Incident

Last spring the pupils of Terra Mala School held elections for student council offices for the next school year. Each candidate was required to have a petition signed by his home room teacher and twenty pupils, and then the petitions were submitted to the incumbent student officers who chose from them three candidates for each office. The candidates so chosen then conducted a campaign in which they made posters to place on school room windows, and in which they spoke to classes. At the end of the two-day campaign, elections were held by secret ballot in home rooms. After the election, the principal was dismayed at the number of protests of the election by students and teachers alike.

Many teachers were disturbed because the boy elected president was not even a "C" student, and was in a gang which had a bad influence on other pupils. Others were upset because some teachers would not permit campaign posters on their windows. Many teachers and pupils complained that the incumbent officers had picked as final candidates pupils who were their personal friends. Some teachers felt that the faculty should serve as the screening committee. When the principal presented these ideas to the vice-principal, Mrs. Goggins, she became very angry and stated that the student council was just one big headache and she wished it would be done away with.

Problem: Defend or refute the attitude of the teachers toward the boy who was elected president. What might the principal have done about the teachers who would not participate in the pupil activity? Defend or refute the vice-principal's attitude toward the student council. Is there a "hidden" problem in this case?

Short Case 2
Mixing Sixth and Eighth Graders

For the second year, the Haverford Elementary School district sponsored a camping program for sixth grade pupils, in cooperation with a neighboring district of somewhat lower socio-economic level. Teachers from the schools accompanied their classes and, in addition to the regular camp staff, student teachers from a nearby teacher-training college were brought in to observe and to act as supervisors in the tent-cabins where the children were housed. When the Greene School sixth grade classes of the Haverford district went to camp, the school from the other district sent eighth grade classes instead of sixth, claiming that those pupils would derive more benefit from the experience.

Prior to the opening of the camp, the Greene School principal and two sixth grade teachers conducted an experiment intended to measure the change in pupil attitudes toward each other; they administered a questionnaire survey to pupils before going to camp, and were to administer the same questionnaire when they returned. Results of the second questionnaire compared with the first one, indicated a trend toward improved attitudes on the part of pupils. Mr. Evans, the principal, believed the camp had been of real value and intended to recommend it for another year.

Then Mrs. Lee, mother of one of the sixth grade girls, in conference with Mr. Evans, related that, due to the distribution of pupils, her daughter, Ellen, and Ellen's closest friend, Dorothy, had been the only sixth grade girls placed in a cabin with four girls from the other school. She stated that during the time immediately after taps, when the staff of the camp was in planning session and when the children were left alone for a while, the eighth grade girls told many questionable tales. The two younger girls had been aghast, and were fearful of going to their teacher about the situation.

Mr. Evans found himself faced with many questions.

Problem: What were some of the many questions which the principal faced? Was the camping situation described here an ideal one? What should the principals and staffs of the two schools do to improve the camp the next year? Should Mr. Evans tell Dorothy's parents about the incident? Why or why not? How could the supervision of the camp be improved? Did the benefits of the camp exceed the disadvantages?

Short Case 3

Lack of Cooperation

At the final faculty meeting of the year, Mr. Hayler, principal of Ellisong School, announced that he would like to have a school newspaper the next year, and invited any interested teacher to talk with him after the meeting. Miss Lees, who was a journalism major in college, indicated that she would sponsor the project. Mr. Hayler told her that he would be happy to have her accept the responsibility, but that he could not arrange released time for her. She would have to take the newspaper activity during her free period, an arrangement to which Miss Lees was agreeable. During the first week of the fall term, a bulletin was sent to the twenty fifth and sixth grade classes asking that each teacher send two pupils to Miss Lees, and stating that these pupils would be out of class three hours a week, and would need to make up any work missed.

At the first journalism class meeting Miss Lees was disappointed when only eight pupils reported. Teachers did not want to send pupils during class time; they seemed so vehement that Miss Lees decided not to bother Mr. Hayler with the problem so that bad feeling among faculty members might be avoided. The eight pupils had little cooperation from teachers during interviews. The proposed first edition had to be postponed for four weeks, after which time the master ditto copies were presented to the principal for approval. He returned the copies with a note indicating that a student gossip column and jokes had no place in a school newspaper and suggested that the paper be re-written. At this, Miss Lees asked the principal to release her from the assignment. Mr. Hayler was disturbed by her lack of cooperation.

Problem: What steps could the principal have taken to assure that the newspaper project would be successful? As principal, what would you have done had you been faced with a staff of teachers with attitudes such as the staff described here? What would you do about the request of Miss Lees?

Chapter Seven

Evaluating the Instructional Program in the Elementary School

Recent events have affected the educational program in the United States. The firing of satellites and men into space has commanded the nation's attention. The United States' successes and failures, as well as those of other nations, have been linked to the educational program.

The United States has been challenged, as never before, by an aggressive world power. Education has a high priority in the thought and action of the nations competing in the fields of scientific and industrial development. Knowledge of such thought and action has caused many citizens to voice a concern over school programs in this country. President Eisenhower's Commission on National Goals advanced the belief that, for the best development of the individual and the nation, the effectiveness of education at every level and in every discipline should be strengthened and enhanced. In 1959, the former president of Harvard University, Dr. James B. Conant, in his widely publicized report on the American high school, advanced a concern for increasing the effectiveness of secondary schools. The Rockefeller

Report, *Pursuit of Excellence: Education and the Future of America,* made a strong plea for "excellence" in education. In 1961, the Educational Policies Commission published their report, *The Central Purpose of Education.* This report suggested that education must be interfused with the process of thinking and the attitude of thoughtfulness. A two-year Joint Interim Committee on Education in California reported to the 1960 California Legislature that the Committee believed there should be greater stress placed on "fundamentals" in the schools. President Kennedy has on several occasions reiterated his belief that the education of our nation's citizens must be strengthened. Typical of numerous recently published books showing that the growth of a nation is dependent on good schools is *America Too Young to Die* by Alexander De Seversky, a noted aeronautical authority.

Civilized man has always been concerned with improving the training of his offspring, but the present sense of urgency is greatly intensified. Much of the recent criticism of education stems from the frustrations and fears of citizens as they witness the revolutionary events of the day, and there has been a developing national consciousness which causes search for better ways of educating the nation's children.

The purpose of evaluating the educational program is to help all persons concerned with the education of children to discover and understand the goals and tasks of schools. It is necessary to create the best possible program of instruction for America's children, youth, and adult citizens. Teachers and school administrators need help and encouragement as they begin to appraise present practices and search for better processes of educating future citizens. The purpose of this chapter is to assist elementary school teachers and administrators, as they seek more logical and workable means to determine what should be taught, and to assure that effective teaching and learning will be a reality.

WHAT IS EVALUATION?

Evaluation has several meanings. An appropriate meaning is determined by a particular experience involving certain circumstances. Evaluation is inherent in every meaningful enterprise in which people engage. As soon as goals or purposes for an activity or enterprise are announced, the question is raised: "To what extent are the purposes or objectives being realized?" The baseball player assesses his batting average and determines whether it is high or low as compared with the other players on his team and the players on the other teams in his league. His predetermined goal is to have a high percentage of hits for the number of times he comes to bat during the baseball season. The salesman makes a daily, weekly, or monthly evaluation of the number of sales he has made. His company has probably given him a quota to reach if he is to be successful as a salesman in that organization. In each of these illustrations a goal or objective is identified, and progress toward that goal is evaluated. Success or failure is measured.

Evaluation is often difficult to define as it relates to education. Stanley[1] explains that educators endow the terms, "measurement," "evaluation," and "assessment," with various meanings. The last two imply predetermined objectives of instruction. Evaluation is a more inclusive term than measurement because it is more than a testing program: it connotes the making of value judgments.

As used in this book, evaluation means the following things:

1. Evaluation is the means by which a school, teachers, administrators, and citizens agree upon the purposes or goals to be sought in the education of children. The determination of the goals to be sought is made within the framework of understanding that the school takes its place with the church and the home as important institutions in American society. The church and the home are guaranteed the right to perpetuate the values peculiar to different religions and various patterns of family life. The public school provides for all the children to acquire the understandings, skills, and values that need to be learned if democratic processes and ideals are to be maintained and extended. The values held by society in general become the goals of education.

It is one thing to state that teachers, administrators, and citizens should agree upon the purposes or goals to be sought in education, and quite another thing to see this objective realized. The process by which these important agreements are to be reached may be long and laborious. This is the place where creative leadership and incisive organization become imperative. Time must be provided for people to sit down and discuss what values they believe are currently held by society, and how these values may be translated into learning experiences for children. A school system will need to perfect an administrative organization that permits these discussions to be held in an orderly, meaningful manner.

2. Evaluation includes the processes a school uses to decide whether the predetermined goals are being realized, and to insure the continued research and experimentation necessary to keep the school

---

[1] Julian C. Stanley, "The Interdependent Roles of Research and Evaluation in Teaching," *Educational Leadership,* XIII (April, 1956), p. 420.

program in conformity with the changing needs. Here the school will make use of all the evaluative instruments and data that may be effectively used to measure the outcomes of the teaching-learning process. The measurement will not be limited to written examinations and objective tests. Records of pupil activities, anecdotal records, interviews, reports from parents, behavior checklists, health records, films and transcriptions, sociometric devices, interest inventories, and projective techniques may be used.

The ultimate purpose of evaluation is to establish, as objectively as possible, a comprehensive picture of each pupil's school achievement in terms of the educational goals the school has accepted. The interpretation of the results of all the findings and experimentation is of prime importance. It is here that decisions are made concerning need for change. The interpretation of the results of evaluation must be made easily accessible to all school personnel and to the citizens of the community. This is the way a school community comes to a rational understanding of the need for change, and when such change is proposed by the school administration the public is usually ready to accept the recommendations.

THE SCHOOL DEFINES THE GOALS OF ELEMENTARY EDUCATION AND DEVELOPS A PHILOSOPHY OF EVALUATION

School systems have often been lethargic in the matter of perfecting sound programs of evaluation. Fortunately, there are numerous exceptions, some of which are documented in this chapter. There seems to be one outstanding reason for the lack of an organized program of evaluation in many schools—the problem has been that administrators and teachers do not have a clear understanding of the ways such a program may be initiated.

INITIATING A PROGRAM OF EVALUATION IN A SCHOOL SYSTEM

The superintendent, or someone delegated from the central office, should initiate the organizational steps necessary in setting up an appraisal plan. Emphasis should be given to the importance of participation of the entire school staff in the initiation of the program. Each staff member should have a part in making decisions concerning the establishment of goals to be sought in the school system, and in the formulation of philosophy which will control the type and amount of evaluation to be made. School staff members will need to examine basic statements of educational goals as they attempt to set up their own objectives.

The Purposes of Education in American Democracy,[2] issued by the Educational Policies Commission in 1938, and *A Framework for Public Education in California,*[3] printed in 1950, are examples of basic statements of the broad purposes of education. The staff should interpret *the goals* in terms of children's behavior. As a result of the study and discussion that precedes agreement, a philosophy of evaluation emerges and criteria are developed for use in the evaluative process. The decision on goals, the development of a philosophy of evaluation, and the selection of criteria presupposes that an administrative organization has been perfected which will permit the school staff to proceed toward initiating a planned and orderly evaluation program.

ADMINISTRATIVE ORGANIZATION AND EVALUATION

The school administration has a vital role to play in setting up a carefully charted plan of organization as the beginning point of an evaluation program. Without organization the plan may be doomed to failure, frustration, and disappointment. The philosophy presented in the proposed organization chart below may be adapted to school systems of varying sizes. Obviously, it would be more detailed for the large city school system.

This administrative chart represents a type of organization in which problem solving may be handled democratically. It permits flexibility in planning, encourages the wide use of committee structure, and allows for the involvement of the entire school staff in decision making.

The following are basic principles which may be used as a guide to serve the staff of a school system where an organized plan for an evaluation program is being perfected:

1. The responsibility of the central office administration to provide instructional leadership is apparent and accepted by the entire school staff.
2. The problems to be solved will determine the structure and details of organization.
3. There will be a clear definition of the areas of responsibility

---

[2] *The Purposes of Education in American Democracy,* Educational Policies Commission, National Education Association, and American Association of School Administrators (Washington: National Education Association, 1938).

[3] *A Framework for Public Education in California,* Bulletin of the State Department of Education, Vol. XIX, No. 6 (Sacramento: California State Department of Education, November, 1950), p. 29.

Figure 4

ADMINISTRATIVE ORGANIZATION FOR EVALUATION IN A SCHOOL SYSTEM

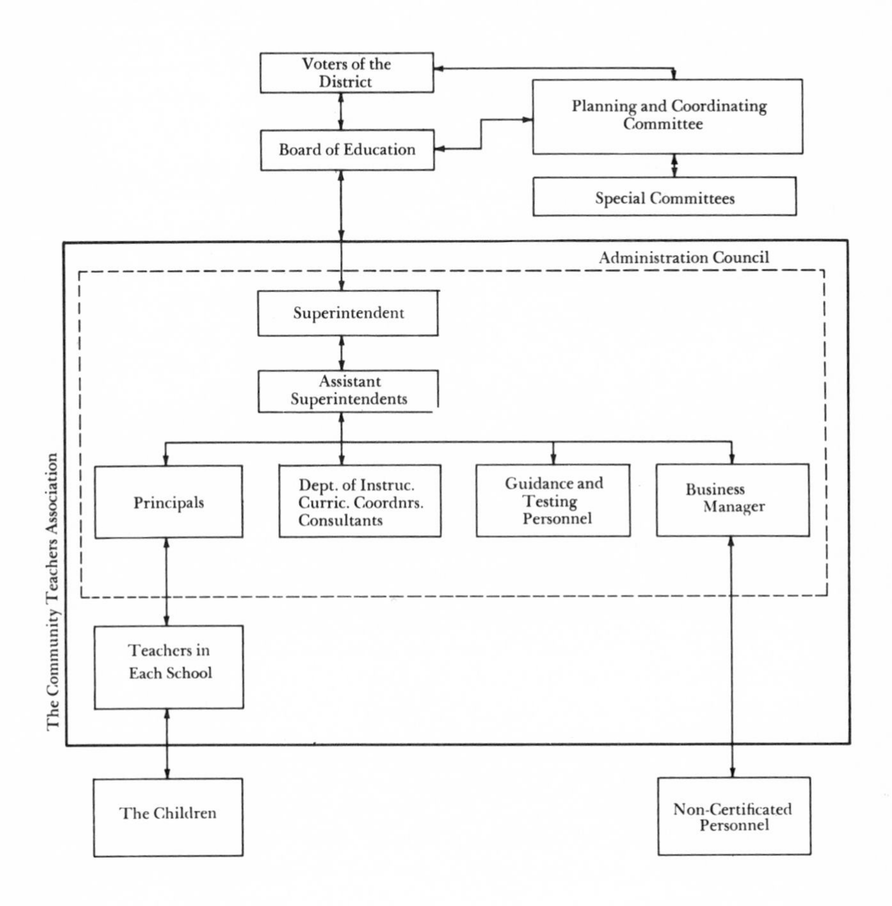

and cooperative working agreements for each officer in the administrative organization.

4. The people to be involved in the problem-solving process are clearly identified.

5. The organizational structure will provide means for a two-way flow of communication between the administrative officers of the school and the other staff members.

6. The organizational plan will identify responsibility for providing resources and facilities to be used in the problem solving process.

THE ROLE OF THE PRINCIPAL IN EVALUATION

It is at the instructional level that the elementary school principalship must justify itself as a profession. The principal must be able to identify a good instructional program if he is to exert leadership in attaining such a program in his school. The school staff has the right to look to the principal for leadership in planning and implementing an evaluation program. He has definite leadership responsibilities for improving the school. These leadership responsibilities, as described by Oberholtzer,[4] fall into two categories.

1. RESPONSIBILITY IN THE SCHOOL SYSTEM

The principal is usually a part of a school system with two or more schools, and his responsibilities encompass what is being accomplished in the entire system. He may contribute to the planning for evaluation by serving as a member of the administrative council or by his membership on the planning and coordinating committee where general instructional policy is considered. He communicates downward to his staff members by keeping them informed of decisions being made by the central office staff and key committees. He communicates upward the ideas, concerns, and accomplishments of his school staff as they proceed to identify and solve commonly agreed upon problems. Not all principals, especially in large city school systems, will be members of the administrative council or members of the planning and coordinating committee, but they will have representation on these councils and committees.

2. RESPONSIBILITY IN THE SCHOOL

The principal can best perform his leadership role in improving the instructional program by centering his major emphasis on the

[4] Kenneth E. Oberholtzer, "What a Superintendent Says," *The National Elementary Principal,* XXXV (October, 1955), pp. 14–15.

particular school he administers. It is in the local school setting that the experimentation, the research, and the important accomplishments are to be made.

The elementary school principal may ask himself the questions on the following check-list to ascertain whether or not he is offering as much assistance as possible in the evaluation process. The checklist may be used as a guide to follow in making plans for evaluation of the instructional program in his own building. The members of his faculty should spend considerable time with him in discussing all the items on the checklist, for in this way they will be able to understand the kind of evaluation program contemplated for their school. It will be through these discussions that the faculty and the principal will come to definite agreements on what they believe are the strengths and weaknesses of their present program. This will help provide the impetus for further research and experimentation. The principal will find the checklist valuable as an instrument for use in checking each step of the evaluation procedure. Not enough schools do effective evaluation, and often the reason is the administrator's lack of understanding of the real meaning and effective use of evaluation.

THE PRINCIPAL AND EVALUATION

A. *Organizing Schools for Evaluation*

Have I:

1. Made an effort to help the school system perfect a well-defined organizational plan for evaluation?
2. Helped the staff agree upon and understand the basic philosophy and objectives of the total school program?
3. Helped determine what problems are most needful of study?
4. Helped to clarify a plan of attack on the problems that have been isolated for study?

B. *The Types of Measurement Data Needed and the Instruments to be Used in Gathering Data*

Have I:

1. Lent my assistance in formulating clear-cut agreements on the kinds of measurement data needed if problems are to be solved?
2. Helped determine what evaluation instruments will be needed to obtain the necessary measurement data?
3. Provided the commercially available measurement instruments to be used in evaluation?

4. Provided time for staff members to construct evaluation instruments which could not be purchased?
5. Provided means for economical use of the teacher's time in scoring certain types of tests?

C. *The Use of Specialized Services in Evaluation*

Have I:

1. Helped make the services of psychologists, guidance workers, consultants, and other specialists available to the staff?
2. Conducted an in-service program to acquaint our faculty with new trends in evaluation and measurement?

D. *The Instructional Program*

Have I:

1. Made provision for carefully planned and controlled experimentation in some aspect of classroom teaching and learning?
2. Provided adequate instructional materials and equipment for the teachers?
3. Offered support and encouragement to the teaching staff as they worked toward the improvement of instruction?
4. Kept in close communication with the central office staff and the special committees in regard to the success or failure of regular and experimental programs in our school?
5. Kept our school staff informed of progress being made in other schools within the system?

E. *The Community and the Evaluation Program*

Have I:

1. Found ways to use the talents of school citizens in the program of improved instruction in the school?
2. Kept the community informed of the school program through personal communication, newspaper releases, and other media?

THE TEACHER'S RESPONSIBILITY IN EVALUATION

The classroom teacher plays a leading role in evaluation, for it is impossible to separate evaluation from the total learning process. The classroom teacher is constantly facing the problem of selecting learning experiences, organizing activities, and selecting methods of instruction. He formulates tentative hypotheses, tests them, and arrives at a conclusion which determines a course of action.

The classroom teacher may use the following check-lists to serve as a guide in determining his responsibilities in an evaluation program. He will use the guide to serve as an evaluative instrument for use in checking his own successes or failures as he works through the year on a project for improving certain aspects of the teaching-learning process in his classroom. The check-list should be used by the teachers in planning sessions with the principals, where they are attempting to reach agreements on what will be done to strengthen their effectiveness as teachers.

THE TEACHER AND EVALUATION

A. *Participation in Cooperative Planning*

Have I:

1. Been active in professional meetings in helping to plan an effective program of evaluation?
2. Offered my time and talents to committee work in which places and procedures for evaluation have been considered?
3. Developed a high sense of purpose as it pertains to improving the teaching-learning process?

B. *The Teacher and Evaluation in the Classroom*

Have I:

1. Determined the academic and emotional needs of the children I teach?
2. Made an assessment of the pupils' interests, skill in critical thinking, and work habits?
3. Isolated problems peculiar to the community in which I teach?
4. Formulated a plan for classroom research whereby problems may be studied by the following procedures:
   (a) recognizing a problem,
   (b) establishing criteria so that the problem may be defined,
   (c) collecting data by testing and observing,
   (d) interpreting the data by comparing pupil behavior patterns specified as desirable,
   (e) planning a course of action following the interpretation of data,
   (f) examining the results of the action program to determine the degree of success obtained.

THE STEPS IN EVALUATION

It has already been suggested that each staff member should take part in making decisions concerning the significance of problems under consideration. The important principle involved when a group initiates a procedure or plan is that it becomes the personal possession of each participant. The members of the group are motivated to work toward the successful conclusion of the project attempted.

There are essentially four major steps in the development of an evaluation program in a school system. The steps are enumerated and discussed here.

1. The first step is to identify the problems. Staff members must sense the existence of the problems that can be isolated and described. In the process of discovering the problems, they will develop the desire to find solutions.
2. The second step is to determine the values the staff consider to be important. Considerable time must be provided for the staff to examine practices, and to determine what they believe is being done right, as well as what practices should be improved. This examination is a critical step in the evaluation process, and it should not be hurried. At this point, research data from the school systems should be considered, to indicate strengths and weaknesses in the instructional program. Teachers will need to discuss the values they hold as related to the purposes of the educational program. These discussions will provide opportunity for individuals to make contributions and resolve differences.
3. The third step is to prepare criteria for guiding action. Shane and McSwain[5] suggest that these criteria are the statements of values to be sought with and for children through significant school experiences. These guide lines are to be followed in changing the curriculum, so that socially desirable outcomes will occur in the behavior of boys and girls, and so that they will learn to think.
4. The fourth step is to plan for and initiate the action program which will modify the curriculum, and thereby bring about the desired changes in children. The success of each program or project will be determined by the use of evaluative instruments and teacher judgments. The process repeats itself as new needs become apparent.

SELECTED EXAMPLES OF EVALUATION IN SCHOOL SYSTEMS

The "Sputnik Era" brought some good to the educational system of the nation by causing many schools to evaluate educational goals

---

[5] Harold G. Shane and E. T. McSwain, *Evaluation and the Elementary Curriculum* (New York: Henry Holt and Company, 1958), p. 111.

and accomplishments. As a result of such evaluation programs, important changes have been made in the primary grades in some schools. Midwest City, Oklahoma, Cedar Falls, Iowa, Sioux City, Iowa, and the Warner School of Nashville, Tennessee, show examples of programs where detailed systems of evaluation and recording have been worked out on a series of progressive achievement levels in the various skill areas. Thus, when each new year starts, the teacher who receives the children can immediately see where individuals are working in each area of growth.

Elmira Heights, New York, Hillsborough County, Florida, and University City, Missouri, are examples of cities having primary programs where reading development is used as the chief focus for recording and grouping, with other skill areas handled in a more standard fashion.

Foreign languages have recently been introduced into elementary schools in many parts of the country. Highland Park, Illinois, has instituted a unique approach for elementary school foreign languages. Approximately one-third of the teachers and the superintendent of schools learned conversational Spanish together. The children, in turn, learn from their teachers in an informal but planned manner.

Evaluation continues to be done at an increasing tempo. There is evidence that more schools are searching for better ways to improve the total teaching and learning process.

A NATIONAL STUDY OF EVALUATION PROCEDURES

The American Association of School Administrators, the National School Boards Association, and many educational leaders of the country have cooperated in supervising the *preparation of a series of publications* which served to emphasize the whole problem of evaluative principles, procedures, and techniques. First, a broad policy statement entitled *This We Believe*[6] was published. This publication directs attention to the general goals of education. A second pamphlet, entitled *Judging Schools with Wisdom,*[7] laid down general principles which must govern sound evaluation.

The National School Boards Association and the American Association of School Administrators received a grant from The Fund

---

[6] *This We Believe,* American Association of School Administrators and National School Boards Association (Washington, D.C.: The American Association of School Administrators, National Education Association, 1958).

[7] *Judging Schools with Wisdom,* American Association of School Administrators and National School Boards Association (Washington, D.C.: The American Association of School Administrators, National Education Association, 1959).

for the Advancement of Education for making a series of firsthand case studies of actual procedures of evaluation in local school systems. Approximately 100 carefully selected school systems in the country submitted information which illustrated their approaches to evaluation. Twenty-eight school districts, representing different types of communities, administrative organizations, and geographic areas in the country, were selected from the original 100 for specific study. Competent observers visited each of the districts and collected firsthand information about evaluative procedures being used. Descriptive reports provided the material for a series of fourteen publications entitled the *Quest for Quality* series.[8] These profiles for evaluation will be useful as a source of ideas and suggestions to local districts as they plan for the evaluation of their educational programs.

Descriptions of the evaluative practices used in a large city and in a suburban community are presented to give a clear picture of how two school systems attempted to improve practices. These practices may serve as a general guide to other schools, but each school system will have its unique problems, and must fashion its own plan.

EVALUATION IN A CITY SCHOOL SYSTEM

There is great diversity in the priorities, procedures, and instruments used in the evaluation of school systems. The plan of evaluation in a specific large city school system and a suburban school system should prove valuable to students of school administration. Although there are many differences in the means of evaluation among the school systems, there are also many common elements that may serve as a source of ideas and suggestions for planning future evaluation programs.

The Vega City schools.[9] Vega City is the fictitious name for an actual city with a school system enrolling 123,429 students in kindergarten through grade 14. It is a rapidly growing community, and the school administration realizes that evaluation processes are factors which will determine whether inevitable changes are orderly, planned, and intelligent, or whether they will be frantic and aimless.

The Vega City School District depends upon a strong research department for the coordination of its evaluation program. The research staff includes a director of research, an administrative analyst, and a systems and procedures analyst. These staff members are drawn from varied fields. The director of research is a clinical psychologist and a

[8] *Quest for Quality,* American Association of School Administrators and National School Boards Association (Washington, D.C.: The American Association of School Administrators, National Education Association, 1960).

[9] *Ibid.* (Booklet No. 1), pp. 15–32.

curriculum specialist. The assistant director has a background in educational administration. The administrative analyst is experienced in industrial management. The systems and procedures analyst, who works out of the administrative analyst's office, is a public administration specialist.

The research department makes an annual study involving 30 districts in the state which are operated under unified boards and administration for the complete program. Information is secured by photocopying the budgets of the cooperating districts, and also by asking the administrators to fill out brief questionnaires. Studies have shown comparisons of such facets of operation as: salary schedule, expenditures, time allotment in elementary schools, methods, programs, and policies. The comparative studies are used by the research department as a necessary part of several different research approaches they have used, including: trends, projections, problem solving, quality control studies, opinion surveys, experimentation, and analysis.

A pattern for the district's evaluative procedure has been established. This pattern includes the following steps:

1. Definition of the problem or center of concern
2. Detailing information needed
3. Background review
4. Analysis of possible problems involved
5. Development of questions to be answered
6. Collection of information
7. Analysis of information
8. Determination of strengths and weaknesses
9. Reporting of findings

The Evaluation program at Vega City includes several different research approaches. They include:

1. Comparative studies
2. Studies of trends and projections
3. Problem solving
4. Quality control studies
5. Opinion surveys
6. Experimentation and analysis

To find solutions to problems dealing with such areas as curriculum improvement, equipment standardization and textbook selection, Vega uses lay and professional committees representative of the various interests involved. Present status is studied; strengths and weaknesses are assessed. Judgments concerning needed steps are pooled, and then the evaluation machinery is set up.

In a sense, each new program introduced into the Vega district goes through an experimental stage. Effort is made to test innovations rigorously before they become a part of the established program. The experimental reading adjustment room program is one example of this type of evaluation. The program was initiated to help second and third grade children who were not making satisfactory progress. The basic procedure was to re-teach the beginning steps of reading. Reading adjustment teachers met with 5 or 6 different groups of children each day for approximately 40 minutes each. The groups were made up of 10 to 12 pupils. After four years of experimentation and evaluation, the program proved to be valuable enough to be continued on a regular basis. The same experimentation and evaluation procedure was followed in establishing a written language program in grades four through six. The evaluation was concerned with the comprehension of the mechanics of English grammar and the ways in which children learn to use language. The first step used in gaining information was a survey of the written language performance of a statistical sampling of fourth and sixth grade pupils in the district. Tests were used to measure the quality, style, and mechanics of essays written by children. A technical check was made in grammar and usage, punctuation, capitalization, spelling, and handwriting.

Generally, the study revealed that pupils in the Vega City Schools were reaching expected curriculum goals in written language. However, there was less growth in the mechanics of writing than in other areas included in the survey. These results prompted recommendations for changes or re-emphasis in this phase of the written language program.

Many policies and decisions must be made with due concern for what people think. Opinions should be known regardless of what is done about following or ignoring them. On several occasions, Vega school officials found it advisable to survey the opinions of one or more segments of the general public. Examples of some of the opinion surveys include: "The New Report Card," "Your Child and the Gifted Program," and "Pupil Behavior."

Vega's evaluation program is undergirded by an outstanding school system information program. The Public Information Department includes a director, an assistant director, two full-time secretaries, and two full-time clerks. This department supplies news and feature material to two daily newspapers, several weeklies, three television, and seven radio stations. More and more the Information Department finds itself involved in servicing requests for information, rather than originating news releases.

The school board and the administration are keenly aware of the need for keeping the school staff fully informed. A weekly bulletin from the superintendent's office includes interpretive articles, expanded coverage of board meetings, actions and deliberations, and articles about staff members. The superintendent makes an annual report to the staff by television on the day the entire staff returns for the start of the new school year. One of the television stations makes available a full hour of time for this purpose. Following the telecast, principals lead staff discussions, based upon the report, in each building. The superintendent's report follows a three-day orientation program for teachers new to the system.

The pattern of evaluation in Vega is a clear one. Coordination of the program is attained through a well-staffed Research Department. Experimentation is going on continuously, and each new experimental project has built into it the means for evaluating what will be done. This guards against perpetuating some new practice or procedure simply because continuation appears to be the best means of justifying the experimental effort. The evaluation of the Vega schools is comprehensive in that it goes beyond re-examination and up-dating curriculum aspects of the program. It goes into such important areas of school operation as business matters, personnel problems, school building adequacy, population growth patterns, and equipment standardization. There is good reason to believe that the Vega School System has an evaluation program which supplies the school staff and the school citizens with many of the answers to such questions as: "What should be taught in our schools?", "How well are we doing?", and "What do we need to do to improve our practices?"

EVALUATION IN A SMALL CITY SUBURBAN SCHOOL SYSTEM

The Apollo school system.[10] Apollo is the fictitious name for a colonial brick-and-stone suburban residential community of 55,872 persons who are largely professional and business people. There are 10,000 students in the Apollo Township School District. Apollo has a definite pattern of evaluation. Not all of the elements in the pattern could be used in many school systems, but certain aspects of the program should be included in all school district evaluation programs. Some of the central features of the Apollo evaluation program are:

1. *The Parent Council.* This organization is the coordinating unit of the Parent-Teacher Association and has representation from all the schools. It is sponsored by the local P.T.A., the building principals, and the superintendent's administrative staff. Four yearly council programs are held. The agenda for the meetings represents a wide range

[10] *Ibid.* (Booklet No. 3), pp. 20–32.

of topics, such as: The organization and administration of the district as it concerns instruction, the professional staff in-service programs, and the salary schedule. The Parent Council serves as a means of informal parent evaluation, and as an important device for informing a much larger group of parents in each separate school district within the city.

2. *The educational program meetings.* Some 500 school-related meetings are conducted in Apollo each year. The largest of the meetings attract 1200 persons; the average is approximately 250. These meetings are built around topics meaningful to citizens studying the workings of their schools. In one recent year the following seven topics were discussed at educational program meetings: "The Educational Program in the Elementary School"; "The Guidance Program"; "The Role of the Principal in Our Educational Program"; "The Educational Program in Our Junior High School"; "The Evaluation of Pupil Progress"; "The Vocational Education Program"; and "The Educational Program in Our Senior High Schools." The Apollo Board and superintendent are convinced that this approach is essential in order to provide and maintain high quality schooling in the community.

Staff members are challenged and motivated as they prepare information to present to parents at the numerous meetings. They are forced to do a sizeable amount of evaluating before they get to their feet to speak. One staff member said that such a presentation affected him in this fashion: "When I am assigned to make a report at one of these meetings, I find myself staying up late at night thinking just how I will describe and interpret my work. I know that the moment I stand up, there will be questions coming at me from all sides. But I have done my night work properly and carefully and have the answers ready. I have examined my job better than would an evaluating expert from outside."

3. *Evaluation by outside agencies.* Apollo can afford to hire outside agencies to survey its schools and methods. This is often done, as was the case when the visitation of an accreditation team showed a clear need for added guidance personnel. In order to make wise decisions, the superintendent recommended that a comprehensive evaluation of the guidance program be made by a committee of the most competent personnel available. His proposal was approved by the board, and a team of three consultants was employed. Although Apollo does not hesitate to employ outside agencies to assist when there is need for help, the district chooses to rely chiefly upon local appraisals and evaluations. The principals and teachers have developed an interest in devising self-evaluative techniques for their own improvement.

4. *Unique board meetings.* The board of education has adopted the philosophy that one of its most important functions is that of helping the school citizens get a more complete understanding and appreciation of the merits and needs of the educational program. It is for that reason that many of the educational program meetings are held in conjunction with the board meetings, and the board devotes one such meeting each month to problems relating strictly to the educational program. At these meetings, round table discussions are held to give representatives of the citizenry a chance to ask questions and share in the planning.

5. *In-service program.* The Principal's Workshop is an in-service program for principals, supervisors and special staff personnel of the school system. It is initiated by the superintendent, is scheduled for late summer, and consists of a full week of all-day sessions. Participants are requested early in May to submit proposed study topics to the workshop planning committee which, aided by the superintendent and assistant superintendent, makes preliminary plans. The final workshop agenda is prepared, printed, and mailed to all professional staff members early in August. Any teacher or staff member may attend, and many interested classroom teachers do attend.

Some of the workshop topics have been: "Audio-Visual Services"; "Administrative Policies Relating to Kindergarten"; "Grouping and Its Related Problems of Evaluation and Marking"; "In-Service Plans in Arithmetic and Mathematics"; "Achievement Test Data and the Improvement of Instruction"; and "The Role of the Helping Teacher in the Improvement of Instruction." Staff members present these topics, and time is provided for discussion and questioning.

The entire professional staff attends two in-service sessions each year to study a single educational topic of current concern. At these meetings the findings of research both from within and without the school system are applied to the topic being studied. If the research indicates need for change, steps are taken to make necessary corrections in the educational program.

The superintendent and the key staff members of this school system will admit that Apollo's evaluative methods are subjective in character. Generally, the studies are designed (1) to determine the effect of certain program changes upon the individual student, and (2) to determine through personal responses the effect of organization changes, new policies, course selection and modification, large group instruction, and parent-teacher interviews.

Evaluation of a program of community education is a complex undertaking that cannot be successfully carried out by the use of any one simple instrument or technique. The examples of practices in the

Vega and Apollo schools will be most useful to local school districts as a source of ideas and suggestions, rather than as examples of processes that can be used in totality.

CONCLUSION

There is general national concern for the development of more effective educational programs at all levels and in all disciplines. If this goal is to be attained, better evaluative techniques will need to be perfected and used.

Evaluation, as the term is used in this chapter, involves the determination of worthy educational goals and the perfection of ways to attain those goals in one school or an entire school system. The ultimate concern is to provide the means for each student to reach his highest educational potential.

Evaluation of the educational enterprise in a school system is the responsibility of the board of education, the central office staff, the principal, the teachers, and the school patrons. If all these people are to share in the responsibilities of evaluation, there must be a well-defined and planned program.

The school principal is once more in a strategic position of leadership. He helps in the basic planning for a program that extends throughout the school system and into each school. He works with the teachers, parents, and pupils to implement the program in the school he administers. The strengths and weaknesses of the educational program will first be discovered in each separate school. The principal is close to the problems the teachers seek to isolate and solve. He is the person to whom the lay citizen responds as reactions and suggestions are offered.

There is still much to be learned about ways of effectively evaluating an educational program. Very recently large and powerful professional and lay organizations have stated their belief in the need for better evaluation of the educational product. They have done some significant research on the problem and have made important pronouncements. There is reason to be encouraged about progress being made.

Short Case 1

Teaching the Fundamental Skills

John Doe is principal of a large elementary school in a suburban community outside a large mid-western city. The city newspapers have been giving considerable attention to public education. There have been some newspaper stories concerning the alleged weaknesses of the city schools in regard to the teaching of the fundamental skills in reading, writing, and arithmetic. The question of whether or not the public schools are doing a good job has been a common topic of conversation in the community.

One afternoon a very vocal professional man from John Doe's school community came into his office and complained bitterly about the quality of instruction in the school John Doe administers.

Problem: What kinds of evidence must John Doe be able to present if he is to make a strong defense of the program in his school? Present your answer in adequate detail.

Short Case 2

A Testing Program in the Elementary School

The entire administrative and teaching staffs of the New Town Elementary School District have been involved in planning for the launching of an evaluation program. One of the most important undertakings in the evaluation process will be determining the effectiveness of the teaching-learning process in the schools. The schools do not have a well-planned testing program.

Problem: The Planning and Coordinating Committee of the school system has been responsible for outlining the various facets of the evaluation program. This committee has selected you to head a special committee to determine the testing program that should be used in the evaluative process. How do you propose to proceed with the planning and organization necessary to accomplish the task assigned?

Chapter Eight

Improving Instruction Through Supervision

From early Greek and Roman days to modern times, educational theory has shifted from a subject-centered to a child-centered emphasis, and back again, never maintaining a middle position for any length of time. Eclectic educators have, however, placed some of the best practices from each of these extreme positions into our public school programs, thus helping to enhance the progress of the educational profession in general. In America, changes in the philosophy of supervision have paralleled the changes in philosophy of education as a whole, from the earliest days in New England to the present.

THE NEED FOR SUPERVISION AT THE ELEMENTARY SCHOOL LEVEL

There is little disagreement among teachers, supervisors, and principals as to the need for effective supervision. At the elementary school level, some reputable programs of supervision have existed for a number of years, but there remains a need for many more such programs.

Fully qualified elementary school teachers generally are well versed in academic and professional areas, but they often need to be relieved of their timidities and freed from traditional controls that inhibit the teaching-learning situation in the classrooms. These are responsibilities of supervision. At the same time, many elementary teachers are not fully qualified because of a lack in academic and professional backgrounds. Here, too, are areas in which supervision can facilitate growth.

As education at all levels becomes more intricate and complex, the need for increased and improved supervisory services becomes greater. Assistance in all areas, particularly those involving human endeavor and cooperation, can be greatly enhanced and fostered through an effective program of supervision in the school system.

With research and experimentation proceeding at rates never before undertaken in the public schools of America, an adequate supervisory program would be needed in every system, if only to aid the instructional staff in keeping abreast of the design and results of such studies. It is impossible, in these days of rapid changes and innovations in the schools, for practitioners to keep up-to-date on what is happening in their profession without the expert technical assistance that is available in an effective program of supervision.

An adequate supervisory program often uncovers hidden sources of leadership and creativity in a school system. When principals and other supervisory personnel make their rounds of elementary classrooms in a district, they are often in positions to discover leadership and creativity that might otherwise lie dormant.

THE CHANGING CONCEPT OF SUPERVISION

The early inspectional and dictatorial concept of supervision, one that is still too often held by present-day educators, may be compared to the mechanistic point of view of learning: that one learns one thing at a time most efficiently through passive listening. Since teachers of an earlier day were largely unprepared and without professional stature, they were expected to listen to the supervisors, and to carry out their directives without question. In contrast to this point of view, the modern concept holds that an individual is unique, dynamic, purposeful, and that he learns and reacts as a "whole" to those things identified with his own purpose. When one applies this organic point of view to supervision, the shift in emphasis moves from subject matter per se to the key factors in the learning process: the teacher and the child. Since improvement of instruction is the primary reason for any supervisory program, and since any such improvement hinges on teacher performance, it follows that the teacher is the key participant in the total program.

In a broad sense, supervision is a school service designed to improve the teaching-learning situation. It is sometimes thought of as an expert service which is provided on a consultation basis. In fact, in some areas of the country the very term "supervision" is being changed to "consultation," and "supervisors" are becoming "consultants," or one of some twenty-five other titles because of the unsavory connotations of the process, which has been identified, variously, as "snoopervision," or "snipervision." In modern supervisory programs, principals and supervisors or consultants serve as skilled resource persons possessing skills which aid administrators, teachers, parents, and children in providing an educational program which will eventually improve the quality of living in the communities in which they live and work.

RESEARCH REPORTS COMPARING SUPERVISED AND UNSUPEPVISED UNITS

A number of studies which compare the achievement of elementary school pupils in supervised and unsupervised units have been made. One of the earliest of these was made by Courtis[1] and Barnes in 1919 when they compared pupil's achievement in geography in supervised and unsupervised schools in the city of Detroit. Under carefully controlled conditions, about 25,000 boys and girls in grades four, five, and six in the Detroit public schools took the geography tests. In a decision based on the results of the tests, the schools were divided into four equal groups: a group supervised by classes, a group supervised by schools, an inspected group, and an unsupervised group. At the end of six weeks of instruction in geography, the groups were retested, original scores were retabulated to maintain original equality of the groups, and comparisons and interpretations were made. The researcher found the following relationships of actual gains made by pupils to gains possible: The unsupervised group made 49.5 per cent of the desired gain; the supervision by inspection group gained 54 per cent; the supervision by schools group raised the percentage to 68; and the supervision by classes group succeeded in making 69.5 per cent of the desired gain. Visits of the supervisor to the group supervised by classes resulted in that group's actual increase of achievement of 40 per cent.

In the same school system an experiment in handwriting was conducted by Miss Lena Shaw,[2] the Detroit system's supervisor of handwriting. Approximately 30,350 students in grades three through eight took penmanship tests at the beginning of a semester and, as a result of the tests, the schools were divided into four equal groups. The same

---

[1] S. A. Courtis, "Measuring the Efforts of Supervision in Geography," *School and Society* (July 19, 1919), pp. 61–70.

[2] Lena Shaw, unpublished materials.

procedures as those in the geography experiment were followed; the results indicated that the unsupervised groups made 30.1 per cent of possible gain, the inspected group made 36.2 per cent, the supervision by schools group made 40.7 per cent, and the supervision by classes group made 37.2 per cent of the desired gain.

Pittman,[3] in a seven-months' study of schools in Brown County, South Dakota, found that boys and girls in supervised schools advanced approximately 194 per cent further in the particular areas concerned than did children in comparable but unsupervised schools. Pittman used the equivalent groups method in conducting his experiment; two equated groups were compared in their ability to achieve. The experimental group received supervision for seven months in the 1919–1920 school year; the differences between this group's achievement and that of the unsupervised control group were credited to the effect of supervision. Supervised children, "when measured by equated differences and by percentages of progress of the experimental group measured in terms of progress of the control group, advanced approximately 194 per cent as far during the seven months in the particular functions under investigation as did the children with whom they were compared."[4] Children were tested and achievement compared in the following areas: reading, spelling, written composition, penmanship, and arithmetic. Children were in grades three to eight, inclusive; 114 children comprised the experimental group, while 225 were in the control group. All test scores of the experimental group were used in the statistical treatment; the scores of 114 control-group children which were most nearly equal to those of the 114 in the experimental group were used. Results of the experiment were obtained by comparing the improvements made by the 114 children in each group.

Hoppes[5] found that the achievement of children in supervised schools in Oakland County, Michigan, was 76 per cent greater than that of children in similar but unsupervised schools. Kinhart[6] conducted a study on the effect of supervision in English and found that the supervised group did significantly better work than did the nonsupervised group. His study was conducted for one semester with a control (unsupervised) group and an experimental group. The latter

[3] M. S. Pittman, *The Value of School Supervision* (New York: Warwick and York, 1925), pp. 1–17.

[4] *Ibid.*, pp. 16–17.

[5] W. C. Hoppes et al. *The Value of Supervision in Rural Schools of Oakland County,* Bulletin No. 7 (Lansing, Mich.: Michigan Education Association, 1926), p. 40.

[6] Howard A. Kinhart, *The Effect of Supervision on High School English* (Baltimore: Johns Hopkins University, 1941), p. 102.

was supervised ten hours per month through group conferences, classroom visitations, individual conferences, examinations of teaching units and texts, study of students' papers and records, intervisitations, and case studies. A study of the effects of supervisory activity in changing the curriculum and philosophy of five elementary school teachers was conducted by Greenfield.[7] He found that as a result of help offered through classroom visitations, individual conferences, professional reading, discussions of items on a teacher rating scale, summer school attendance, and teacher selection of tests and reference materials, a new program was initiated without loss of subject-matter learning by pupils.

It is understandable that studies of the degree to which supervision is effective are limited, when one considers the complexity of such studies and the resulting disadvantages to pupils in the unsupervised situations. It is interesting to note, however, that available studies indicate that supervision is definitely helpful. It is quite evident, though, that more research which will compare the supervised situations with unsupervised ones needs to be conducted.

THE KINDS OF SUPERVISORY HELP NEEDED BY TEACHERS

Teachers are individuals, and their interests and needs vary as much as those of their students. Typically, in almost any elementary school in the nation, there are teachers who have been in the particular school or system for many years, and there are teachers who are spending their first year in the profession. The needs and interests of these two groups of teachers, to say nothing of the many with varying lengths of tenure in between, are quite different. Then there are the mature, settled teachers, the young, energetic newcomers, and many in between, with varying needs and interests. Some of the teachers in the system or building have their master's degrees and work beyond, while others may not yet have completed their baccalaureate degrees. Some are "old timers" in the district's professional growth program, while at the other end of the scale are novices to the profession who scarcely know what the in-service program is all about. In the same way that teachers should be aware of individual differences in their pupils, principals and supervisors who are "teachers of teachers"

[7] B. L. Greenfield, "Study of the Effectiveness of a Program of Elementary School Supervision," *Journal of Educational Research,* XXVII (1933), pp. 123–126.

should be aware of the differences that exist among and between members of the staff. Staff morale depends to a good measure upon the principal's and supervisors' ability to recognize teachers' desires, and upon their ability to help meet them.

People of all ages have the same kinds of basic needs, varying only in degree. Teachers desire and need security, the freedom from fear and uncertainty. While this is never wholly attainable, administrative and supervisory staff can help in this area by treating teachers with fairness, while giving them recognition for accomplishments in the classroom and elsewhere about the school. Teachers also gain an intrinsic satisfaction when they are provided with: good working conditions, a feeling that they are an integral part of the school, and a voice in the administration of the school.

In a study by Lowe,[8] the opinions of 284 teachers in Indiana regarding practices employed in supervision were reported. The researcher found that the practices which gained favor with the teachers included: participation in professional organizations and conventions, committee work for teachers and supervisors, classroom visitations, help on administration and evaluation of tests, individual conferences, recognition of good work, and bulletins prepared by the supervisors. The practices for which they expressed dislike included: demonstration teaching, inter-school visitation, planning graduate study, professional libraries, excursions, radio and television programs, research and experimentation, and teachers meetings called by the supervisors.

It is interesting to note that in another study conducted by Palmer,[9] there appeared to be some contradiction of Lowe's findings, but at the same time expressions of basic needs and desires were once again shown. Palmer's survey was broadened to include not only elementary school teachers, but also elementary principals and consultants, whose opinions concerning supervisory practices were also included. Palmer concluded that teachers wanted more written evaluation, more demonstration lessons, better professional library facilities, and assistance in art and music. Teachers in their first year wanted more experience with intervisitation and aid in individual work. Consultants place more value on classroom visitations than did the teachers, and they also thought more help was given than the teachers thought they received.

---

[8] Joe Lowe, *Status of the Work of the General Elementary Supervisor in Indiana* (unpublished Doctoral dissertation, Bloomington: University of Indiana, 1952).

[9] Wayne R. Palmer, *A Study of Existing and Desired Supervisory Services in the Indianapolis Public Schools* (unpublished Doctoral dissertation, Bloomington: University of Indiana, 1952).

Trennepohl,[10] in a study conducted in schools in Kansas, found that teachers needed, but seldom received, help in planning activities for both dull and bright pupils, help in developing and maintaining a workable concept of discipline, and help in learning how to conduct successful interviews or conferences with parents. The help that teachers needed and most often received from supervisors included preplanning sessions prior to the opening of the fall semester, individual conferences, faculty meetings, handbooks and directories, special bulletins, group conferences, and professional organization membership. Teachers and supervisors in the Kansas study indicated that teachers needed, but seldom received, help with educational films, classroom observations by the supervisor, workshops for teachers, teacher visits to other schools, and demonstration teaching.

In a study by Daines[11] of supervisory practices in Idaho, it was found that the major needs of elementary school teachers in that state were: help in teaching slow learners, help in teaching fast learners, help with understanding needs of children with behavior problems, help in developing skills for independent work at different reading levels, and help in developing feelings of confidence, security, and belongingness in children.

Santos[12] found that teachers in a fast-growing area of California rated the following supervisory techniques as highly desirable: demonstration lessons, directed visitation of other teachers from other districts, classroom observations, directed reading, directed study, bulletins, and evaluation conferences.

THE INDUCTION OF NEW TEACHERS

With the rapid growth in population and accompanying growth in school enrollments, the problem of inducting new teachers into professional service has persisted as a supervisory activity. New teachers may find themselves beginning their work in a system that has many policies, procedures, and services which are unfamiliar to them. The period of adjustment to their new responsibilities may be one filled with frustrating experiences unless effective induction is a well-defined part of the supervisory and in-service education program.

Teacher drop-outs may be partially alleviated if more adequate in-

---

[10] Harlan Trennepohl, *Supervisory Assistance Needed and Received in Kansas* (unpublished Doctoral dissertation, Boulder: University of Colorado, 1956).

[11] Delva Daines, *Analysis of Fifty Instructional Problems of Elementary School Staffs in the State of Idaho and the Implications for In-Service Growth Problems* (unpublished Doctoral dissertation, Pullman: Washington State College, 1956).

[12] Donna Santos, *A Cooperative Analysis of Supervisory Practices in a Growing Elementary School District* (unpublished Master's thesis, San Jose, Calif.: San Jose State College, 1956).

duction programs are effected. Here, again, the desires and needs of teachers should be taken into consideration, and steps to help meet them must be initiated by the principal. The simple procedure of helping new teachers become acquainted with administrative, supervisory, and instructional personnel sometimes is significant in helping new staff members become adjusted to their situations. Additional help can be offered them if administrators and supervisors will take time to explain policies affecting teaching personnel, as well as to explain the school system's educational philosophy, whether it is published or not. Administrative and supervisory personnel can assist new instructors to become adjusted by acquainting them with curriculum guides and how they may be obtained, and also with records, forms, and reports for which the teachers are partially or wholly responsible.

New teachers want and need to learn about the services which the school provides, such as health services, guidance services, general supervisory services, special education services, instructional materials services, and the like. They should also learn about the community in which the school is situated—its problems, needs, and resources that provide services for children. They need to learn about parent-teacher activities, and the parts they are expected to play in the programs of parent and teacher organizations.

This orientation is a mammoth task, and it is not expected that all of these things can be accomplished in the course of a few days. One week prior to the opening of school should be devoted to the induction of new teachers, and a continuing program of orientation should be carried on throughout the first year or two of a new teacher's service. It is the principal, of course, to whom the responsibility of providing an effective orientation program falls.

Some schools hold two-day workshops just prior to the opening of school, and new teachers are encouraged to attend and to prepare instructional materials to use in their classrooms during the ensuing year. Principals, supervisors, and "master teachers" are usually available to give assistance. Second workshops, usually one-day affairs, are sometimes held about mid-year.

Social events are often planned to help the new teachers get acquainted. Local administrators and teachers' associations often treat the new staff members to lunches, dinners, barbecues, and other affairs.

Some districts have adopted a "master teacher," or "helper teacher" program, which provides an opportunity for an experienced classroom teacher to work closely with a small group of new teachers throughout their first year. The master teacher is released from his own classroom responsibilities for the year, and he works on a two-grade span in the field in which he has had experience. Master teachers are on call, and are available whenever the new teachers need help. Some of the duties of master teachers are: taking part in preschool activities involving new teachers; helping new teachers plan and organize the year's work; serving as resource persons in obtaining materials and giving information about available materials; giving demonstration lessons; helping explain district policies and philosophy; helping teachers organize their classes, and suggesting ways of meeting individual differences and handling programs; making classroom visitations and providing for follow-up conferences; serving on curriculum committees for revising the program and for preparing units of work; helping plan and organize such in-service activities as grade level meetings and workshops; and serving on programs, panels, and informative groups for P.T.A. and board of education meetings.

The master teacher programs show promise of success, as new teachers often feel more at ease, and more willing to work closely with one of their peers who has had recent classroom experience. Personal relationships are most important; often the master teacher must serve as a source of encouragement and as a true friend.

WHAT IS INCLUDED IN SUPERVISION?

Supervision, although clearly a part of the administrative structure in the field of education, is probably the least understood of administration's components. Basically concerned with the improvement of the teaching-learning process, supervision sets about to develop a structure in which individuals help each other, and in which persons themselves feel more adequate and worthy of achieving the goals of education. Working with school personnel to cooperatively develop and produce an outstanding educational program provides a real challenge for the principal and others concerned with the supervisory process.

Burton and Brueckner emphasize that supervision, if it is to achieve its central purpose of improving instruction, must provide:

1. Leadership that develops a unified school program and enriches the environment of all teachers.
2. The type of emotional atmosphere in which all are accepted and feel that they belong.
3. Opportunities to think and work together effectively as a faculty group.

4. Personnel procedures that give the teacher confidence in the school system.
5. Program change based on honest evaluation.[13]

The function of supervision is to help the teacher grow in ways which stimulate learning; this being true, it follows that the main function of the principal and others involved in supervising is leadership, and the discovery and motivation of leadership in the group.

Whatever the techniques used in a school district's supervisory programs, they should provide for the entire teaching-learning environment through democratic action and good human relations. Good supervision provides for the involvement of the total staff in the group-study-discussion approach to planning. As these individuals cooperatively identify common goals and work toward their fulfillment they can pave the way for all-around improvement.

The supervisory techniques in current use by principals and other personnel are legion and varied. Some of the more common ones include: curriculum improvement programs, workshops, committee work, classroom visitations, demonstration teaching, extension courses, visiting days, bulletins, experimental units, development of service materials, conferences, professional meetings, study groups, supplementary and adopted materials evaluation, use of consultants, use of tests, and in-service education. Use of these techniques should be determined cooperatively and based on the learning environment, with special concern for facts about the needs of individuals.

The really effective programs of supervision are those which operate at the local or individual school level. There are, however, certain supervisory activities at the national, state, and county levels which are either directly or indirectly available to the local units, and thus have their place in the over-all supervision picture of the public schools.

THE UNITED STATES OFFICE OF EDUCATION

In a strict sense, all national professional organizations are resources which can be helpful in local supervision programs. The national meetings and publications of these large bodies are, in themselves, media of considerable import in the improvement of the teaching-learning situation; they all include programs or suggestions that are designed to improve the education of America's boys and girls. Principals should see that the resources of the national organizations are made available to their local staffs.

---

[13] William H. Burton and Leo J. Brueckner, *Supervision* (New York: Appleton-Century-Crofts, Inc., 1955), p. 127.

The United States Office of Education of the national Department of Health, Education, and Welfare provides services that are of a supervisory, rather than an administrative nature. Through its Division of State and Local School Systems, the United States Office provides educational leadership in both elementary and secondary education. It maintains relationships with, and furnishes advisory services to, state and local school systems and professional organizations; including organization and administration of state and local systems, organization and administration of schools, supervision, curriculum and instruction, and auxiliary services.

The functions of the Office are to collect and disseminate educational information, to publish educational documents, and to assist the states and local school systems by carrying on research studies and offering consultative service. Information from the Office is disseminated through publications of various kinds, conferences and workshops, and by means of direct answer to some half-million inquiries each year. The federal agency also provides financial assistance for different projects and experiments in education throughout the country.

A number of national studies have been conducted by the Office with respect to organization, administration and supervision of elementary schools. A well-known study is that reported at mid-century by Effie G. Bathurst[14] and others in which the following concepts were revealed: (1) only three sampled cities in the 1948 study were using the platoon plan of school organization, and of these cities one had already converted primary grades to the self-contained classroom units, one had about one-fifth of its schools still using the platoon plan, and one had converted all primary units to the self-contained plan, with some platoon and departmentalization organization still existing in the intermediate grades; (2) departmentalization was still present in most cities reporting, predominantly in intermediate and upper grades, but was used chiefly as an expediency measure until a complete change-over to the self-contained plan could be affected; (3) the self-contained classroom was the "overwhelming choice" of persons responding to the study's inquiry; and (4) 28 of the 52 cities studied provided for "ungraded" classes for slow-learning children.

A study made for the Office by Professors Getzels and Jackson of the University of Chicago has just recently (1961) been completed. While the report was not published at this writing, preliminary releases indicate that many ideas held by educators concerning intelligence and

[14] Effie G. Bathurst et al, *Fourteen Questions on Elementary School Organization,* Pamphlet No. 105, U.S. Office of Education (Washington, D.C.: Government Printing Office, 1948), pp. 14–15.

creativity will no longer prevail, since the two are not necessarily related, and since the more creative youngsters need not be the more intelligent ones. Such findings portend changes in the organizational structure of certain classes in elementary schools.

SUPERVISION AT THE STATE LEVEL

Creative leadership functions are the keys to a state department of education's potential in providing services for the schools within a state. Excellence in education is obtained through leadership, and in recent years more and more state departments have exerted their influence through excellence in leadership and guidance.

The advising and consulting function of state departments of education provides areas of leadership for local school districts which, alone, could not provide them. The extent of the departments' capacity for providing such leadership functions depends, however, upon the size and quality of their staffs. It is the goal, therefore, of most state departments to develop a reservoir of the most competent professional staff in order to serve the educational needs of all areas of service in which the departments have been given responsibilities.

The improvement of educational programs within the state requires that consultative services be directed primarily to local school districts. Some state departments provide the consultative services directly to school teachers through classroom supervision, and directly to local school administrative and supervisory personnel through individual and group conferences. However, major attention from the state departments is given to groups working on common educational problems by providing for carefully planned workshops, institutes, or conferences, in all areas of the school community. Such techniques develop sound proposals for educational policy, based on combined experiences and judgments of state department consultants and the school representation.

Included among the supervisory activities of state departments of education are the following: conducting and advising on pilot and experimental programs; preparing and publishing resource materials for teachers and administrators; maintaining liaison with professional groups in the field; developing leadership programs through workshops, conferences, and materials; coordinating the professional educational leadership of colleges, public schools, and educational associations through commissions and state committees; stimulating the development of programs of child study to be used as a basis for curriculum development; substituting for existing programs of accreditation and standardization a program leading to local evaluation and individual progress in keeping with the principles of child growth and development; developing basic and instructional policies on local and state levels; and conducting a clearing house for sharing up-to-date information on new developments in education. If principals do not take advantage of the state assistance available to them in the most important area of instructional improvement, they are not adequately fulfilling their responsibilities.

SUPERVISION AT THE COUNTY LEVEL

Most states provide for an intermediate county school organization which operates between the state department of education and the local school district. Under this structure, county supervision was developed for the purpose of serving many small school districts with low average daily attendance, which could provide no supervisory help for teachers. Since there are still many small school districts that cannot supply supervisory services comparable to those available in most large city school districts, the need remains for the county to provide such services.

The county offices provide supervisory and consultative services to the fiscal, administrative, and educational programs of two or more local school units. Most of the supervisory time is directed toward classroom help by general and special area or special subject supervisors who visit classrooms, arrange for conferences, assist in group planning by grade level, and provide for demonstration teaching. Curriculum development is carried on in summer workshops and conferences by a supervisor in charge of this area. In-service education programs are also provided by county supervisors. Most county offices maintain an audio-visual library with materials available to all teachers in the county. County supervisors assist in grouping children for instruction, evaluating programs, ordering books and materials, introducing new methods and techniques of instruction, and aid in professional growth. Principals should be aware of and make use of county instructional services in their buildings.

SUPERVISION AT THE DISTRICT LEVEL

Supervisors in most local school districts are usually attached to the central staff of a school system rather than assigned to a single building. In a typical local district, general supervisors deal with general questions of methods and materials, while special supervisors are concerned with special subject matter or grade level areas. Large school systems are likely to have one or more general elementary supervisors as well as several special supervisors. As leaders with unique skills in matters of curriculum, supervisors play a special role in the program of the local district for the improvement of instruction. It is at the district level that a principal may receive the greatest amount of supervisory assistance for the instructional program in his building. In the supervisor's work of helping to develop a better educational program for children and of helping staff members in their professional growth, he must also strive to develop an atmosphere of mutual respect and confidence. When individuals have a voice in planning various activities, they also contribute more to them. As one of the school's professional leaders, the supervisor must spark the staff into a cooperating team in which each member, along with pupils, parents, and administrators, may contribute his talents in improving the school's curriculum. Motivating others to see their responsibilities is a most important supervisory skill. Effective supervisors will take advantage of every opportunity to allow teachers to be recognized for their accomplishments, while the supervisors themselves keep out of the limelight.

Supervisors must also be able to promote an environment which will provide teachers with freedom to experiment, to evolve new ideas, to work out their own problems, and to feel that they are important to the successful operation of the entire school program. Effective supervision will give attention to the reduction of teacher loads and the improvement of the teachers' status in the school and community.

The effective supervisor will *use* his intelligence and creative ability as he faces problems of curriculum improvement. He will make it a point to be thoroughly familiar with the school's community and its resources, and will know how to use these resources to the benefit of the educational program. He will be adept in the process of evaluating the school and its curriculum as he pursues a program of continuous study of curricular procedures, of human relations and group dynamics, of problem solving techniques, and of social changes and their impact upon the school's program.

Supervision at the local district level does not differ substantially from that at the county level; many of the same services are provided by both units, with county services available principally to the smaller and more rural districts, and the local central office serving the schools within the single large district. District supervisors call grade-level meetings when there are special needs in certain subject areas, direct the work of committees working on curriculum problems, issue special bulletins containing information in a number of areas, conduct workshops at the beginning and during the course of the school year, meet with faculties of the schools several times a year, visit in classrooms within the district, give advice and assistance with new teaching techniques, and generally provide for in-service education for members of the teaching staff.

The skills necessary for effective supervision must be employed in many areas of the total school situation. Successful supervisors sponsor a mutually-cooperative approach to all problems in their districts; they respect the worth and dignity, and accept the personalities, of all persons in the school community. They employ skills that result in effective group organization and action, while utilizing participation of the group's individual members in working toward solutions of the school's problems. They educate teachers in the use of scientific, problem-solving techniques to the end that success in the teaching-learning situation may be realized. The really effective supervisors use every resource and tool at their disposal in furthering the wholesome development of teachers, and thus ultimately, of boys and girls.

Figure 5 shows the organization of a small or medium-sized school district. It may be seen that the district's general and special supervisors are directly concerned with instruction and may be considered as staff officials to assist building principals and teachers with responsibilities in the education of pupils. In extremely small districts, the director of instruction may be the assistant superintendent, a building principal, or even the district superintendent.

THE PRINCIPAL'S SUPERVISORY ACTIVITIES

As the director of instruction in the elementary school, the greatest responsibility for supervision usually falls upon the principal. As he tries to better the educational program as well as the teaching-learning situation in his school community, the principal must see to it that an effective program of supervision exists in his building. Currently, authorities in elementary school administration and supervision subscribe to the policy of the national Department of Elementary School Principals of the National Education Association, when it proposes that at least 50 per cent of the principal's time be spent in supervision. The elementary school principalship is defensible as a vital professional position only at the instructional level.

As elementary schools continue to grow, both in number and effectiveness of programs, principals must be equipped to coordinate the work of increasing numbers of specialist services; they must be prepared to work with better-prepared teachers; they must be better able to provide leadership in a school-community that gives promise of be-

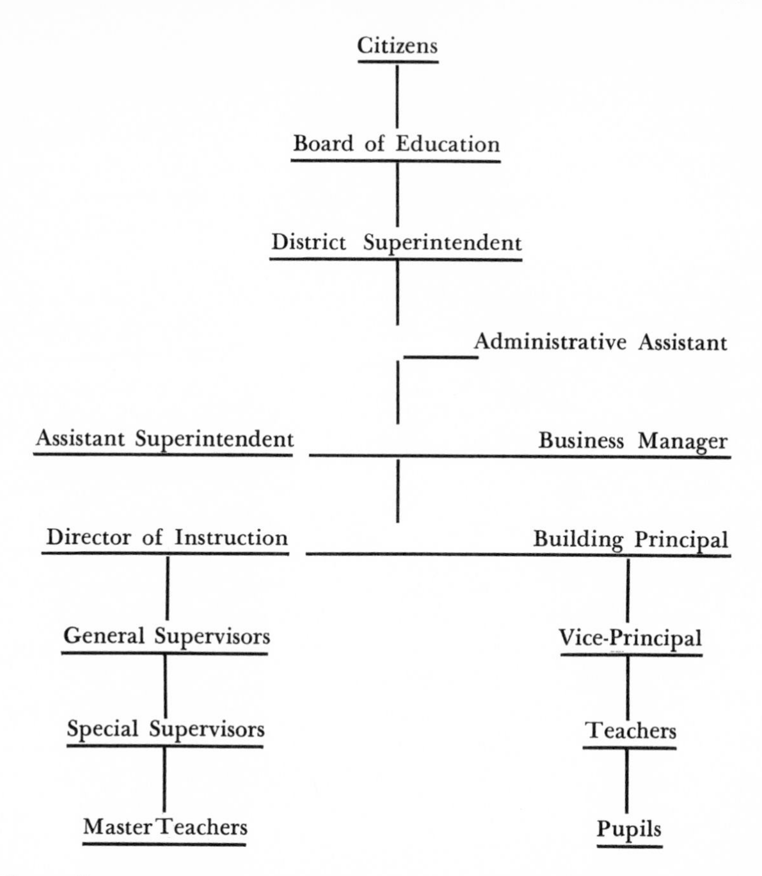

Figure 5. ORGANIZATION CHART OF A SMALL OR MEDIUM-SIZED ELEMENTARY SCHOOL. SUPERVISORS ARE CONCERNED WITH INSTRUCTION AND SERVE AS STAFF OFFICERS TO ASSIST TEACHERS IN THE LEARNING SITUATION FOR PUPILS.

coming more and more autonomous; and they must be ready to do their part in articulating the levels of instruction in their buildings, and throughout the system, as they recognize the importance of unity in education.

The modern elementary school principal must know what a good instructional program is, and recognize the steps that must be taken to evaluate and effect continual improvements in the curriculum. To realize these important goals, the school's leader must know the community in which the school is situated, and the community's relationship to the school and its program; he must be able to work with pupils, teachers, and parents so that a sound program of instruction is built and maintained in his building; and he must know what resources are available in the school community and how they can best be used in building a program of highest quality.

THE PRINCIPAL LENDS LEADERSHIP FOR CURRICULUM IMPROVEMENT

The modern concept of the curriculum is that it includes all experiences of children while they are under the influence of the school, including their interactions with, and reactions to these experiences. As the trend toward autonomy in the local elementary school building continues, responsibility for the improvement of the curriculum rests increasingly with the individual principal. The basic goal of curriculum improvement in the elementary school is to improve the learning situation so that each child may grow, develop, and learn to the maximum of his capacity in mental, social, emotional, and spiritual areas.

Since no one person possesses all the necessary abilities to make this goal a reality, it is up to the principal to coordinate the many talents of the several persons involved in the teaching-learning situation. Thus, the instructional leader of the school must be able to identify the abilities of others and to develop their potential for the forward progress of the instructional program.

Improvement of the curriculum or instructional program of a school implies change. The principal is the key person involved in this changing school situation. His attitude toward curriculum improvement is reflected throughout the school—in the teachers, in the pupils, in the parents, and in the non-certified personnel; and if he starts with "where they are" and proceeds from there, he is well on his way toward bringing about effective change in the school's program and in the members of the staff. In order to effect desirable change or growth in his school, the principal will strive for a satisfactory emotional climate among the personnel. He will understand the goals and purposes of elementary education; he will accept the teachers as peers; he will encourage teachers to carry on active research in their classrooms to develop new ideas and more effective teaching techniques; he will make materials available for classroom activities, and will expedite schedules so that teachers may work together in effecting desirable curriculum changes.

CURRICULUM IMPROVEMENT IN BALTIMORE[15]

The program of curriculum improvement and the place of the elementary school principal in the program is exemplified in the elemen-

[15] Adapted from Mary A. Adams, "Technics for Working Together in Baltimore, Maryland," *The National Elementary Principal,* XXXV (April, 1956), p. 11.

tary schools of Baltimore, Maryland. The more than 135 schools of the system have been divided into five regions, each headed by a director, and served by a staff of two elementary supervisors, two elementary specialists, and consultants in the fields of art, music, and physical education. This team plans learning experiences cooperatively, and involves members of the schools' faculties, so that individual teachers receive specific help in terms of their interests and needs. The principal is the key member in inter-relating the resource team and the members of the faculty, and in seeing that the plans set up are carried forward.

The work of all area directors and resource staff members in the Baltimore program is coordinated, and all principals are brought together in unified relationships. Staff meetings and principals' conferences are particularly valuable.

As a result of the Baltimore plan, there is a closer knowledge of individual teachers by supervisory personnel, there is more effective use of resource services by the schools and faculties, and there are closer interpersonal relationships than were possible before the introduction of the plan.

Much of the cooperative planning in Baltimore originates in the individual elementary schools; many principals have faculty advisory committees which work strictly with the instructional programs of the individual schools. In many instances, faculties of neighboring schools initiate projects of joint interest, and frequently joint faculty meetings are held, involving staffs of several neighboring schools. Programs arise from commonly considered interests and the suggestions for dealing with them. Teachers and children are often encouraged by principals to engage in intervisitations among the schools of the area. In these visits they share common interests and gain new ideas.

THE PRINCIPAL VISITS THE CLASSROOM

The supervisory technique most frequently practiced by elementary school principals is the classroom visitation, or observation. Originally used as a device to eliminate incompetent teachers, and later to discover teachers' weaknesses or problems with a view toward correcting them, modern visitations are considered a part of an over-all view of teaching techniques which considers both strengths and weaknesses. Once the strengths and weaknesses of teaching techniques have been assessed, the principal is considered to have a background for proceeding with a program of follow-up activities to improve the total program of instruction in the school.

A prerequisite to effective classroom visitations is cooperative preplanning by the principal and teachers. Gone are the days when the little red eraser was passed from one teacher to another when the principal or supervisor was sighted arriving on the scene to "inspect" the classes. Ideally, teachers will feel at ease with the principal in their rooms studying the teaching-learning situation with an eye toward improvement, not toward "rating" the individual teacher. Unfortunately, it may take some time before this objective can be realized, because so many teachers are schooled in the tradition of the rating visitation. A paradox is becoming evident in many school systems; in those systems in states having tenure laws and regulations for teachers, the rating is often being done approximately as it was twenty-five years ago. There is much need for better ways of determining how to grant tenure status for teachers.

Scheduled visitations are often the most worthwhile; in these, the principal or supervisor visits the room with his attention centered on specific problems. This is not to imply that scheduled visitation is the only defensible method; many teachers operate under considerable emotional strain when the visit is definitely scheduled. For these staff members, it is probably a more valuable experience if the principal or supervisor "drops in" to observe the teacher in his most effective work. It is a comparatively simple matter to ascertain which type of visit the teachers prefer.

Principals should keep adequate records of each visit to a classroom. Included in the records are such items as class reaction to the lesson, class participation, and other pertinent data. While it is not always considered good practice to take notes during the actual visitation, it is important that the principal make his report in writing soon after the visit. The most important reason for making the report is to provide background information for the principal-teacher conference, which should follow soon after the visit. After the principal commends the positive qualities viewed in his visit to the classroom, he should encourage the teacher to analyze her own weaknesses. The teacher and principal can then plan cooperatively for correcting weaknesses and improving teaching.

OBSERVATION AT FAIRFIELD, CONNECTICUT[16]

Principals in the elementary schools of Fairfield, Connecticut, make frequent supervisory visitations to the classrooms of their system. During the course of the school year, principals participate in both general

16 Adapted from W. H. Hellman, "Technics for Working Together in Fairfield, Connecticut," *The National Elementary Principal,* XXXV (April, 1956), pp. 15–17.

observations of the entire instructional program and planned observations of specific aspects of the program.

For the general observation of the entire program made by the principal, the school leaders, teachers, and pupils meet early in the school year, and at occasional times during the year, to plan the kind of school atmosphere they feel is desirable. Short, daily visits to all classrooms, the playground, the corridors, the lunchroom, the bus-loading platforms, the lavatories, and all other parts of the physical plant while they are in use are made by the principals in the Fairfield elementary schools. These visits are a part of the cooperative evaluation which takes place as the school year progresses. Varying the time of their observational visits, the principals note items needing attention, so that conferences with appropriate staff members may be held at a future time.

Principals in Fairfield also make planned visitations with respect to the specific aspects of the educational program associated with the basic purposes of the school: the fundamentals such as reading, writing, spelling, arithmetic, social studies and science; the personal and social development of pupils; citizenship; and physical and mental health. As in the general observational visits, cooperative planning determines the type of program the staff desires in the basic objective areas; as a result of the pre-planning sessions, all staff members know the kind of teaching-learning situation that should prevail. Prior to their visitations, the principals announce which particular area will receive their attention. Deviations from the desired program then become the source of cooperative action on the part of teachers, principal, and pupils.

THE PRINCIPAL CONFERS WITH TEACHERS

Earlier in this chapter, several references were made to principal-teacher conferences as important aspects of the administrator's supervisory activities. Cooperating with personnel to develop methods of communication in working together provides a real challenge for the school's principal. If he can establish satisfactory working relationships with staff, pupils, and the community, he can make a long stride toward stimulating teacher growth, thereby achieving more effective learning situations, with the community's understanding and approval. If the principal is to fulfill his responsibility for encouraging leadership in members of his staff, he must create an atmosphere in which constructive, free-flowing ideas are presented by the individuals on the staff. The principal-teacher conference is one technique through which this objective may be fostered.

Through individual conferences with members of the staff, the elementary school principal may be effective in establishing widely agreed-upon purposes for the school's program. In this way, the stage may be set for creative and cooperatively-arrived-at changes to be made in the instructional program.

Whether the principal is the conference leader in an individual, small-group, or large-group meeting, and whether the conference be with teachers, pupils, parents, custodians, cooks, lay persons, or other administrators, he must provide for an atmosphere in which all may benefit as they encounter problem-solving situations together. Provision must be made for all to learn from the conference proceedings. The principal must accept the possibility that other previously-unthought-of problems may arise before any progress is facilitated. The principal who is an effective conference leader will make certain that all persons involved share ideas. His chief contribution will be through the stimulation of thinking and talking on the part of the conferees. It is important, however, that he guide the thinking of the conferees to some kind of conclusion, in order to avoid the popular conception that a good deal of time is wasted and nothing accomplished in conferences.

A principal should operate under the assumptions that (a) the teachers are willing to entrust themselves and their problems to a supervising principal, and (b) they are willing to be influenced or changed by this relationship or, at least, through principal-teacher conferences. With the goal of mutual understanding uppermost in the minds of both parties, the principal can then:

1. Assign the proper importance to each teacher's problems.
2. Establish rapport through proper communication by close listening, remembering what the teacher has said, and displaying a sincere interest in the teacher's problems.
3. Propose a scientific problem-solving approach to the questions posed by the teacher, whereby she might see how she can solve her own problems, or, undertake a discussion of the questions in such a light that the teacher has a better outlook as a result of seeing her problems more clearly.
4. Promote the possibilities of further teacher-principal conferences with respect to the teacher's professional and, perhaps, personal questions and problems.

THE PRINCIPAL PROVIDES FOR IN-SERVICE EDUCATION

In-service education is a concept and practice that has wide acceptance in school situations today, and many elementary school administrators give top priority to the continuous learning of their staff members. Every elementary school, as well as every educational system, should strive to promote continuous improvement of all persons on the staff so that they keep abreast of advances in subject areas, as well as in the theory and practice of teaching. With the large number of new elementary school teachers who have been integrated into school systems throughout the nation, a successful orientation program for new members undertaking first teaching assignments has had to be developed in modern districts. This program has become a basic aspect of in-service education. Deficiencies in the background and preparation of members of the staff, both certified and non-certified, have also necessitated programs of in-service education for persons who would profit by an on-going and well-planned program to improve their efficiency.

The principal is the key person in an effective in-service education program in his building. The role he plays is determined by his concept of the nature of in-service education, by his understanding of the dynamics of change, and his attitude toward individuals working together in groups. Besides the principal's responsibilities for providing inspiration for in-service education and creating a climate for growth, he must spark the effective organization of an in-service program and facilitate the work of the various groups of individuals involved in the program.

It is important to emphasize that only through shared responsibility and mutual cooperation of the administrator and the teachers in the planning, organization, and evaluation of in-service activities can a really successful program evolve. The principal's enthusiasm and general attitude for in-service education, as well as for all other aspects of the elementary program, will usually be reflected by the teachers. Improvement in the teaching-learning situation as a result of in-service education is the result of the teachers' desires to use the most effective procedures in their classrooms, and their appreciation of the social significance of their work.

The administrator's role in the in-service program is described in some detail in Chapter III. Literature abounds with the types of activities which are included in in-service programs, such as: teacher institutes; workshops; pre-school conferences; monthly grade level meetings; observation of lessons; intervisitations and excursions; lectures or speakers; curriculum-development programs; development of resource units and courses of study; conferences with faculty, parents, and pupils; study groups; provision of professional reading materials; participation in public relations programs; attendance at professional meetings; extension classes or summer school courses; and provision for sabbatical leaves for travel or continuing education.

There is presently a trend toward universities and colleges providing less instruction in the techniques of teaching and methodology.

This trend sharpens the need for more and better in-service programs for beginning teachers. There is considerable evidence to show that beginning teachers are not as well prepared now, professionally, as they were before many universities began to increase academic training and decrease professional training for elementary school teachers. It is likely that this situation will be corrected in coming years when it is realized that an elementary teacher needs to have a balanced professional and academic pre-service program. Until such time as this is accomplished, however, the need for in-service education in the various local districts is strongly evident.

The faculty meeting, properly planned and carried out, is one of the most effective means of supervision and in-service education at the disposal of the principal. Too often, however, elementary administrators use the faculty meeting to discuss routine aspects of administration which could better be disposed of in a faculty bulletin. As an effective part of an in-service or supervisory program, the faculty meetings should be cooperatively planned by the principal and the teachers to the end that the meetings have a common purpose. A faculty meeting committee, elected by the teachers, can plan for the year's meetings and prepare each session's agenda to be distributed to the staff prior to each meeting.

The setting of a definite time and place for faculty meetings is an important morale-building aspect, but the teachers themselves should have a say as to when and where the meetings are held. The optimum time, according to teachers and administrators, is after school is dismissed. Ideally, if possible, the faculty meeting should be made an integral part of the school day, with the children being dismissed an hour early once or twice a month, and the meeting usually consuming an hour or an hour and one-half. Experience has taught, also, that teachers appreciate a definite time to begin and a definite time to end a meeting. Refreshments of coffee and cookies at the beginning of the session serve a useful "ice-breaking" purpose at the meeting.

Demonstration lessons are an especially effective supervisory technique at the principal's disposal. Such lessons, carried on by the principal, a supervisor, or a teacher, are means of providing teachers with ideas of superior teaching skills and methods which may be adapted to meet their individual needs and situations. It is the principal's responsibility to see that such demonstrations represent superior teaching, and that they are well planned and evaluated by his staff.

Closely associated with the demonstration lesson is the intervisitation, in which teachers visit other teachers' classrooms either inside or outside their own building or district. This technique requires careful planning since arrangements must be made for substitutes to release the teachers who participate in the intervisitation day. Evaluations, again, are important aspects of intervisitations.

Other less obvious but important techniques of the in-service education or supervisory program are: well-prepared bulletins from the principal's office, suggestions for professional reading, and publicity concerning a college's offerings of interest and value to the staff. The supervisory bulletin is an effective means of relaying communication on matters of administration and supervision affecting the entire faculty.

Regardless of the techniques and media used in supervisory and in-service education programs, they must be constantly and continually evaluated. It is the responsibility of the principal to see that this is accomplished, but the actual evaluation is most effectively performed in cooperation with the teachers. On the basis of results of the evaluation, the staff should revise and strengthen the supervisory program to better meet the needs of the staff. A detailed description of the process of evaluation is included in Chapter VII.

CONCLUSION

Supervision, concerned with improving the teaching-learning situation, is at the heart of both the instructional program and the productive organization of the elementary school staff. The principal who conscientiously and effectively spends at least 50 per cent of his time in supervisory activities finds that those affected by his activity improve their performance and effectiveness. Success in the principal's supervisory activity depends upon how well he performs his tasks, how well he can develop the cooperative spirit in his team of teachers and other school personnel, and how well he understands them. The principal, as a supervisor, has a right to expect *performance* from the persons on the certificated and non-certificated staffs; he also has a right to expect information from those persons on how the education of children might be accomplished more efficiently and effectively. The teachers and other personnel should expect to perform efficiently and to make suggestions for the more effective implementation of the teaching-learning situation. Since the principal expects to receive the same things that staff members expect to give, the sole remaining objective is to clarify these expectations. This, in essence, is the principal's supervisory responsibility.

The principal expects to acquaint teachers and non-certificated employees with their jobs, to provide them with supplies and materials with which to perform their work, to provide for in-service education so that they may improve their performance, and to give them information about school policies and procedures. The staff members expect these things from their principal and, in addition, have a right to learn from him how well they are performing their work. Staff members can assist the principal in the communication of these things through conferences, questions, and inviting him for visits to their classrooms; the principal helps staff members by encouraging them to raise problems for possible cooperative solution.

Finally, it is the joint responsibility of principal and teachers to continually evaluate the teaching-learning situation, working toward the ultimate goal of improving the education of the students in the school.

Short Case 1

Supervision Is Needed

Mr. Keller was principal of the Ellinwood Elementary School. He recently had employed a Mrs. Davis, who had not taught for several years, but had previously taught in grades two and three in a different district. Mr. Keller wanted one of the older teachers in the school to take a vacancy in second grade, and he assigned Mrs. Davis to grade four. Soon it became apparent that Mrs. Davis was not doing well in the areas of arithmetic and social studies. Mr. Keller scheduled a conference with her at which he tried gently to discuss the deficiencies and suggest that supervisory assistance was available.

Mrs. Davis was re-employed for the next year at the same grade level. The elementary supervisor visited her class and made suggestions for improvement in arithmetic and social studies, but Mr. Keller was certain the suggestions went unheeded. There was an undercurrent of dissatisfaction among the parents of both her former and present pupils concerning the two subject areas. However, Mrs. Davis was employed for a third year to teach the third grade, but dissatisfaction resulted in her not being rehired for the fourth year.

Problem: What help might a supervisor give in this situation? Could another type of curriculum organization in an elementary school possibly have utilized Mrs. Davis' competencies in areas other than arithmetic and social studies? Describe such a curriculum structure.

Short Case 2

The Supervisor Intervenes

Ted Scott had been an outstanding principal at Seaview Elementary School for eight years, and in that time had won the respect and admiration of the teachers in the school and most of Seaview's citizens. Under his administration, some very worthwhile educational innovations had been introduced into the school, and were well accepted.

When Jim Smith, a former disgruntled bus driver, was elected to the board of education, he told his friends he was "out to get" Mr. Scott. The latter resigned, taking a principalship in a nearby city at a higher salary. Then Ralph Jones was elected principal at Seaview. He proved to be a pleasant man on the surface, but his administration was autocratic and his philosophy strictly subject-centered. As many unsavory situations arose, the morale of the staff was completely shattered, and six teachers resigned at the end of the first year of the new administration. All would have been complete chaos had not a supervisor from the central office intervened in many of the problems.

Problem: What do you think the supervisor did when he "intervened in many of the problems"? What are some areas in which a supervisor might help solve problems in a school and still not go over the head of the principal? What would you have done about Mr. Jones had you been superintendent of the district?

Short Case 3

Teachers Oppose Veteran

For a number of years Miss White had been the undisputed unofficial leader at the Washington Elementary School; she had been quite influential with parents and teachers. Though she had not finished the baccalaureate degree, she maintained that she knew more about teaching than the administrators and supervisors who had completed higher degrees in education. She refused to take further professional training, and discouraged other teachers in the school in this undertaking.

In the past two years, Washington's pupil population had been growing steadily, and so had the size of the teaching staff. Some of the new teachers opposed Miss White, and the latter retaliated by criticizing teachers before parents, individually and in groups. Mr. Gray, the principal, decided that something had to be done about Miss White.

Problem: What should Mr. Gray do about Miss White? Are there any implications here regarding a teacher's tenure at a particular school in a particular district? What might Mr. Gray and the staff do to try to interest Miss White in improving herself professionally?

Chapter Nine

Pupils with Problems: Providing for the Mentally Superior

The practice of providing for gifted children and youth is not a new one. In fact, the story is told of the Mohammedan ruler who, in the sixteenth century, selected only the fairest, strongest, and most intelligent youth to train as leaders of his kingdom.

Since the earliest days of education in America, public demand has made the schools aware of the need for a well-planned program for the gifted youth. Originally used to indicate mentally superior pupils, the term "gifted" now includes all children with special talents in creative fields as well as those who are intellectually superior.

It is a rare school system that does not accept, at least theoretically, the principle of individual differences; anyone associating with groups of children for a number of years realizes that boys and girls are not born with identical traits; and the longer they live the more different they become, as home and early school training provide opportunities to learn. It is a rare school system, too, that does not put this principle into practice insofar as children with serious mental or physical handicaps are concerned; many classes are devoted to the education of mentally deficient, retarded, and physically handicapped children.

There are considerably fewer schools, however, that have seriously applied the principle of individual differences to the gifted or "mentally superior" students of their population. Because of their abilities, gifted children are usually able to succeed satisfactorily with a minimum of effort and assistance from adults. If uninspired and unmotivated, however, they often become satisfied with a level of achievement somewhat below their capabilities. It has been only in relatively recent years that the demand for specialists, the extension of required schooling, and the increasing pressures of mass education have focused attention on the needs of the mentally superior pupils in our schools.

Since the 1950's, more and more schools have initiated experiments with special programs for the mentally superior students within their jurisdictions. Such programs have been intended to challenge the superior boys and girls to a more effective use of time, effort, and talent, thereby conserving our greatest human resources. Such programs have been intended to provide opportunities for the development of the abilities of gifted children through special activities not usually found in the average classrooms of the nation. Such programs have been intended to provide mentally superior pupils with training in leadership in a democratic culture, and to maximally develop their individual potentials for service in our society.

INTELLECTUAL GIFTEDNESS DEFINED

A review of professional literature on the subject of the "mentally elite" reveals that there is no clear-cut, totally agreed-upon definition for intellectual giftedness. During the early years of the current emphasis on the education of the gifted, the American Association for Gifted Children defined the academically gifted as a person whose performance in any line of socially useful endeavor is consistently superior,[1] while the Educational Policies Commission of the National Education Association suggested that pupils with IQ's of 120–137 be identified as moderately gifted.[2]

DeHaan and Havighurst propose that the gifted be considered as those who are in the top ten per cent of their age group in one or more areas of talent: general intellectual ability; ability in science, mechanics, social leadership, or human relations; talent in creative arts, music, graphic arts, creative writing, or dramatics. They conclude, "We shall consider any child who is superior in some ability that can

1 Paul Witty, ed., *The Gifted Child* (Boston: D. C. Heath and Co., 1951), p. 8.

2 Educational Policies Commission, *Education of the Gifted* (Washington, D.C.: The National Education Association, 1950), p. 11.

make him an outstanding contributor to the welfare and quality of living in our society."[3]

While it is generally agreed that the intelligence test score does not enable us to identify all gifted children, and while there is considerable disagreement as to what minimum intelligence quotient constitutes that of a gifted child, it is relatively safe to presume that the intelligence test score is the most objective means of identifying the mentally superior in comparison to average or below-average individuals in intelligence. In short, intelligence test scores have been found to be the most valid single criterion for indicating the gifted; they make it possible for school personnel to predict rather early in the child's life certain abilities that may lead to important contributions to society in any of several different areas.

It is interesting to note that the range of intelligence quotients of gifted children participating in special programs in the nation's schools varies widely—often from 110 to 160 and above—with cut-off points varying according to the percentage of gifted children in the population of a school district, with the type and objectives of the programs offered, with the district's general philosophy of education, and with the amount of funds available.[4] Kough and DeHaan declare that the solution in each case depends upon local school conditions.[5] How many gifted children can be given special attention in the classroom or school? How much can the school give these children? The answers to questions such as these will determine how much can be done for the gifted children, and will help determine what IQ level should be used as a cut-off point.

Much has been learned about general characteristics of gifted children. Contrary to the once-popular belief, intellectually gifted children are not physically retarded, unsocial misfits. Terman and Oden's 25-year study of 1500 gifted children, corroborated by many other investigators making similar studies, indicates that mentally gifted boys and girls are generally physically attractive and well-adjusted socially, and are generally superior to their peers of similar age in size, strength, and general health. The gifted may be highly superior in some ways and average or below in others; their best accomplishments are in reading and language, their poorest in penmanship and spelling. They

---

[3] Robert F. DeHaan and Robert J. Havighurst, *Educating Gifted Children* (Chicago: University of Chicago Press, 1957), p. 1. Copyright 1957 by the University of Chicago.

[4] California Elementary School Administrator's Association, *The Gifted Child—Another Look* (Palo Alto, Calif.: The National Press, 1958), pp. 1–2.

[5] Jack Kough and Robert F. DeHaan, "Identifying Children with Special Needs," *Teacher's Guidance Handbook,* Vol. I (Chicago: Science Research Associates, 1955), p. 23.

often show evidence of unusual imagination and resourcefulness, and possess remarkable ability to apply their new-gained information to other situations.

Several districts have developed their own checklists to aid teachers in observing pupils for traits that might bring out early identification of giftedness. Most authorities agree that early identification is essential if the full value of a program for gifted children is to be realized; superior children need special guidance. Early identification is also important because acceleration by grade skipping, if it is to be done at all, is more advisable in the lower grades.[6]

The following 16 characteristics are most often found on checklists for early identification of the gifted:

As a group, the majority of the intellectually gifted:

1. Are interested in a wide variety of things and have knowledge of many things of which other children are unaware.
2. Are able to generalize and rationalize.
3. Are very curious; ask why.
4. Have a good memory; retention comes readily without much rote drill.
5. Read two grades above their grade level; read early in life.
6. Verbalize; possess advanced vocabularies; talk at an early age.
7. Are more sensitive, self-critical, and trustworthy.
8. Show originality, imagination, and creativity.
9. Tend to seek older companions; those in the higher IQ ranges (150 and up) tend to engage in solitary activities.
10. If between IQ 130–140, tend to be better leaders and to have a good social adjustment; above IQ 140, this may be less true.
11. Come from all races, creeds, environments, economic brackets.
12. Have high ability regardless of sex.
13. Are emotionally relatively stable.
14. Have similar play interests to those of average ability, but desire more complicated games, rules, and standards.
15. Desire to do things differently.
16. Are superior in height, weight, and general health.[7]

Teachers can often most easily identify children gifted in art, writing, or social leadership by observing the performance of these boys and girls. Intelligence tests, while enabling adults to identify most of the boys and girls potentially gifted in abstract intelligence, often fall far short in the measurement of other potentials. Since intelligence tests and teachers' judgments are not infallible, consideration should also be given to personal health data, data on social-personal develop-

[6] Lewis M. Terman et al, *The Gifted Child Grows Up, Genetic Studies of Genius,* Vol. IV (Stanford, Calif.: Stanford University Press, 1947), p. 231.

[7] California Elementary School Administrator's Association, *op. cit.,* p. 5.

ment and emotional maturity, a social history, pre-school growth and development records, school history, lists of interests and hobbies, and records of special abilities. Attitudes and values may be measured by sociograms, diaries, autobiographies, open themes, anecdotal records, discussions, and interest surveys.

While it is generally agreed that teacher observation of characteristics is the most effective method of identifying specially gifted children, the teacher needs help from other sources. The Philadelphia Suburban School Study Council's Committee on the Gifted Child, from experiences and wide reading by members of the group, has suggested eleven identification techniques: (1) group intelligence tests; (2) individual intelligence tests such as the Stanford-Binet or Wechsler-Bellevue; (3) reading tests; (4) teacher judgments; (5) judgments by peers; (6) special aptitude tests, such as tests in music, mathematics, mechanical aptitude; (7) cumulative records; (8) early choice of career; (9) parental observations; (10) case studies, such as special detailed studies of the individual in all his relationships; and (11) free-expression compositions, which are unusually revealing in disclosing just what an individual is like.[8]

It is, of course, admitted that any one of these techniques used in isolation is unreliable, nor will the combination of only two or three infallibly identify the gifted. When several are combined in focus upon one individual, however, a reasonably accurate picture of the subject will begin to emerge.

EMERGING CONCEPTS INVOLVING INTELLIGENCE AND CREATIVITY

Evidence from recent studies conducted in school situations and among some of the professions is throwing new light on the nature of intelligence and its relationship to creativity. In the Getzels and Jackson study referred to in the previous chapter, two groups of high school boys and girls were considered; one group of students in the top 20 per cent in IQ scores and in the bottom 20 per cent in creativity marks, and another group of students who ranked in the top 20 per cent in creativity marks and in the bottom 20 per cent in IQ measures. The two researchers found that both groups ranked equally superior in academic achievement to the school student body as a whole, and concluded that one possible explanation for the latter group's high achievement may lie in the fact that it did include the most creative students. It is interesting to note that, generally, the high IQ

8 Philadelphia Suburban School Study, *Guiding Your Gifted, A Handbook for Teachers, Administrators and Parents* (Philadelphia: Educational Service Bureau, School of Education, University of Pennsylvania, 1954), pp. 8–9.

students tend to be the convergent thinkers, while the highly creative students tend to think divergently.

In another study recently concluded in the Institute of Personality Assessment and Research at the University of California in Berkeley, some 600 persons who were adjudged creative in the professions of writing, architecture, research in the physical sciences and engineering, and mathematics were studied. The study, made by a group of psychologists, was part of a nation-wide study of human creativity, and revealed that highly creative persons are, in the main, well above the average in intellectual capacity. Since, however, there are many factors involved in intelligence, the relationship between intelligence and creativity is not clear-cut. For example, in the verbal section of the intelligence test, creative writers scored higher than other groups being studied, but in the spatial relations section of the intelligence test, the writers gained the lowest score. Creative persons scored well above average on the intelligence tests, but their scores, individually, had a wide range; among some of the creative groups, the correlation of intelligence and creativity is essentially zero.

TYPES OF PROGRAMS FOR EDUCATION OF THE GIFTED

Education of the gifted is a complex problem. Programs designed to attain this important objective vary widely due to differences in philosophies held by teachers, parents, administrators, and special interest groups, the financial ability of the district to support a program, and many other factors. Generally, however, the classes fall into three general types: enrichment, acceleration, and special classes.

Enrichment. Wherever school districts undertake programs for gifted children, enrichment is found to be one of the principal techniques employed at all grade levels. Implementation of this technique is achieved simply by enriching the regular classroom program in such a manner that the mentally superior children are challenged at their level of accomplishment.

Significantly affecting the enrichment program is the manner of class grouping. In schools where heterogeneous grouping of children in the classroom is the mode, relatively homogeneous chronological ages result, but a wide range of ability and achievement and a diversity of interests inject real problems in providing a program for those children at the top of the scale. This, however, may be the most practical approach to providing a program for the gifted in small schools or in schools where the number of superior children is small. In many instances, too, a community or staff may have strong feelings against segregation of superior pupils.

Even though most gifted children provide a measure of their own enrichment, as a result of their increased understanding and differentiating ability, increased curiosity, and broader ability with abstractions, the need for stimulating and nurturing their cognitive abilities still demands a planned approach. In an effort to extend the child's environment into new dimensions, some schools provide children the opportunity of using research skills; others allow children to expand and delve deeper into special interests.

Acceleration. One of the earliest efforts to provide for mentally superior children involved acceleration: a program, currently being discouraged, in which pupils were promoted on the basis of high quality performance or mental maturity into classes of a higher level than their chronological ages would normally allow. In districts where effective acceleration programs are being practiced, due consideration is also given to social and emotional maturity, and physical development.

In some districts employing acceleration programs for the gifted, children are advanced to higher grade levels; in other districts, they are assigned more advanced subject matter within a class if their abilities and interests render such assignments feasible. In still other districts, acceleration programs provide early entrance into school for children of mental superiority, provided they also display superior social, emotional, and physical maturity, and advanced reading aptitudes.

Administratively, a program of acceleration is probably the simplest method of providing for gifted children in a school. Under such a program, children are simply placed into a group at their achievement level, with due consideration to social, emotional and physical maturity. Such a program has the additional advantage of enabling these children to get at their life's work at an earlier age. In acceleration programs, the frustration of bright children who must remain with slower pupils is alleviated. Such a program requires no differentiation of school curricula, though this may promote the intolerable practice of attempting to adjust the child to the school rather than the school to the child.

Special classes. For many years one of the most controversial methods of providing for mentally superior children has been that of special class groupings, or segregation. Such special classes run the gamut from entire schools made up of high mental ability pupils in advance-level classes to single classes of pupils having superior mentality or high interest in special areas, who are taken from their regular classes and placed in accelerated classes in the subject areas.

The most common programs of special classes are part-time plans in which pupils are taken from the classroom and placed in special classes for an hour or more one or more times a week. In this manner, children are provided with enrichment-type work intended to broaden and deepen their information and interests, by being placed with specially trained teachers who have only the responsibility of planning and preparing lessons for mentally superior children.

Some types of special classes for the gifted are more adaptable to the elementary school than to the secondary school, since these programs use teachers to guide the superior pupils full-time through the regular required curriculum, demanding as a result that such teachers guide learning in all curricular areas.

Adaptations of the special classes plan are utilized in interest grouping where special interest groups are organized to bring added enrichment to classroom activities, in summer school programs planned specifically to serve the needs of the mentally superior, and in special classes organized to meet adjustment needs of gifted boys and girls with academic, social, or emotional problems.

THE FUNCTION OF ADMINISTRATION

There are several facets of administration, some frequently misunderstood, which are involved in programs specifically designed for mentally superior children in the elementary schools.

Primarily, it is the administrator's function to stimulate interest and action among school personnel and lay persons in a program which will meet the needs of gifted youngsters. As a logical follow-up to this function, the administrator may then guide faculty and lay persons into formulation and actual implementation of plans for such a program.

It is necessary for the school administrator or principal to have a thorough knowledge of plans for providing for gifted children and, particularly, to be fully cognizant of current trends in this area. At the same time, the administrator must maintain an open mind in considering faculty and lay persons' suggestions concerning such a program for mentally superior students.

The administrator must also provide for constant evaluation of the program for the gifted child, and the achievement of the persons concerned. Suggestions for changes and improvements should come from the administrator as he observes the program in action, and from the administrator, the staff, and lay persons as the program progresses.

Gunn suggests that the principal is the key to a successful program of providing enrichment in classrooms for mentally superior children. Some of the enrichment activities which Gunn suggests are: (1) stimulation of a wider use of the library; (2) organization of field trips as they are especially meaningful to gifted children; (3) organization of creative activities or interest group programs; (4) provision of more opportunities for work in science; and (5) enrichment of the creative arts program in the elementary classroom.[9]

ENRICHMENT PROGRAMS IN ACTION

School district programs involving enrichment for their mentally superior pupils are varied and widespread; in fact, it is doubtful that any program for the gifted, regardless of how it is "typed," exists without employing some manner of experiences intended to enrich the curricula of the children affected. Some schools employ the technique of a "club period" such as that of Hunter College Elementary School students' participation in special group activities which eventually are shared with other boys and girls; other schools use the "extra work" project of the type employed in the Malvern School in Shaker Heights (Cleveland), in which abler students head committees for group projects, perform experiments for the class, and engage in many other similar activities. Regardless of form, however, all enrichment-type programs have incalculable value.

PORTLAND'S "LATERAL" ENRICHMENT PROGRAMS

The enrichment program in the Portland, Oregon, schools begins in the fifth grade and continues through the senior high school. Though teachers in that city's schools are constantly on the lookout in all grades for children who are mentally superior, it is at the fifth grade level that screening begins in earnest, utilizing scores from the California Test of Mental Maturity and certain other achievement tests and teacher judgment. Following this initial screening, the children selected are given the Thurstone Primary Mental Abilities Test, and those children having consistently high scores on one or more tests are identified for further study. At the same time, children are screened for exceptional talent in creative areas such as art, music, mechanical comprehension,

[9] Henry M. Gunn, "The Gifted Child and the Responsibility of the Elementary Principal," *California Journal of Elementary Education,* XXVI (May, 1958), pp. 222–223.

creative writing, drama, and social leadership. Standard tests and other techniques developed by school committees are used for this screening.

The type of enrichment program carried out in each building in Portland depends upon the community served by the school, the school's physical facilities, the faculty, and the children. Methodology in carrying out the program varies within the classrooms, but emphasis is placed on use of a variety of materials, independent explorations, critical thinking, and attention to leadership capacities.

While enrichment within the elementary school classrooms of Portland is the primary concern of school personnel, some special-interest groups in such areas as mathematics, science, foreign languages, creative writing, music, drama, and social leadership are formed and meet for short periods two to five times a week for special study.

Children are grouped by age with minor adjustments for differences in intellectual capacities. Though by no means the only teaching technique employed, the major portion of the children's learning experiences are centered about specific units of work. Individual, small group, and class projects form the basis for learning experiences, and each pupil is encouraged to contribute to the common theme in ways best suited to his interests, aptitudes, and capabilities.[10]

THE GIFTED IN SAN DIEGO

The program in the San Diego, California, city schools is limited to the top one-half of one per cent of the total school population, all with scores of 148 or above on individual intelligence tests. The reasons for using this score—three standard deviations above the mean—for selection of pupils were: the necessity to limit the size of the group for this experimental program and the observation that children in this group appeared to have more difficulty in their school adjustment than did those in the lower ranges of measured intelligence.

The responsibility of directing the program in the different elementary schools rests with the building principals, who are encouraged to experiment with the programs in their buildings, enlisting the aid of psychologists, teacher-consultants, visiting teachers, and supervisors and various specialists. The gifted children are placed with teachers

[10] Robert J. Havighurst, Eugene Stivers, and Robert F. DeHaan, *A Survey of the Education of Gifted Children,* Supplementary Educational Monographs (Chicago: The University of Chicago Press, 1955), pp. 87–89; and Clifford W. Williams, "Organizing a School Program for the Gifted," *Education for the Gifted,* 47th Yearbook of the National Society for the Study of Education, Part II (Chicago: The University of Chicago Press, 1958), p. 399; and, in the same Yearbook, Dorothy E. Norris, "Programs in the Elementary Schools," pp. 246–257.

who are deemed most capable of working with them. In-service education is provided for the teachers; San Diego State College offers summer workshops and classes on the mentally superior child. Three teacher-consultants carry responsibilities in major areas of curriculum and enrichment planning, interpreting policy, planning meetings for parent and school personnel, preparing and introducing lessons that provide enrichment for small groups of superior and gifted pupils, and providing assistance for teachers in effective use of enrichment materials. The teacher-consultants develop special assignments which the teachers can suggest to a single child or a group of superior pupils, most of the assignments being major undertakings which could last from three to twenty weeks.

The San Diego program is primarily one of enrichment, in which pupils continue in regular classes, with the number of superior pupils being limited to two or three per class. A unique characteristic of the program is that of cluster-grouping, in which individual classes contain either the high ability through the low-average ability, or the high-average through the extremely low. Classes are reorganized each year so that the "average" pupils attend variously with the high groupings and the low groupings. An evaluation of each school's program is made each year, and continuous planning is carried on so that the program may be improved.

ACCELERATION OF THE GIFTED

A second general method of providing for mentally superior boys and girls is that of acceleration. Though seldom used in isolation, this approach emphasizes the child's advancing to the next higher level or grade when his achievement indicates he is ready to undertake more advanced work.

A type of acceleration program found in Pittsburgh's schools provides that a child may enter school at an earlier age than he normally would. The University of Chicago Laboratory School has an accelerated program which covers the usual eight grades of elementary school in seven years; in this plan the superior child, with an IQ averaging 125 or 130, completes high school a year earlier than he normally would.

Junior high school pupils in New York City's "special progress classes" complete the three-year junior high program in two years, and enter the high schools one year ahead of "average" pupils. These special progress classes include about 3,000 pupils in 62 New York transition schools. A similar program exists in Baltimore's junior high schools. Careful consideration is given to the physical maturity of boys and girls who are accelerated according to this plan.

ACCELERATION OF PALO ALTO PUPILS

While the program for the education of gifted children in Palo Alto, California, Unified School District does not emphasize acceleration to the exclusion of enrichment and special classes, it does give a great amount of attention to the aspect of acceleration. The program in that district was initiated in 1953 with the formation of the District Gifted Child Committee for the purpose of studying existing provisions and methods of instruction for able pupils. By 1955, the process of determining the number of gifted children in the district had been completed by the school's psychological services. Individual intelligence scores based on the California Mental Maturity Test, plus the advice of teachers, counselors, and principals, were the criteria which determined the pupils to be included in the program. The committee collected information concerning other gifted programs in the nation, studied the data, and made recommendations. The committee's recommendations were: (1) that the problem be attacked through three avenues—enrichment, acceleration, and grouping; (2) that special attention be given the gifted student who achieves below his potential; (3) that a thorough evaluation be designed to parallel each aspect of the program, with special emphasis on what effect it would have on the social relations of the children involved; (4) that a director be appointed to establish, administer, and supervise a well-defined program; and (5) that a handbook be written which would state the district's policies governing this program, purposes in pursuing it, techniques for more precise identification of gifted children, and suggestions for ways in which a teacher could better provide for his most able students. All of these suggestions received administrative approval, and were implemented.

The Palo Alto schools use two approaches to acceleration: grade level acceleration and subject area acceleration, the latter having become known as the Advanced Standing Program. Here, as well as in the regular grade-skipping phase of the program, gifted pupils are accelerated after serious consideration of the pupil's mental, physical, social, and academic status by his principal, teachers, and parents. The percentage of pupils who have been accelerated has increased from the original five to ten per cent to the present 18 per cent of the gifted children, and indications point to a possibility that 25 per cent may be accelerated within the next few years. This represents the goal of the Palo Alto System.

Acceleration is used extensively in the area of mathematics, a program which starts in grade six when pupils showing high aptitude in arithmetic are encouraged to do seventh grade arithmetic in their sixth grade classes. Those who do superior work are given a seventh grade arithmetic examination in May; if the results indicate a thorough understanding of seventh grade arithmetic, those pupils are programmed into eighth grade arithmetic when they reach grade seven. Algebra is begun in grade eight, and the regular mathematics sequence is followed through grade eleven. In the twelfth grade, calculus or analytic geometry is offered as an advanced study course on the college level. Similar programs have been developed in areas of social studies, English, sciences, and foreign languages.[11]

SPECIAL CLASSES FOR THE MENTALLY SUPERIOR

Many school districts in the nation have initiated special classes for gifted children in an attempt to improve their educational opportunities. Hunter College Elementary School is a special school for the gifted; Allentown, Pennsylvania, Brockton, Massachusetts, Birmingham, Alabama, and Indianapolis, Indiana, bring gifted children from several schools together into a single special group. Colfax Elementary School in Pittsburgh supports a program of workshops for gifted children during a part of the day. University City (St. Louis) provides "enrichment classes" for about ten pupils who meet once or twice a week with a special teacher, and later share their special projects with other classes in the school in assembly programs or presentations to a particular grade group. Los Angeles elementary schools conduct a Special Work Program for Rapid Learners, involving pupils from some 24 schools who meet one morning a week in groups of 12–15 with special teachers.

THE MAJOR WORK PROGRAM IN CLEVELAND

One program for gifted children which dates its origin back to the 1920's still continues to the present. This is the Major Work Classes in the Cleveland, Ohio, school system. In this program, enrichment is stressed, but the principal emphasis is upon special groups of mentally superior pupils; there is no acceleration. Begun in the elementary grades, the "work" classes are carried on into the junior and senior high schools of the city.

The purpose of the special classes for gifted children with IQ's of

[11] District Gifted Child Committee, Palo Alto School District, *Improving the Instructional Program for Able Students* (Palo Alto: Professional Library, 1958), pp. 1–4.

125 or over is to cover more material than is covered in the regular classroom, and to cover it more thoroughly and meaningfully.

In order to determine pupils eligible for Major Work Classes, Cleveland school children are given group intelligence tests when they are in the high second, high fourth, and low sixth grades. Children whose scores are 125 or above are considered for the special classes; if their scores range between 110 and 120 IQ, they are included in enrichment groups within the regular classroom, there to study courses in the regular curriculum and to become involved in some features of the Major Work program. The school psychologist administers the Stanford-Binet individual intelligence test to those pupils in the group-tested higher echelons of measured intelligence. If the child maintains an acceptable score on this test, the home is contacted by the Major Work supervisor, and all of the child's potentialities are evaluated by a council composed of teachers, parents, principals, psychologists, and others.

Once accepted into the Major Work program, a child is placed in a combination 1–2–3 grade, a combination 4–5–6 grade, or a junior high, lower high school, or senior high school group, depending upon his age. Pupils in Major Work Classes tend to remain together during the elementary school experiences; they have constant contacts with other pupils in the school through regular physical education classes, club periods, orchestra, crafts, and the student council.

Regular courses of study set up by curriculum committees for the "average" child are the bases of study for children in the Major Work Classes. Enrichment of this program is left to the discretion of the specially trained teachers in charge of the classes, with due consideration of desires, needs, and interests of the pupils. Some areas of special instruction in music include singing, dancing, playing, listening, and creating; special art is under the direction of special art teachers; special language training for each Major Work Class includes a 45-minute period of conversational French each day. Methods of instruction include the discussion method, the research method, and the problem solving method, among others.

A commendable feature of the Cleveland program is its follow-up technique for Major Work Class pupils. Postal cards are mailed biannually, and the data on the returned self-addressed postal cards are studied by the school. Questions on the card include: (A) Name? (B) Address? (C) Where employed? (D) Position? (E) Where in school? (F) Present status? (G) Training for what? (H) Present ambition? (I) Remarks: (marital status, family, important events).[12]

[12] Theodore Hall, *Gifted Children—The Cleveland Story* (Cleveland: The World Publishing Company, 1956), pp. 1–90.

CONCLUSION

Part of the success of the foregoing programs of education for gifted children stems from the fact that the professional staffs involved realize that their particular programs are not the complete and positive answer to the education of mentally superior boys and girls. These programs are, as all should be, in a constant state of experimentation, and the curricula involved constantly emerge in improved forms. There now exists no positive best way to educate the gifted—or, for that matter, the lesser mentally endowed children. The sooner educators fully realize the implications of this statement, the sooner they will initiate programs in their schools which will meet the needs, interests, and potentials of our nation's greatest natural resource, our children.

Late research findings in the relationship between intelligence and creativity are pointing up some important implications for the work of elementary school principals, teachers, and lay persons. Recent studies indicating that grade point averages have a zero correlation with over-all ratings of success on jobs, and that creative pupils—possibly with intelligence quotients below the "gifted" range—often achieve equally high in scholarship as pupils with high intelligence but relatively low creativity, may necessitate a shift in thought by some school personnel. For one thing, principals and teachers will need to broaden their consideration of children and their progress through school beyond the results of intelligence and achievement tests. Secondly, principals will need to exert leadership in motivating teachers to encourage divergent thinking among pupils in the school; this will demand the ultimate in understanding on the part of adults in the school community, for creative children are less willing to accept adults' reasons for doing things, and are thus more difficult to handle. Children who are creative can no longer be termed "nuisances" in the classroom, and compelled to conform to all standard norms. They should be encouraged to be "different" within acceptable limitations, and to find answers for themselves.

Short Case 1

Pupils Progress Too Fast

Mr. Waters, principal of Dundee Elementary School, participated in a laboratory school experimental program for gifted children during the summer session. Many new materials were employed in this program, among them a reading kit, and Mr. Waters was enthusiastic about the possibilities for growth in reading skills resulting from proper use of the kit. He determined to secure several of the kits for use in his school's gifted reading program in the fall. Armed with statistics related to reading growth by the laboratory school youngsters who had used the kits, Mr. Waters called upon the superintendent.

Mr. Waters presented statistics concerning success of children who had used the kit in comparison with expected growth of the same children based upon national school samples, summarized the specific uses of each part of the reading program for the kit, and quoted the school price of the kit. The superintendent, however, disapproved the plan. He stated that teachers didn't like them, and complained that teachers in neighboring districts who had used the kits claimed the children progressed too fast, were no longer satisfied with the basal texts, and became discipline problems during reading period.

Problem: What is the crucial problem in this case? If you were Mr. Waters, what would you do now? Should Mr. Waters have used another approach to getting the kits in the schools other than going directly to the superintendent? How could Mr. Waters work through the faculty of his school to further encourage use of the kits? If teachers resist much teaching media for the reason indicated by the superintendent, how can the administrator help effect a change in their attitude?

Short Case 2

T.V. for Mentally Superior

Mr. Teller, principal of Grange Elementary School, called a faculty meeting during the pre-school orientation week in September. He told the teachers that for the present academic year the school would be included in a pilot television teaching plan for gifted children. The school was to be equipped with television sets for the four sixth grade and the four fifth grade rooms, and through using closed circuit programming, all fifth and sixth grade gifted children would have a course in literature. The sixth grade classes were also to have a televised course in South American history to be given three days a week for one semester.

An hour after the teachers received this information, a delegation of angry fifth and sixth grade teachers went to Mr. Teller's office and told him they highly resented this television nonsense and that they felt that they had always done a good job with mentally superior boys and girls in the areas to be covered. Three of the teachers went so far as to announce that if their teaching were considered to be so inferior that they needed television, they would offer their resignations immediately. The other teachers present seemed very sympathetic toward this attitude.

Problem: What, essentially, is the problem in this case? In this particular case, might the teachers' anger be justified? If so, how? How would you present the program for gifted children in a faculty meeting so that this situation would not occur? Try a role-playing situation in which you conduct a faculty meeting at which the proposed program for gifted children is presented. What might Mr. Teller do now to reassure the teachers?

Short Case 3

Against Segregation

The school board and administrative staff of Greenlawn Elementary School district decided during the summer recess that they would initiate special classes for gifted children for the next school year. They had studied this type of grouping and decided that it was a favorable plan. Teachers were contacted during August and informed of the change in structure. They were asked in the letter to prepare materials in order to teach the classes. Parents were informed of the plan the first day of school when the children concerned brought home a mimeographed letter.

At the end of the first day of school, many disturbed teachers sought out the principal to express their dislike for this program. They said they felt lost at sea, and just didn't know where to begin or how. The next morning principals of the district were summoned to an emergency meeting at the superintendent's office and were informed that parents had been flooding the switchboard with calls since the pupils had arrived home the day before. The parents, he stated, demanded that their children not be segregated at school.

Problem: What could have been done to prevent this situation? What must the superintendent do now in order to calm the storm of parental and teacher protest? How do you think teacher participation in policy planning operates in this district? How else might the school district have planned for special education for its mentally superior pupils? What are advantages and disadvantages of these plans?

Chapter Ten

Pupils with Problems: The Maladjusted and Handicapped

In Chapter IX the authors presented a treatise on one type of exceptional child, the mentally superior. There remain, however, still other children who deviate from the norm to such an extent that programs of special education must be provided for them if the American ideal of education for all the children of all the people is to be realized. Thus, many school systems in the nation provide programs for the mentally retarded, physically handicapped, and emotionally disturbed boys and girls in their districts.

Since the turn of the century, many of America's public schools have made provisions in their curricula for almost all levels of physically handicapped boys and girls, and some limited provisions for children who are mentally retarded. Still, it is estimated that well over half of the maladjusted and handicapped children in the United States are not being provided for in special programs in the schools. Slow-learning and handicapped children must receive more support from school-communities in America if their efforts are to result in productivity.

Handicapped children have the same basic needs as all other children. It is more difficult for maladjusted and handicapped children to meet the normal needs of growth and development, but their needs in these respects are no different from those of other children. Children who have crippling conditions of mind or body want to be considered as individuals and as contributors to democratic groups, as do all children, and they should be. Maladjusted and handicapped children, like all other children, will sooner or later find themselves in a world that extends beyond the limits of the family circle, and all must learn to live in that world. In short, the needs and interests of maladjusted and handicapped children are exactly the same as those of "normal" or "superior" children; the difference in most instances is not in kind, but in degree. The means adults employ in helping maladjusted and handicapped meet their needs and satisfy their interests are different in degree and in aims and outlook. In most cases, identical means are used to assist the maladjusted or handicapped child in growth, development, and learning as are used with other children.

In becoming well-adjusted individuals in a democratic society, children must learn to accept their particular handicaps. There is, however, a real difference between an attitude of blind, defeated acceptance and that of knowledge that one has gained mastery of his environment.

MALADJUSTED AND HANDICAPPED DEFINED

It is impossible, of course, to state a sweeping, all-inclusive definition that would properly describe all children who have handicaps of one sort or another. Included, then, in this section are separate definitions of three types of maladjusted and handicapped children: the mentally retarded, the physically handicapped, and the emotionally and socially maladjusted.

THE MENTALLY RETARDED

Most authorities agree that it is impossible to draw an exact line between borderline and mentally defective individuals. This is due, principally, to our inadequate means of measuring intelligence. Authorities agree, also, that an intelligence quotient of about 70 is usually acceptable as the bottom level for "normal" mental ability. Using that IQ as a standard, then one might arbitrarily place the mentally retarded individuals within the range of 50 to 70 IQ, as children with quotients below 50 are rarely found in public schools. Children within this arbitrary IQ range are usually educable to a limited degree, but are recognized as needing special instruction in separate class groups.

About 2 to 3 per cent of children are considered to be mentally retarded—one to every classroom, were the school population evenly divided.

Children in the 50 to 70 IQ range, sometimes referred to as morons, may learn reading in a mechanical manner, but should not be expected to achieve a great deal in comprehension. As adults, they may be adept at menial tasks, such as farm chores, doing simple sewing or carpentry, or rough painting. Children with IQ's between 25 and 50, often referred to as imbeciles, cannot be expected to cope with the demands of reading and arithmetic in the elementary schools but, with special instruction, they may learn to do very simple cooking, wash dishes, do very simple sewing, and certain extra-menial jobs around a farm. Very little learning is possible for children with IQ's below 25. Often individuals in this category, usually referred to as idiots, cannot learn even to dress themselves or to care for their ordinary cleanliness needs.

It is important for administrators and teachers to bear in mind that intelligence testing is not a tried and true procedure of measurement; the results of such testing can, at best, be considered only as an approximate index of a child's mental ability. A number of extrinsic or accidental factors may play a part in the measurement of intelligence; thus it is necessary that school personnel proceed with extreme caution when considering and acting upon the results of intelligence tests.

PHYSICALLY HANDICAPPED

Physically handicapped children in the schools are those who have orthopedic, heart, hearing, sight, speech, or certain other types of defects. Since the handicaps in this area are so varied, the schools must provide a varied program in helping individual children live with their defects and achieve to the best of their abilities.

Orthopedic defects appear in about one out of 100 persons below the age of twenty-one, and there are some 550,000 cases in this age bracket in the United States. Some children with these types of handicaps require bedside instruction. Children with orthopedic defects tend toward overageness and low IQ's.

Children afflicted with glandular or cardiac handicaps are provided for in the school, if possible, but they must be cared for in strict compliance with doctors' or hospitals' orders. Hearing defects can often be remedied by classroom seating arrangement, provided the defects are not too serious. Often hearing equipment in the classroom is necessary, and the mode of instruction should always be intelligent and sympathetic. Serious hearing cases may need to be referred and placed in special classes or schools.

Children with tuberculosis will require rest periods during the school day, and special classes and special food services may need to be provided. Special instruction in hospitals or homes may be necessary for tuberculosis patients. Children who are subject to epileptic seizures must have teachers with utmost competence in handling the situation during and following such seizures. If epileptic children are not admitted to the school, and there are many systems in which they are not, the school may provide a home consultative service.

If children experience difficulty by the age of five, six, seven, or eight years in making such consonant sounds as *P, B, M, W, H, T, D, N, G, K, NG, Y, F, V, TH* (as in *this*), *AZ, SH, L, S, Z, R, WH,* or *TH,* they probably are in need of help from the school's speech therapist. While many apparent speech defects appear in young children, they normally are outgrown in the first two or three years in school. But there are sometimes psychological reasons for speech difficulties, most often detected when a child hesitates in his speech or has a tendency to repeat words. Often such difficulties are caused by the child's being rejected, neglected, overprotected, or pressured, and it is the responsibility of the school personnel to make the child feel as secure as possible, to make him feel wanted and important. Children need to feel relaxed, not embarrassed because of their speech.

Special classes are necessary for the blind and partially blind children in the schools. Children defined as blind are those having, usually, not more than 20/200 visual acuity in the better eye with correcting lenses; or having a visual acuity greater than 20/200, but with a limitation in the field of vision such that the diameter of the visual field subtends an angle not greater than 20 degrees. These children will need Braille classes.

Policies of the school should favor leaving physically handicapped children in regular classes with proper safeguards whenever possible. Such children may spend most of their day in the regular classroom and have special periods when they will be provided with the necessary special help from a visiting teacher. Many physically handicapped children have made satisfactory adjustments in regular classroom situations.

EMOTIONALLY AND SOCIALLY MALADJUSTED PUPILS

Emotionally and socially maladjusted pupils include children who are psychotic, nervous, retiring, socially negative, or have problems of truancy, incorrigibility, or delinquency. Teacher-psychologist cooperation is necessary in most instances of these kinds, but in extreme cases of incorrigibility and delinquency, special classes are called for.

Many emotionally and socially handicapped children do not represent a problem for the teacher, but rather represent, now or in the future, a problem for themselves. These boys and girls may never succeed in making a satisfactory adjustment to society without trained assistance.

THE ROLE OF THE ELEMENTARY SCHOOL PRINCIPAL

Education for the maladjusted and handicapped is an area with which every elementary school principal should become familiar if he and his staff are to provide the best program possible for all the children of all the people. The principal, certainly, need not be a specialist in the treatment of ailments of maladjusted and handicapped children; indeed he cannot possibly be such an expert. However, planning the administration of a program which will best help such children meet their needs will be more successful if the principal has some knowledge of the characteristics and abilities of these boys and girls, and of how they can best achieve goals under the circumstances.

How the school and community accept and help children who are mentally retarded, have physical disabilities, or are emotionally and socially maladjusted, depends to a large extent upon the administrator's attitude and philosophy with respect to these boys and girls. A proper attitude toward maladjusted and handicapped children must permeate the entire elementary school if "normal" children are to accept the deviates into their social spheres; aims and objectives of special activities or classes for handicapped children must be clearly understood by all personnel in the elementary school building; teachers and their classes of children must develop a sympathetic understanding toward the special problems of maladjusted and handicapped students. Children in the "normal" categories in the school must learn to appreciate the pupils in special classes; see their problems; and understand that as individuals they are as important as anyone else, and deserve the same considerations and courtesy.

Socialization is an important aspect of handicapped children's development; with many it is a much more important area than is academic achievement. Success in life depends on an adequate socialization program for many children who are maladjusted or handicapped. Elementary school administrators must provide these children with opportunities for the development of good work habits, dependability, adequate body and eating habits, proper table manners, and other attributes of good citizenship in a democratic society. Integrating handicapped children into activity classes such as art, physical education, and music for periods of time, provided they can withstand the stress and strain of the activity, will help them learn to get along with others, and this concomitant learning will be carried over beyond school age.

Providing proper equipment for maladjusted and handicapped children in the classrooms and on the playground is within the realm of responsibility of the elementary school principal. Besides the usual equipment, such as cots, folding screens for individual work without interruption, work benches, and the like, the administrator should be aware of new equipment which is constantly being produced by manufacturers and which may bear trial. Where necessary, too, the principal must see that transportation for the pupils is provided.

One of the administrator's most important responsibilities with respect to maladjusted and handicapped children is that of establishing rapport with the parents. Often parents have guilt-feelings with respect to their handicapped children, and it is important that the principal transmit to these parents the feeling that he understands their situation and is willing to cooperate with them to the fullest to do whatever is best for the child. Good relationships between the school and the parents sometimes result in a lessening of tensions on the part of parents or of school personnel. It would not be amiss for the principal to visit the parents in the home, or to contact them at school when they come for conferences with the teachers regarding their children.

If a principal properly discharges his responsibilities with respect to maladjusted and handicapped children, they are much less likely to leave the school as misfits in the community and burdens upon society.

SPECIAL EDUCATION

A program of special education is generally accepted as the most effective means of providing for pupils with problems. Through such a program, the school community attempts to adjust its offerings to children's disabilities so that the abilities of exceptional children may be developed, just as the regular program attempts to provide for the needs of so-called "normal" children. Thus the democratic ideal of equal educational opportunity for all may be effectively achieved.

In addition to a program which will help children develop certain skills, a special education plan will provide boys and girls with opportunities to develop habits and attitudes essential for effective social adjustment. The philosophy of such a plan, it may easily be seen, is not different from that of a program for pupils in the normal educational procedure. An adequate program of special education will provide for instruction particularly adapted to maladjusted and handicapped children, but not at the expense of a broad basic education.

Such a plan will enable the pupils to adjust satisfactorily to their present environment, and will also assist them in finding means of effectively meeting new problems they will face in the future.

Some authorities favor programs of special education as carried out in special schools or segregated classes, where handicapped children will be free from the competitive aspects that creep into regular classroom situations, and thus be at liberty to pursue their individual problems and to meet their unique needs. In such an environment, proponents maintain, there is a smaller chance that the effects of social stigma will be in evidence, and the children will benefit from more attention as individuals. The chance that they will find they cannot succeed becomes lessened in such a segregated situation.

Opponents of segregation, however, point out that such a plan raises questions of psychological import. Some pupils, particularly boys, tend to revolt against the isolation and distinction of special classes or schools. Also, opponents of segregation hold that teachers feel less responsibility for handicapped children as individuals, and as a result tend to stress subject matter and to de-emphasize social development. Furthermore, segregated classes often tend to concentrate problems of behavior in groups where examples of good behavior are most needed.

School administrators and other personnel, then, are often faced with the dilemma of whether to provide for segregated schools or classes for maladjusted and handicapped children, or to intermingle these children having special physical, mental, or emotional needs with boys and girls who are deemed "normal." The best answer to this problem rests in the individual situation. In very small districts, of course, there is no need or occasion to establish segregated schools or classes, nor is it economically feasible. In large districts where the number of handicapped children is quite large, separate schools or classes are probably the more effective plan. There are studies which indicate that exceptional children, the gifted as well as the maladjusted and handicapped, are educated better, academically and socially, if they are segregated into schools or classrooms which are specially suited for learning experiences appropriate to their abilities or disabilities.

The special class, then, should be retained as a part of the elementary school building organization, with the teacher a regular member of the teaching staff directly responsible to the principal. In this way the children in the special education classes will be housed in a room especially adapted for their needs and located in the regular school building, and they will be accepted as a part of the regular school organization in the various activities which the attendance unit promotes. If the number of children involved is sufficient, a "center" might be organized by combining four or more special education classes in a regular elementary school with classes occupying the same position in the school as any of the individual graded classrooms. The center would be under the administrative leadership of the school's principal, and children in the classes would use the school's regular equipment and materials. Children in the center would have just as free contact with children in regular classes as the latter do with each other, but the teachers in the center would be trained in their specialized work. Class sizes within a school usually range from ten to eighteen, with the average being fifteen. From the point of view of the curriculum, the organization should be very flexible; far less ground will be covered than in the regular classroom, and emphasis will be placed on concrete, utilitarian aspects rather than on abstract, academic areas, though the latter will not be wholly neglected.

Selection of pupils for special education classes should come from recommendations of faculty members and the administrator, in collaboration with specialists in the various problem areas. Criteria might include oral and written examinations, physical examinations, psychological examinations, and subjective evaluation, with the child's mental health and home environment being areas of special consideration.

More than half of the states have set special requirements for teachers of special-education classes. In addition to the usual requisites of patience, understanding, and sympathy with special problems required of all teachers, teachers in special education should be persons who possess a high degree of contagious enthusiasm, and who maintain an exceptional ability to motivate children. Such teachers must incline slightly more in the direction of the practical than the academic, and possess a talent for manual work and artistic expression. Some states require that teachers have a master's degree; most require at least one year or more of regular teaching experience.

Methods used in teaching special-education classes must be indigenous to a school program that will ensure the maladjusted and handicapped boys and girls that school is both possible and worthwhile. The use of juvenile techniques and materials below the age level of maladjusted youngsters has a tendency to humiliate and insult rather than to help. Teachers of special education classes should constantly be on the alert for new techniques, approaches, textbooks, and subjects which will be beneficial in guiding the learning of their pupils. Instruction should be planned through the use of projects arising from the children's own needs and interests in everyday life, and audio-visual and other concrete aids should be used unsparingly to facilitate learning through the senses. A great deal of emphasis in programs for pupils with problems must be directed toward growth in social adjustment; handicapped and maladjusted boys and girls must learn the value of contact with others. This is the basis of an effective and happy life in a family and in a community.

Many excellent special education programs are in operation throughout the United States. Representative of programs found in the Far West, the East, and the Middle West are those in the Fresno, California, New York City, and Oak Park, Illinois, school systems. Discussions of those three fine programs are presented here to illustrate the fact that a recognition of the importance of special education for maladjusted and handicapped children exists in most areas of the nation.

Fresno's special education program.[1] Special education for maladjusted and handicapped children in the Fresno, California, City Unified School District includes separate programs for cerebral palsied children, the physically handicapped, the blind, the educable mentally retarded, and children needing assistance with speech and hearing. In addition, the district operates a work experience program for mentally retarded students at the secondary level.

Cerebral palsied children's program. The Sunshine School for cerebral palsied children, a cooperative program sponsored by the California State Department of Public Education and Public Health, is operated jointly by the Fresno City Unified School District and the Fresno County Health Department, with children from the city or the county being eligible for enrollment. Children who have been diagnosed as cerebral palsied may be referred to the admissions committee, which will screen the referrals by studying medical and psychological records and evaluations by teachers and therapists, when they are available. All placements in the program are on a trial basis, and any orthopedically handicapped child from age three and one-half to approximately fourteen years may be considered for placement in this school. However, priority is given to cerebral palsied children.

Requests for placement in the cerebral palsied children's school may be made by parents, physicians, crippled children's services, teachers, principals, or school nurses. Referral to the admissions committee is made by the Fresno system's director of special education at the request of the examining orthopedist, who also determines the eligibility of students for physical or occupational therapy.

Home and hospital instruction for physically handicapped. Any home or hospital bound school-age child in the Fresno district is eligible for home instruction if it is necessary for him to be out of the classroom for three weeks or longer. The child must, of course, be free from communicable or infectious diseases, and referral for the home

---

[1] Adapted from Board of Education Policy Handbook, Fresno City Unified School District.

instruction may be made immediately upon the child's withdrawal from school.

Referrals for home instruction are made directly to the Fresno district's Department of Special Education by the home, the family health adviser, or the school's principal or dean. Contact with the family health adviser is made by the Department of Special Education to secure permission to work with the child, and teaching service is begun immediately upon receipt of a medical recommendation for instruction. The school principal is notified when a student is accepted for home instruction, and before the student can be readmitted to school, a medical adviser's release should be obtained.

Oral training classes for the deaf. In the Fresno system, classes for deaf or severely hard of hearing children are available for those from the age of three and one-half through high school grades. Lip reading and skills of oral communication are taught along with regular academic subjects. Recommendations for placement in this program are made by an otologist at the request of parents, physicians, or school personnel. Referrals are made to the school nurse and to the department of special education; consultation with the special class teacher is necessary before placement is made.

Resource program for the blind. Educational provisions are made for blind children living in Fresno City or Fresno County at both the elementary and secondary levels. A resource teacher is available to work with the pupils, training them in techniques of Braille writing and Braille reading, securing for them necessary special materials, and guiding them to live and learn in a sighted society. Children in this program are enrolled in a regular class in the school for as much of the day as can be arranged, considering their academic development, knowledge of Braille skills, and social development.

Children who are eligible for the program for the blind in Fresno are those with 20/200 vision or less in the better eye after correction, those with a progressive eye condition as determined by an ophthalmologist, those who are educable as determined by all available information about the child, and those with the ability to adjust socially and emotionally to regular classroom programs. Referrals are made to the district's Department of Special Education by anyone in the community who knows of a blind child in the Fresno area.

Classes for the educable mentally retarded. Children of compulsory school age (eight to eighteen) are considered for placement in the classes for educable mentally retarded if they have been identified as mentally retarded through individual psychological study conducted by the Fresno district's Department of Guidance. When a teacher or principal finds that a child is not progressing normally, he makes the referral to the Department of Guidance on a form requesting individual study of the child. Arrangements are made for the child to be studied in school; if the results indicate a need for placement in a special training class, parents are contacted, the problem explained to them, and their cooperation enlisted. Prior to the child's placement, a letter of request is signed by his parents.

Speech and hearing service in the regular school program. The Fresno district, through its speech and hearing department, offers special help to the 7 to 10 per cent of the children in the district who have speech that is different from their classmates. A hearing screening program is conducted during the school year, and youngsters with a hearing loss are referred for medical care. If the hearing impairment has caused a speech difficulty, these children are included in the remedial speech program. If the hearing loss is severe enough to affect school work and the child cannot hear the teacher's directions or classroom discussions, he is referred for lip-reading instruction. These cases are accepted for special training after conferences with teachers, parents, and the school nurse.

One of the speech and hearing consultants visits each school once a week and makes arrangements with the principal for a room in which to work with small groups at the most convenient time. A referral sheet is left with each teacher, and she lists any children who have a noticeable speech problem. The consultant then plans with each teacher a twenty-minute period for these children to participate in a speech class of not more than five students. The consultant goes into each kindergarten room at least once a month to work with the entire class, on the theory that preventive measures may alleviate later problems, and so that children will realize that speaking correctly is fun.

Speech difficulties are classified as follows:

a. Stuttering: The stuttering child is usually nervous, tense, and excitable. Stuttering is characterized by:
   1. repetitions (My name is T-T-T-T-Tommy)
   2. prolongations (mmmmmmmmmmmy nnnnnnnname is Tommy)
   3. blocking (the mouth opens and contorts, but no sound is forthcoming)

b. Delayed speech: The child, because of shyness, emotional upsets, or immaturity, talks very little or not at all.

c. So called baby talk: The child has many sound substitutions such as "wed" for "red," "yitto" or "witto" for "little," "tum" for "come." He may leave out consonant sounds and have speech consisting mainly of vowels. He may use immature expressions, such as "Me do it."

d. Omission of sounds: He may say "ky" for "sky," or "ike" for "like."

He probably leaves off the endings of words. This could indicate a hearing loss.

e. Substitutions of sounds: He may lisp (th for s); other common substitutions are f for th, w for r or l, t for k, d for g, s for sh.
f. Organic speech problems due to cleft palate or cerebral palsy.
g. Voice disorders: Extreme nasality, highness or lowness of pitch, huskiness or hoarseness which is not the normal temporary change of puberty. An unusual quality of voice sets the child apart from his fellows.

If a speech problem becomes apparent, teachers and parents in the Fresno program are encouraged to arrange for an interview with the school consultant. Materials are available to help the child in the regular classrooms and at home. The curriculum speech and hearing committee has prepared a series of pamphlets, "A Guide for Parents," on stuttering, lisping, hearing, and sound substitutions. For the classroom teacher, "We All Speak, Why Not Speak Well," a handbook on helping in the classroom with the child's speech problems is available at the offices of the school principals.

In-service education is available to all teachers who serve on the speech and hearing curriculum committee. As a result, they are in a better position to differentiate between those children with speech problems which can be helped in the classroom, and those children who need additional help from the consultant.

New York City's special education program. In the past half-century, New York City's vast educational system has made great strides in its program of special education for the maladjusted and handicapped children and youth of the nation's largest metropolis. Among the varied aspects of the program are those dealing with the physically handicapped, the disturbed, and the mentally retarded. Begun in the city's elementary schools, the special education program extends, whenever possible and desirable, into the secondary schools of the system.

Program for the physically handicapped. The board of education's Bureau for the Education of the Physically Handicapped serves children with cardiac involvements, orthopedic conditions, neurological impairment, lowered vitality and/or nutritional deficiencies, and with such conditions as diabetes, hepatitis, epilepsy, arrested tuberculosis, skin disorders, allergies, and postoperative cases, at elementary, junior and senior high school levels. The Bureau strives to achieve as nearly as possible the general objectives of education: to aid pupils in their adjustment to their limitations; to maximally develop their residual powers in school, family, and community life; to provide continuity of education for children; and to promote education of and assistance from parents and lay persons with respect to the program for the physically handicapped.

The Bureau establishes special classes for the physically handicapped within the regular schools of New York City, where activities of these children are integrated with the regular school programs insofar as possible. Included in the integrating activities are assembly programs, audio-visual programs, excursions, shop work, special school events, and lunch periods. Children who are homebound are encouraged to affiliate with a neighborhood school so that they may participate in various activities.

Referrals for placement into the program for physically handicapped children are made by educational and medical authorities in New York City, and final approval for placement is provided by the Bureau for the Education of the Physically Handicapped. The school system provides special forms, available from school nurses or from the appropriate bureau of the Department of Health, for admission into and discharge and transfer from classes in the various areas of disability.

A wide array of services is available to the New York Bureau for the Education of the Physically Handicapped. The local board of education services include instruction by specially licensed teachers; guidance and counseling; itinerant teachers for the visually handicapped; special in-service courses; bus transportation; educational and vocational placement services; testing, research, and evaluation; curriculum coordination and materials; speech and lip-reading; audio-visual instruction; psychiatric services; radio and television; and availability of typewriters, radios, and sewing machines to homebound pupils. From the Department of Health Services, the Bureau has access to screening, referral, and follow-up by school nurses and physicians; medical recommendations for school placement; dental care; and provision for help by the medical director, psychologists, therapists, and attendants. Services provided by the State Department of Education include the provision of bulletins and curriculum materials; consultation with specialized personnel; guidance services; and teacher training through grants and workshops. A number of private agencies and parent groups are also available to provide services for the Bureau for the Education of the Physically Handicapped.

Additional services to physically handicapped children are provided in New York City's so-called "400 Schools," those designed to effect and maintain continuing education to children who are confined to hospitals or convalescent homes for two weeks or more, and to those placed in institutions and shelters for neglected and/or dependent children. The major considerations of the "400" schools are: to help the child adjust to the current situation in his new environment; to adapt the educational program to each child's total needs; to help the child grow and develop as normally as possible; and to provide specific materials of instruction, services, and guidance to facilitate the continuity of the child's educational program while in the "400" schools and upon his return to school and home.

Admittance to the "400" schools is made with the approval of the attending physician. The child is placed on the school register, and the teacher notifies the school from which the child came, requesting that the child's records be sent to the "400" school and that the transfer be made effective as of the date on which the child was placed on the "400" register. Appropriate forms are provided.

The curriculum of the "400" schools in New York City is essentially that of the regular schools, with curriculum adjustments and adaptations made in accord with the specific situation. Teachers who hold the health conservation license, indicating training in special health and related emotional problems, are appointed to classes in hospitals and convalescent homes. The common branch license entitling them to teach in the school subject matter areas, makes a teacher eligible for appointment to child care centers. Teachers assigned to either area are required to have personalities and training which equip them to work with children who have special health or emotional problems. Much of the professional growth of teachers in hospitals and institutions is achieved through close association with administrators, specialists in other professions, social workers, and parents; in-service courses, workshops, and conferences are often held for their benefit.

Services available to the "400" schools in New York are approximately the same as those described above which are accessible to classes provided by the Bureau for the Education of the Physically Handicapped.

New York's "600" schools for disturbed children. Approximately twenty-five schools in the New York City system are devoted to caring for boys and girls who are disturbed, and who have been unable to succeed in previous schools. The so-called "600" schools provide these children with treatment and rehabilitation in smaller classes with teachers who care about them, and with a curriculum comprising activities and experiences which are geared to the children's interests and needs. The pupils, who have experienced few emotional, educational, or social satisfactions in their lifetimes, come from homes and neighborhoods that are disturbed, tense, and disordered.

Teachers in the "600" schools approach their task from several levels or points of view: by considering each child as a unique personality affected by problems of deep concern to himself; by procuring the cooperation of various agencies in the city, such as child caring agencies, the Youth Board, Bureau of Child Guidance, youth squad of the police department, probation officers, mental hygiene clinics and vocational guidance counsellors; by enriching the backgrounds of these children so they may achieve a fuller life with greater satisfactions through exposing them to good music, literature, art, and various places of interest in the city; by giving them worthy models to emulate through units of instruction, assembly programs, examples of their teachers, and introduction to children of members of auxiliary groups who point up to these deprived children that life is a cooperative venture; by developing their interests through questioning and conversation, and through a variety of classroom and school activities in such areas as art, arts and crafts, various socializing activities, and a remedial reading program.

The curriculum of the "600" school provides for experiences in academic subjects, industrial arts, music, crafts, art, athletics, field days, trips, assembly programs, panel discussions, and many club activities. Units of instruction of interest to the children, encompassing a wide variety of activities and integrating all the curricular areas, are an important aspect of methodology in these special classes.

In-service education is carried out for teachers in the "600" schools, and consists of detailed discussions of the nature and background of the children in the schools; implications with respect to teachers' attitudes toward children, parents, clinics, welfare and social agencies, community groups, the courts, probation officers, attendance bureaus, and all other agencies having contact with the child and his family; readings and a discussion of the most recent literature dealing with the maladjusted child; visitations to classrooms in "600" schools; assignment of each trainee to full-day observations in a specific classroom to note routines, planning, manner of working with children; talks by the Bureau of Guidance team concerning its role in the "600" schools; and detailed discussions of specific case histories.

Education of the mentally retarded.[2] When the New York City Board of Education opened its first public school class for retarded children in 1902, the class proved to be the forerunner of one of the nation's current leaders in this area of special education. From that first class with its single teacher, the program has developed until today it employs more than 750 specially trained and licensed teachers to man the classrooms where more than 11,000 children and youths between the ages of five and twenty-one report each day for instruction and guidance in learning activities. Providing the program for children

[2] Bureau for Children with Retarded Mental Development, *Overview of the Work of the Bureau for Children with Retarded Mental Development* (New York: Board of Education of the City of New York, May, 1960).

of limited mental ability in New York is the responsibility of the Bureau for Children with Retarded Mental Development of the Division of Child Welfare, which plans, organizes, administers, and implements the facilities of special education for retarded children.

Children with Retarded Mental Development (CRMD) classes are provided for qualified pupils from kindergarten through high school levels in the New York system. Vestibule classes, for the youngest educable retarded children, with chronological ages from five to ten years and with mental ages up to about six years, offer a pre-school or kindergarten type program which helps the mentally retarded child become aware of himself as an individual, and introduces him to his responsibilities in relation to other persons in his immediate environment. Specially trained teachers and supervisors are given the first opportunity to evaluate the whole child in terms of his functioning level and indicated potential. When ready, the children are then promoted to the appropriate primary class in the Track I or Track II program.

Included in Track I are the educable mentally retarded children whose social adjustment, emotional stability, academic achievement, and intellectual potential indicate they would profit from a curriculum designed to take them through junior high school, and either the vocational or academic high school special class program in preparation for independent functioning with limited supervision on unskilled or semiskilled levels. Children in Track II are the educable mentally retarded who exhibit more limited social and emotional maturity and primary academic achievement, incompatible with success in a high school special class program. This curriculum is designed to offer pupils a classroom program through the junior high school level, and to prepare them for the specialized training program for pupils seventeen to twenty-one years of age that will ready them for employment in a closely supervised, sheltered, or partially sheltered working situation.

The Track II program for trainable severely retarded pupils is designed primarily to develop the self-help skills of the child and train him to operate more effectively, with direction and supervision, in his home and immediate neighborhood, or possibly in a very sheltered workshop or public or private residential school.

The special class program for Track I is based on a core curriculum which serves to integrate the eight curricular areas: social living, health and hygiene, social studies, language arts, mathematics, science, fine arts, and practical arts. The core program builds on the child's known environment from the limited circle of his home and family to his eventual adjustment in the community, and includes the following eight cores: home and family; the neighborhood; the larger community; the city; study of job areas; choosing, getting, and holding a job; spending one's income; and the worker as a citizen and social being. The Track II program proceeds more slowly than that of Track I, yet uses the core approach following the maturational development of the child in five major areas with descending order of emphasis: health and physical development, personal competency, social competency, avocational and vocational skills, and academic skills.

Referral to classes for the mentally retarded may be initiated by the parent or school principal, after initial screening by regular grade teachers or guidance counselors on the bases of observation, group tests, or other evaluating criteria. Eligibility for the classes is determined by the Bureau of Child Guidance, also a branch of the Division of Child Welfare, which makes its recommendations on the basis of specific eligibility criteria mandated by New York state law. The Bureau of CRMD determines suitable class placement on the bases of social and emotional development, chronological age, and physical and psychological findings. Educable mentally retarded children are defined as those with intelligence quotients of between 50 and 75; trainable mentally retarded have IQ's of below 50.

Twice each year, each teacher is required to review pupil profiles as indicated on her class personnel sheet, and recommend for retest pupils who seem to be functioning above or below their indicated expectancies. It is recommended that CRMD pupils be retested at three-year intervals. Inter-class changes, promotions, and transfers are authorized on the basis of chronological age, readiness, and pupil needs. Normally, a child spends three years with any one teacher; clustering of classes within a school provides for promotions within each school level and to the next higher level.

Legally, communities in New York State where there are ten or more pupils eligible for instruction in mentally retarded classes must provide classes for "educable" or "trainable" pupils, and the state provides financial aid to local communities to ensure implementation of the law. Legislation provides that classes be located in school buildings where there are classes of regular grade pupils of similar ages, and that the chronological age range of pupils within a class shall not exceed four years unless approval is given by the commissioner of education. To qualify for state aid, special classes must be limited to a maximum enrollment of fifteen for elementary school classes, eighteen for secondary classes, and ten for trainable mentally retarded classes.

A comprehensive program at Oak Park, Illinois. Based on the premise that the concept of education of the exceptional child is the recognition of a need for procedures for working with individuals in small groups, and holding a high regard for the rights of individuality which characterize a free society, the Oak Park, Illinois, public school system provides a comprehensive program in special education. The program, in addition to serving pupils in Oak Park, reserves space on a first priority basis to River Forest, Forest Park, and Berwyn, which are nearby neighboring suburbs. Children from twenty or more other suburbs are also taken on a tuition basis, thus enabling the neighboring communities to provide a convenient and quality facility for their special education needs. Consultative services to the nearby suburbs are also provided by the Oak Park office.

The Oak Park program provides special classes for the partially sighted, the orthopedically handicapped, the educable mentally handicapped, and the acoustically handicapped deaf and hard of hearing. Clinical services are also provided in speech correction, home tutoring, psychological services, and counseling services.

A child may be referred for special education services by the classroom teacher and/or the school nurse, through the building principal, parent, or a social welfare agency. The references are made to the Office of Special Education in Oak Park central offices. Following the study, which may involve conferences with parents, teachers, and physicians, as well as psychological examinations, recommendations for special placement are made to the teacher and parents. This information is returned to the building principal so that he may inform all persons concerned.

The various special education programs have been organized under the "Illinois Plan for Special Education of Exceptional Children," and have been developed according to standards set forth in each plan with modification as indicated by the unique needs of Oak Park children. Each program is located in a regular school building. When children are enrolled in a special program, it may be necessary for the child to remain in the special room placement for most of the school day because it is impossible for him to make a satisfactory adjustment in the regular classroom. However, arrangements may be made for a child to be enrolled in the special room, but to attend class for part of the day in the regular classroom. In the event that handicapped children have multiple handicapping conditions, the placement of the child in a special program is determined by the handicap which appears to be most pronounced. When an additional service is required for a child, that service is either brought to him, or he is transported to the location of the service; for example, a deaf child who is also cerebral palsied would be enrolled in the class for the deaf, but would be transported to the orthopedic center for physical therapy on an outpatient basis, upon the physician's recommendation.

The orthopedic program. In Oak Park's program for the orthopedically handicapped, children with the following types of handicaps are eligible for placement: convalescent-rheumatic fever; kidney infections; virus infections; long illnesses; postoperative cases; accident victims and those in casts; delicate children with cardiac cases or low vitality, or who are undernourished; cerebral palsied; spastics; athetoids; and congenital cases including dislocation, amputation, spina bifida, flat feet, club feet, post-polio, arthritis, diabetes, epilepsy, bone tuberculosis, Erb's palsy, muscular dystrophy, and torticollis.

Included in the orthopedic services are: home teaching for any child of school age of sound mind who may be absent from school because of illness, injury, or convalescence for a period of four weeks or more; physical therapy for children who are enrolled or who may come on an out-patient basis; enrollment in one of the orthopedic rooms with possible placement in the regular classrooms for part of the day; hot lunch program; additional resting facilities; and transportation to and from school.

The enrollment procedures in the Oak Park orthopedic program begin with the usual referral from the school nurse and/or teacher through the school principal, from a parent, or from a social welfare agency. A physician's report, plus a psychological report in appropriate cases, recommending that the child be enrolled in the program, must accompany the application for placement in the program. In addition, a request for a transfer from the school of residence must be submitted to school authorities. All children are placed in the orthopedic service with the approval of the director of special education.

The educable mentally handicapped program. Children who have been examined and recommended by a qualified psychologist are eligible for placement in the Oak Park mentally handicapped program. The school district provides a special curriculum for these children, designed to meet the needs, interests, and abilities of each child; individual case study records are kept to adapt the educational program to the pupil's changing needs, interests, and abilities. Transportation to and from school is provided by the Oak Park system.

Eligibility for the mentally handicapped program is determined by a state certified psychological examiner, with final decisions concerning eligibility made by a staff member of the state office of public instruction. Most children are eligible for re-examination every three years; however, in some instances in which eligibility is doubtful, the psychological examiner may recommend re-evaluation at the close of a six-month or one year period.

The partially sighted program. Children who are eligible for the Oak Park partially sighted program include: any child who, in the opinion of an ophthalmologist, would benefit by special class placement; children suffering from non-communicable diseases of the eye, or diseases of the body that seriously affect vision; children with serious progressive eye difficulties; children having a visual acuity between 20/70 and 20/200 in the better eye after refraction; and children who, on recommendation of an eye physician, can be placed in the sight saving class as a temporary measure if they are found to be in any of the following groups: children who have had eye operations, particularly enucleation, as a result of which readaptation in eye use or psychological readjustment is necessary; children under ten years of age having amblyopia exanopis or squint, when the good eye is being excluded; and children recovering from diseases such as measles or scarlet fever, which are likely to affect the eyes.

Included in the services of the Oak Park partially sighted program are: instruction with a minimum of eye strain; opportunity for sight-saving children to be normally adjusted educationally, socially, and emotionally by participation in regular class recitation and other activities not requiring close use of the eyes; teaching for conservation of remaining vision; and provision for vocational guidance to enable the child to occupy a useful place in an adult society.

All children seeking placement in the class for the partially sighted must be of normal intelligence, which may necessitate an examination by a state certified psychologist before or shortly after a child has been admitted to the program. As a part of the enrollment procedure, the child's eye physician completes the ocular report designed by the Illinois Society for the Prevention of Blindness. A new physician's report is required each year.

The acoustically handicapped program. In its acoustically handicapped program, the Oak Park school system provides for children who have not, or cannot, react to spoken language understandably through the use of a hearing aid. These children, designated as "deaf," must acquire language and speech skills by tactual, visual, and auditory methods. The program provides, too, for the "deafened"; children who have acquired language and speech naturally, but who have lost their hearing through illness or accident, and can no longer react to speech understandably through amplified sound. Also included in the program are the "educationally deaf," those children who have not learned to react understandably to language, but who can learn to understand language through amplification, such as a hearing aid. The program also provides for the "hard of hearing," those children who have acquired language and speech naturally and react to spoken language understandably, provided the source is brought near their hearing range, either by speaking loudly or by the use of a hearing aid.

Children who have these hearing handicaps are provided educational experiences in rooms for the acoustically handicapped, but attend some regular classes with hearing children of their own age. In this way they will have the opportunity to work, play, and socialize with hearing children so that they may progress both academically and socially. Children who are hard of hearing attend regular classes as well as the class for the acoustically handicapped, where they are given auditory training, lip reading, and other special help. The school district provides transportation to and from the center, when necessary.

An otologist's report, providing the diagnosis and recommending placement of the child, must accompany the application for admission to the acoustically handicapped program in Oak Park.

CONCLUSION

School services have steadily increased for children who are acoustically handicapped, visually handicapped, speech handicapped, orthopedically handicapped, mentally retarded, and emotionally disturbed. Desirable education in the modern American school is that which will develop the potentials of each individual to the optimum level. Elementary schools in this nation must extend the scope of education outward from the academic areas to include a real concern for each child and his total adjustment; they must provide opportunities for each child to achieve according to his individual and unique needs so that he can develop into a useful and happy member of society. Elementary school principals can spark these objectives by providing for flexible, continuous programs of special education, well-formulated and specific, with periodic evaluations. Administrators must provide for the special education program as an integral part of the regular classroom work wherever possible.

Short Case 1

He Can't "Catch up"

Jim Trueblood was placed in the special education program in Eventown's elementary school because of low scores on group and individual intelligence tests. Mr. Hadley, the principal, had encountered a very difficult time in convincing Jim's mother that the program was the best thing for him. The mother had finally consented, but had made it perfectly clear that she expected that Jim, within a short time, would "catch up" with his class again.

As time passed, it was found that Jim was falling further and further behind his class, and it became evident that he would never be able to rejoin his class or any other class in the regular program of the school.

Problem: How can Mr. Hadley explain the real situation with respect to Jim to Mrs. Trueblood? Try a role-playing drama in which Mr. Hadley and Mrs. Trueblood discuss Jim's situation. What implications are included in this case for all mentally retarded youngsters?

Short Case 2

Teacher Doesn't Adjust

Miss Lew had taught the special education room of Darlington school for twenty-two years. She had a group of children varying in number from twelve to eighteen over a period of years. Special education in the K–6 school included children who had physical, mental, and emotional disabilities or difficulties.

When Miss Lew was advised by her physician to take a year's leave of absence from the school, Miss Smith, a regular second grade teacher, agreed to teach in the special education room for the year. After a month in the room she became discouraged at the lack of evident achievement on the part of the pupils and decided that her disposition was not such as to cope with the demands of the special education program.

Problem: What can the school's principal do to help Miss Smith become better oriented, adjusted, and satisfied in the special education program? What are some grouping techniques with which Miss Smith might experiment with the children in her room? Are there implications here for others interested in this type of teaching?

Short Case 3

The Faculty Proposal

At Sunset School, in grades kindergarten through six, there are about fifteen to twenty children with serious problems in learning. The faculty, in a recent meeting, proposed that twelve of the children be selected for work in a new Opportunity Room which was to be opened in the school in September. The teacher for the room was to be named from one of the twenty-two teachers now employed at Sunset. After due process, the twelve children selected would be removed from the regular classrooms and placed in the new room. In this manner, the faculty thought that the children could receive special training in arts and crafts, music, and some of the less academic areas of school.

Problem: How do you feel toward the proposal of the faculty? What should be involved in the "due process" mentioned in the case? What are the implications involved in the curriculum proposed by the teachers?

Chapter Eleven

Guidance: The "Coming" Area in the Elementary School

A few years ago the curriculum director of a state department of education, while visiting a midwestern elementary school, mentioned to the principal that if he were a young man starting out in elementary education he would go into the field of guidance. "This," he said, "is the *coming* area in elementary education."

Such a statement has interesting implications for young people who are about to enter the teaching profession, or for those with considerable experience who would like to "branch out" into a relatively new area in the elementary school. Or is it new? Have not conscientious elementary school teachers through the years offered individual child guidance as an integral part of each school day? So they have—but this phase of their job has never been specifically listed as a part of the school curriculum. There is, however, a growing recognition of the necessity for a planned program of elementary school guidance: one aimed at achieving the primary need of children to be an important and accepted part of society. It is this more formal aspect of elementary school guidance to which the curriculum director referred.

With the growth of school populations and increase in the size of school units and school districts, there has come recognition of the need for special help for teachers, as well as for children, in the areas of child guidance and counseling. Society all around us gives evidence of the need for guidance in personal, social, educational, and vocational areas. Statistics reveal that juvenile delinquency is on the increase; diseases caused by tension incapacitate, or even kill, many persons; there is a heavy demand for psychological and psychiatric services; there is waste of ability. All of these factors emphasize the need for increased formalized guidance services during a child's formative years as he progresses through the elementary school.

WHAT IS GUIDANCE—AND COUNSELING?

Child guidance in the elementary school is, simply, a process of helping each child to discover and develop his potentials to the fullest. Guidance, as a process by which direction is given to the curriculum, assists in individualizing the educational experiences of children in the schools.

Froehlich states that "guidance services may be defined as those services which are designed to help the school adjust the pupil, and to help the pupil to make adjustments to the school and to life."[1] Mortensen and Schmuller define guidance as "that part of the total educational program that helps provide the personal opportunities and specialized staff services by which each individual can develop to the fullest of his abilities and capacities in terms of the democratic idea."[2]

Over a period of time, the scope of education has been extended to include a concern for the child and his total adjustment. Educators have recognized that a child must have good physical and mental health as well as sound social and emotional development if he is to learn to the optimum of his capacity. Even though an emphasis upon sound, formal guidance programs at the elementary level has been delayed, educators have recently become more concerned with this area, textbooks on elementary school guidance have been published, colleges have developed courses devoted exclusively to the subject, and many school systems have set up organized guidance programs for their elementary units.

The heart of the guidance program is its counseling services, the person-to-person aspect of this program. Counseling is that part of the guidance program intended to offer a specialist's assistance to another

---

[1] Clifford P. Froehlich, *Guidance Services in Schools* (New York: McGraw-Hill Book Company, Inc., 1958), p. 8.

[2] Donald G. Mortensen and Allen M. Schmuller, *Guidance in Today's Schools* (New York: John Wiley and Sons, Inc., 1959), p. 3.

person in increasing the latter's understanding and ability to resolve his problems.

Currently there are three areas of thought with respect to types of counseling: (1) the non-directive or client-centered approach; (2) the directive or clinical approach; and (3) the eclectic approach. In the non-directive approach, originated by Dr. Carl Rogers at the University of Wisconsin, the counselor encourages the individual to express freely his thoughts and feelings, and the counselor himself does not direct, but merely reflects these thoughts and feelings. This reflection allegedly aids the individual in understanding himself and his problems. The structure of the counseling sessions is a free, permissive, and acceptive atmosphere. The directive or clinical process is characterized by a definite procedure which the counselor follows. These steps have been listed by Williamson and Darley as follows:

1. Analysis of data concerning student.
2. Synthesis of data so as to reveal assets and liabilities of the student.
3. Diagnosis of the problem by clinicians.
4. Prognosis or prediction by clinician of the future development of the problem.
5. Counseling to improve the student's adjustment.
6. Follow-up to further assist student and check on counseling.[3]

The eclectic approach to the counseling process assumes the point of view that both directive and non-directive procedures have good points, and the more desirable aspects of both are used. Proponents of this approach believe it more readily lends itself to the specific situation at hand.

WHY GUIDANCE IN THE ELEMENTARY SCHOOL?

There are many characteristics of the elementary school which make it an ideal beginning place for guidance in the educational framework. Because elementary school children are still young, guidance for these children can be preventative as well as remedial in approach. If the child of elementary school age does have problems, they are usually of fairly recent origin, and can usually be solved much more easily than problems of longer duration. In addition, since he is so young, the elementary pupil is not as fixed in his behavior patterns as an older child, and any unacceptable behavior patterns can be altered more quickly and easily. Because elementary school teachers generally teach children in self-contained situations, they have more opportunity for study of the whole child. They can recognize problems peculiar to

[3] Mortensen and Schmuller, *op. cit.*, p. 316.

individuals, and can work steadily with the child for resolution of these problems.[4]

Frequently, the remedial function of guidance programs receives the greatest emphasis in elementary schools, although it is considered to be the least effective of the functions. It is important for the teacher and others working in a program of guidance to know the developmental patterns of children, and to be able to distinguish short term upheavals in behavior as part of the regular maturation process, or as warning signals that something is really wrong. It is tragic when a child with problems too big to handle alone gets no real or lasting help until he is picked up by the law. Then the pattern of his life is set, and it is often too late for assistance with troubles that are deep-seated. If guidance in the elementary schools could be a continuing, developmental, preventative program, the need for remedial guidance would be greatly alleviated.

Effective programs of guidance are based on the premise that human beings need help—that all persons, regardless of age, have certain basic needs that must, and will, be met. How they will be met depends upon the guidance a person provides for himself, or that which is provided for him by someone else. Children, especially, are often too immature to recognize and isolate their problems, much less solve them, without the aid of adults. How much better it is, for example, when a child, through assistance, learns to channel his energy to learn to read or to solve arithmetical abstractions, rather than to throw rocks on the playground in order to satisfy the universal need of gaining status with peers. Experience has proved that when a child attempts the rock-throwing method of gaining status, the exact reverse of what he wishes occurs—but a second or third grader is unlikely to know this unless some mature adult helps him establish a more socially acceptable and intellectually satisfying pattern of behavior. Situations occur in children's lives, as well as in adults', when it becomes necessary to seek aid in order to make wise decisions. A child may find this aid in the school if an effective guidance program is in operation. A good guidance program is concerned primarily with the outlooks, insights, attitudes, appreciations, and behavior of pupils in their process of growth and development; it seeks to assist individuals or groups in choosing a line of action, a method or procedure, a goal.

The needs and values of our society in general provide the bases for effective school guidance services. Technological advancements have catapulted our culture into an age of specialization and automation. This, along with the rapid tempo of modern, urban life, has tended

---

[4] Ruth A. Martinson and Harry Smallenburg, *Guidance in Elementary Schools* (Englewood Cliffs, N.J.: Prentice-Hall, Inc., 1958), pp. xiv-xv.

to increase the number and depth of individual problems, even within the elementary schools. Statistics record the rising incidence of mental illness. Something must be done to help preserve the mental health of coming generations! Part of the answer lies in effective programs of guidance in our schools.

Guidance services rendered to the individual involve counseling which stimulates the child to evaluate himself and his actions, decide upon a course of action, accept responsibility for his choices, and initiate a course of action related to those choices. Guidance services rendered to the instructional staff involve assisting teachers in understanding pupils, providing in-service education activities, and providing a ready referral service. Guidance services rendered to administration include assistance in curriculum development or improvement, provision of pertinent pupil personnel data, and provision of a liaison with the community.

Peters lists these tasks of guidance personnel which point up tacitly the reasons for guidance in an elementary or secondary school:

1. Pre-registration advice
2. Admission and registration advice
3. Orientation of students to their new surroundings
4. Receiving, making, and keeping up-to-date complete cumulative records
5. Intelligence and achievement testing (kept to a minimum)
6. Securing educational and occupational information and making it available to students, teachers, and counselors
7. Counseling each student regarding:
   a. Personal and social adjustment
   b. Vocational plans
   c. Educational orientation
   d. Health problems
8. Coordination of the efforts of administration, teachers, and guidance personnel as regards the guidance program.[5]

COLLECTING AND USING DATA ABOUT CHILDREN

Before school personnel can adequately guide children in their school-connected activities, it is necessary that as much information about the pupils as possible be obtained through a systematic procedure. Anecdotal records, obtained through teacher observation of

[5] D. M. Peters, "Guidance, A Basic Need," *Illinois Education,* XLVIII (October, 1959), pp. 56–58.

the child, are probably the most common and valid means of data-recording. Daily classwork, including creative activities, is a fruitful source of information. Sociometric devices, such as the sociogram, role-playing, classroom social analysis, and the sociodrama, are useful devices in determining the child's behavior in relation to his peers. Achievement tests and diagnostic tests, judiciously used, reveal much information about the pupils' problems of learning in the academic areas. The information gathered from all of these sources, and possibly others, is generally kept in the pupils' cumulative folders which are readily available to teachers or others involved in the guidance program.

Parents, doctors, school psychologists, nurses, psychologists, social workers, visiting teachers, churches, youth organizations, and various other specialists are all potentially helpful sources of information regarding children in the school.

The information gathered by the above-named means assists teachers and other guidance personnel in what Cottingham refers to as the three functions of the guidance program: (1) assisting children in personal adjustments; (2) assisting children in social or group adjustments; and (3) assisting children with academic or learning problems.[6] In Cottingham's opinion, the groups of inventory data proposed by Wrenn and Dugan offer a satisfactory framework for collecting facts for the guidance of children. This framework includes: (1) scholastic aptitude; (2) scholastic achievement and basic skills; (3) special abilities: clerical, mathematical, artistic, and the like; (4) interests and plans; (5) health and physical status; (6) home and family relationships; (7) emotional stability and social adjustment; (8) attitudes; and (9) work experience.[7]

In well-organized guidance programs, the amount of paper-work involved in record-keeping becomes quite voluminous and time-consuming. Sometimes such preparation of data is delayed to the point where it becomes of little, if any, use to teachers, counselors, or others directly involved in the guidance program. For several years guidance personnel have sought a means of keeping current records readily available, thereby making information available when it is most useful, and thus most able to benefit students. Recently, guidance personnel have been investigating the possibility of using modern data-processing machines to assist in collecting and recording pupil personnel data.

In the spring of 1960, the Bureau of Guidance of the California State Department of Education initiated a study of the processing,

---

[6] Harold F. Cottingham, *Guidance in Elementary Schools* (Bloomington, Ill.: McKnight & McKnight, 1956), p. 2.

[7] *Ibid.*

recording, and utilization of pupil personnel information, the study being financed by funds from the National Defense Education Act of 1958. Purposes of the study were: (1) to secure data on current pupil personnel practices, and determine the feasibility of setting up a state-wide integrated data processing system; (2) to establish a pilot data processing center to test procedures in an operational setting; and (3) to consider the establishment of a state-wide network of data processing centers.[8] A committee was selected by the state superintendent of schools to investigate programming, pre-registration and registration, testing, reporting to parents, attendance accounting, statistical reports, and cumulative records. While this particular study dealt with guidance at the high school level, it was expected that many findings would be applicable to a program for elementary schools.

WHO PERFORMS THE GUIDANCE ACTIVITIES IN THE ELEMENTARY SCHOOLS?

Personnel involved in planned guidance activities at the elementary level vary with each individual situation. The principal or administrator certainly has an important role to play if the guidance program of the school is to be a success. A bulletin issued by the California State Department of Education lists these major functions of the principal in developing and carrying out a satisfactory guidance program in his elementary school:

1. The principal helps the staff to develop a sound philosophy of guidance.
2. The principal takes the initiative in organizing the school's program of guidance services.
3. The principal provides for in-service education of the staff in guidance principles and procedures.
4. The principal coordinates the guidance program.
5. The principal provides direct counseling services to pupils when needed.
6. The principal encourages the staff to evaluate the effectiveness of the guidance services.[9]

Foster has pointed up the duties of the principal in the guidance program, as follows:

[8] Alvin Grossman, "Integrated Data Processing Study," *California Schools,* XXXI (June, 1960), pp. 304–305.

[9] California State Department of Education, "Good Guidance Practices in the Elementary School," *Bulletin,* XXIV (Sacramento: the Department, August, 1955), pp. 3–4.

1. Provide personnel for the guidance program.
2. Provide facilities (office space, secretarial help, tests, and supplies).
3. Help in program planning so that teachers can have free time for guidance functions.
4. Help in organizing and supporting a guidance committee to serve as a policy-making and advisory body in the area.
5. Contribute professional leadership to the guidance program by suggesting activities and by helping carry them out.
6. Contribute professional judgment to the handling of guidance situations through helping in group and individual counseling as necessary.
7. Help to provide for the in-service education of the school staff in guidance activities as one of the important areas of education through providing for consideration of this work in staff meetings; through occasional scheduling of extension courses, workshops, or other in-service training programs; and through cooperating with staff members who are furthering their training by university class attendance and other means.
8. Help in interpreting the guidance program to the public.[10]

The counselor aids the principal in planning and evaluating the elementary school guidance program. Counselors have been growing in number and effectiveness throughout the country in the last few years. The counselor's role in the program, according to Foster, is (1) to counsel with individuals and with groups; (2) to work as an adviser to teachers regarding guidance; (3) to give leadership to the guidance program; (4) to provide testing services and analyses; (5) to provide record services and interpretations; (6) to provide educational and occupational information; and (7) to know the guidance resources of the school and community.[11]

William Newman has provided a description of the various jobs of the counselor and the approximate percentage of time spent by the counselor in each area at the Potomac School in Bakersfield, California.[12] The following is a summary of the counselor's duties as reported by Newman:

Individual counseling (12 per cent). Counseling with children comprises the major job in this area. Home calls and interviews with parents of children with problems are also included.

Records and reports (12 per cent). Written reports help keep teachers fully informed of the counselor's activities and progress with

---

[10] Charles Foster, *Guidance for Today's Schools* (Boston: Ginn and Co., 1957), pp. 16–25.

[11] *Ibid.*

[12] William H. Newman, "A Full-Time Counselor in an Elementary School," *Elementary School Journal,* LVI (April, 1956), pp. 355 ff.

children from their classes. Some time is spent completing interview reports for filing in case folders. These reports are necessary for a continuous smooth-running program and for any study and evaluation of cases. A few reports are required for the principal and the district's central office.

Administrative assistance (12 per cent). Although undesirable, it seems the counselor is often called upon to fill the role of administrative assistant. For example, when the principal is absent from the building the counselor often acts as head of the school. Many counselors also display a tendency to go ahead and do something that needs to be done, even though it is an administrative or clerical chore.

Group counseling (8 per cent). Two groups were formed for children whose behavior took an aggressive form. Another was organized for the shy, withdrawn child. By being organized into school "helper" clubs, these children were provided with opportunities for expression without engaging in aggressive activities at the expense of the more "normal" children in the classrooms.

Health (8 per cent). It is the counselor's job to screen all referrals from teachers regarding the health of children. He takes care of those cases in which he is able or qualified. The others he refers to the nurse, who comes to the school two half-days a week.

School-wide guidance programs (5 per cent). As a co-worker with the principal, teachers, supervisor of instruction, and supervisor of child welfare and attendance, the counselor, in grade-level meetings, works on school-wide guidance needs. School-wide emphasis might be given to "Don't Be a Litterbug Week," "Please and Thank You Week," and others. The counselor spends some time implementing the plans made cooperatively by the staff group.

Attendance (5 per cent). Clerks do the routine attendance work, but the counselor makes home calls in case of unverified absence, absence of truants, and absence of considerable length. The counselor works closely with the child-welfare and attendance supervisor on the problems that arise.

Welfare (5 per cent). The counselor serves as welfare chairman for the Parent-Teachers Association; and in this connection has processed short-term lunch loans, the giving of used clothing to children who would be unable to attend school without it, and the referral of more serious cases to other agencies through the child-welfare and attendance supervisor.

Planning (5 per cent). Included in planning is evaluation. Past activity must be evaluated in order to make the best plans for the coming week. Long-term planning includes deciding proportionate amounts of effort to be expended in each broad area, and it deals with how emphases are to be varied in each area during the progress of the school year.

Teacher consultation and case conferences (5 per cent). This area includes conferences involving teacher, principal, director of special services, supervisor of child welfare and attendance, and parent; also, informal talks with only one or more of these persons about a particular child or guidance problem.

Student activities (5 per cent). City-wide activities involve school participation in such events as spelling bees, talent contests and the like. The counselor helps organize these functions which give him the opportunity to meet and know more children in the school. The counselor also works with the student-body organization.

Safety committee (3 per cent). This committee is made up of a group of children elected as representatives from various classrooms to encourage safe and proper conduct in the halls and on the playground. The counselor is the adviser to this group.

Referrals to other agencies (3 per cent). Cases for which the counselor is not qualified must be referred to psychological, health, and welfare organizations. All these referrals are re-screened by the director of special services.

Talks to classes (3 per cent). The counselor often speaks to various classes in an effort to promote some type of better behavior.

Testing (3 per cent). The counselor does not take any of the testing load from the teacher's shoulders, but he does give leadership in the testing program. He is a resource person on test administration, interpretation of results, and analysis of group data. A small amount of his time is spent in giving additional tests where previous results have been doubtful.

Enrollment (3 per cent). Enrollment after the beginning of school is the responsibility of the counselor. He does some testing to insure satisfactory placement.

Informal contacts and observations (3 per cent). The counselor spends some time in the classroom and during recesses observing children whom he is studying.

Of all school persons, the elementary school teacher, because of his strategic position, has the greatest guidance potential and responsibility. The most widely used approach to elementary school guidance is through the classroom, in which the teacher is made the primary agent in the use of guidance techniques, with the specialist being used only on a referral basis, or when problems are beyond the teacher's competencies. Foster points up the role of the teacher in guidance, as follows:

1. To know the students as individual personalities.
2. To orient them to their work in the class.
3. To help them develop effective ways of working.
4. To help provide good learning conditions.
5. To conduct and participate in group guidance activities.
6. To counsel students as individuals and in groups.
7. To secure information about the students.
8. To know the guidance resources of the school.
9. To consult with parents and other teachers.[13]

Guidance activities of a teacher are illustrated by the activities of a second grade teacher who read the story, "I Want to be a Teacher," to her children. Following the reading of the story, she developed an interesting discussion motivated by the questions: "How many of you want to be teachers?" and, "Have you thought about what you want to do when you grow up?" Then she directed the children to write a creative story or poem using the title, "When I Grow Up."

Later, the same teacher read, "I Want to be a Pilot," and in role play the children became pilots, stewardesses, and tower control men. They had fun, and they learned. They built an airport to extend their knowledge. One little boy read the book, "I Want to be a Baker," to the class, and surprised his classmates by passing a pan of rolls he had made.

Teachers should learn to use guidance techniques to supplement and extend their effectiveness as teachers by acquiring a thorough knowledge of how children grow, develop, and learn, and then by following a definite plan that will meet the needs of each particular child and group of children.

There appears to be a significant trend in the field of elementary school guidance work toward the inclusion of social workers in the program. The school social worker supplements the work of the teacher, aiming to make her work more effective within the framework of the classroom. School social work is an inter-disciplinary approach to helping and understanding children. It employs members of related professional disciplines, who bring their specialized knowledge and services to the program to cope with problems that interfere with the child's use of educational opportunity.

The school social workers are assigned to the schools of the system as members of the school staff. They work with individual children in regularly scheduled interviews, hold conferences with parents, refer to and hold conferences with community agencies, take care of attendance problems, take care of welfare need referrals, hold conferences with classroom teachers, and conferences with administrators

[13] Foster, *loc. cit.*

within the schools. In a study of fourteen communities, made by one of the authors' classes in 1960, it was found that the majority of the school systems required the school social worker to hold a regular elementary school state teaching credential. In addition to professional education, school social workers specialize in areas of the understanding of human behavior, facility in the effective use of community resources, and skill in the social casework method.

School social workers are known by a variety of names, but their functions are basically the same. Originally designated as "visiting teachers," they are now commonly referred to as "adjustment-remedial teachers" or, simply, school social workers. Typically, children are referred to the school social worker by the teachers, parents, principals, supervisors, other school personnel, by the child himself, or by community agencies. Referrals are made on the basis of any difficulty which appears to be affecting the child's general adjustment. The social worker makes a clear case study of each child so referred, and initiates a plan of treatment or action. He may refer the child and his family to an outside community agency, or to professional psychological or psychiatric services outside the school. He may make home visits to confer with the parents. He may have some cases which must be handled through the juvenile courts and child welfare agencies. He may refer the parents to a marriage counseling service. Whatever the plan of treatment, the collaboration of other special service personnel within the school is vital to the effective functioning of the school social worker. Often the school social worker is expected to engage in research, to help train those new to the services, to participate in curriculum planning, and to handle certain not-too-well-defined administrative responsibilities.

In general, school social workers are under the same basic personnel policies as a regular classroom teacher. The length of the school year and the school day are the same for both types of school employees; attendance by social workers at professional meetings on local and state levels is required. Housing for the social work program appears to be a major administrative problem in the systems studied; most are housed in whatever left-over space is available, with workers interviewing behind screens in the halls, in boiler rooms, in janitorial supply closets, and in the social workers' cars.

According to the results of this study, school administrators and social workers alike seriously questioned the value of time spent in keeping records in the majority of school systems. Only one of the fourteen school systems studied provided clerical assistance to the social workers. Caseload size varied from system to system, according to the types of cases and the number of schools assigned. Five of the systems indicated a caseload size of between 35 and 50 but, in general, no standard figure for caseload had been set. In the majority of the systems studied, four days a week are spent in direct service to children, parents, and school personnel, and a fifth day is reserved for office work, administrative planning, and supervision.

The school administrator is the key person in the social work program. He should not blindly accept the program because it has worked elsewhere, but should work out a program to meet the specific needs of his own school.

HOW ARE GUIDANCE ACTIVITIES CARRIED OUT?

Many elementary schools and school districts have some form of guidance program or facilities now in operation. The special staff personnel range from one psychologist or psychiatrist to a specialized department of such personnel. The size of the department depends mainly upon the size of the school or district itself. There is considerable variation, however, in the facilities available for guidance even among districts of approximately the same pupil population size. These appear to be due principally to differences in administrative philosophies in regard to the need for guidance services in the particular district involved.

All schools have the basic ingredients for a guidance program. If these schools are to help children come safely and happily through the crucial formative elementary school years, they must provide realistic guidance to help students achieve mental, emotional, and social well-being. But guidance must remain what it has long been—an intrinsic part of teaching.

Wrenn sees both the individual and team functions of teachers and counselors when he states,

> A teacher stimulates intellectual understanding, helps with mastery of knowledge, arouses curiosity, and provides students with a sense of achievement. A counselor contributes to students' self-understanding, to the making of realistic and personally meaningful life plans, to growth in social maturity. He helps the student discover who he is and how he can become what he wants to be within limits of his capacity and needs of our culture.[14]

An effective guidance program in any school depends not only upon the organization, but also upon the personnel working together in the

[14] C. Gilbert Wrenn, "Guidance—an Overview," *National Education Association Journal,* XLVIII (January, 1959), pp. 16–18.

school district. The classroom teacher serves as the core of the elementary school guidance program, but the best idea of the roles of the school personnel in guidance can be gained by thinking of them as a team which consists of the school administrators, the teacher, the counselor and special guidance personnel, the supervisor of curriculum, the supervisor of instruction, the parents, and the pupils.

The manner in which guidance activities are carried out—the manner in which these teams actually operate—may best be observed by noting brief descriptions of the organization and functions of the guidance services of several school districts. But before that is done, it may be in order to note what Barr states are guide-lines to guidance philosophy:

1. Guidance should help people to assess their abilities and liabilities and to use that knowledge effectively in coping with their environment. Both the welfare of the individual and of the group must be considered.
2. Guidance is developmental, preventive, and remedial in nature. The more effective the developmental phase, the less emphasis will need to be put on the preventive and remedial.
3. Guidance should recognize the maturation level of the pupil and expect performance in keeping with that level.
4. Guidance should attempt to locate the assets of each child and capitalize on those assets. Success in one area tends to generalize into other areas.
5. Guidance services should be for all children: the typical, the gifted, and the maladjusted. Frequently the maladjusted receive most of the attention.
6. Teachers should be aware of the needs of their pupils and know methods for meeting those needs. They should realize that unsatisfactory behavior usually indicates that those needs are not being met satisfactorily.
7. There are few "wonder drugs" in the field of guidance. Attitudes and problems which have taken a long time to build are not ordinarily subject to quick change. They take time and patience to alter.
8. The teacher should be a professional person. Professional ethics demand that teachers keep information about students and parents confidential. It is also expected that teachers will be as objective as possible in dealing with both data and with counselees.
9. The teacher should recognize his limitations in dealing with guidance problems, and should make referral to the proper agencies when necessary.
10. Many factors may influence the pupil's behavior. Guidance,

therefore, is concerned with the home, the community, the peer group, and the school as each affects the child.[15]

CLINICAL SERVICES AT NEWARK

The city of Newark, New Jersey, was one of the first large cities to develop a center of clinical services, for many years a function of the Bureau of Child Guidance. Newark has now integrated its special services under the leadership of an assistant superintendent.

The *Administrative Guide for Special Services* in the Newark Public Schools indicates that the range of services includes: (1) Bureau of Attendance, dealing with child welfare and school census; (2) Bureau of Health Education and Service; (3) Bureau of Child Guidance (clinical services); (4) Department of Secondary School Guidance; and (5) Department of Special Education (speech therapy, and services for handicapped children).

The purpose of the Bureau of Child Guidance is to provide services to teachers and children through visiting teachers (psychiatric case workers), clinical psychologists, and a psychiatrist. Visiting teachers are assigned to two elementary schools each. Psychologists are responsible for problems involving questions of learning capacity, intelligence, and placement.

Visiting teachers assist the classroom teacher "to bring about a better school adjustment with children who have personality, emotional, or behavior problems."[16] The visiting teacher studies the home and the child and works with the classroom teacher to achieve an understanding of the case at hand.

Following are types of problems which are referred to the visiting teacher (psychiatric case worker):

1. Behavior problems.
    - (a) The child who "shows off" or who annoys constantly by his demands for attention.
    - (b) The child who lies or steals.
    - (c) The child who resents authority.
    - (d) The bully or braggart.
2. Personality problems.
    - (a) The sensitive child who cries easily.
    - (b) The daydreamer.
    - (c) The immature child who does not fit into the group and who is too dependent.
    - (d) The child who has fears.

---

[15] John A. Barr, *The Elementary Teacher and Guidance* (New York: Holt, Rinehart and Winston, Inc., 1958), pp. 11–12.

[16] Foster, *op. cit.*, p. 116.

3. Scholarship problems.
   (a) The child of average intelligence whose school failure has no obvious cause.
   (b) The child of superior ability who is careless and uninterested in his school work.

The Bureau of Child Guidance has developed a classification of levels of treatment which range from what is known as the "full-study" case, involving the work of the visiting teacher, the psychologist, and the psychiatrist, to the "advisory case," which may involve just one problem in which advice is given to the teacher in a single interview with no record-keeping involved.

In the Newark program the principal of each school is responsible for seeing that the individual classroom teachers administer group tests, and that records are kept for each child in the school. He is also the liaison officer between the assistant superintendent's Bureau of Special Services and the teachers, counseling them in individual cases, and helping with referrals for those needing a visiting teacher. The principal also helps the classroom teacher in carrying out the recommendations made by the visiting teacher.[17]

GUIDANCE IN CHAMPAIGN, ILLINOIS

The purpose of guidance in the elementary schools of Champaign, Illinois, is to aid each child in better understanding himself as an individual and as a member of the group. To meet the physical, intellectual, social, and emotional needs of each child, careful teacher-pupil planning is practiced. All of the available resources of the school and community are utilized.

Figure 6 shows a breakdown of the guidance personnel, administrators, teachers, and pupils in the Champaign school district. The function of the central guidance council is to assist and inform the superintendent on matters of guidance. The elementary schools are represented by one primary teacher and one intermediate teacher selected from the guidance committee of the elementary schools.

The guidance committee of the elementary schools has a specific make-up in the guidance program. The personnel consists of one person from each elementary school in the city and one representative from the rural area. Four parents are included on the guidance committee, three from the city and one from the rural area. The duties of the guidance committee of the elementary schools are as follows: (1) to evaluate the guidance program; (2) to discover and discuss problems;

[17] Foster, *op. cit.*, pp. 116–118.

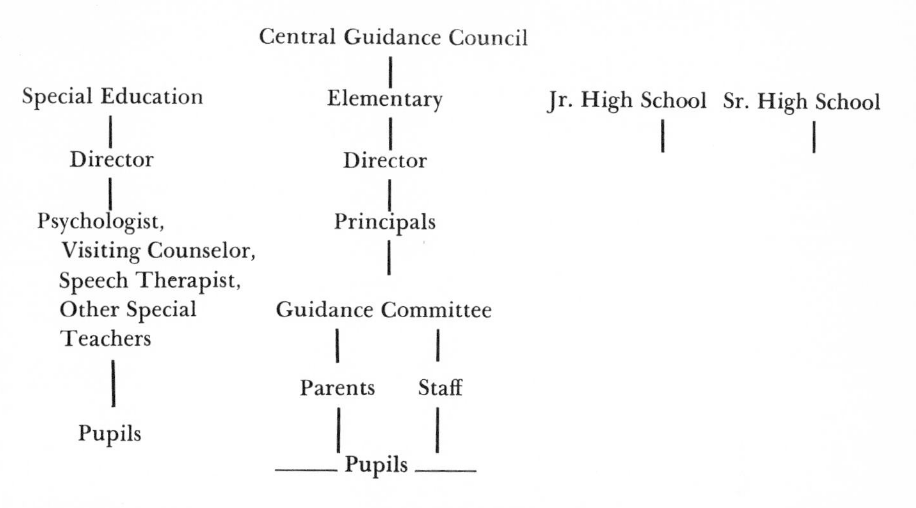

Figure 6. BREAKDOWN OF GUIDANCE PERSONNEL IN CHAMPAIGN, ILLINOIS, SCHOOL DISTRICT

(3) to plan ways of improving the guidance program; (4) to suggest teaching procedures that will make the guidance program more effective; (5) to plan administration of the testing program; and (6) to set up new policies to be presented and approved by the staff and the central guidance committee.

The consultant of the elementary guidance committee is the director of elementary education, and is also a member of the central guidance committee. The director also serves as a consultant to the principal, teachers, pupils, and parents in all phases of guidance. He is available for conferences to discuss specific problems needing special attention. The director works with the teachers in planning an instructional program, and confers with the staff in the selection of teaching materials. He provides leadership in the selection and administration of the regular testing program, and tabulates all test results for the system. He also aids the teachers in using these test results.

Schools with large enrollments have full-time principals. The smaller schools have principals who also teach. The principal is responsible for providing leadership and supervision of the guidance program in his building. The principal administers placement tests to all new pupils before they are placed permanently in a class. He confers with the teachers on all referrals, and sends the referrals to the appropriate persons. The principal also cooperates with the director of elementary guidance in appointing a teacher to the elementary guidance committee.

As in all good guidance programs, the classroom teacher is the key person in the Champaign operational program. She is responsible for promoting an atmosphere in the classroom that leads to good mental health. The classroom teacher participates in studies of the curriculum. She cooperates in the testing program; studies the cumulative record folder; and is responsible for keeping these up to date. The teacher is the important person in identifying the specific problems of the children. The visiting counselor, school psychologist, speech correctionist, and other specialists depend upon the teacher to refer cases requiring special help. The teacher discusses with the principal the problems of her students. These cases may also be discussed with the director of elementary guidance, the director of special education, or both. All referrals for specialists are routed through the principal, then to the director of special education, who sets up priorities for special testing with the cooperation of the director of elementary guidance, the principal, and the teacher. The teacher may be asked to keep an anecdotal record on a specific child so his behavior patterns and educational progress data will be available for conferences, and for the evaluation of the child's development.

The Champaign guidance program starts at the first grade level. Pre-admission services are provided for parents of incoming first graders. These pre-admission services are designed to acquaint parents with the program their children will meet, and to encourage the cooperation of parents in helping prepare their children for entrance into the first grade. At a tea held the preceding May, each parent is given a booklet entitled, *Getting Your Child Ready for School.*

In all schools, the individual grades hold parent-teacher conferences to supplement report cards. The purpose is to develop a mutual understanding between home and school, and to help parents better understand their child's abilities and stage of development. A home visit is made by the teacher if the parent is unable to come to school.

Standardized tests are given once a year in all grades. These tests are usually given the last of September or first of October so that teachers can have the results early in the school year to use in their planning. All first, third, and fifth grades, and all new second, fourth, and sixth grade children are given a group intelligence test. All second grades are given a reading test, and reading and language tests are given in the third grade. Achievement tests in reading, arithmetic, and language are given in the fourth, fifth, and sixth grades. All the schools follow flexible grouping in the classroom, especially in the skill areas.

A cumulative folder is begun on each child when he enters school, and is continued until he leaves the school.

It is apparent that much time and planning have gone into the guidance program of the Champaign schools. Although the program seems highly centralized, emphasis is still placed on the individual school keeping in close contact with the parent, and on keeping the program child-centered.[18]

THE CUPERTINO, CALIFORNIA, ADJUSTMENT-REMEDIAL PROGRAM

A unique program in elementary school guidance is the Cupertino Union Elementary School District Adjustment-Remedial Program which was designed in the closing years of the 1950's to assist children who are currently unable to profit adequately from their regular classroom programs.

Teachers in the Adjustment-Remedial Program are freed from regular classroom responsibility to work in identifying and helping unhappy and disturbed children make a more adequate social, personal, and educational adjustment. These teachers identify fast-learning children, and assist in developing challenging programs for them; they discover children with bilingual or limited backgrounds, and offer experiences involving both cultures; they study to understand the slow learning child so that they may help him through a supportive program as he learns; and they identify and give remedial help to children with educational difficulties. In effecting the child's optimum condition for learning, and helping establish an appropriate instructional program, the Adjustment-Remedial teacher may work with the classroom teacher, the pupil, the parent, the school personnel, and community resource leaders.

Careful screening in choice of personnel is carried on in an effort to secure teachers who have had successful classroom teaching experience, and who have the warmth and flexibility of personality to be able to relate comfortably and productively to the persons with whom they will work. Once these teachers have been chosen, in-service education in case work techniques and remedial methods is carried on in two-hour sessions weekly.

In the Cupertino program, master teachers are used as guidance personnel, in the belief that the chief task of the school is education. Once better understanding of the child is gained through the many facets of the cooperative effort, the master teacher has the skill to create an effective schoolday program.

---

[18] Board of Education, *The Guidance Program in the Champaign Community Schools* (Champaign, Illinois: Community Unit School District No. 4, 1956).

A case history synthesizing the significant accumulated information is used by the Adjustment-Remedial personnel to understand the child better. As the Adjustment-Remedial teacher begins to help a child, he records significant data about him, which eventually becomes the case history, to be used in diagnosis or in evaluation of the child's progress. It may be used in a case review to help other significant persons in the life of the child to better understand him. With parental permission, it may be sent to a community resource to aid in diagnosis.

The special teacher receives from the classroom teacher a referral which includes identifying information and the reason for referral, recorded in behavioral terms by the teacher. Upon receipt of the referral, which becomes the first page of the case history, the Adjustment-Remedial teacher adds a cumulative record of tests and comments by previous classroom teachers, and a health record. If the child is thought to need only remedial instruction, the next recorded step may be a diagnostic work-up, then a plan of action recorded over a period of time, eventually a record of evaluation of progress and, later, a noted follow-up to see if the progress is continuing.

If the child is in need of a more intensive plan, then the gathering of data includes material regarding personal information, family background, developmental history, and a further statement of the problem.[19]

Several facets of the Cupertino program are considered to be "pioneering" in guidance techniques. The Class Survey Chart shown in Figure 7 is an interesting innovation. Upon the child's referral, the Adjustment-Remedial teacher makes an evaluation of the child's strengths and weaknesses, and possibly gives the child additional tests in certain areas. The adjustment teacher may call upon the services of the consultants if she needs help with individuals or with groups.

The consultation program personnel includes, besides the Adjustment-Remedial teachers, a general Adjustment-Remedial Consultant and a Director of Special Services (a psychologist). The Adjustment-Remedial teachers can work directly with other agencies of the community, though the referrals to other agencies are usually handled by the general consultant. The A-R teachers act as psychometrics in giving individual tests, and in interpreting the tests given by classroom teachers. Much work is done by the A-R teachers in helping slow learners, as well as in providing enrichment experiences for the mentally superior children.

The Director of Special Services has done a great deal of work in perfecting forms for recording test data quickly and permanently for

---

[19] Norma Randolph, ed., *The Adjustment-Remedial Program.* (Cupertino, California: Cupertino Union Elementary School District, 1959), pp. 1–16.

each child. He has devised forms to be used by data processing machines for recording, as well as for scoring, individual tests. He has also used parents in scoring some of the group tests—a unique innovation—and a helpful one from the point of view of public relations.

Figure 8 projects the operational structure of the Cupertino program.

CONCLUSION

Guidance services are in their infancy in the elementary schools of America. These services are, however, increasing in number with each new school year; and training programs in colleges and in-service education should continue, so that teachers who aspire to be counselors and guidance directors may prepare for these important positions.

Guidance services in the elementary schools have, in recent years, been directed toward helping children solve their educational, social, and emotional problems. There is a current trend, however, toward including vocational guidance services at the lower school level. This trend has been prompted, in part, by the great change in the American cultural life caused by the advent of automation. Children need to learn at an early age about jobs, job requirements, and tasks which have been altered, eliminated, or created as a result of new advances in technology and other aspects of the American society.

A key person in the elementary school guidance program is the principal. He should be included in all planning and execution of plans in the guidance services area. Besides being active in the initial steps of setting up a guidance program, the principal must be the leader in programming, coordinating, and evaluating the program in his school after it has officially begun. The problem of providing proper personnel and physical facilities comes under the jurisdiction of the principal. Not the least important of the principal's responsibilities in the area of guidance services is that of lending his inspirational leadership in a continuous and constructive manner, so that the program will be successful in helping students grow toward useful and complete adulthood.

Short Case 1
The Discipline Problem

L.B. is a 10-year-old boy in the third grade, physically well-developed and tall for his age. He had been retained once in the first grade; he does not perform up to his ability as indicated by scores on achievement tests. L.B.'s

Figure 7

Class

NAME	I Learning Power					II Special Abilities										III Educational Development									
	1	2	3	4	5	6	7	8	9	10	11	12	13	14	15	16	17	18	19	20	21	22	23	24	25
	Learns Very Slowly (50–69)	Learns Slowly (70–89)	Learns at Average Speed (90–109)	Learns Rapidly (110–129)	Learns Very Rapidly (130–150) Above	Has Intellectual Curiosity, Drive & Motivation	Shows Scientific Interest	Shows Leadership	Expresses Artistic Ability	Can Write Creatively	Has Dramatic Talent	Has Musical Ability	Has Talent for Dancing	Shows Mechanical Ability	Shows Physical Prowess	2 Years Below (−2.5 to −1.6)	1 Year Below (−1.5 Yrs. to −6 Mos.)	At Grade Level (−5 Mos. to +5 Mos.)	1 Year Above (+6 Mos. to 1.5 Yrs.)	2 Years Above (+1.6 Yrs. to 2.5 Yrs.)	Needs Reading Skills	Needs Spelling Skills	Needs Arithmetic Skills	Is Under-Achieving	Is Over-Achieving
1. Sandra Jones					X	X	X	X		X		X	X							X					
2. Bob Blake		X							X						X	X					X	X		X	
3. Carol Bailey			X															X			X	X	X	X	
4. Ferne Brown																									
5. Edna Cardle																									
6. Jane Morris																									
7. Dean Russell																									

A CLASS SURVEY CARRIED ON BY THE ADJUSTMENT-REMEDIAL TEACHER AND THE CLASSROOM TEACHER, PICTORIALLY PORTRAYED ON A SURVEY CHART, GIVES A PICTURE OF INDIVIDUAL DIFFERENCES WITHIN THE CLASS. CHILDREN HAVING PHYSICAL, EMOTIONAL, EDUCATIONAL, OR CULTURAL PROBLEMS OF SUFFICIENT MAGNITUDE TO RETARD LEARNING ARE

Survey

IV Cultural Level			V Personal & Inter-Personal Relation						VI Physical Development					Comments
26	27	28	29	30	31	32	33	34	35	36	37	38	39	
Has Rich Background	Has Bi-Lingual Background	Has Limited Background	Excessive Mobility	Shows Withdrawn Behavior	Shows Aggressive Behavior	Tends Toward Negative Self-Image	Tends Toward Positive Self-Image	Enjoys Free Flowing Relationships	Visual Handicaps	Hearing Handicaps	Speech Handicaps	Crippling Handicaps	Special Health Problems	
X							X	X						Enter in Extra Work Group
					X	X							X	Asthma—Refer to A-R
				X							X			Refer to A-R Program

IDENTIFIED. REFERRALS ARE MADE TO THE ADJUSTMENT-REMEDIAL PROGRAM FROM THE CHART THROUGH PRINCIPAL, ADJUSTMENT-REMEDIAL AND TEACHER JUDGMENT. AT THE SAME TIME, THE PRINCIPAL IS GIVEN A BIRD'S-EYE VIEW OF THE DIFFICULTIES FACING THE TEACHER IN ESTABLISHING EFFECTIVELY EDUCABLE GROUPS.

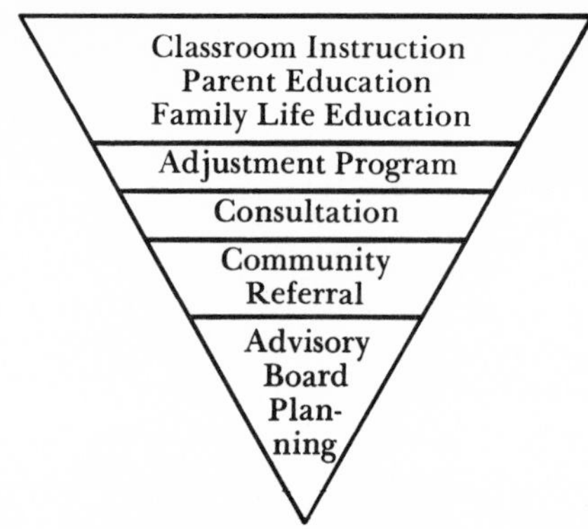

Figure 8. OPERATION PLAN OF CUPERTINO, CALIFORNIA, ADJUSTMENT-REMEDIAL PROGRAM

score in reading tests shows him to be achieving at grade level, but his performance in class is high first or low second grade; his IQ is about 105. He demands constant attention from the teacher, the children in his classroom, and his mother; he became quite a "discipline" problem this year, though his mother says he is happier than he was in school last year. L.B. is good in sports and on the playground, but he often gets into trouble because he wants to "run the show."

During the course of the year the teacher and principal conferred several times regarding L.B.'s progress and problems; at one of these conferences the school psychologist sat in. The psychologist gave L.B. an individual test, in which the child said the psychologist just talked to him, and he had a lot of fun. The psychologist was to have followed this up with class observations, but his load was so heavy that he never did this. In a final conference between L.B.'s parents, the principal, and the teacher, the child's need for academic and social help was exposed, but it was agreed that L.B. should not be retained in grade three if the parents would agree to special tutoring in an attempt to bring the child up to grade level. The school also recommended that L.B. attend remedial classes during the summer, and that he become involved in the reading improvement program that would be initiated in the fourth grade.

Problem: What provision could have been made for helping L.B. in grade two? What was the role of the teacher in this case? Of the administrator? Of the psychologist? What place in the modern curriculum is made for "discipline" problems of this type?

Short Case 2

Teacher-Psychologist Non-Cooperation

Mrs. Vancer found it impossible to teach her fifth grade class with Tommy Dinkens in it. No matter what was happening in the classroom, Tommy would very likely get out of his seat and skip around the room once. He contradicted everything the teacher said; he lied frequently; he blamed "accidents" on other children; and he cried if the teacher tried to discipline him. When the principal asked about Tommy's abilities, Mrs. Vancer replied that she just didn't pay any attention to those test scores because they didn't mean anything, and that she did not know anything about Tommy other than what she observed in class.

The principal asked if Mrs. Vancer didn't think it might be a good idea to submit a referral concerning Tommy to the district psychologist. She replied that she certainly didn't see any sense in it, that all the teachers knew such a procedure was useless. When the principal asked why this might be, Mrs. Vancer replied that it was because all the psychologist wanted you to do was fill out a lot of silly forms. She further indicated that she didn't think the psychologist knew much anyway, because the first question on the form asked, "What is this child's problem?" and "Why do you think it exists?"

Problem: From this brief description, how might the principal have explained to Mrs. Vancer how the techniques of the psychologist could have been really valuable? What techniques not mentioned here might the psychologist have used? What are the purposes of the first two questions on the form?

Short Case 3

The Social Isolate

Bobby was in second grade. He was large in comparison to his classmates since he had been retained once in kindergarten. His parents did not give him the attention and the affection that he needed. He was achieving at a low first grade level and, due in part to his previous failure, did not have "status" with his classmates. He tried to gain this status through his physical prowess, and was constantly throwing rocks and starting fights on the playground. A sociogram showed him to be a social isolate.

The school guidance counselor found that Bobby's IQ was a little above 120. A test with a mirror showed him to be a mirror reader. He seemed to have a valid interest in space ships.

Problem: What techniques might the teacher, or others, have employed that might have been effective in Bobby's situation? What other media or resources should or could have been used to obtain more information about Bobby? Did the counselor have any further role to play in this case?

Chapter Twelve

Accounting for Our Potential Products

There are differences of opinion in defining the "products" of the elementary school. Some authorities maintain that the school's products are the boys and girls who progress through six to eight years of learning within its walls. Others support the idea that the products are the intangibles, such as learned skills and understandings, which those children acquire and carry with them as they proceed into the higher grades in the educational system, or into life outside the system. This is actually a moot point; the pupils and what they acquire through their learning activities in the school are inseparable; the children who leave the elementary school are still the same children who entered; but, because of the learning that has taken place, their behavior is different than it was at the time they began kindergarten or first grade. In the following discussion, then, when the school's "products" are spoken of, the term identifies those students or ex-students, complete with all of their skills, understandings, physical features, appreciations, attitudes, and other characteristics of typical American children.

The school's "products," then, must be of primary interest to the staff if the pupils are to be afforded an educational program which will be most beneficial to each of them. Elementary school children must be placed in a situation which will serve the best interest of each individual, and maintain his uniqueness in spite of the sheer numbers of pupils confronting the staff. While the "products" are in the school, the staff must place them in accordance with the school's educational philosophy. Grouping children according to their ability will probably result if the school's objectives lean toward an emphasis upon academic achievement; less stress on ability grouping will result if the school's goals include social and emotional development in addition to mental and intellectual growth.

CLASSIFYING CHILDREN FOR GROUP ASSIGNMENTS

Many kinds of grouping for instruction exist in the elementary schools of America, depending, among other things, upon the patterns of organization of the schools. If the organizational structure is an ungraded plan, as described in Chapter IV, children will be grouped according to achievement, or, in the kindergarten or first grade, according to mental maturity test results. If the typical graded plan is the mode of organization, pupils will be grouped largely according to chronological age and evidences of subject matter mastery. Within each classroom in the school, children are placed into still finer groups, based variously on ability, special interests, heterogeneity, friendships, and, on occasion, alphabetical order. It is a responsibility of the principal to provide the leadership necessary to inspire teachers to be flexible in their classroom grouping, without allowing the inspiration and achievement level to dwindle to a point that is less than desirable.

With no clearcut evidence on the subject of optimum grouping, the matter of whether to group heterogeneously or homogeneously will depend upon an individual school's philosophy. If children within the classroom are grouped according to the results of intelligence or achievement tests, it will be found that there will be almost as great a range in performance of pupils in the "slow" group as in performance of those in the "fast" group, though, of course, there most likely will be significant differences in the average scores of the two groups. The small reduction in range will not allow a teacher to differentiate between groups of bright and dull pupils. It is difficult to accept the grouping of children on the basis of subject matter achievement alone, if one accepts the growth and development of all aspects of the child's being as an objective of the elementary school.

Even though children in slow groups may feel a stigma and their parents may feel resentment, it is probably best to do a certain amount of ability grouping, particularly in reading and arithmetic, and especially in the primary grades. Such a plan of grouping has a tendency to allow the more able pupils to proceed according to their pattern of growth, while it offers slower pupils needed assistance in the subject areas. If a school staff is planning to utilize ability grouping, it should remember that the important thing in such grouping is to adapt the content and method so that children in each group will be helped in meeting their individual needs. Sometimes this procedure requires a very radical adaptation, and certainly includes a good deal more than simply varying the pace and amount of material covered. A wide variety of instructional materials is of paramount importance if effective ability grouping is to be achieved.

One interesting experiment in arithmetic ability grouping was that reported by Smith as carried on at the Lake Charles, Louisiana, City Schools, Grades 2 through 5, in 1959–60.[1] Experimental and control classes in these four grade levels were formed, the former classes spending at least 75 per cent of the daily arithmetic period working in intra-class groups—A (high), B (average), and C (low)—formed by use of grade placements in arithmetic average, while the control classes were taught by the "class-as-a-whole" procedure. The results of the study indicated that the experimental classes achieved significantly higher gains than did control groups in: arithmetic average, Grade Two, Grade Four, and Grade Five; computation, Grade Two, Grade Four, and Grade Five; and problem solving, Grade Two. The intra-class Group A (high) made significantly higher gains than did matched partners in the control groups in computation and arithmetic average, Grade Five; intra-class Group B (average) achieved significantly higher gains than did control group matched partners in computation, problem-solving, and arithmetic average, Grade Four; and intra-class Group C (low) achieved gains that were significantly higher than did control group matched partners in computation and arithmetic average, Grade Four. The one area where matched partners in control classrooms made significantly higher gains than intra-class groups was in problem solving, Grade Three, where the matched control-group partners did better than intra-class Group B (average).

While this experiment concerned only the area of arithmetic, it is probable that experimentation in the other subject areas of the elementary schools would reveal similar results: that intra-class ability grouping is a technique which will improve achievement in elementary school subjects in the primary and intermediate grade levels.

Grouping children according to their interests is often an effective

---

[1] William Maurice Smith, "The Effect of Intra-Class Ability Grouping in Arithmetic Achievement in Grade Two Through Grade Five" (Unpublished Doctoral dissertation, Louisiana State University, 1960)

method of classifying students for instruction. While it is always rewarding to see children achieve above their ability level because of their interest in learning, it is often difficult for teachers to find pupils' interests and connect the learning to them. It is often difficult to determine whether a pupil's attention indicates genuine interest, or only a passing whim. Effective teachers, however, can determine real interests through the use of a number of techniques, such as interest inventories, original art work, original literary pieces, and others. If it is determined, for example, that certain children in the class are genuinely interested in heroes or other important persons, that some are interested in geographic areas, or in art, music, or mechanics, a classroom divided into groups according to these particular interests possesses great potential for learning in such areas as social sciences, language arts, sciences, and others.

Many times, grouping children within the classroom for specific tasks proves to be an effective technique. One first grade teacher developed an effective method for conducting a lesson in reading. Rather than calling the children to the reading circle by "Redbirds," "Johnny's Group," "Group Number One," or some other fatuous method, the teacher spoke each child's name, and he took his place in the group for instruction in one of the reading skills for which he had a special need. In the next reading session, the teacher emphasized another reading skill, and only those children who had a special need for instruction in that skill were called to the reading circle for that particular lesson. Thus, the teacher kept the grouping completely flexible, and no child had occasion to say that he was in the "first" reading group, or the "low" reading group. Instruction was channeled toward the children's individual needs in the important skills of reading.

Within certain limitations, grouping according to friendships within the classroom often produces desirable outcomes. Just as adults often enjoy doing things together, so, too, do friends in the class, and children will often accomplish far more individually and as a group if they are allowed to work with close acquaintances. Of course, teachers know that if children had complete freedom to choose their associates, some would certainly choose unwisely; consequently, important and long-range groups should probably not be formed with friendship as the sole basis.

The types of grouping just discussed point up again the importance of flexibility in providing for instruction. Sub-grouping within a heterogeneous classroom provides for the free movement of children from one group to another, depending upon the prevailing circumstances. Elementary school principals should understand that their decisions will be called for many times in respect to grouping, because it is absolutely necessary that some useful arrangement be carried out in the classrooms of their schools. The welfare of the child should be in focus when decisions of this kind are made; the range of achievement among children is great regardless of the type of grouping agreed upon, and individualization rests upon many considerations other than grouping alone. Elementary school principals must provide leadership that will result in the upgrading of education for America's boys and girls, regardless of the type of grouping that is followed in the school.

MARKING AND REPORTING PROGRESS OF PUPILS

When a school considers a change in its system of marking and reporting to parents, it invariably finds itself involved with everything that concerns policy and philosophy of education, including curriculum, teaching methods, size of classes, and qualification of teachers. It is natural to desire a new and better reporting system, but when the project is actually undertaken, the foreseen problems become greatly magnified, and the unforeseen problems become legion. No one has yet found the *one* best way of marking pupils and reporting to parents, but it is a worthy enterprise with which to experiment, perhaps to find the method best suited for the local situation, perhaps even to make some progress toward *the* ultimate answer to the problem. The quest for discovering more satisfactory marking systems and provisions for reporting to parents seems to be an almost universal problem; some researchers find that as high as 90 per cent of the schools in their studies are undertaking projects which may result in better procedures of marking and reporting.

With the vast number of possible marking systems which a school system might use, it will be difficult for a committee working on the problem to arrive at a method which will be acceptable to a majority. Such a committee will need some guides by which to determine the system of marking best suited to a particular school situation; it will need to consider the purposes which marks are assumed to serve and whether or not they meet the purposes, which system of marking best meets the needs of the local community, and whether there are better ways of evaluating growth and development of children.

Marks on report cards are purported to show achievement of the child in relation to his grade group or his ability, to provide information for guidance purposes, to provide information for prospective employers or higher educational institutions, to motivate the child to higher achievement, to assist in communication between home and school, and to identify the child's strengths and weaknesses. Experience shows that marks do not achieve these purposes; at least, the traditional letter marks or numerical or percentage systems do not. They do not relay adequate information about pupils' general development and, in fact, ignore important areas of growth. The school that believes in developing individual differences and in helping children achieve their best capabilities will undoubtedly find traditional methods of marking to be inadequate for the school's broad objectives. In fact, there is some evidence to the effect that report cards with traditional markings may do more harm than good, contributing to truancy, making children unhappy, and producing unhealthy rivalry among children.

When children receive marks in any subject they are pursuing, those marks do not represent pure achievement in the subject. They reflect other unknown elements such as pupil effort or lack of it, obsequiousness, and personal antagonisms.

The same fixed standard cannot be used to measure the achievement of each unique child. Children, furthermore, all go through the same stages of growth, but they do not all go through those stages at the same rate. This makes reporting decidedly more difficult; certainly it is almost impossible to describe a child's achievement by use of symbols.

The crux of the whole matter seems to lie in the answer to this question: what do parents *really* want to know about their child? Kingsley made a study of the reactions of teachers, pupils, and parents to a number of different reporting procedures and techniques and found that more than 75 per cent of both parents and teachers wanted the following factors in the reporting program: statements explaining the meaning of symbols used in marking, absent and tardy records, personality trait ratings, "S" and "U" marks to show progress in music and physical education, space for teacher comments, warning slips, parent-teacher conferences, a "Back-to-School Night" Parent-Teacher Association meeting, and one afternoon a month for parents and teachers to hold brief conferences.[2] Agreeable to a large extent, the pupils expressed a desire for ratings in personality traits and work habits, effort marks in each subject, space for teachers' comments, different cards for elementary and junior and senior high schools, a "Back-to-School Night," monthly parent visits to teachers, and warning slips. Interesting contrasts revealed by the study included: in

[2] Howard H. Kingsley, "Communication Between the School and Home: A Study of Teacher-Pupil-Parent Reaction to a Variety of Reporting Procedures and Techniques" (Unpublished Doctoral dissertation, Boston University School of Education, 1959).

contrast to parents, more than 75 per cent of the teachers favored a message from the superintendent, space for parent comments, and different report cards for the elementary, junior high, and senior high schools. On the other hand, more than 75 per cent of the parents, in contrast to the teachers, were in favor of an effort mark in each subject and one in work habits.

Other surveys have shown that parents have indicated their three principal concerns as being the knowledge that their child is acceptable to others in his class, that he is normal socially and academically, and that he is succeeding. Since these questions cannot be answered adequately by percentage or letter grades, it would appear that personal letters or individual conferences with parents are much preferred for clear, two-way communication.

Some modern writers regard letters to parents as the best method of reporting. These provide opportunities for including many different types of information which vary according to parents' understanding and the values of the school. Diagnostic letters, now used more widely than symbols, contain many facts about the child and his work, indicate growth socially, physically, and emotionally as well as intellectually, and make comparisons with the child's own previous accomplishments. Such letters also may make evaluations according to the child's ability, and may offer suggestions for home guidance. Some teachers, however, show poor judgment in what they put into letters, and letters often become stereotyped. A high degree of skill in communication is required of a teacher to adequately report on individual differences in the child's performance. Furthermore, statements written in a letter often do not convey the same meaning to a reader that the writer intended.

Some school systems use a system of marking pupils on check lists, in which teachers make check marks in various squares indicating that the child is either achieving satisfactorily or is not achieving as he should in the various subject areas and other areas which are being evaluated. Such a system has not proved particularly superior to the traditional three- or five-letter marking system.

The medium of reporting which is considered by most authorities to be the optimum method for avoiding misunderstanding and promoting good feelings between home and school is the parent-teacher conference. A study by Robitaille attempted to determine whether or not the conference method of reporting pupil progress in the elementary school is justified by objective data as the superior method.[3] Robi-

[3] Joseph Philip Robitaille, "An Analysis of the Effect of Parent-Teacher and Parent-Teacher-Pupil Conferences on the Problems of Intermediate Grade Pupils" (Unpublished Doctoral dissertation, University of Connecticut, 1959).

taille used the experimental-control group technique with three classes of fourth, fifth, and sixth grade pupils, and concluded as a result of his study that the superiority claimed for the conference method of reporting pupil progress appears justified when it is combined with a written report. He also concluded, among other things, that conferences have a definite, positive effect in reducing the number of problems which display evidence of poor mental health; that conferences help a child free himself of negative attitudes toward school; that parents are aware of the advantages of conferences, and do believe they provide for better relations between home and school; and that intermediate grade pupils are capable of participating in the evaluative process. Parent-teacher conferences are not a panacea for all reporting ills, and some few reporting problems still remain after this technique is employed by a school; but these conferences do appear to be superior to other systems which have been employed.

In the environment of the child's own classroom, where his work can be seen, answers to such questions as these may evolve: How does the child work as a part of the group? How does he work as an individual? Is he becoming more responsible in his behavior? Does he talk and listen well? Does he show an increasing creative ability? Does he understand the essentials of health and safety? Is he showing an increasing ability in using his knowledge of reading, numbers, writing, science, and social living? Teachers and parents, in discussing such questions together, can formulate the best plan for facilitating the growth and development of the child, both at home and at school.

A large amount of prior preparation, particularly on the part of the teacher, is necessary for a successful teacher-parent conference. The teacher must have skill in interviewing, and have an intimate knowledge of the child which he is capable of communicating to the parents. Many teacher-parent conferences have been ruined by a teacher's inability to communicate properly, with the result that the parent is dissatisfied with the teacher's analysis. Parents need to understand that they may raise any questions they wish, and also that they may be free to offer any information pertinent to the child's education.

Development of a satisfactory reporting system is primarily an administrative problem, but in this area, as in all others in the elementary school, the principal must seek the cooperation of teachers and lay-persons in the planning if real progress is to be realized. The revision of a system of marking and reporting to parents is not likely to be successful if it is imposed upon a group. A change in such a system calls for an examination of the school's educational philosophy. Teachers, parents, and pupils must be prepared for a change in the marking and reporting system, and this calls for a series of question-answer sessions so that the use and interpretation of the new system will be understood. In accord with the idea that everyone who is affected by evalution should have some say in it, the principal and his staff should consider the possibility of pupil participation in whatever system is adopted.

THE USE OF MECHANIZED RECORD-KEEPING TECHNIQUES

A great amount of time is involved in the keeping of records, marking of grade cards, and other "paper administration" activities of the classroom teachers, supervisors, administrators, and office employees in school systems over the nation. In some schools, the tallying of registration cards alone requires a staff of several clerks working a minimum of two weeks following the opening of school. Report cards often consume five or six hours of the teacher's time, a large portion of which is expended during the school day. The amount of time spent by teachers, clerks, and sometimes by administrators in counting lunch money, school bank deposits, and milk pennies is sometimes phenomenal; such activity is necessary, but it takes valuable time that could more profitably be spent in activities which improve the teaching-learning situation in the school.

Some elementary, and many secondary, schools have begun to use mechanized record-keeping techniques and tabular equipment in order to minimize the amount of valuable time spent by individuals in these bookkeeping activities. In addition to saving time by use of machines, school districts are also turning to such devices in an effort to improve efficiency and accuracy.

A reference was made in Chapter XI to data processing methods that are being tried by guidance personnel in collecting and utilizing information about pupils. Machines are also being used for gathering data regarding registration and attendance, for making alphabetical listings, for producing grade cards, and for handling and counting of coins. Schools or districts that are too small to finance their own machines sometimes make use of nearby service bureaus that provide the machine services.

In school districts where machines are available, elementary school teachers can have a complete, reliable class roll on the opening day of school. Late registration cards, even those that come in on Friday before the opening of school on Monday, can be processed so that the names, in alphabetical sequence, can be included on multiple copies of an up-to-date roll for each teacher.

The machine-operated report card system is especially helpful in secondary schools, and in elementary schools which have a departmentalized or semi-departmentalized organization. In such situations, the school's enrollment files are sent early in the fall to the office where the machine is located, or to a service bureau which handles the records for the school, and there a master card for each pupil is punched, complete with name, address, class, homeroom number, telephone, date of birth, and distance from school. The school prepares curriculum cards for each subject, which include the teacher's name, subject title, period and room number; then the machine imprints on these cards the name, sex, homeroom, class, and code of each pupil enrolled in the course. Finally, students' master cards and curriculum cards for each subject are merged; each student card is grouped with cards for each subject for which he is registered. At grade card time, teachers simply mark, with an electrographic pencil, each student's grade, citizenship mark, and number of days absent under the appropriate heading on his subject card. The cards are then sent to the machine or service bureau, where they are punched and report cards prepared. With grades for all subjects collated, the cards are sent back to the homeroom teacher for distribution in person, or to the office where they can be mailed to parents. Extra copies of the grade cards are prepared so that the office will be able to distribute them to the cumulative folder, the homeroom teacher, and to other appropriate sources. Incidentally, the machines also provide, at the same time they are producing the report cards, an alphabetically arranged list of those pupils who are doing unsatisfactory work, or whose course-work is incomplete.

Automated grouping is another experimental innovation in some school systems. Where this technique is being tried, pupils are grouped into classes on the basis of the elements of a subject field which they have not learned, regardless of the grade level of the children or the subject, and these classes are assigned to teachers already aware of their needs. Since progress of pupils is measured by what they have learned, a glance at their machine punch-cards reveals where they stand with respect to learnings in a certain subject area, and also what they have yet to learn in the areas. A sorting machine automatically assigns children to groups after the skills, understandings, and concepts which they have not mastered have been identified and punched on the pupils' cards. Regrouping of pupils, based on the information they have learned during the past eighteen weeks, occurs at the end of each semester. While a machine system of grouping is based on achievement in subject matter, it precludes one of the basic principles of evaluation, namely that it must be continuous. With elementary schools under continual evaluation, the public schools can ill-afford to limit the surveillance of pupils' progress to only twice a year.

Some elementary schools are also reproducing records on microfilm. By such a procedure, records are centralized and readily available for reference. Additionally, record microfilming releases floor space for other needs of the school, and overall economies are effected.

THE PRINCIPAL'S RESPONSIBILITY FOR ACCOUNTING

As the elementary school principal sincerely strives to help all teachers in the school improve the instructional program, he must constantly be thinking of the placement of students, as well as the best plan of reporting to the parents in his school-community. He must be aware of the wide diversities of experience and home background that have shaped the lives and personalities of the pupils in his building; he must take all facts into consideration as he solves the problems involved in providing the best possible instruction for all his pupils.

The principal should plan a balanced heterogeneity as he pursues the organization of classroom groups for the most effective instructional program. Such heterogeneity does not just happen; rather, it comes from consistent, systematic planning. Imbalance in the form of too great a majority of boys or girls, a preponderance of minority background children in one class, or a collection of problem children in another, often results from haphazard or alphabetical sectioning. With planning, the principal can achieve proper balance between the sexes in any one classroom, can assign minority background children to various sections, and can see that children with problems are placed in classrooms where their needs can be met most expeditiously.

Another of the principal's administrative responsibilities in accounting for the school's products is that of providing high-quality supervision. He must consistently find ways to help teachers understand, in all of their complexity, the children they teach. He must set the pace and the example of respect for individual differences among adults on his staff, as well as among children, so that such respect will permeate his attendance unit. His goal must be for higher teaching competence through proper planning, guidance, and assistance.

A third responsibility is, of course, that of providing the physical necessities for carrying out an adequate system of accounting. Some amount of instructional supplies is a necessity, regardless of the type of grouping arrangement which the school adopts; any adaptation of grouping arrangement will be unsuccessful unless the teacher can be supplied with materials appropriate to the system decided upon. The principal must also provide a plentiful supply of appropriate forms for the successful operation of a reporting system.

TYPES OF RECORDS NEEDED BY THE ELEMENTARY SCHOOL

The kinds of records used in elementary schools vary almost as much as the elementary schools themselves, and this is as it should be. The types of records a school keeps are determined by such factors as its curriculum, size, philosophy of the school and community, level of development of the staff and community, amount of time available, amount of secretarial help, amount of office space and equipment, and length of the school year. There are certain basic records, such as those involved in enrollment, attendance, pupil classification, withdrawals, transfers, and tuition fees, which all schools maintain for all pupils. In addition, some schools also keep records dealing with trends in enrollment; age-grade distribution; promotion and retention; teacher certification, professional, and personal status; funds received and distributed; inventories of supplies and equipment; and cumulative records, with pupils' permanent record forms attached. Each school determines the data to be included on the permanent records, but the forms usually provide information relative to pupils' names, dates and places of birth, names and addresses of parents, results of standardized tests, summaries of absences, data on achievement, ratings on personal traits, special awards and activities, nationality, color or race, sex, and health data.

THE CUMULATIVE RECORD

The cumulative record is probably the most important that an elementary school keeps for each pupil, because on this form is recorded all the information which the school feels is important about the child. Some states have adopted a uniform cumulative record form for the use of all schools within their boundaries. Among the types of cumulative forms in use are the ledger or card-type, and the folder-type—the latter being the more functional because of its flexibility. Besides containing a myriad of information recorded directly on the folder itself, this type of record may also be used as a file for anecdotal records, notes from parents, and other informative materials regarding the child. The folder type of cumulative record, printed on cardboard, is easily kept in a file cabinet and, because of its comparative sturdiness, can be used for the entire time that the pupil is in the public schools. Whether cumulative records are stored in the central office, the principal's office, or in the pupil's classroom, they should be kept in a fireproof vault or storage cabinet. All personnel should bear in mind that the cumulative records contain some confidential information regarding the pupil, and abuses should not occur.

Most cumulative records contain information such as the following:

> Family background: names of parents or guardians; occupations of parents or guardians; marital status of parents; with whom the pupil lives; economic conditions of home; number and ages of brothers and sisters; attitude of family toward pupil.
>
> Data about pupil: name; age; appearance; color and race; place of birth; church affiliation; picture of pupil.
>
> General health of pupil: past illnesses; pupil's health habits, such as food in his diet, amount of sleep, and the like; absences and tardinesses; physical examinations; physical handicaps.
>
> Personality traits and work habits: record of developing interests; reports of interviews; teachers' observations of work habits; reports of home visits, and visits and correspondence from parents.
>
> Out-of-class activities: summer activities; hobbies; clubs; spare-time activities.
>
> Work experiences and vocational preferences (entered at junior and senior high school levels): part-time work activities; summer work; student's expressed goals and purposes.

Figure 9 is a reproduction of the cumulative record forms for the elementary and junior-senior high schools in Duluth, Minnesota, through the courtesy of school authorities in that city, who state that these particular forms "have been very valuable in connection with our guidance program." It will be noted that the front and back pages of Form 14B refer to the elementary grades kindergarten, one, two, three and four. Form 14C refers only to elementary grades five and six and junior high school grades seven and eight; and Form 14D, the reverse side of Form 14C, refers to junior and senior high school grades nine, ten, eleven, and twelve. It may be seen that the Duluth forms are very complete, and include all the elements of good cumulative record forms discussed above.

ATTENDANCE RECORDS

Since aid from the state is based largely on average daily attendance in the various school units within the state's boundaries, it is vitally

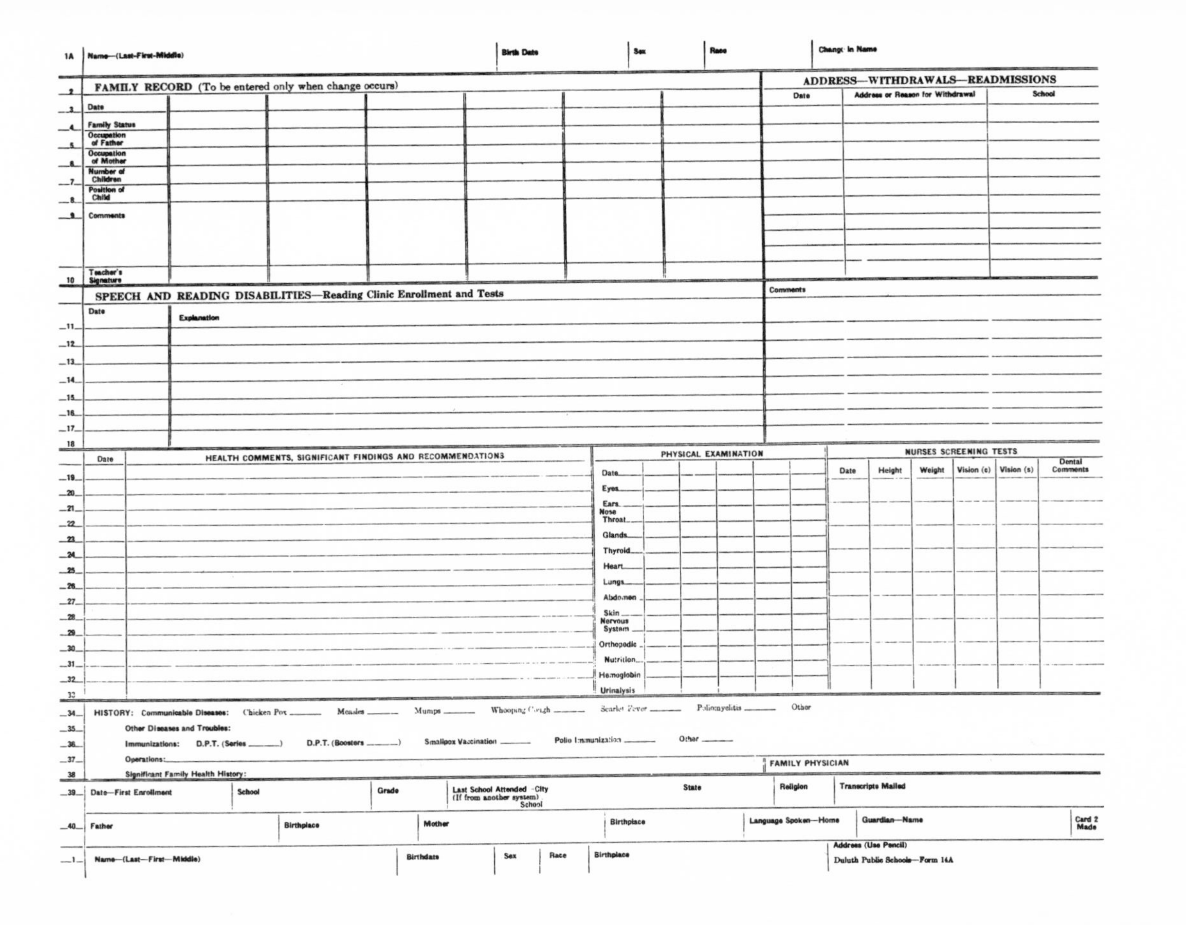

1A Name—(Last-First-Middle) | Birth Date | Sex | Race | Change in Name

2 FAMILY RECORD (To be entered only when change occurs)

3 Date
4 Family Status
5 Occupation of Father
6 Occupation of Mother
7 Number of Children
8 Position of Child
9 Comments
10 Teacher's Signature

ADDRESS—WITHDRAWALS—READMISSIONS

Date	Address or Reason for Withdrawal	School

SPEECH AND READING DISABILITIES—Reading Clinic Enrollment and Tests

Date	Explanation

11 12 13 14 15 16 17 18

Comments

Date	HEALTH COMMENTS, SIGNIFICANT FINDINGS AND RECOMMENDATIONS

19 20 21 22 23 24 25 26 27 28 29 30 31 32 33

PHYSICAL EXAMINATION

Date
Eyes
Ears Nose Throat
Glands
Thyroid
Heart
Lungs
Abdomen
Skin Nervous System
Orthopedic
Nutrition
Hemoglobin
Urinalysis

NURSES SCREENING TESTS

Date	Height	Weight	Vision (c)	Vision (s)	Dental Comments

34 HISTORY: Communicable Diseases: Chicken Pox ____ Measles ____ Mumps ____ Whooping Cough ____ Scarlet Fever ____ Poliomyelitis ____ Other

35 Other Diseases and Troubles:

36 Immunizations: D.P.T. (Series ____) D.P.T. (Boosters ____) Smallpox Vaccination ____ Polio Immunization ____ Other ____

37 Operations:

38 Significant Family Health History: | FAMILY PHYSICIAN

39 Date—First Enrollment | School | Grade | Last School Attended—City (If from another system) School | State | Religion | Transcripts Mailed

40 Father | Birthplace | Mother | Birthplace | Language Spoken—Home | Guardian—Name | Card 2 Made

1 Name—(Last—First—Middle) | Birthdate | Sex | Race | Birthplace | Address (Use Pencil)

Duluth Public Schools—Form 14A

Figure 9

Figure 9 (continued)

41A Name—(Last-First-Middle) Form 14B	Father	Mother	Birthdate	Sex	Race

ELEMENTARY GRADES (Kindergarten—One—Two—Three—Four) | GRADE 4 OR 6 AS NEEDED

42	Year						
43	Grade						
44	Schools						
45	Days Attended						
46	Absent—Tardy	Abs. / Tardy	Abs. / Tardy	Abs. / Tardy	Abs. / Tardy	Abs. / Tardy	Abs. / Tardy
		SUBJECT / S.T. / Av.	SUBJECT / S. T. / Av.	SUBJECT / S. T. / Av.	SUBJECT / S. T. / Av.	SUBJECT / S. T. / Av.	SUBJECT / S. T. / Av.
47	Marks in School	Reading Readiness	Reading (Final Level___)	Reading (Final Level___)	Reading (Final Level___)	Reading (Final Level___)	Reading (Final Level___)
48	Subjects	English	English	English	English	English	English
49	and		Spelling	Spelling	Spelling	Spelling	Spelling
50	Standardized	Numbers	Arithmetic	Arithmetic	Arithmetic	Arithmetic	Arithmetic
51	Achievement	Social Studies	Social Studies	Social Studies	Social Studies	Social Studies	Social Studies
52	Tests	Natural Science	Natural Science	Natural Science	Natural Science	Natural Science	Natural Science
53							
54			Penmanship	Penmanship	Penmanship	Penmanship	Penmanship
55		Art	Art	Art	Art	Art	Art
56		Music	Music	Music	Music	Music	Music
57		Rhythms	Physical Education	Physical Education	Physical Education	Physical Education	Physical Education
		NAME / Date / CA / MA / IQ	NAME / Date / CA / MA / IQ	NAME / Date / CA / MA / IQ	NAME / Date / CA / MA / IQ	NAME / Date / CA / MA / IQ	NAME / Date / CA / MA / IQ
58	School Ability						
59	Tests						
		Gr. / TEST / Date / Gr E	Gr. / TEST / Date / Gr E	Gr. / TEST / Date / Gr E	Gr. / TEST / Date / Gr E	Gr. / TEST / Date / Gr E	Gr. / TEST / Date / Gr E
60	Educational						
61	Tests—						
62	Standardized						
63							
64							

65	SOCIAL	POSITIVE	1-Adaptable	3-Aggressive	5-Conformist	7-Cooperative	9-Courteous	11-Dependable	13-Diplomatic	15-Friendly	17-Industrious	19-Leadership	21-Obedient	23-Respectful	25-Self-confident	27 Self-controlled
66	QUALITIES	NEGATIVE	2-Stubborn	4-Retiring	6-Individualist	8-Uncooperative	10-Rude	12-Erratic	14-Tactless	16-Aloof	18-Lazy	20-Followership	22-Disobedient	24-Disrespectful	26-Timid	28-Uncontrolled

67	Social Qualities Rating						
67A	Conduct						
68	Individual Development						
69	Special Abilities and Interests						
70	Personality Assets						
71	Needs Help With						
72	Behavior Modified By						
73	Referred to						
74	Teacher's Signature						

41 Name	Father	Mother	Address (Use Pencil)	Phone

Figure 9 (continued)

75A Name—(Last-First-Middle)	Father	Mother	Birthdate	Sex	Race

	ELEMENTARY—Grades Five and Six		JUNIOR HIGH SCHOOL—Grades Seven and Eight							
SEMESTER			1	2	1	2	1	2	1	2
76 Year										
77 Grade										
78 Schools										
79 Days Attended										
80 Absent—Tardy	Abs. / Tardy	Abs. / Tardy	A / T	A / T	A / T	A / T	A / T	A / T	A / T	A / T
81 Room or Teacher										

	SUBJECT / S. T. / Av.	SUBJECT / S. T. / Av.	SUBJECT / S. T. / 1 / 2	SUBJECT / S. T. / 1 / 2	SUBJECT / ST / Cr. / 1 / 2	SUBJECT / ST / Cr. / 1 / 2
82 Marks in School Subjects	Reading (Final Level___)	Reading (Final Level___)	English	English	English	English
83 and	English	English	Arithmetic	Arithmetic		
84 Standardized	Spelling	Spelling	Social Studies	Social Studies		
85 Achievement Tests	Arithmetic	Arithmetic	General Science	General Science		
86	Social Studies	Social Studies				
87	Natural Science	Natural Science				
88 Picture Grades 7-8-9						
89	Penmanship	Penmanship				
90	Art	Art				
91	Music	Music				
92	Physical Education	Physical Education	Physical Education	Physical Education	Physical Educ.	Physical Educ.

93 School Ability Tests 94	NAME / Date / CA / MA / IQ	NAME / Date / CA / MA / IQ	NAME / CA / MA / IQ / %ile	Music	NAME / %ile	NAME / CA / MA / IQ / %ile
Other Educational 95 Tests— 96 Standardized	Gr. / TEST / Date / Gr E	Gr. / TEST / Date / Gr E	Gr. / TEST / Gr E / %ile		Gr. / TEST / Gr E / %ile	Gr. / TEST / Gr E / %ile

97 Social	POSITIVE	1-Adaptable	3-Aggressive	5-Conformist	7-Cooperative	9-Courteous	11-Dependable	13-Diplomatic	15-Friendly	17-Industrious	19-Leadership	21-Obedient	23-Respectful	25-Self-confident	27 Self-controlled
98 Qualities Rating	NEGATIVE	2-Stubborn	4-Retiring	6-Individualist	8-Uncooperative	10-Rude	12-Erratic	14-Tactless	16-Aloof	18-Lazy	20-Followership	22-Disobedient	24-Disrespectful	26-Timid	28-Uncontrolled

99 / 99A Social Qualities Conduct						SEQUENTIAL TESTS OF EDUCATIONAL PROGRESS
100 Individual Development						PERCENTILE BANDS GRADE
101 Special Abilities and Interests						Fall Spring / Fall Spring / Fall Spring / Fall Spring
102 Personality Assets						LISTENING COMPREHENSION
103 Needs Help With						READING COMPREHENSION
104 Behavior Modified By						
105 Referred To						WRITING (English)
106 Clubs and Offices						SCIENCE
107 Work Outside of School						
108 Educational Plans						MATHEMATICS
109 Vocational Plans						SOCIAL STUDIES
110 Teacher's Signature						

75 Name—(Last-First-Middle)	Father	Mother	Address (Use Pencil)	Phone
			Duluth Public Schools—Form 14C	

Figure 9 (continued)

111A | Name—(Last-First-Middle) | Father | Mother | FINAL RECORD

Form 14D

JUNIOR AND SENIOR HIGH SCHOOL (Grades Nine, Ten, Eleven and Twelve.) | Birth Date | Date of Grad.___ Score___ Rank___ No. in Class___ High School Percentile___ M.S.A.T.___ Coop. English___

	SEMESTER	1	2	1	2	1	2	1	2	1	2
112	Year										
113	Grade										
114	Schools										
115	Days Attended										
116	Absent—Tardy	A T	A T	A T	A T	A T	A T	A T	A T	A T	A T
117	Room										

		SUBJECT	Cr.	1 Av.	2 Av.	SUBJECT	Cr.	1 Av.	2 Av.	SUBJECT	Cr.	1 Av.	2 Av.	SUBJECT	Cr.	1 Av.	2 Av.	SUBJECT	Cr.	1 Av.	2 Av.
118	Marks in School	English				English				English				English				English			
119	Subjects																				
120																					
121																					
122																					
123	Picture Grades																				
124	10-11-12																				
125																					
126																					
127		Physical Education				Physical Education				Physical Education				Physical Education				Driver Training—Date			
128		CREDITS				CREDITS				CREDITS				CREDITS				CREDITS			

		NAME	CA	MA	IQ	%ile	NAME	CA	MA	IQ	%ile	NAME	CA	MA	IQ	%ile	NAME	CA	MA	IQ	%ile	NAME	CA	MA	IQ	%ile
129	School Ability Tests																									
130																										

		Gr.	TEST	Score	%ile	Gr.	TEST	Score	%ile	Gr.	TEST	Score	%ile	Gr.	TEST	Score	%ile	Gr.	TEST	Score	%ile
131	Educational Tests																				
132	Standardized																				
133																					

134	Social Qualities Rating	QUALITIES LISTED—REVERSE OF CARD				
135	Individual Development					
136	Special Abilities and Interests					
137	Personality Assets					
138	Needs Help With					
139	Behavior Modified By					
140	Referred To					
141	Clubs and Offices					
142	Work Outside of School					
143	Educational Plans					
144	Vocational Plans					
145	Teacher's Signature					

111 | Name—(Last-First-Middle) | Father | Mother | Address (Use Pencil) | Phone

important that accurate, complete records be kept on pupil attendance. Most districts provide each teacher with an attendance record book, or register, in which spaces are provided for attendance data and, usually, spaces for the pupil's date of birth, address, and parents' and guardians' names. District-adopted attendance summary sheets are also provided teachers so that at the end of an attendance period, usually a month or six weeks, the instructors may turn in to the principal's office the total class attendance for the month, along with the average daily attendance for each classroom. Since it is the responsibility of the principal to see that such summary reports are accurate, many administrators have clerks check the summaries against the teachers' registers. Usually, then, the principal turns in to the superintendent the overall attendance summary of his unit for each attendance period, again on forms provided by the district or the state. A final attendance report is also turned in to the superintendent at the end of the school year.

OTHER TYPES OF RECORDS

As indicated earlier, many schools maintain a number of different types of records regarding their pupils. So that teachers may adjust instruction from time to time according to pupils' physical condition, many units keep rather elaborate health records; some schools have separate health cards, others use a type of anecdotal record for this purpose, and still others keep an accurate and up-to-date section concerning health on the cumulative records. Reports of communicable diseases are usually kept in the records, as are height and weight data, and results of physical examinations. Accident data are important to protect the well-being of pupils, and to insure that the school and staff will be protected against claims of negligence.

Many schools maintain achievement profiles of pupils so that their achievement level in the various areas of learning may be maintained. Such profiles indicate acceleration or retardation by years and months in the various areas, and also provide an opportunity for teachers to compare growth as shown by results of tests taken at two or more different times.

Everyday experiences of pupils are recorded in many schools in the form of anecdotal records. Teachers write the anecdotes, recording positive and negative behavior patterns of children in different situations and activities over a period of time, dating each anecdote. Such records aid the teachers in conferences with parents as well as in helping pupils pursue activities to meet their individual needs. Anecdotal reports often indicate pupils' expressed interests and attitudes, and enable teachers to know their pupils better, and so better guide their learning experiences. Anecdotal reports are usually kept in the students' cumulative record folder.

The curriculum record, a little-used but valuable report, is a teaching log indicating group activities of all kinds. Problems of curriculum and instruction are often brought to light when records are kept of field trips, social activities, health and safety experiences, lunchroom activities, and experiences in language arts, arithmetic, social studies, and science.

CONCLUSION

One of the principal's prime responsibilities in respect to accurate record keeping is to clearly explain the purposes of such records to his staff, since it is they, after all, who keep the records and make the reports. He must impress the faculty with the importance of the reported information, and demonstrate how it can lead to improved facilities and services in the school. He must not only inform the faculty that accurate reporting aids in securing financial assistance from the state, but he must also lead the staff into seeing the value of reports in providing a better educational program for the students. Ideally, the principal will provide teachers with release time from teaching so that they can work on time-consuming reports and, if possible, he will see that teachers have clerical assistance in preparing records and reports. An in-service education program in the keeping of records would not be amiss in most elementary schools.

Elementary school principals can further improve the record-keeping system, and help keep teacher tempers in check, by scheduling the school's reporting activities, providing and making readily accessible all forms that will be needed as they make their reports, and providing easily accessible storage space for the report forms. A continual evaluation of the records and reporting process by the principal and the staff may result in more efficient and time-saving ways of keeping records and reporting information.

Some reports and records in the elementary school are the sole or main business of the school's administrator. These include financial reports, inventories, requisitions, certificated and non-certificated personnel records, schedules of various kinds, public relations releases, operational reports of the attendance unit, and reports for outside agencies, among others. A large proportion of the principal's routine record-keeping and reporting may be done by office clerks and secretaries; in districts where there is no office help, the principal must keep records and complete reports himself.

The new principal should, as one of his first duties, acquaint himself with the state, county, and local board of education requirements with respect to records and reports to be submitted from his attendance unit. Whenever he and his staff have a voice in what records and reports should be compiled, they should bear in mind that the forms should be consistent with the school's objectives, and should contain spaces only for significant facts and figures in pupil's educational lives and experiences. The number of forms should be kept to a minimum, consistent with the demands of the school and its community. And, most important, the records should be used for the promotion of the welfare of the boys and girls in the school.

Short Case 1

Emphasis on Academics

Emily Fort sat down in the teachers' room. It seemed her first moment of relaxation since parent conferences began two weeks before; the new first grade teacher noted that only two parents had failed to keep their appointments. The majority of her pupils were children of professional people, and Emily felt that she had gained much during the conference periods. She was somewhat disappointed, though, at the emphasis most of them had placed upon academic progress. The parents indicated little concern over other areas of growth. Eager to discuss this with the principal, Earl Halpen, she had stopped by his office only to learn that he was attending a district staff meeting. Another question was in Emily's mind. Should she make home visits if the parents failed to respond?

The following morning, Mr. Halpen stopped by Miss Fort's room before school. "Oh, I'm so glad you came," said Emily. "I did want you to give me some help with respect to a couple of problems that arose during my parent conferences." The principal interrupted: "I am sorry. I continue to apologize, but I just can't stay; I have to see another teacher about a problem."

Problem: Why were the parents of Miss Fort's pupils interested mainly in academic progress? What particular responsibility did the principal have regarding the new teacher? What educational philosophy apparently abounded in this elementary school? What could the principal have suggested that might have been helpful in Miss Fort's dilemma?

Short Case 2

Inadequate Health Records

Julia Lanyon had just returned to teaching after an absence of six years. As a new teacher in the area, she was assigned to a school in the lowest socio-economic area of the city. Most of the parents were itinerant workers, and drifted in and out of the area rather aimlessly. Shortly after the fall term began, Miss Lanyon noted that one of her best fourth grade pupils was unable to do his work much of the time. Upon questioning him, she found that he was constantly in pain with severe tooth-ache. Looking at his teeth she discovered that nearly all of them were badly decayed and surmised that several might be abscessed.

Miss Lanyon wondered how many others in the class needed dental work, so she checked health records of all children in her room. Much to her dismay she found that records of dental examinations and referrals were seriously lacking. When she had finished checking on the health records of all of her children, Miss Lanyon was disturbed because of the obvious lack of keeping up-to-date health records on children in the school. She approached the principal and described her findings. The principal replied that he didn't know what she wanted him to do about it as the district had no adequate health records and no funds with which to purchase forms for this purpose. He said he guessed that it was up to the parents to take care of their children.

Problem: By what authority or reason did Miss Lanyon question the school's lack of health records? What is the principal's responsibility to his staff in this respect? What steps should Miss Lanyon take at this point? What can a principal do whose school has "no adequate health records and no funds with which to purchase forms for this purpose"?

Short Case 3

Non-Use of Records

During November of his first year as an elementary school principal, Mr. Neummil was surprised to find a very dejected Miss Kringli at his office door. Usually Miss Kringli was so full of enthusiasm and good spirits that it had never occurred to Mr. Neummil that she might be depressed upon occasion. During the conversation, the principal learned that Miss Kringli's mood was occasioned by the fact that several of her sixth graders were making virtually no progress in arithmetic; even in addition and subtraction they made numerous and frequent errors. She was beginning to feel that she was a failure in her third year of teaching.

When Mr. Neummil asked what the cumulative record indicated about these pupils' ability levels and problems that they had shown in earlier grades, Miss Kringli replied, much to his bewilderment, that she had not really thought of consulting the cumulative records for this information. She told the principal that hardly any of the teachers used them, that they didn't feel the records seemed worth the trouble involved in consulting them.

Problem: What steps could Mr. Neummil take to remedy the situation that exists in his elementary school? Does Miss Kringli have any responsibility in this situation? If so, what is it? What should the school principal do to change teachers' attitudes toward reporting and keeping records?

Chapter Thirteen

Pupil Services at the Elementary Level

The thousands of elementary schools in operation all over the United States exist for just one purpose: to serve the boys and girls who attend them. A statement of this purpose seems simple and self-evident; its implementation is quite another thing. When a school's avowed purpose is to *serve* its pupils, much more is implied than the sole objective of meeting children's intellectual needs; though this, it is agreed, is the primary task. Services for pupils include not only the academic activities of the classroom, but also all other activities which provide for growth and development in social, emotional, mental, and physical areas. If the classroom alone could provide for all the needs of boys and girls, there would be no occasion for such other provisions as the school office, transportation, food services, health services, and library services. The fact is, however, that these services have actually become increasingly important in recent years, and it is safe to assume that they will not become less so in the years immediately ahead. Their place in the elementary school program has become fixed and secure.

Certain of the school's provisions for the welfare of students were discussed in previous chapters. Those described here might be referred to as classroom-supporting activities, or activities whose centers of operation are located outside the classroom, but which exist to supplement and implement the procedures of the classroom. It is the responsibility of the school's administrative officials to make sure that they function effectively.

THE PRINCIPAL'S ROLE IN PUPIL SERVICES

Office, transportation, food, health, and library services are a part of the school program because far-sighted individuals saw a need for such services and took steps to provide them. If such services do not now exist in some elementary schools of America, the principals of those schools could make a genuine contribution to their systems and to their communities by taking steps to assure their establishment. This procedure would require, of course, close cooperation between the people of the school-community, the superintendent of schools, the board of education, and other school personnel. Their planning, led by the principal, can assure either the *provision* of such services, or the *maintenance* of such activities, or both. It is the authors' firm conviction, as a result of experience, that when lay persons and school personnel are brought together in mutual trust and confidence to consider a program which will benefit the children of the community, great things can be accomplished.

Besides the responsibility of planning and working for a program of school services, a second task of the elementary principal is that of making certain that the services work for the best interests of the children in the school. There have been instances of special-interest groups who have offered their "services" to the schools, but such services have proved to be for the welfare of the groups rather than for the welfare of the children. Principals must be overly cautious in such instances; one elementary school principal had an experience in which a certain organization, with its "altruistic" aims, was traced through the local community's organizations, the state department of education, the state teachers' association, and finally through the National Education Association, only to find that the "services" being offered were not in the best interest of children. Needless to say, the "services" of the organization were not accepted in the school.

The third responsibility of the elementary school principal in respect to services for children is that of making sure that they will be utilized effectively, and in accord with proper teaching principles, by members of the staff. The finest school library in America, for instance, is of no earthly value in and of itself; teachers must be motivated to use it themselves and to inspire their classes to use it. Essentially, the same statement could be made with respect to the office, the health clinic, the cafeteria, and even the transportation services. None of these service facilities exists in an elementary school building simply to make the school appear more modern, up-to-date, and progressive. The only defensible reason for the existence of such services is that they are used effectively for the welfare of the boys and girls in the school. In most instances, it is the teachers who see to it that the services are used by their pupils when the need arises.

THE SCHOOL OFFICE

Until recently, the typical elementary school principal's office was a room equipped with the bare essentials of office furniture, where the head of the school performed the necessary clerical duties connected with the operation of the attendance unit. It was a place for teachers to avoid, and most certainly it was one office for pupils to shun at all costs. One principal vividly recalls a visit from a second-grade pupil in which the little fellow asked, as he pointed to the fire-proof vault in which the cumulative records were kept, "Is that where you keep the spanking machine?" This, no doubt, points up the attitude toward the principal's office that was held by the pupil's parents when they attended elementary school and, unfortunately, was the attitude of many children in the schools a generation ago.

Research in education since the turn of the century has influenced school practices and, additionally, the functions of the office of the principal. Today, rather than spending a great deal of time in performing routine clerical tasks, the principal is expected to assume the role of an educational statesman; in essence, this means that his function is that of carrying out responsibilities essential to the improvement of the education of pupils in his school. The equipment in his office consists of a myriad of facilities designed to expedite administrative and supervisory services which are an integral part of a modern elementary school's operation. All of these services exist for the primary function of the school: the education of boys and girls.

This is not to imply that a functional office of the elementary school principal need take on the spaciousness and luxury of a large corporation president's, but neither should it be some unused corner in the building equipped with only a desk and a book case. Whether the room arrangement provides for a suite containing private offices for principal, vice-principal, specialists, lounge, and health clinic, or whether it provides for a more modest arrangement, the concept of the principal's office should be that it is the instructional and administrative center of the building.

Since the office is often the place where first impressions of a school are formed, it should be warm, cheerful, colorful, neat, and interesting. Here many person-to-person relationships are developed, so comfortable chairs, including some small ones, should be provided so that a visitor to the office may be relaxed and at ease. But, with all of its cheerfulness and warmth, an office also needs to be business-like and efficient.

It is in an environment of warmth, sincerity, and efficiency that a principal can best discharge his responsibilities as leader of the school in promoting a high morale among all who come into contact with the school; as curriculum coordinator responsible for implementing and coordinating the school program; and as supervisor of instruction for various types of learners. In such an environment, the principal can best direct the activities connected with his office, such as public and professional relations, records, instructional materials, health services, and pupil, parent, and teacher counseling.

When a list of the general physical requirements for a principal's office is anticipated, due consideration should be given to the administrative personnel and services to be housed, as well as what is needed in the way of work stations, storage, and equipment; in short, the uses to be made of the office and the persons who are to use it should be prime considerations. The office, too, should be located in a part of the building which is easily accessible to the general public, but not so distant from the classrooms that the teachers and pupils lose a feeling of closeness to persons responsible for certain special services. In the outer office there should be a reception area equipped with three or four chairs, one or two of which should be child's size; this should be separated from the general office by a counter space, part of which should be of child's height. The general office should house a clerk and secretary with their desks, files, and work tables, complete with duplicating equipment. Here, also, the telephone switchboard and public address system console should be located. Mail boxes should be placed in a location convenient for both the staff and the clerk.

The principal's private office should be located so that it is adjacent to the outer office, but his desk should not be in the line of vision from the counter. Two doors should be provided, one leading to the outer office, the other leading to the outside of the building. If there is a vice-principal, his office should have the same facilities as the principal's, and his office should be separate from that of the principal.

A desirable feature of an administrative suite is a conference room in which meetings between the principal and pupils, the principal and parents, staff and parents, or principal and small staff groups might be held. Here, also, tests might be administered to individuals or to small groups. Furniture should include a large conference table, preferably round, and eight or ten comfortable chairs, some storage files or cabinets, and facilities for audio-visual aids and testing machines.

A room for storage of instructional supplies and certain movable equipment should be located near the outer office, convenient for staff and for the office clerk who holds the key to the door. If the supply shelves and cabinets are located in a teacher's work room, the master keys that unlock classrooms should also unlock the doors to the supplies. A teachers' lounge is almost a necessity in an elementary building. It should be attractive and have comfortable, easy-to-maintain furniture, including a small range and refrigerator. Magazine racks holding professional periodicals should be placed in the room, and a bulletin board should be provided.

A health clinic, complete with facilities for testing vision and hearing, and other equipment recommended by medical authorities and manned by the school nurse, is an important part of the general office suite. It should be located so that children occupying the two beds in the unit may be observed from the outer office, but not from the reception area, so that the children may be observed by the school clerk if the nurse is temporarily absent. The usual toilet and washing facilities should be included in the clinic, along with medicine cabinets and testing equipment.

A SCHOOL OFFICE IN IOWA

An example of a functional elementary school office is that found at Pleasant View School near Pleasant Valley, Iowa. Completed in 1959, along with the rest of the $698,000 building, which contains 31,000 square feet, the office is the result of considerable planning between the architects and officials of the school.

The administrative unit of the building consists of a principal's office, an outer reception area, a walk-in vault work-room, an intercommunication room, and a storage area. The area of the unit is approximately 16 feet by 42 feet.

Advanced planning made possible the following advantages of this office unit:

1. The main playground and play areas are visible from the administrative office.
2. The busport where students enter and leave the building can be supervised from the office area.
3. Communications can be made with the play areas and busport from the intercom panel which also faces these imporant areas.
4. The foyer where students wait before regular classes is clearly visi-

ble from the administrative area through glass areas in the aluminum wall partitions.

5. The school clinic is adjacent to the administrative area and readily available.
6. The area contains built-in cupboards, file cabinets, bulletin boards, automatic bell equipment, teacher mailboxes, and bookshelves.
7. The office area is located directly adjacent to the main entrance, and is easily accessible to visitors.
8. The principal's office provides complete privacy, with entrances both from the outer office and from the adjacent corridor.[1]

TRANSPORTATION SERVICES

A once familiar scene in the "good old days" was that of boys and girls walking or riding horseback or in animal-drawn carriages one, two, three, or even more, miles to school through foul weather as well as fair. In place of this, a huge fleet of the familiar yellow and chrome buses now transport children safely from their homes to school and back again. As consolidation of school districts continues and one-room schools and other small attendance units close their doors, more children of the community board the fast, safe, and comfortable buses to attend classes in buildings some distance from their homes.

The proportions which the transportation services have attained in recent years are revealed by the fact that more than 12 billion boys and girls, representing one of every three pupils, ride on 171,000 buses as they travel about three and three-fourth million miles each day over all kinds of roads in all kinds of weather at a cost of little more than $35 per rider per year. And yet, with the latest in bus construction engineering, and with the emphasis upon more rigid driver examinations, training, and supervision, the school bus is the safest mode of transportation today.

At one time, most schools contracted with private carriers to transport pupils, but with the trend toward more school-operated and maintained vehicles, principals are assuming additional responsibilities in transportation service. Additional responsibilities accrue, also, with the trend toward the schools' use of large capacity buses of the transit type, as well as small vehicles for small groups of pupils.

Since everything that takes place in the program of the elementary school is a part of the curriculum which the principal administers, he is, therefore, responsible for the supervision of the bus operation at his school. He is charged with seeing to it that statutory and board rules

[1] Ed Fauble, "A Functional School Office," *The National Elementary Principal,* XL (October, 1960), pp. 20–21.

and regulations regarding transportation are carried out; he is expected to see that children's safety and well-being are protected while boarding, riding, and alighting from the buses. The principal, usually in collaboration with bus drivers and teachers, builds the bus schedules, and alters them when necessary in the best interests of efficiency and safety. He maintains the same relationship with drivers of the buses as he does with other members of the instructional and non-certificated staffs.

Good pupil attitudes help promote good pupil behavior on the buses; the principal, together with the drivers and teachers, shares the responsibility for motivating children's proper attitudes. Some authorities advocate written rules of behavior for children who ride the buses; others maintain that handing children a written list of "do's" and "don'ts" for bus travel is probably the least effective method of promoting good behavior. At any rate, the children should know what is expected of them; they must *learn* what good standards of behavior are before they can be expected to exercise them. It is the principal's responsibility to see that they have the opportunity to learn them.

Assignment of teachers to "bus duty," supervision of the loading and unloading of children on the buses, is also the responsibility of the school's administrator. He must, in some way, instill in teachers charged with this duty an appreciation of the importance of the safety and welfare of the students; together they must implant in the minds of young people the importance of learning socially-acceptable and safe modes of travel in public conveyances. This, of course, is part of the education of children, and it can be accomplished principally inside the classroom, without lessening the child's enjoyment of riding on the bus with classmates and friends.

Seeing that driver's reports, accident reports, and principal's reports to the central office get in on time is another of the principal's transportation service responsibilities. Some authorities recommend that the principal provide the superintendent of schools with a regular weekly report on the status of the school's transportation services.

Finally, it is the principal's responsibility to see that the school buses help extend and enrich the educational program of the district. In modern schools, the buses are used to a far greater extent than for the sole purpose of transporting pupils to and from school. The vehicles are used for educational field trips taken by pupils and adults in the community; they transport new teachers through the district as part of an orientation indoctrination; they provide transportation for various groups in the community when certain of their activities require such service. The school's transportation facilities can be used by the principal as an effective public relations medium.

ADEQUACY OF BUS SERVICE

A problem with which the administrator must inevitably grapple is that concerning who shall ride the buses. It would be well if the school system's administrative officials would initiate a campaign to persuade the board of education to adopt written transportation eligibility standards to be distributed in the community. Such standards should be based on the school's enrollment, distance children live from the school, presence of various types of hazards, and ability of children to walk to school.

Following are the transportation eligibility standards adopted by the San Luis Obispo, California, school system:

> Bus transportation is available to all regularly enrolled pupils of the San Luis Obispo City Schools whose residence is outside of the 1947–48 city limits. Any exception to this rule shall be by written permit only. Bus transportation is offered only provided a pupil conforms to all rules and regulations regarding bus transportation. If there is any question regarding eligibility of a passenger, the bus driver should require a written permit from the school principal. Pupils are picked up only at regular stops as designated by school officials. School buses are to be used for transporting school pupils from home to school and from school to home only. Any exceptions must be authorized by the office of the Superintendent of Schools.
>
> *Conduct of passengers.* While riding on a school bus, students should be expected to conduct themselves in a manner similar to that which is expected of them in a regular school classroom—with the exception that normal conversation should be permitted. Loud talk, whistling, or shrill noises of any type are not allowed. Such things are a hazard to the safety of passengers. Passengers are to remain in their seats while the bus is in motion. At no time shall passengers be permitted to extend hands, arms, or other portions of their bodies outside of the windows.
>
> *Discipline.* Good discipline in a school bus is essential to the safety of passengers. Riding on a school bus is a privilege. Furnishing bus transportation for school pupils is optional with the governing board of the district. Failure on the part of a bus passenger to conform to rules and regulations may result in the loss of school bus privileges.
>
> The bus driver is "captain of his ship." All bus passengers are responsible to the driver for their behavior while riding on a school bus. The driver must have the respect of all passengers. Discipline cases should be referred immediately to the school principal.[2]

---

[2] San Luis Obispo City Schools, *Instructions for School Bus Drivers,* duplicated, undated, pp. 1–2.

Such a set of standards might serve as a guide to other administrators and school boards as they strive to resolve the problems involved in providing adequate transportation services.

FOOD SERVICES

The cafeteria is another service of the school which is the direct responsibility of the principal. While the cafeteria exists to provide hot lunches for students, it is by no means limited to that objective alone. As an integral part of the school program, the cafeteria provides opportunities for instruction in eating and health, citizenship education, sociability, and certain aspects of economics. Children are given the opportunity for certain types of work experiences in the cafeteria; and they may also improve their social skills by serving as hosts and hostesses when adults visit the school, as well as in everyday associations in the lunchroom with their classmates. Children and teachers of various grade levels can plan and implement the decorations in the cafeteria, and thus provide for more pleasant surroundings in that room.

While the ultimate responsibility of operating the cafeteria is that of the building principal, the usual practice is for the school's officials to employ a cafeteria manager whose duties include the planning of menus in compliance with proper children's dietary requirements, and general supervision of the operation of the lunchrooms and kitchen. Since the manager is an employee of the school district and will associate directly with children, he must be friendly with children and strive to know and understand them. He purchases all foods for the cafeteria, with an eye toward high nutritional standards as set forth by various state and federal agencies. He provides a statement of the cafeteria's operations, usually on a monthly basis, for the state department of education and for the local board of education, and he cooperates with teachers who wish to carry out units on foods and health. While the manager of the lunchroom operation carries out most of the actual responsibilities for the operation of the cafeteria, the principal ultimately is held accountable for the successful operation of the service unit, so it behooves him to keep in close contact with the activities of that unit.

There is no universally accepted practice with respect to the length of the lunch hour; some schools allow as little as twenty minutes, and others as much as sixty or more minutes for children to eat. Experimentation within the local building is perhaps the best method of determining the optimum time that certain classes should be allowed for lunch, since such factors as age of children and distance from classroom to cafeteria must be considered. At any rate, adequate time for proper eating should be provided, but not so much time as to encourage "playing" or other socially unacceptable behavior at the tables. Some schools are experimenting with a "closed" noon-hour at the elementary level, in which case the lunch hour essentially becomes another "class" during the time allotted for this activity. Cooperative planning by teachers and the principal is necessary in the important area of scheduling.

In some schools, teachers eat with the children all or part of the time, while in others they do not; here, again, there is no universally accepted pattern. There are arguments for and against either practice. Those schools whose policy it is for teachers to eat with children hold that in this way table manners and acceptable social graces can best be developed in children. On the other hand, there are those schools which hold that teachers need a rest period away from children at some time during the day, and in self-contained classroom situations the noon-hour is about the only time in the daily schedule that can be set aside for teacher relaxation. Both points of view have merit. Again, cooperative planning and experimentation may point up the best policy for a local attendance unit. In cafeterias which provide a separate room for faculty, use may be made of parents, teachers' aides, or substitute teachers to supervise the eating activities in the dining room.

Financially, the basic cafeteria problem in most schools is to make the food services operation pay its own way without jeopardizing the nutritional value of the lunches served to the children. A portion of the principal's responsibility in this respect is to keep the food services operation as free from financial burdens as possible, so that the quality and quantity of the lunches may be continuously improved, and at the same time to keep the cost of the meals within the range of pupils and teachers. The Federal government, through the National School Lunch Act of 1946, and the local districts, through subsidization of a portion of the cafeteria's operation, have enabled many school officials to meet this responsibility. In past years, the Federal government, operating through the state departments of education, has provided surplus food commodities and monies to help defray costs of meals, thus enabling most children to have a warm, well-balanced noon-day meal at a minimal price.

An important phase of the cafeteria operation involves obtaining a desirable environment. In this respect there exists an almost universal teacher complaint that there is "too much noise in the lunchroom." It is true, of course, that a desirable environment would be devoid of flying food and cutlery, and excessive pushing, shoving, tripping, and boisterousness. At the same time, however, it should be pointed up that a desirable environment does not preclude a lunchroom situation in which children converse in a normal manner in much the same way that adults converse in any public eating place. When 200 to 500 boys and girls of elementary school age are assembled together to eat, there is bound to be a considerable amount of "noise" from just the simple act of talking together. But careful attention should be given to what is a normal amount of talking, as opposed to an excessive amount of noise. If the noise is truly excessive, the staff might consider answers to some of the following questions:

Are children given an opportunity to share with teachers and parents in the planning of cafeteria operations and activities? Is the lunchroom generally a pleasant place to eat? Is the cafeteria free of unsavory odors? Are children treated fairly and justly while they are in the dining room, and are they given adequate time to complete their meal? Do children from different rooms sharing the lunchroom at the same time cooperate with and respect each other as they remain in food lines and as they move to and from tables? Are the tables of proper size; are they kept clean and inviting? Are the walls and ceilings acoustically treated, and are they pleasing to the sight through appropriate colors and decorations? Do teachers eat with children? The correction of adverse conditions is bound to improve the lunchroom environment and lead to more socially acceptable behavior on the part of children.

THE MARYVILLE, MISSOURI, CAFETERIA

Typical of effective food service operations is the one located in the public schools of Maryville, Missouri, adjudged by supervisors from the state department of education as one of the best-equipped and operated cafeterias in the state. This operation, established in newly-constructed quarters in the mid-1950's, serves children in the public elementary school building, where the cafeteria is situated, and also students in the public high school building located about one block distant.

Children eat a plate meal planned to meet nutritional standards set by federal and state home economists and nutritional experts. By meeting such standards, the Maryville schools are entitled to cash reimbursements for each plate served, in addition to food commodities distributed by the state department authorities. This subsidy, plus the fact that the cafeteria manager successfully integrates the surplus foods into the menus, has resulted in meals of quality and quantity for students and teachers in the schools at a very low price. Children are encouraged to pay for two weeks in advance for their meals, though they may purchase them daily if desired. Teachers keep lunch records for the individual classrooms, which are turned in to the principal's office at the end of the month on forms provided for the purpose, and from which his monthly reports to the state department and the local board of education are prepared.

Classrooms are dismissed for lunch on a "staggered" basis to prevent long lines and an overflow of pupils into the cafeteria. In order to speed up the service, first and second grade children's trays are placed by upper-grade kitchen help at the tables so that when the younger children enter the dining room they simply sit at their places before a steaming hot lunch. They, like other patronizers of the cafeteria, "bus" their own trays and silver service to the receiving window, where upper grade students dump the scraps into garbage pails and place the trays and silver into the dishwasher baskets. A number of needy children are provided with free lunches.

The adult kitchen staff consists of the manager, himself an experienced restaurant operator, and two assistants. Some upper grade and high school boys and girls assist with minor tasks in the operation of the food service under the direction of the cafeteria manager.

Special tables are prepared for staff members, though they often eat with their children. Teachers spend considerable time in classrooms with units on food, health, social amenities, and proper eating habits, and they have access to the cafeteria whenever such facilities are a useful part of their classroom projects. Teachers, on a schedule, serve as supervisors in the cafeteria. Special holiday lunches have become traditional at the Maryville School, but the quality of the daily lunches has caused the patronage of the cafeteria to grow in numbers each year since the operation began.

The building, utilities, custodial services, and kitchen personnel wages are provided for from district funds, as was the initial capital outlay for cafeteria equipment.

HEALTH SERVICES

Administrators have long been concerned about the mental and physical health of the boys and girls in America's schools, but at no time in the history of public education have administrators been completely satisfied with the results of the schools' health services and health instruction. Despite the emphasis given through the years to the development of a healthy mind and body, the mental institutions are crowded and becoming more so, and it is a rare medical hospital that has an oversupply of empty beds. Some astounding statements have recently been issued by authorities concerned with the health of

America's citizens; for example, one authority predicted recently that at the present rate, by the year 2060 half of the people in this country will be in hospitals and the other half will be taking care of them! Obviously, if there is any semblance of accuracy in such a prediction, something has to be done about the present trend in public health.

The very first objective of the first set of educational goals ever published in this country was that of "Health." When the report of the Commission on Reorganization of Secondary Education, National Education Association, was presented in 1918 as the *Cardinal Principles of Secondary Education,* there was an emphasis upon health instruction, good health habits, health in work and play, and health in the home and community. In the widely-circulated objectives of education as formulated in 1938 by the Educational Policies Commission of the National Education Association, under the initial listing of the Objectives of Self-Realization, these three may be found: *Health Knowledge*—The educated person understands the basic facts concerning health and disease; *Health Habits*—The educated person protects his own health and that of his dependents; and *Public Health*—The educated person works to improve the health of the community. It is doubtful that there has ever appeared a list of objectives of education in which health was not among the most important in the group; yet, the results of health programs in the schools and elsewhere leave much to be desired in this important area.

While there is almost universal agreement that children's health is of paramount importance, there is wide misunderstanding and difference of opinion regarding the organization, administration, and implementation of the modern school health program. Some possible causes of this dilemma are the following:

1. The schools have been placing too much emphasis upon the theory of health practices instead of upon the individual well-being of pupils.
2. Teachers are generally not well-versed in the subject of health; many are at a loss as to how to supplement and implement textbooks and other materials in health, even if they have such materials.
3. School officials fail to utilize the services of other agencies of the community, such as the health department, and the medical and dental professions, in the planning and carrying out of the health services of the attendance units.
4. In-service training programs in health education are not provided; failure to evaluate the current health services results in the school's failing to keep in step with changing needs and trends.
5. Much misunderstanding exists among school personnel, including the school nurse, as to diagnosis and treatment of pupils' ills; in

some states teachers could find themselves involved in real problems as a result of simply administering aspirin or attempting to set splints on a broken arm.

6. There is little agreement on the extent of responsibility of boards of education and official community health agencies for the school's health service.

Several factors condition the type of health service organization which is most practical for any particular elementary school. Some of these conditioning factors are: size and location of the school, financial status of the district, state and local legal provisions and restrictions, availability of specialists in the various health areas and, most important of all, the attitude, interest, and leadership of the school's administrators. Responsibility for the ultimate success or failure of an elementary school's health program rests squarely upon the shoulders of the principal, who either does or does not disseminate his interests to the instructional staff, and who does or does not extend to the community his concern for the physical and mental well-being of the students in his building.

If the principal is serious about bringing his school's health services out of the realm of the theoretical, to the practical level where it is of real service to pupils, he will be instrumental in providing action in several areas. First, he will see that a continuous day-by-day program of observation of children by their teachers is carried out; staff members are in a position where it is a relatively easy thing to detect early signs of communicable diseases, uncleanliness, poor mental health, and certain physical impairments, such as difficulty in seeing and hearing. A program of in-service education, utilizing community medical and psychological authorities, would be of great help to teachers as they endeavor to detect and refer cases needing attention.

Secondly, the principal who is genuinely concerned with the physical and mental well-being of the children in his school will provide adequate first-aid services. When a child is seriously injured, it is often necessary for the school to take immediate steps for providing relief until proper authorities can be summoned and arrive on the scene. In such cases, parents should be notified immediately.

The good principal will also regard adequate health records as his responsibility. In cooperation with the staff, parents, and other affected persons, the principal will provide forms carrying a complete health history of the children, and will see that they are sent along with the boys and girls as they progress through the school.

Finally, the principal will make provision for periodic physical examinations for the children in the school, and see that the results of the examinations are made known promptly and confidentially to the children's parents. Medical and dental examinations made even once each school year will work wonders in upgrading pupils' general well-being, including their academic achievement, all other things being equal.

DENVER'S SCHOOL HEALTH SERVICES

An effective school health services program is found in Denver, Colorado, where more than 50 nurses work some time every week in modern health rooms in every school in the city. In the elementary and junior high schools, each nurse carries an average pupil load of from 1200 to 1600, and each nurse considers herself a member of both the teaching and nursing professions, with some social work also included.

In Denver, the school nurses assist classroom teachers by: (1) helping to relieve their concern for individual children; (2) planning with teachers the classroom teaching units concerned with health service activities that involve the children; (3) planning with the teachers time for vision and hearing tests, weighing, dental examinations, inspections for skin infections, and medical examinations; (4) planning with the teachers all classroom first-aid procedures for the care of minor injuries; and (5) planning the major first-aid program for the building, ordering supplies, and supervising the health materials used by the classroom teachers.

The school nurses assist principals and teachers in Denver in the procedures of admitting and excluding children who are ill or injured. When children are excluded, the nurses counsel with the parents regarding further steps to take in the case. Nurses assist medical examiners in conducting examinations when given at school, encourage referrals to the family physicians, and follow through with parents and teachers on medical recommendations for the children. The nurses are responsible for selecting and scheduling children to be screened in the areas of weight, vision, hearing, and oral hygiene by technicians when they come to the school.

The nurses have charge of the health service rooms in the buildings, including activities carried out in the clinic, supplies and equipment, and room appearance. They keep records and reports on the children; each child has a cumulative health record which follows him throughout his entire public school experience.[3]

ELEMENTARY SCHOOL LIBRARY SERVICES

Almost as conspicuous by its absence as the hickory stick and the dunce cap, is the elementary school pupil with a single book in read-

[3] Gertrude E. Cromwell, "School Nurse Is Part of the School Program," *The Nation's Schools,* LIX (February, 1957), pp. 63–64.

ing, another single book in arithmetic, and a third in history. Recent research and experimentation in child growth and development and the process of learning have made the single textbook approach to learning antiquated; in its place a concept of library services has emerged which helps children meet their needs in a much more adequate manner.

One of the greatest contributions the public schools can make toward the perpetuation and defense of the American way of life is to foster the practice of critical thinking by children and youth. If educators can cultivate in students a continuing attitude of questioning that which they read and hear, of checking on the authority of the statements made by individuals in books and in discussions or speeches, of examining all aspects of problems with which they are faced before arriving at a final conclusion or solution, then there is little danger that subversive influences will be successful in their attempts to undermine the democratic social order. The development of adequate library services in the elementary schools has paralleled the introduction of activities connected with the teaching of critical thinking, of problem solving methods, and of various other learning projects and curriculum innovations.

Modern library services in the elementary schools embrace a number of aids to the instructional program. First of all, they provide a suitable, adequate, and well-selected number of supplementary books and other references of the printed type which can be used in the classroom learning situation. Whether the school has a "central" library, or whether the organizational structure emphasizes the individual classroom library, many materials are classified as being a part of the library services of a school. There should be a balance between informational materials, reference materials, and types of fiction; there should be materials for the slow learners, the mentally superior pupils, the average children; there should be books and magazines and bulletins of learned organizations and government agencies to supplement reading, writing, arithmetic, social studies, science, language arts—all of the academic areas of the elementary schools; there should be books for potential professional persons, craftsmen, laborers, scientists, musicians, artists, firemen, postmen, milkmen, and other workers. Two dollars per year per pupil is none too large an allocation for such library materials.

Secondly, modern library services provide an adequate selection of audio-visual aids and materials. Projectors, recorders, films, slides, pictures, maps, charts, and other instructional materials of this type should be readily available to pupils and teachers so that they may be used to supplement the other materials in the learning situation. The library can be of inestimable assistance to a classroom teacher if, when notified by the teacher of an upcoming unit of work or problem situation, the librarian is able to provide many books, magazines, newspapers, pamphlets, bulletins, films, film-strips, charts, and pictures relating to the classroom activity.

A third provision of modern library services is that in which children learn how to use books, libraries, and audio-visual materials, how to develop better reading habits and tastes, and how to share reading experiences. The most effective type of structure to further these objectives is the centralized library room, where all library materials are at the disposal of all pupils and teachers. There is a trend toward the centralized library, manned by a full-time librarian.

The success or failure of modern library services depends, to a large extent, upon the disposition of the elementary school principal; his attitude toward the services, along with his leadership ability, can assure the realization of functional library services. The effect he has in assuring the board of education, school personnel, and pupils of the importance of adequate library services, together with his ability to encourage the use of the library by careful scheduling, will spell progress or lack of it in the adequate provision of this important aspect of elementary education.

The elementary school library should be located so that it is convenient to all classrooms in the school, including the kindergarten rooms, and arranged so that future expansion is possible. Lighting, heating, and sanitation should be adequate, and there should be a minimum of disturbing noises in the library areas. The minimum room size should be about 1300 square feet, about 30 square feet per pupil using the room being the ideal. Chairs and tables and book stacks of sizes suitable for elementary age children should be provided. Card-catalogs should be suited to the needs of the children in the school; even kindergarteners can learn to match pictures in the card catalog with pictures on the book cover. The library should have magazine racks, bulletin boards, chalk boards, display cases, and similar equipment.

Selection of books for the elementary school library is an important part of the service. Vocabulary and interest levels of pupils in the various grades, quality of materials, usefulness to the learning program, and durability are all aspects to be considered in selecting the materials. The principal would do well to involve the teachers in this process, since they know what materials would best serve the instructional program in the classroom; the school librarian can be a valuable aid in the selection of books, and the pupils themselves can also make valuable suggestions in this activity. Sources that are helpful in selecting books include: the *Children's Catalog,* published by the H. W.

Wilson Company; the *Handbook for the Teacher Librarians,* published by the American Library Association; the American Library Association's monthly bulletin, entitled *The Booklist;* and *Five Hundred Books for Children,* by Nora Beust, available through the United States Office of Education.

School personnel may find the chart in Figure 10 helpful in determining the skills to be developed in grade levels 1 through 6.

MIAMI SHORES, FLORIDA, LIBRARY SERVICES

The story of the initiation and maintenance of the elementary school library services in the Miami Shores, Florida, system exemplifies what can and is being done to provide excellent services of this type. To begin the project there, committees from the Parent-Teachers Association and the faculty, together with the principal, collected books from individual classrooms, discarded some, repaired others, and cataloged the remaining ones. Then they visited several established libraries, consulted with a trained librarian and followed her advice in using the *Children's Catalog* as a guide in ordering, processing, and cataloging. The P.T.A. supplemented the meager county appropriations for books for a number of years.

After operating for four years without a trained librarian, the school board employed a full-time, trained librarian. The P.T.A. provides a library committee which processes, catalogs, and mends the materials under the librarian's supervision. When the central administration office's appropriations became adequate, the P.T.A. undertook the building up of the collection of supplementary readers, filmstrips, films, recordings, maps, globes, flannel boards, and similar materials. Parents, teachers, and pupils built up the vertical file and a picture file. The art consultant took much of the responsibility for collecting the first pictures and directing the P.T.A. art committee in mounting them. This service has continued. Two upper-grade teachers allowed pupils who had the time and interest to clip and put tagboard covers on material from magazines like the *National Geographic* and *Life.*

A Classroom Planning Chart, where teachers list the units which they expect to teach for the next four to five weeks, was started as one means of insuring the availability of many materials for each unit, and to assist the librarian, physical education teachers, and consultants in art and music to plan ahead for better correlation with the classroom.

The selection of books, as well as of all other materials housed in the library, is a cooperative process; the faculty, parents, and children are encouraged to drop suggestions in a suggestion box, and to make

Figure 10. SKILLS TO BE DEVELOPED THROUGH THE USE OF THE SCHOOL LIBRARY

This chart outlines the skills to be developed in each grade level as the pupil uses a school library.[4] The points of emphasis are in italics. Both continuous growth in skills already learned and development of new skills are taken into account on each grade level.

Grade I

(1) *Library citizenship*
(2) *Care and appreciation of materials*
(3) Locating library materials
(4) Borrowing materials from school library

Grade II

(1) Library Citizenship
(2) Care and appreciation of materials
(3) *Locating library materials*
(4) *Borrowing materials from school library*
(5) *Discussing books*

Grade III

(1) Library Citizenship
(2) Care and appreciation of materials
(3) Locating library materials
(4) Borrowing materials from school library
(5) Discussing books
(6) *Reporting on books*
(7) *Using an index and a table of contents*

Grade IV

(1) Library Citizenship
(2) Care and appreciation of materials
(3) Locating library materials
(4) Borrowing materials from school library
(5) Discussing books
(6) Reporting on books
(7) Using an index and a table of contents
(8) *Using a juvenile encyclopedia*
(9) *Using a card catalog*
(10) Borrowing books from public libraries
(11) Taking notes
(12) Using pamphlet and picture materials

Grade V

(1) Library Citizenship
(2) Care and appreciation of materials
(3) Locating library materials
(4) Borrowing materials from school library
(5) Discussing books
(6) Reporting on books
(7) Using an index and a table of contents
(8) Using a juvenile encyclopedia
(9) Using a card catalog
(10) *Borrowing books from public libraries*
(11) Taking notes
(12) Using pamphlet and picture materials
(13) *Using an atlas and a globe*
(14) *Using an unabridged dictionary*

Grade VI

(1) Library Citizenship
(2) Care and appreciation of materials
(3) Locating library materials
(4) Borrowing materials from school library
(5) Discussing books
(6) Reporting on books
(7) Using an index and a table of contents
(8) Using a juvenile encyclopedia
(9) Using a card catalog
(10) Borrowing books from public libraries
(11) *Taking notes*
(12) *Using pamphlet and picture materials*
(13) Using an atlas and a globe
(14) Using an unabridged dictionary
(15) *Using WORLD ALMANAC*

---

[4] Virginia State Board of Education, *School Library Guide,* XXXVIII (September, 1955), p. 57.

suggestions during Book Week. Good books and other materials are adequately publicized. The librarian sends notes to teachers about books of special interest to them, and often refers enthusiastically to materials which are available. Teachers are encouraged to browse, and may borrow new materials before they are processed. New books are kept on display for one week. Each classroom is encouraged to keep a book collection in its library corner, and to change it at least once a month. The library at Miami Shores is open before and after school. The teachers and the librarian are constantly working together to improve the reading level and broaden the interests of the pupils; there is much book sharing in the classrooms, many book talks, much storytelling in the library, and much individual guidance by the librarian and teachers.

The library welcomes displays in classrooms, where pupils responsible for each display must exhibit with it appropriate books or other library materials.

All routine work in the Miami Shores library is done by pupils: from the third grade up, each room has its pupil librarians who supervise charging of materials, sign and shelve all materials returned, and check an assigned section of bookshelves weekly. First and second grade librarians return their class books before their class comes to the library, check on overdues for their group, and act as general liaison persons between their classroom and the library. Two literary groups, a Third-and Fourth-Grade Club and a Fifth-and-Sixth-Grade Club, meet monthly to plan and produce original programs and discuss library problems, and thus get experience in parliamentary procedure. Teachers give much library instruction by showing and discussing filmstrips on library tools, and other classroom instruction. This instruction begins during the second half of the third grade, and individual instruction goes on constantly, as the need arises. The librarian attends all faculty meetings, and the faculty is occasionally asked to evaluate the library.

The Miami Shores library, which serves more than 1,000 children, includes a reading room, a conference room, a workroom, storage room for old magazines and extra audio-visual machines, and a room for supplementary readers, maps, and other teaching aids. There is only one librarian, but he works closely with the curriculum consultant of the school system. Principal, parents, faculty, pupils, and librarian have all had a part in building the Miami Shores library and in making it an exciting and rewarding factor in the school.[5]

---

[5] Lois McAlister Pilson, "Cooperation Developed an Elementary School Library," *Instructor,* LX (November, 1958), pp. 79 ff.

CONCLUSION

Office, transportation, food, health, and library services each plays its unique role in the growth and development and learning of boys and girls in the elementary schools of America. With the possible exception of the library service, these areas are not generally considered to be a direct part of the academic achievement machinery of the school; but they do, nonetheless, contribute to the overall development of children. They are necessary and important to the elementary school program that strives to meet the basic needs of boys and girls as they progress through the school. Principals in modern progressive elementary schools will take appropriate steps to initiate and maintain these several services as a part of their schools' programs.

Short Case 1

A Health Problem

The nurse in the Monte Vista Elementary School called in Mrs. Felter and informed her that she should keep her four children out of school until their skin ailment, which was contagious but easily cured, was cleared up. The nurse had excluded these children on numerous occasions before; the mother had been very uncooperative about the matter. This time was no exception.

Mrs. Felter, her patience at an end, said that she would not take the children out of school again, despite the fact that the disease was still clearly existent. She claimed that the children had contracted the disease in the "dirty school," though examinations of all children in the school revealed no other cases. Despite pleas for cooperation on the part of the school nurse, the mother would not keep her children at home; rather, she personally brought the children to school and sat in the health clinic with them when their teacher sent them there, since the nurse had not given them clearance to attend classes.

Problem: What can the nurse do about this situation? What can the principal do to help resolve the problem? What laws in your state are applicable to a situation such as the one described in this case? What are the parents' responsibilities, and how can they be made to see and meet their duties? Are there other sources or referrals to whom the nurse and the principal can turn? Who are they, and what might be their recourse?

Short Case 2

An Incapacitated Bus

Morton School was the only public elementary school in a community of about 10,000 inhabitants. The first item on Superintendent Blake's agenda of the first meeting with Principal Curtner after the Christmas holidays referred to a problem that had arisen during the vacation: the oldest of three buses had been ruled unsafe for transporting pupils to Morton School. It was a 53-passenger vehicle, and was used on two different routes each morning and evening. There were no funds available with which to purchase a new bus, and additional monies would not be forthcoming until the coming summer. It appeared that the school would have to operate for the remainder of the year with but two buses. No public transportation facilities existed in the community.

There were several possible courses which the administrators decided they could pursue: (1) Re-schedule the two remaining buses' routes in such a manner that they would transport the pupils normally carried by the out-of-service vehicle, in addition to their regular passengers; (2) Employ private carriers to transport the pupils; (3) Appeal to parents to deliver their children to school and home again; (4) Ask teachers to cooperate in the emergency and to deliver the children in their private automobiles; (5) Re-route all bus schedules so that more children would be required to walk to school.

Problem: Which alternative should the administrators choose? Support your answer and explain in detail why this alternative would be better than any of the others. Can you think of any other possible alternatives? Explain in detail.

Short Case 3

Makes Haste Slowly

Ed Farr was ready to begin his second semester as principal in the Prairie Valley Elementary School. He had had four years of elementary school teaching experience, and two years of administrative experience at a small school in a community near Prairie Valley. During the first semester in his new situation, he had "made haste slowly," becoming acquainted with and gaining the confidence of the 27 teachers in Prairie Valley, acquainting himself with the school and its problems, and getting settled in a new community. He believed, as a result of studying achievement tests which had been administered in the school during the past four years, that the school's greatest challenge was to improve the reading program. Mr. Farr felt he was now ready to begin fulfilling his responsibilities as a supervising principal.

He motivated the faculty to elect a steering committee, and its first responsibility was to sound out the teachers as to what they felt were the school's most pressing problems. To Mr. Farr's surprise, the problem judged unanimously most important was the noise in the cafeteria.

Problem: If you were in Mr. Farr's position, which problem would you have the staff work on first—the reading problem or the one concerning noise in the cafeteria? Why? How would you proceed in introducing and pursuing your choice? When and how would you introduce the problem of reading achievement in the school?

Chapter Fourteen

Organizing for Effective Personnel Administration

No workers in any other profession serving the people need greater understanding of human relations than do the administrators of our public schools.

Edwin Stevens studied the administration of personnel policies in the schools of one state. He came to the conclusion that personnel functions are still treated in an incidental manner in far too many school systems of that state. It seemed evident to Stevens that business and industry were years ahead of the schools in this respect. There is no particular reason to believe that the findings in this particular state are significantly different from those in the majority of states.[1]

Maxine Robbins made an analysis of critical incidents in administration which were reported as affecting professional actions of teachers. A list of twenty-five requirements for an effective principal of an elementary school was compiled. Two important conclusions resulted from the study: (1) The most important area of requirement for elementary school principals is that of personal relationships; (2) Ineffective principals have more critical incidents in the area of personal relations than in any other area.

---

[1] Edwin Dillion Stevens, "Selected Personnel Policies and Practices Used in Business and Industry and Their Implications for Educational Administration" (Unpublished Doctoral dissertation, University of Connecticut, 1957).

Robbins recommended that institutions responsible for educating administrators should give more attention to the development of abilities in the field of human relations.[2]

THE CHANGE IN MANAGEMENT OF HUMAN RESOURCES

It is encouraging to note recent indications that school boards and school administrators have become interested in attempts to integrate the work of people in ways that motivate them to be productive and cooperative. These recent experiments in human relations have gradually evolved from examples set by business organizations and forward looking school systems. Human relationships have been with us as long as there have been people, but the attempt to deal with them on a planned basis is relatively new.

Records show that in the early part of the twentieth century some men in industry were becoming interested in people as important factors in their attempts to increase production.

In the 1930's Elton Mayo, a Harvard sociologist, and his colleagues became keenly interested in the thesis that the worker was the most important element in business, and that no one knew very much about the worker.[3] The work of Mayo and others caused human relations to become a concern of business executives. It became a common occurrence during the 1940's for respected managerial executives to lecture on the importance of understanding human relations as an essential factor in the successful management of a corporation. An example is a statement by Clarence Francis, made in 1947 when Francis was Chairman of General Foods Corporation:

> The problem of individual productivity is primarily and fundamentally one of human relations. People are composed of body, mind, and spirit, all of which, but particularly spirit, should be applied to executing assigned tasks if maximum productivity is to be attained.[4]

Statements such as this reflected increasing public concern for the rights and privileges of the employee. The public had been aroused about "sweatshops" and poor working conditions.

---

[2] Maxine Hazel Robbins, "An Analysis of Critical Incidents in Administration Reported as Affecting Professional Actions of Teachers" (Unpublished Doctoral dissertation, Indiana University, 1959).

[3] Elton Mayo, *The Human Problems of Industrial Civilization* (Cambridge: Harvard University Press, 1933), p. 47.

[4] Clarence Francis, "What's Ahead for Those in Industrial Relations Work?" *Industrial Relations,* Vol. V (October, 1947), p. 8.

The federal government had passed significant labor laws. In 1908, the Employer's Liability Act was passed covering accidents to railroad employees. The National Industrial Recovery Act in 1933 included a section on the rights of employees to organize and bargain collectively. The Social Security Act in 1935 provided certain benefits to workers and their dependents.

It was natural then that the leaders of business and industry would begin to spend time, money, and effort in an attempt to find new ways of coping with the need for improved relationships between administration and the worker.

The administration of school personnel has been subject to many of the same influences which have affected general public personnel administration. Personnel administration in schools has generally lagged behind the same type of administration in business and public service, but school systems have tended to pattern their personnel plans along lines similar to those found in industry and public service.[5]

PRESENT STATUS OF THE ART OF HUMAN RELATIONS

During World War II, great impetus was given to the actual formulation of programs of management and employee cooperation. The capitalist was no longer caricatured as a portly man smoking a long black cigar and wearing a huge twenty-four carat gold watch chain. He had become a man of meditation and thoughtful action. The symbol had changed to that of a serious and determined man seated at the mahogany conference table, surrounded by persons who could assist him in determining the right course of action. He was now regarded as having an interest in the employees of the company.

The changes in human relationships in the world of business were also arriving in the field of educational administration. The Ichabod Crane symbol of the pre-civil war headmaster had given way to one of the principal with the high starched collar and a Phi Beta Kappa Key dangling from his watch chain. By the early thirties the new symbol for the school executive had come to be quite like that of the executive in business. The principal, too, was seen as a person spending several hours each week at the conference table, assisted by teachers and other administrators in the problem-solving process. The elementary school principal today finds this symbol a fact as he works with committees

---

[5] B. J. Chandler and Paul V. Petty, *Personnel Management in School Administration* (New York: World Book Company, 1955), p. 27.

around the conference table in an attempt to solve the problems of his particular school.

By the end of World War II the literature describing practices in many of the high quality school systems in our country emphasized the concept that the most important job of the schools was to improve instruction. The superintendents and principals in these schools were realizing that one of their main functions was to find ways of working with and through people to obtain answers to instructional problems. If the improvement of instruction was a team-work endeavor, the superintendent and principal had to discover ways in which school staff members could attack the problems in a planned and logical manner. It meant too that there had to be mutual faith, confidence, and respect among all staff members.

GUIDING PRINCIPLES IN SOUND PERSONNEL ADMINISTRATION

The focal point of all activity in a school system should be the classroom where the learning experiences of pupils take place. The remaining functions, services, and plant facilities should be justified on the basis of their contribution to the effectiveness of the teacher and his work with pupils.[6] This means it is necessary that a prevailing philosophy should be at work in the schools. This philosophy may dictate that the school system is to be organized on the line-and-staff principle, or it may be a philosophy in which the line-and-staff organization does not completely satisfy the desire to give priority to human needs and values.

There is ample reason to believe that a majority of school administrators today are recognizing the importance of democratic organization and administration of schools. Now it is necessary to perfect school organizations where this philosophy may be put into practice. In order that the democratic concept may become a fact in the organization and administration of the schools, it is necessary to formulate some principles of action. These principles should give emphasis to each individual as an integral part of the team working to improve the teaching-learning process in the schools. It is significant that the formulation of principles governing personnel administration is a common problem in the administration of schools and in industry.

David C. Yang selected twenty-six industries, and collected personnel policy statements from each company. He also examined authoritative

[6] Roland F. Campbell and Russell T. Gregg, *Administrative Behavior in Education* (New York: Harper and Bros., 1957), p. 292.

statements from available literature on industrial and educational personnel management. He then derived a set of principles practiced in industry, and another set in use in educational administration.[7] The two sets present an interesting parallel:

Principles Derived from Industry

1. Principles should recognize and respect the worth and dignity of the individual.
2. They should provide opportunity for self-fulfillment and advancement.
3. They should be based on mutual responsibility.
4. They should provide security for all employees.
5. They should insure flexibility.
6. They should pave the way for group concern and participation.
7. They should help meet social and psychological needs of employees.
8. They should be based on fairness of pay and treatment.
9. They should be based on better working conditions.
10. They should promote job satisfaction.

Principles Derived from Education

1. Principles should be based upon respect for the worth of the individual.
2. They should provide opportunity of advancement and self-fulfillment.
3. They should encourage mutual responsibility and group welfare.
4. They should provide a sense of security.
5. They should develop adaptability to changing conditions.
6. They should emphasize participation and group concern.
7. They should foster respect for personal feelings and attitudes.
8. They should rely on the intelligence of man.
9. They should emphasize cooperative action.
10. They should emphasize democratic leadership.

In the above stated principles it is apparent that the first seven pairs are so similar that they can be treated as identities.

ORGANIZING FOR EFFECTIVE ADMINISTRATION OF PERSONNEL POLICIES

It is not enough to say that the school system should have a planned program of personnel administration. Such a program will not come into being without planning. The philosophy of the school system will determine how the administration of personnel problems will be handled. Attention should be given to keeping the plan as simple as

[7] David C. Yang, "A Study of Principles, Policies and Techniques of Personnel Relations in Industry and Their Implications for Personnel Relation in Education" (Unpublished Doctoral dissertation, Florida State University, 1957).

possible. As school systems grow large the organizational structure tends to grow more complex. This is apparently one of the reasons that it is more difficult to keep good staff relations in a large city school system.

FORMAL PLANS OF ORGANIZATION

The formal organization is that which can be drawn on a chart or described in writing, and which forms the structure used to allocate assignments and duties to personnel. The formal organization may provide for channels of communication, but too often that channel runs only one way, from the top down.

One plan of formal organization is that of the highly centralized school system. In this approach the program is initiated, planned, and managed by persons in the central office of the school system. Another approach could be called the decentralized approach. In this organization the initiation, planning, and management is primarily the responsibility of each school and the teachers in that school. The third approach could be called the centrally coordinated approach. This approach appears to maintain the strengths of the centralized and decentralized approaches, and to avoid some of their inherent weaknesses.

The centrally coordinated approach. The ideal formal organization is one that makes provision for the establishment of a central policy in all matters that concern the certificated and non-certificated employees of the school system, and yet which provides for the employees in each individual school. The centrally coordinated approach offers a way to capitalize on the efforts of individual schools and individual teachers, and yet utilize the central office personnel. It provides a way for all segments of the school system to work as a team in the cooperative attempt to solve problems. General authority is recognized and welcome: individual responsibility is recognized and accepted. Problems on an individual school basis and on a system-wide basis may be met and solved through the centrally coordinated approach.

Figure 11 illustrates a plan which a system or a school may use to conduct research to find the strengths and weaknesses of the prevailing personnel administrative structure. Such a project illustrates how cooperative planning may bring about workable policies and plans for more efficient personnel administration.

Staff participation in decision-making. In a study designed to gain insight into the elements of the work situation which tend to produce satisfaction and dissatisfaction, Margaret Browne used the non-directive interview technique with all agriculture, home economics, and 4-H club program leaders, district supervisors, and district administrators

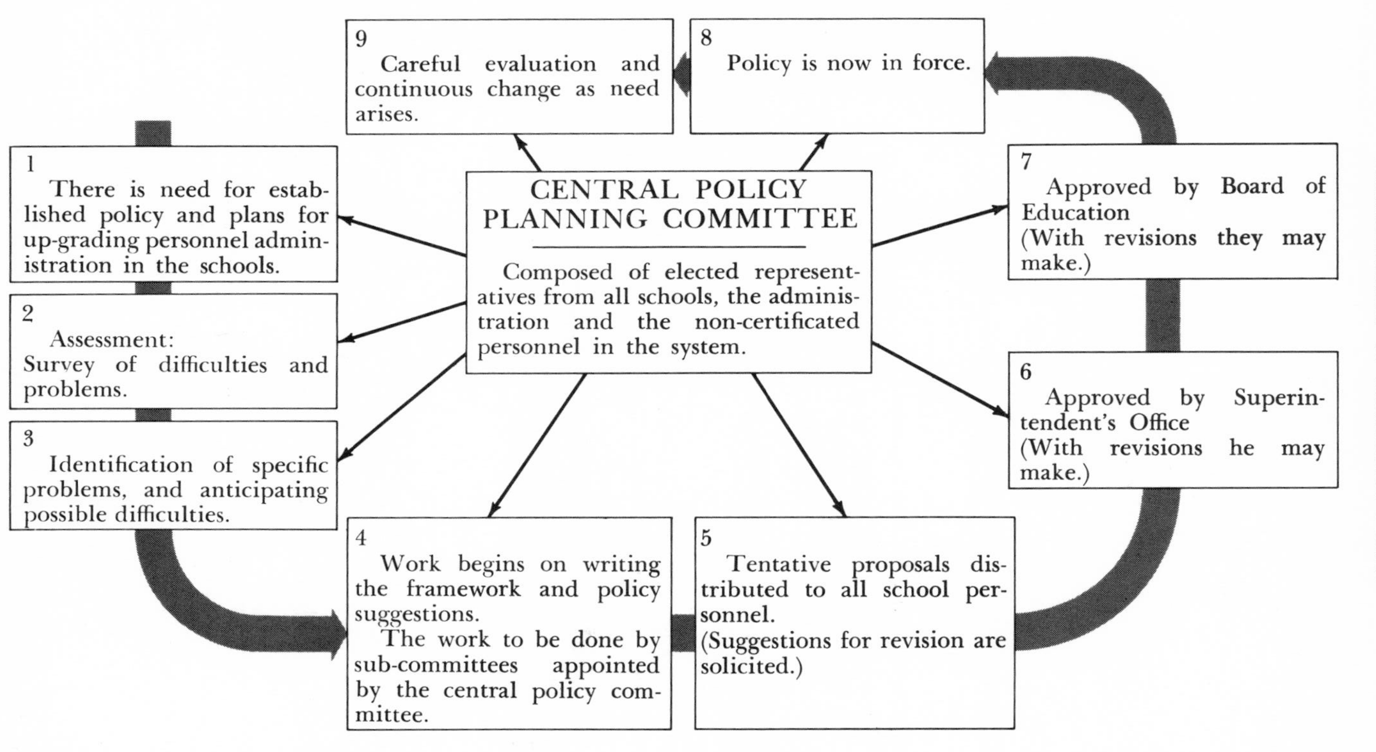

Figure 11 CYCLE OF COOPERATIVE PLANNING FOR ESTABLISHMENT OF PERSONNEL POLICY

in the extension services of three states. Her findings are significant as they relate to the importance of cooperative planning and decision-making in the schools.

Job satisfactions appeared to be lowest where: (1) respondents felt least involved in decision-making; (2) communication was judged to be inadequate; (3) there was the largest number of levels in the hierarchy.[8]

Harry H. Houston studied the administrative process as it relates to decision-making. He identified and classified the factors that affect centralized and decentralized administration. The factor most closely examined was that of decision-making. He found that:

1. Decentralized administration is identified with democratic administration.
2. Professional people need the freedom and autonomy that accompanies decentralized administration.
3. Apathetic, autocratic people do not feel free to be creative; they are dependent upon leadership.
4. Strong teachers place above everything else the freedom to plan and experiment.
5. The quality of decisions increases with decreasing leader domination.
6. The individual must have an identification with the total operation if he is to possess a feeling of accomplishment.
7. Through freedom of decision the submissive person develops a new feeling of adequacy.
8. The most outstanding results will be realized if teachers are permitted a high degree of latitude in decisions.
9. Satisfaction of the needs of teachers is bound up with the needs of pupils.
10. Leaders make their greatest contributions by permitting free expression of opinion and unity of purpose.[9]

QUALIFICATIONS AND DUTIES OF SCHOOL PERSONNEL

There is definite evidence that some personnel problems arise because there is no clear-cut job description available when a candidate for a school position is interviewed and employed. One study showed

[8] Margaret Carlson Browne, "Job Attitudes of Middle Management in Three Cooperative Extension Services" (Unpublished Doctoral dissertation, University of Wisconsin, 1959).

[9] Harry Herbert Houston, "An Inquiry into the Administrative Process as It Relates to Decision-Making" (Unpublished Doctoral dissertation, Rutgers University, 1959).

that forty-two per cent of the people employed as Directors of Elementary Education in city school systems reported that their duties were not clearly defined.[10] It is important that accurate descriptions of jobs and statements of qualifications be formulated for use in employing and classifying personnel in school systems.

JOB DESCRIPTIONS

The job description form should contain the following information:

1. Name and location of school and school system.
2. The job title, including a reference to the department in which it appears.
3. A job summary that, in one to three paragraphs, outlines the grade or subjects, the extra-curricular responsibilities, and any other specific duties expected of the applicant.
4. A description of the physical working conditions, the materials, the equipment, and the specific location.
5. The specific type and amount of supervision to be expected.
6. The community living conditions (type of housing accommodations, and prevailing prices).
7. The training, skill, experience and other personal qualifications required.
8. The salary range.
9. Provisions for tenure, retirement, and other benefits.
10. The usual working hours.
11. A statement of any unusual working conditions.
12. Address of person to whom application should be made.

JOB CLASSIFICATION

Too few school systems have spent the time and effort required to work out job classifications for the certificated positions. An organizational pattern must be formulated if a school system expects to write job classifications. One way to describe major administrative divisions of a school system would be as follows:

1. All instructional services would be regarded as a part of a major administrative division known as the Educational Division.
2. All services in business would be a part of a major administrative division known as the Business Division.
3. All custodial and upkeep services would be a part of a major division known as the Maintenance Division.

After the organizational pattern has been determined, the job descriptions and classifications may be written.

---

[10] Lowell G. Keith, "The Position of Director of Elementary Education in Cities of over 35,000 Population," *American School Board Journal,* CXXVIII (April, 1954), p. 51.

The Salem, Oregon, Public School System has a well-defined classification system for its administrative and consultative personnel.

CLASSIFICATION OF POSITIONS IN THE SALEM PUBLIC SCHOOLS

The following classification is hereby established as constituting the positions of administrative and consultative personnel in the Salem Public Schools: Superintendent, Assistant Superintendent, Manager, Principal, Assistant Principal, Teaching Principal, Director, Supervisor, Consultant, Coordinator, Dean. The distinguishing characteristics of each position are as follows:

a. Superintendent:
   1. Is the chief administrative officer of the District.
   2. Is responsible directly to the District School Board.
   3. Holds a Superintendent's Credential.

b. Assistant Superintendent:
   1. Is in charge of a variety of specified areas of responsibility which may extend through all levels of the school system.
   2. Is responsible to the Superintendent and, through him, to the Board.
   3. Holds a Superintendent's Credential.

c. Manager:
   1. Is in charge of a specified field of responsibility outside the instructional program which extends throughout the School District.
   2. Is responsible to the Superintendent, either directly or through an Assistant Superintendent.
   3. Is not required to hold a state teaching or administrative certificate.

d. Principal:
   1. Is the chief administrative officer of one or more school buildings where the total full-time teaching staff is more than eight.
   2. Is responsible to the Superintendent, directly or through an Assistant Superintendent.
   3. Holds a regular Principal's Credential for the level to which he is assigned.
   4. The following types of principals are authorized:
      a. High school principal.
      b. Junior high school principal.
      c. Elementary school principal.

e. Assistant Principal:
   1. Is the administrative assistant to the Principal in a building where the staff and the enrollment is such that one administrative officer cannot perform the duties of the office effectively.

2. Holds the required administrative credential for the level to which he is assigned.
3. The following types of assistant principalships are authorized:
   a. High School assistant principal.
   b. Junior high school assistant principal.

f. Teaching Principal:
1. Is the administrative assistant to the Director of Suburban Schools, and is in charge of the building to which he is assigned.
2. Teaches a full class load in addition to his administrative responsibilities.
3. Holds required teaching certificates for position to which assigned.

g. Head Teacher:
1. Represents the principal of a building in cases of emergency, or in the absence of the principal when one principal is assigned to more than one building.
2. Teaches a full class load.
3. Holds required teaching certificates for position to which assigned.

h. Dean:
1. Serves as administrative assistant to the building principal or assistant principal in a high school in dealing with problems of pupil personnel.
2. Holds the required certificate from the State Department of Education.

i. Director:
1. Is an administrative officer having an area of responsibility, under an assistant superintendent, which includes a defined range of grade levels and of school buildings.
2. Holds the required credential from the State Department of Education.
3. The following directorships are authorized:
   a. Director of Special Education.
   b. Director of Physical Education, and Recreation.
   c. Director of Music Education.
   d. Director of Suburban Schools.

j. Supervisor:
1. Is a supervisory officer, under an assistant superintendent, of a function of the school system other than in the fields of curriculum or instruction, which requires professional leadership and centralized coordination. His rank is below that of a Director.
2. Holds the required certificate from the State Department of Education.

3. The following positions are authorized as Supervisory:
   a. Supervisor of School Lunch.
   b. Supervisor of Instructional Materials.
   c. Supervisor of Adult Education.

k. Consultant:
1. Is an instructional specialist assigned to promote the improvement of teaching and curriculum by advising with teachers, principals, assistant superintendents, and others.
2. Is concerned with the discovery and use of instructional aids, supplementary materials, teaching guides, methods of teaching, and resource units, and the use of such items by teachers.
3. Holds the required credentials from the State Department of Education.
4. The following positions as consultant are authorized:
   a. Consultant in Music.
   b. Consultant in Physical Education and Health.
   c. Consultant in Art.
   d. Consultant in Audio-Visual Aids.

l. Coordinator:
1. Is an administrative worker under an assistant superintendent or a building principal who is responsible for the development and continuation of a program of instruction in an area in one or more high schools and one or more junior high schools.
2. Has limited but specific administrative responsibilities in both the junior and senior high schools assigned to him.
3. Promotes integration between units or buildings of the school system.
4. Holds the required certificate from the State Department of Education.
5. The following positions as coordinator are authorized:
   a. Coordinator of Health, Physical Education and Athletics.
   b. Coordinator of Industrial Arts.[11]

Figure 12 shows the duties outlined for an administrative assistant, superintendent of schools, a business manager, a director of personnel, and a director of school planning services. This functional statement of duties was prepared for an elementary school system in the San Jose, California, area. It is intended to serve the needs of an elementary school district with an enrollment of between 6,000 and 15,000 students. The school district has another assistant superintendent in charge of instruction.

Statement of qualifications and duties for an assistant superintendent for instruction. The following description of the suggested

[11] Salem Public Schools, *Rules and Regulations* (Salem, Oregon: Board of Education, 1956), pp. 7–8.

Figure 12. MORELAND SCHOOL DISTRICT*

ASSISTANT SUPERINTENDENT FOR ADMINISTRATIVE SERVICES

Business Management	Personnel	School Planning Services
Accounting	Recruitment of Certificated Personnel	Building Planning
Transportation Director	Determination of Personnel Needs	Supervision of Construction
Cafeteria Director	Job Interview and Selection	District Maps
Budget Preparation & Control Purchasing	Evaluation	Research
Distribution of Supplies	Assignment	Surveys
Plant Operation	Salary Schedule	School Census
Building Maintenance	Promotion & Transfer	Community Information
Supervision of Custodians	Termination of Employment	Bond and Tax Service Programs
Personnel, Classified	Professional Relations	Site Selection
Warehousing	Selection and Training of Administrative Personnel	Real Estate Purchasing
Pupil Attendance & Accounting	Substitute Teachers	Community Services—Management Use of School Facilities
Property Appraisal & Insurance		
Financial Reports		
Property Accounting		
Inventory Control		
School Census		
Community Services Mgt.—Use of School Facilities		
Production of Annual Reports		

* This chart was prepared for the Moreland Elementary School District by Lowell Keith, San Jose State College, San Jose, California, and Walter Garcia, Stanford University, Palo Alto, California.

qualifications and duties of an assistant superintendent for instruction was prepared as a guide for a school board in the process of selecting a person to serve in that office. It is an example of the type of statement which should be prepared for most of the certificated personnel in a school system. It is becoming increasingly important as school districts begin to employ more people with special qualifications, who are to be assigned special duties. The "master teacher" serving as the director of the teaching team is an example of a new specialty in teaching.

QUALIFICATIONS: THE ASSISTANT SUPERINTENDENT OF SCHOOLS FOR INSTRUCTION

Professional Training

The training necessary for one serving as Assistant Superintendent for Instruction in the ______________ School District should include at least a master's degree in professional education with a specialization in curriculum and supervision. In addition, this person should have additional professional training beyond the master's degree. Ideally, he should possess or be working toward the doctorate. He should have, or be able to obtain, a valid credential.

Personal Qualifications

The person to be selected for the position of Assistant Superintendent for Instruction should have the following personal qualifications:

1. He should have demonstrated ability to work effectively with teachers and other professional staff in developing and implementing a sound and imaginative educational program.
2. He should be of sufficient maturity so as to have had successful experience as a classroom teacher and a building principal.
3. He should be in good physical condition.
4. His personal integrity and fairness should have been amply demonstrated.
5. He should be a person who has the intellectual capacity and the highly developed professional skills which will enable him to provide direct leadership in every phase of classroom instruction.

Experience Background

The person to be selected for the position of the Assistant Superintendent for Instruction in the ______________ School District should have the following experience background:

1. He should have a record of successful experience as a classroom teacher in the elementary grades and as a building principal of an elementary school. (This statement of qualifications was written to describe the qualifications and duties of an assistant superintendent for instruction in an elementary school district.)
2. His experience record should show, in general, a pattern of in-

creasing leadership in curriculum development and the improvement of instruction.

3. His experience background should show a clear success record in the following areas:
   (1) Promoting and securing a high degree of professional teamwork among all staff members in providing a sound instructional program.
   (2) Possessing skill in working with parent groups and the public in securing understanding and acceptance of the instructional program.
   (3) Demonstrating at least sufficient familiarity with the duties of the superintendent of schools in order that he may act in the absence of the superintendent.

DUTIES: THE ASSISTANT SUPERINTENDENT OF SCHOOLS FOR INSTRUCTION

The Assistant Superintendent of Instruction shall perform such duties and exercise such authority as may be delegated to him by the Superintendent. The definition of duties of the Assistant Superintendent of Instruction will permit the Superintendent to make additional assignments or transfer temporarily some specific duties to another department or person if, in his opinion, such changes are necessary for the good of the District.

The primary duties of the Assistant Superintendent of Instruction shall be as follow:

1. To administer the instructional program within the framework of policies established in the district by the Board of Trustees.
2. To coordinate the efforts of all who provide instructional services to the teaching staff.
3. To exercise leadership in curriculum development by providing for staff participation in setting up the goals of instruction.
4. To serve as a resource person for building principals and teachers.
5. To encourage professional growth on the part of the professional staff through in-service training programs, workshops, and the like.
6. To provide an adequate list of qualified substitute teachers.
7. To guide the work of any special teachers in the school district.
8. To keep records and make reports required by the superintendent.
9. To keep the superintendent fully informed on developments in the areas of curriculum and instruction in the district.
10. To assist the superintendent in interpreting the instructional program to the public, and to help communicate to the instructional staff the public's concern with the schools.[12]

---

[12] This statement of qualifications and duties of an Assistant Superintendent for Instruction was prepared by Lowell Keith, San Jose State College, San Jose, California, and Walter Garcia, Stanford University, Palo Alto, California.

The point has been made in this chapter that the qualifications and duties of the majority of the school personnel in a school system should be clearly stated. Further clarification of the administrative organization will be attained when school districts prepare charts of administrative organization. Figure 13 is an example of a proposed administrative organization for a Department of Instruction to be administered by an Assistant Superintendent for Instruction in an elementary school district enrolling from 6,000 to 15,000 students.

CONCLUSION

There is a growing need to discover and solve problems in the area of school personnel administration. Some promising research in this area has been presented here. In order to recruit better qualified employees and to help them understand their specific duties after they are employed, considerable emphasis is being placed on the necessity for administrators to write clear job descriptions and job classifications. In Chapter 15, the importance of sound personnel policy will be shown, and the essential elements of personnel policy will be examined in detail. Examples of policy statements from some selected school systems will be presented as models for study.

Short Case 1

The New Director of Personnel

The New Town School System had become aware of the need for someone to be employed as a Director of Personnel. The school system had approximately 400 certificated and 150 non-certificated employees. The superintendent of schools and the board of trustees realized that there was need for clarification of many policies pertaining to personnel. New plans and policies were needed. Employee morale was not exceptionally high in the school system.

A Director of Personnel was employed. One of his first actions was to send a questionnaire to most of the administrators, directors, consultants, and non-certificated employees requesting that they outline the tasks they were actually performing. When the results came in he asked the superintendent, the assistant superintendent for instruction, the administrative assistant, and the business manager to comment. In a number of instances it was obvious that employees said they were performing tasks which the administration did not regard as being a part of their duties. In some cases, the administrators agreed that the employees were doing what they claimed but said that they should not be doing some of the tasks.

Figure 13. PROPOSED ADMINISTRATIVE ORGANIZATION FOR A DEPARTMENT OF INSTRUCTION IN AN ELEMENTARY SCHOOL DISTRICT*

ASSISTANT SUPERINTENDENT IN CHARGE OF INSTRUCTION

Research & Public Information	Instructional Materials and Services	Consultant in Charge of Coordination of Instruction	Guidance & Special Education
Interpretation of the School Program	Libraries & Library Services	Supervision of Instruction	Health Services
Issuance of News Releases	Audio-Visual Services	In-Service Education	Guidance & Counseling
Preparation and Dissemination of Publications	Radio and Television	Recreation Program	Group Testing
	Textbooks and other Classroom Materials	Inter-Scholastic Activities	Psychological Services
	General Instructional Supplies and Equipment		School Social Work Services
			Cooperation with Other Youth Service Agencies
			Summer School
			Special Classes
			Adult Education

* Prepared by Lowell Keith, San Jose State College, San Jose, California, and Walter Garcia, Stanford University, Palo Alto, California.

Problem: On the basis of this limited summary of the situation, what course of action would you suggest for the new Director of Personnel? How should he move to resolve the discrepancy between what certain employees say they are doing and what the top administration believes they should be doing?

Short Case 2

Changing the Organizational Pattern of a School

In the New Town School System, the fifth and sixth grades of the elementary schools had been departmentalized for several years. The policy of the school system had encouraged this plan of organization because it was thought that such a plan prepared children for the experiences and problems they would meet when they moved into junior high school. There was a prevailing belief among some of the teachers and administrators that such departmentalization insured higher quality instruction. A heavy majority of the teachers and the principal of the Walnut Grove Elementary School in New Town were dissatisfied with departmentalization in the fifth and sixth grades. They wanted the fifth and sixth grades placed on a self-contained classroom basis.

Problem: Should the Walnut Grove School be permitted to change from an organizational pattern which is followed by other schools in the system? Justify your answer in light of our present knowledge of grouping children for purposes of instruction.

Chapter Fifteen

Policies, Rules, and Regulations in School Personnel Administration

FORMULATING POLICY

The time is past when a school system can be managed in an efficient manner without the combined efforts of all personnel. The idea of one man formulating all school policy may have been tolerated in the past, but many modern teachers have been taught aspects of democratic school administration which cause them to object to dictatorial policy making. We are aware, however, that some school administrators still fail to realize the true meaning of democracy in school administration. Lloyd and Elaine Cook express the idea clearly:

> Autocratic control is a technique of ignorance, a scheme that defeats itself in the end. *Laissez faire,* "the good fellow gone wrong," does not even realize the mental hygiene values now stressed so roundly by group workers as essential in our life. Democracy, while demanding skill and insight, is productive of high morale, a marked degree of teamwork, and creative talent. Judged by all its products,

it would be hard to argue for any other way of conducting school life.[1]

THE ELEMENTS TO BE COVERED BY POLICY

Specific elements of personnel administration need to be covered by school policies, which are outlines for guiding administrative operations. Because established policy enables both the administrator and the school personnel to operate on the same basis in similar situations and allows administrators to offer the same consideration and treatment to all staff members, school personnel policy should be arrived at in a cooperative manner between staff members and administrators. School districts need to establish policies covering the elements of human relations that contribute to the improvement of teaching and learning. The following areas of personnel administration should be covered in school district policy:

1. Written statements of rules and regulations
2. Recruitment, selection, and placement procedures
3. Scheduling and administering the salary program
4. Promotions, transfers, and terminations
5. Evaluation of performance
6. Publications
7. Employee benefits and services
8. Relations with professional and non-professional organizations

There is still a place in school administration for leadership, and for men and women who can make firm decisions. The board of education and the community charge one individual with the responsibility for the school system's accomplishments. The role of this individual, the superintendent of schools, includes the responsibility of identifying the school system's problems and selecting the most important tasks to be performed. Because he cannot do the job by himself, the superintendent creates other positions of leadership by selecting sub-groups which he charges with certain decision-making responsibilities. The worth of the decisions made by the sub-groups is measured by the degree to which they fulfill the superintendent's original goal. The role of the administrator in decision-making is not one of eliminating authority, but one of perfecting a system of administration in which authority and participation are interwoven to create a spirit of teamwork in the problem-solving process. After all the group discussions have been held and some kinds of authority have been delegated, the administrator must still make definite de-

[1] Lloyd and Elaine F. Cook, *A Sociological Approach to Education* (New York: McGraw-Hill Book Co., Inc., 1950), pp. 321–322.

cisions and accept responsibility for them. If administrative decisions are made within a framework of definite board policy, they are easier to communicate to the staff and to the community.

Personnel policies of a school system serve as guides to the actions of employees and employers. Working together, the administrator, the board, and the staff form policies derived from experience and sound theory. Based on sound concepts of human relations, personnel policy concerns the informal as well as the formal aspects of employer-employee relationships. Policy formulation, a means for a constructive rather than a restrictive guide to thought and action, is a positive step in administrative leadership. The fundamental purpose of framing personnel policy is to increase the understanding and cooperation of school staff members. As the society, the community, and the schools change, personnel policy should change. Chandler and Petty give this interpretation:

> Personnel policy may be rigid or flexible. A point somewhere between absolute rigidity and meaningless flexibility is desirable. This implies that at least the most important statements of policy should be written in reasonably specific terms. Flexibility allows for changing conditions that arise from time to time. Rigidity gives permanency and a degree of continuity to the operation.
>
> Well established policy practices should function with a smoothness that will leave most members of the organization unaware of their existence.[2]

WRITTEN RULES, REGULATIONS, AND POLICIES

In Chapter 14, considerable stress was given to the importance of having the right kind of administrative organization for effective personnel administration. It is necessary for a school district to write clear-cut, objective statements of qualifications and duties expected of all school personnel. It is equally important that explicit rules, regulations, and policies be formulated, communicated, and implemented by the school administration and the board of education.

We have already pointed out the necessity for the entire school staff to be active in the formulation of policy affecting working conditions. The rules, regulations, and policies should be printed and made available to all staff members. There is need for a system of keeping them up to date, because changes may be necessary every year. The entire printed statement should be completely revised every three or four years so that all staff members are aware of the

[2] B. J. Chandler and Paul V. Petty, *Personnel Management in School Administration* (New York: World Book Company, 1955), p. 15.

changes brought by board of education action. The alternative would be to use a loose-leaf system, toward which there is an evident trend.

The statements of personnel policy included in this chapter serve to guide the administrators in hundreds of school districts now in the process of formulating such policies. It is becoming an established practice to include principals on planning committees where such policy is being written. The modern elementary school principal should be vitally concerned with the establishment of sound personnel policy. Efficient management of the school he administers depends to a large degree on the way he meets and solves personnel problems.

SELECTED EXAMPLES OF POLICY STATEMENTS

A statement of policy for a large city school system. Some outstanding examples of school board policy statements have been examined. The Detroit school system has printed a manual of personnel practices which represents the work of a large city school system. It is evident that there is need for greater detail in the large city schools than in the smaller school systems. An examination of the table of contents of the *Detroit Manual of Personnel Practices* reveals the thorough job that has been done in this school system.

Personnel Practices in the Detroit Public Schools[3]

Table of Contents

Chapter One. How New Teachers are Chosen

1. The Qualifications of a Detroit Teacher
2. The Selection Process
3. Procedural Steps for the Applicant
4. Procedural Steps by the Personnel Department
5. Probationary Period of Service
6. Emergency Substitute Teaching
7. Conclusion

Chapter Two. Our Team

1. The Sense of Being Professional
2. The Detroit Board of Education
3. Central Administration
4. Field Administration and Supervision
5. You

Chapter Three. Personnel Procedures

1. Contracts
2. Salaries

---

[3] Detroit Public Schools, *Personnel Practices in the Detroit Public Schools,* Publication 389 (Detroit, Michigan: Board of Education, 1955).

3. Length of Teaching Service
4. If You Wish to Be Transferred
5. An Unsatisfactory Rating
6. When Promotion Is Merited
7. If Things Are Going Wrong
8. Your Good Health
9. Your Credentials

Chapter Four. Your Responsibilities

1. Teaching
2. Your Allegiance and Fidelity
3. As to Classroom Discipline
4. Safety
5. As You Grow Professionally
6. Your Relations with the Public

Chapter Five. Your Privileges and Opportunities

1. Holidays
2. When You Are Sick
3. If You Must Take Leave
4. Sabbatical Leave
5. Exchange Teaching
6. Professional and Other Affiliations
7. Insurance and Hospital Benefits
8. If You Are Injured
9. Your Retirement Benefits
10. Adult Education and Summer Schools

Chapter Six. Information

1. Special Offices and Services
2. When You Need Professional Help
3. Informational Publications
4. Instructional Publications

Chapter Seven. How Our School System Grew

1. Yesterday's Growth
2. Today's Developing Pattern

A statement of policy for a middle-sized city school system. The Austin Public Schools, Austin, Texas, published an administration handbook describing the policies, rules, and regulations adopted by the school board of that medium-sized city school system. This work was done with evident care. The personnel of that school system have a guide to follow in meeting the problems they encounter. The contents of that handbook are listed below:

ADMINISTRATIVE HANDBOOK[4]

AUSTIN PUBLIC SCHOOLS

TABLE OF CONTENTS

[4] Austin Public Schools, *Administrative Handbook* (Austin, Texas: Board of Education, 1958).

ments of Debts and Credit Rating—Attendance at Meetings—Complaints and Grievances—Temporary Suspension—Dismissal—Basic Salary Schedule—Handbooks and Manuals

IV. Sites, Buildings, Equipment and Other Physical Facilities
Site Selection—New Construction—Building Alteration—Vandalism and Entry—Purchase of Non-Standard Equipment—Non-School-Owned Buildings on School Sites—Street Paving

V. Miscellaneous
Scholarships and Awards—Community Activities: Drives, Contests, Promotions, Collections, Etc.—Selling Merchandise in Schools—Card Games—Smoking—Refreshments—Loitering—School Telephones—Organizations—Police Services—Commercial Enterprises

A statement of policy for a small city school system. One of the most effective means of keeping all school personnel informed of policies, rules, regulations, and general information is the publication of a handbook. The handbook is usually issued from the central administrative office. If such a handbook is not available from the central office, some building principals issue handbooks for the personnel in their own buildings.

An example of such a handbook issued from the central office to the personnel in a small city school system is the one devised by the Harrisonburg Public Schools, Harrisonburg, Virginia. The handbook contains the following items of information for the school staff:

HANDBOOK, 1958–59[5]
HARRISONBURG PUBLIC SCHOOLS
HARRISONBURG, VIRGINIA

Section I
School Board Members—Administrative and Supervisory Staff—Purpose—School Calendar—Attendance Report Days—Pupil Progress Reports—Orientation for All New Teachers—Pre-School Conferences

Section II
Contract Days—Length of the School Day—Submitting of Reports—Requisitions for Supplies—Callers—Fire Drills—Teachers' Physical Checkup—Payment of Salary—Professional Meetings—Handling of Finances—Campaigns—Substitute Teachers

Section III
Rental of Textbooks—Schedule of Rental Fees—Free Textbooks for Indigent Children—Tuition—Typing Fees—Additional Fees

Section IV
Age of Pupils at Entrance—Pupil Insurance—Physical Inspection—Medi-

[5] Harrisonburg Public Schools, *Handbook, 1958–59* (Harrisonburg, Virginia: Board of Education, 1958).

cal Care and Vaccination—Compulsory Attendance Law—Daily Attendance

Section V

Teacher Retirement and Social Security—Compulsory Retirement—Teacher Tenure—Teacher Hospital Insurance—Renewal of Certificates—Revival of Elementary and Elementary Professional Certificates—1958–59 Teacher's Reading Course

Section VI

Harrisonburg Education Association

Section VII

Professional Study Groups and Committee Work—Teaching Aids and Materials—Professional Library—Special Education—Safety Education

RECRUITMENT AND SELECTION PROCEDURES

The staffing of a school system is a complicated and expensive undertaking. Finding and hiring a single staff member may cost several hundred dollars. There is general agreement among educators that there is a direct relationship between successful recruitment and selection of capable staff members and the quality of the educational program in a school district. Men and women must be located, identified and encouraged to apply for the available jobs. The importance of the entire process of recruitment and selection of school employees calls for the setting of definite policies to guide the procedure. Such policies, if properly formulated, will offer a better opportunity for a school system to employ superior candidates. There is a distinction between recruiting and selecting. The term recruitment describes the process of finding a potentially available pool of applicants for the positions in the school system. The term selection describes the procedure of screening and ultimate employment or rejection of individual applicants. The two processes are so closely related that they are interdependent. The screening of applicants begins early in the relationships with potentially employable applicants. Since preliminary selection does start early in the recruitment process, great care should be taken to maintain good human relations with potential applicants and good public relations with the systems or institutions with which the potential applicants are connected. Recruitment and selection must be a detailed process.

The elementary school principal has become a key person in the recruitment and selection process. He is usually brought into the administrative planning sessions with the superintendent or with the assistant superintendent in charge of personnel. It is in such planning meetings that policy is determined to cover the entire recruitment and selection process. After policy has been established, the principal generally screens the application forms, conducts some of the interviews, and makes recommendations to the superintendent or to his assistant. Quite often the principal uses some of his building teachers to help him do the screening of applications and interviewing. It is now common practice for principals to go on recruiting trips to other cities and states.

The first step in an effective recruitment process is to formulate job descriptions. This process has two major aims, the first being that of measuring the personal qualifications needed for each new recruit, and the second being the determination of the kind, quality, and amount of work to be expected of each new employee. A detailed presentation of job descriptions and job classifications was made in Chapter XIV.

When a school system considers the problem of getting new employees, it should consider policies that will serve as appropriate guides in the recruitment program. Such policies will describe the objectives the district hopes to attain in filling positions with candidates having the best possible qualifications. The following considerations may serve to guide a school district in recruitment:

1. Policy may determine whether applicants for administrative and supervisory positions will be sought from within and/or without the school system.
2. Policy may determine whether the search for new employees will extend beyond the file of applicants.
3. Policy may determine which persons on the staff will actively search for new recruits. (It has become common practice for principals, personnel directors, and designated classroom teachers to be active in recruitment.)
4. Policy may determine whether recruitment teams will go into classrooms and offices to observe prospective applicants.
5. Policy may determine whether there will be selection based on race, religion, or nationality. (The application forms used must be in harmony with the stated policy.)
6. Policy may determine what type of teacher placement bureaus will be used.
7. Policy may determine whether the school system predetermines that teachers will be appointed from a wide geographical area.

Preliminary interview. The preliminary interview may precede the applicant's completion of the school district's application form, or it may follow completion of the form. Both plans are followed. It may be obvious in the preliminary interview that the applicant is deficient in qualities or skills required for the position, or the applicant may discover aspects of the position which do not please him. In either situation, waste of time and effort will be prevented if consideration of the applicant is terminated at this point.

In some situations, the preliminary interview is the only one necessary because the applicant is found to be well qualified for the position. The preliminary interview may be conducted by the personnel officer of the school system, the superintendent, a principal from the school system, an interview committee, or a combination of any or all of these officials.

A *Candidate Interview Record Form* used by the Ithaca, New York, Public Schools is shown here as a good example of a concise, easy-to-use instrument for recording impressions of an applicant.

ITHACA PUBLIC SCHOOLS

CANDIDATE INTERVIEW RECORD

Candidate ______________________________

Position ______________________________

EVALUATION

Encircle the letter which best represents your rating of the candidate in each of the following traits.

	A Excellent	B Good	C Average	D Fair	E Poor
Personal appearance	A	B	C	D	E
Speech and conversation	A	B	C	D	E
Evidence of culture and refinement	A	B	C	D	E
Personal animation, responsiveness	A	B	C	D	E
Attitude toward teaching	A	B	C	D	E
Tactfulness	A	B	C	D	E
Sense of humor	A	B	C	D	E
Estimate of professional worth	A	B	C	D	E

Should the applicant receive further consideration in the event a vacancy exists?

YES NO

REMARKS: (Use back if needed)

Date ______________ Interviewer ______________

References. After the preliminary interview, or after the written application forms have been completed, communication is made with all references. These are persons who know the candidate. As a statement, the reference is a letter or oral expression describing the applicant's character, skill, and experience.

Important principles of sound practice with respect to references need to be mentioned. Dale Yoder offers several such principles. They include the following:

1. "To whom it may concern" letters are of little value.
2. Few people will write a critical evaluation of a candidate and give the statement to the person to be carried by him.
3. A simple request for information is not likely to secure too many facts unless the person to whom the inquiry is directed knows the inquirer.
4. Reliability of reports from references is greatly improved when they are questioned in a face-to-face visit. As a substitute, many school administrators use a telephone interview.
5. Inquiries addressed to a present employer always face the possibility that he may overstate the applicant's qualifications to facilitate his resignation.[6]

The best confidential recommendation form is one that is brief, to the point, and easy to complete. The *Confidential Recommendation Blank* used by the Ithaca, New York, Public Schools is shown as a model.

ITHACA PUBLIC SCHOOLS

ITHACA, NEW YORK

CONFIDENTIAL RECOMMENDATION BLANK

Name of Reference ....

Address ....

M ....

is an applicant for ....
position in our school system and has given your name for reference. We shall appreciate the receipt of your estimate of the candidate's fitness as indicated by your answers to the following questions, and any further information which will help us in making a decision.

Very truly yours,
W. L. GRAGG, Superintendent

---

[6] Dale Yoder, *Personnel Principles and Policies* (2nd ed.; Englewood Cliffs, New Jersey: Prentice-Hall, Inc., 1959), pp. 246–247.

Encircle the letter which best represents your rating of the candidate in each of the traits listed below:
A - Excellent B - Good C - Average D - Fair E - Poor

Character	A B C D E
Scholarship	A B C D E
Health and vitality	A B C D E
Teaching skill	A B C D E
Personality	A B C D E
Success in discipline	A B C D E
Culture and refinement	A B C D E
Tact	A B C D E
Cooperative attitude	A B C D E
Voice	A B C D E
Initiative	A B C D E
Understanding of children	A B C D E

Is the applicant

discreet? ....

cordial? ....

neat? ....

professionally alert? ....

prompt in meeting financial obligations? ....

the type of person you would employ? ....

Has the candidate any physical defects, mannerisms, or peculiarities? ....

....

The following questions are designed to provide information necessary to enable the Ithaca Board of Education to observe the Laws of New York State and the Rules of the Board of Regents with respect to the record (if any) of candidates for appointment in the matter of subversive activities.

(Encircle one)

1. To the best of your knowledge and belief has the above named candidate for a position in the Ithaca Public Schools ever advocated, advised or taught the doctrine that the Government of the United States or of any state or political subdivision thereof be overthrown or overturned by force, or any unlawful means? YES NO

2. To the best of your knowledge and belief has the candidate participated in the preparation, publication or distribution of written or printed matter advocating such a doctrine or advising its adoption? YES NO

3. To the best of your knowledge and belief has the candidate organized or helped to organize or become a member of any society or group of persons which teaches such a doctrine? YES NO

4. To the best of your knowledge and belief has the candidate uttered any treasonable word or words, committed any treasonable or seditious act or acts? YES NO

5. Do you consider the candidate to be a loyal citizen of the United States?
YES NO

Signed .... Position ....

and ....

Date .... Address ....

(Reverse side for remarks)

Application forms. Great care should be used in preparing the application form, the real intent of which is to aid in the selection of applicants. Application forms tend to be too conclusive. The permanent personnel records will contain certain information that does not need to be on the application.

There is good reason to believe that the forms should be specifically designed for the type of position or positions to be filled. This does not mean that a different form will be provided for each position, but that distinctive forms will be provided for each group of jobs having distinctive personnel requirements. The forms used for teacher applicants would not necessarily be the ones used to collect information from an applicant for a principalship or a supervisory position.

The application form used by the Palo Alto, California, Public Schools is presented as a model for teacher application forms.

Observation of the applicant. It is good practice to arrange for a team of three persons to observe the applicant in an actual work situation. These observation teams are usually composed of a principal and two classroom teachers. There is professional courtesy involved in making arrangements for such an observation. The administrator in the candidate's district should be contacted and his permission obtained for the visit. The same arrangements should be made with the building principal in the school where the observation is to be made.

Second interview. If the members of the visiting committee are favorably impressed after seeing the applicant in his work situation, they may call him for a second interview. At this time, the interview committee goes into much greater detail than in the preliminary meeting. The second interview may not be held if there is a pressure for time in making the appointment, or if it is difficult for a candidate to travel a long distance for the second meeting.

Health examinations and tests. The next step in the selection process is that of having the applicant take the health examination and any other tests the district may require.

It is fairly common practice, especially in the larger cities, for the

16

PALO ALTO UNIFIED SCHOOL DISTRICT

Post Office Box 450

Palo Alto, California

Name (Mr., Miss, Mrs.) ______________________ Date ______
Last First Middle

Present Address ______________________ Telephone ____
Number Street City State

Permanent Address ______________________ Telephone ____
Number Street City State

______________________ Date of Birth ____________ Age ____

PLACEMENT SERVICE:

____
Name Address City State

CONFIDENTIAL PAPERS:

Being Forwarded ________
Will Be Requested ________
District Request ________

CREDENTIAL(S):

California Credential(s) ______________________
Type Expiration Date

Credential Applied for: ______________________
Type When?

______________________ ______________________
Major Major

TEACHING PREFERENCE:

1 ____________ 2 ____________ 3 ____________

SPECIAL TRAINING: (indicate by underlining)

Art Crafts Drama Physical Ed. Science Music ______ Language ______

TEACHING EXPERIENCE: (Start with most recent experience). Students list all student teaching.

Position	Grade/Subject	Credential	School	Location	Years From To	Total Months	Annual Salary
							$
							$
							$
							$
							$

EXPERIENCE . . . OTHER THAN TEACHING

Position	From To	Employer Address	Salary
			$
			$
			$

PROFESSIONAL REFERENCES: (List those who have observed your work, include last principal)

Name	Present Address	Official Position

PERSONAL INFORMATION

Marital Status (underline appropriate one)

SINGLE MARRIED WIDOWED SEPARATED DIVORCED

Number and ages of children (if any) ____________

Weight ______ Height ______ State of Health ____________

Normal Hearing? _____ Normal Vision? _____ Wear•Glasses? _____

Illnesses (during last 3 years) ____________ Time Lost ______

Comments: ____________

____

____

PROFESSIONAL MEMBERSHIPS	ACTIVE COMMUNITY MEMBERSHIPS
Organizations ____________	____________
Societies ____________	____________
Other ____________	____________

AVOCATIONAL INTERESTS OR HOBBIES	EXTENSIVE TRAVEL (approximate dates)
____________	____________
____________	____________
____________	____________

PROFESSIONAL CONTRIBUTIONS: (articles, books, periodical literature, etc.)

____

Do you sing? _____ Play the Piano? _____ Can you teach your own classroom Music? ____________

What Extra-Curricular activities do you feel qualified to direct? ____________

____

PERSONAL REFERENCES:

Name	Address	Relationship to Applicant

PERSONAL INTERVIEW

Could you arrange to come to Palo Alto for an interview? Yes__ No__

When? ________________________________

____
SIGNATURE OF APPLICANT

EDUCATIONAL AND PROFESSIONAL PREPARATION

	Institution	State	Attended from	to	Years	Degree	Major or Minor
Elementary							
High School							
College							
and/or							
University							
Graduate Work							
or							
Special							
Training							

NUMBER OF SEMESTER UNITS BEYOND A.B. DEGREE ____

(Must be completed by each applicant)

ORIGINAL STATEMENT

Write a brief statement concerning some noteworthy experience you have had, or an interesting activity in which you have been engaged within the last three years.

applicant to be required to take some kind of examination. In several cities the National Teachers' Examination is used for testing all teaching applicants.

The recommendation. If the candidate has survived each step of the selection process, the time has come for the formal recommendation for appointment. The essential personal data is compiled and made available to the board of education through the office of the superintendent of schools. The superintendent makes the formal recommendation, or it may be made by the director of personnel in some city school systems.

SOUND POLICY IN SALARY SCHEDULING

There was a time in the past when salary scheduling was a simple matter. The superintendent of schools, at the direction of the board of education, determined the salaries to be paid. For the most part there were no salary schedules as we know them today. Some of the decisions by superintendents in the past were made in an arbitrary fashion, and teachers were prone to accept the decisions because there seemed to be no recourse.

The day of the one-man decision is history. Now the standard practice usually takes into account the work and the deliberation of many people. The board of education, the superintendent, the administrators' organization, the salary committee of the teachers' association, the salary committee of the local chapter of the American Federation of Teachers, citizens committees, and employed salary consultants all may have a part in the formulation of the salary policy and schedule.

One of the most important considerations in the building of a satisfactory and workable salary schedule for a school system is to determine a statement of principles to serve as a policy guide. A board of education cannot legally bind successive boards of education to any specific course of action. The schedule does not create a long-term contract, but it does express policies which the present board of education will make a reasonable effort to maintain.

The Grosse Pointe, Michigan, Public Schools have developed an outstanding salary schedule which should be examined carefully for the statement of principles underlying that schedule.

Grosse Pointe, Michigan Salary Schedule[7]

PRINCIPLES UNDERLYING THE SCHEDULE

1. A salary schedule should contribute to an improvement in the quality of service rendered by the schools through heightened morale among employees. We believe that establishment of definite policies relating to the compensation and working conditions of employees contributes significantly to this improvement of our schools.
2. We believe that a salary schedule should be democratically evolved through cooperative consultations involving both laymen and professional educators. During the developmental period, ample opportunity should be provided for employees, either individually or through their representatives, to present specific requests and points of view with respect to personnel policies.

[7] The Grosse Pointe Public School System, *Salary Schedule and Personnel Policies* (Grosse Pointe, Michigan: Board of Education, 1959–1960), pp. 2–4.

3. It is the declared ambition of the Board of Education to pay salaries to all employees which are in line with those paid by the better school systems of Metropolitan Detroit and the Middle West. This desire is based upon our intention to staff our schools with superior personnel in all classifications.
4. The minimum salary paid all employees should provide reasonable recognition of training, experience, and job values, and should provide a living wage for a metropolitan area. Maximum salaries for all employees should be set at levels which will enable the school district to attract and hold superior personnel in job classifications. Such maximum salaries should enable all employees to meet the increasing economic responsibilities which normal adults are expected to assume as they grow older.
5. The salary schedule shall provide for annual increases in compensation to the stated maximum if satisfactory professional growth and service are rendered by the employee. The number and size of such annual salary increments shall be adjusted in-so-far as possible to the normally expected growth in worth to the school system of the average employee in each job classification.
6. The classification of employees and the pay differentials which are recognized in this schedule shall be based upon a scale of job values which is derived from carefully written descriptions of all jobs existing in the school system. Such written job descriptions shall be subjected to careful analysis and evaluation by democratically selected representatives of employee groups. The Superintendent of Schools will base his recommendations concerning the classification and compensation of all employees upon the results of this evaluation process, or if he disagrees with such results, he will report his reasons for a different recommendation to the Board of Education and to employees. The criteria which were cooperatively developed in November, 1946, for evaluating the worth to the school system of all recognized jobs are grouped into the following divisions:
   a. Required training and proficiencies
   b. Mental requirements
   c. Vitality demand
   d. Responsibilities
   e. Diversity and complexity of duties

   A complete copy of the job measurement guide used in evaluating all jobs will be available at all times in the offices of the Board of Education at 339 St. Clair.
7. Provision shall be made for an annual review of job classifications and evaluation if new jobs have been created, or if there is evidence that significant changes have been made in the activities of any job. The results of such job reviews will have no official status unless they have been specifically approved by the Board of Education as revisions of the salary schedule.
8. No discrimination shall be made in the initial employment, rate of

compensation, or retention on the staff of any person because of sex, marital status, or the grade level of children with whom the employee works, unless specific provision to the contrary is included elsewhere in the schedule.

9. The salary schedule should encourage continued growth and training on the part of all employees through affording ample opportunity for upgrading and promotion of qualified persons within the school system.
10. While there is no legal obligation on the part of the school district to pay employees for absence during illness, it is a good policy to allow a reasonable absence for personal illness and for death in the immediate family, without salary deductions.
11. The salary schedule should provide for the recognition of outstandingly meritorious service to the school system by individual employees. This principle should be implemented with great care in order to insure that the policy not be so administered as to create problems of morale which might outweigh the advantages resulting from such merit recognition.

The building principal and the salary schedule. The building principal has an important responsibility in administering the district salary schedule. His efforts may mean the difference between good and poor faculty morale, since the teachers know he has the responsibility of appraising the performance of those under his supervision. There is a slowly increasing tendency for school systems to stress teacher efficiency as an important determinant of granting tenure and advancement on the salary schedule. The principal, the key administrator in making such evaluative judgments, has the following tasks to perform in relation to the salary schedule:

1. He will find a way to channel the constructive ideas of his faculty members into salary considerations.
2. He will see that district salary policies are interpreted and understood by the members of the faculty in his school.
3. He will assist the central school office administration in administering the salary program in order that inequities may not arise.
4. He will search for ways to improve salaries and working conditions of the entire staff in the school system.

Merit pay in salary programming. The merit-pay plan is an innovation which has proved unpopular in some school districts. Merit-pay is a new name for an old idea. For more than fifty years school systems, recognizing superior teachers among their staffs, have been concerned with ways and means for increased salary as a reward for those superior teachers.

The majority of school systems have not adopted merit-pay plans. There are several vexing problems related to the adoption of any plan that proposes to pay some teachers more than others. Most teachers are aware of the difficulties involved when attempts are made to reward alleged outstanding performance. This awareness is probably the reason that the teaching profession, through its national organization, The National Education Association, has been cautious about supporting a movement for the wholesale adoption of merit-pay salary schedules. State teachers' associations have been reluctant to campaign for merit-pay schedules because the rank-and-file members of the profession have been suspicious of such plans.

The complications involved in formulating and administering a merit-pay plan have caused many districts to refuse, or to avoid the adoption of the idea. The value of rewarding superior teachers must be weighed against the risks to maintaining a communal confidence among all teachers. Some of the outstanding problems involved in attempts to formulate a merit-pay plan include workable answers to the following questions:

1. How does a school district determine objectively that a teacher is deserving of merit-pay?
2. Are the evaluative instruments and methods used in the evaluation of the teacher proved to be fair, reliable, and statistically valid?
3. Who will rate the teachers considered for merit-pay?
4. How does the average school district pay a defensible basic salary schedule for all teachers and still have enough money to pay merit schedules?
5. Is the competition inherent in merit-pay plans conducive to building and keeping good faculty morale?
6. Is there conclusive evidence that merit-pay produces better teaching?

The current educational literature reflects a generally optimistic attitude toward the eventual possibility of finding effective ways to pay merit salaries for superior work. The N.E.A. Research Division[8] reports a slight upward trend in the number of urban school districts having superior-service maximum provisions in their salary schedules. In the districts studied, there was an increase from 4 per cent in 1952–53 to 6.2 per cent in 1958–59 of the number offering superior-service maximum provisions in their salary schedules. More small than large urban districts provided the superior-service maximums.

The tenor of local and national thinking indicates an intensification of the search for better teachers and better teaching. Many procedures in administering a school program include the services of master

[8] National Education Association, Research Division, "Salary Provisions for Quality of Service," *Research Bulletin* (December, 1959), p. 108.

teachers. Recent experiments in team-teaching point up the necessity of outstanding teachers. The instruction of all children calls for superior teachers. Teachers should be rewarded for superior work. It is incumbent upon more school districts to search for ways of perfecting merit-pay programs.

EVALUATION OF TEACHING

Although there has always been a need for teacher evaluation, this evaluation has in too many instances been based on social mores or economic standards. In informal and subjective evaluations, teachers have been dismissed from their positions because they failed to pass the test of persons evaluating their performance. Too many instances reveal that evaluation was not carried on in a professional manner. Although the profession is obligated to identify and release the incompetents to protect the student from inadequate teachers, the teaching profession cannot afford to lose effective teachers through faulty systems of evaluation. Furthermore, a majority of states now offer some kind of tenure provision for teachers. In order to protect teachers as well as students and to insure the effectiveness of tenure laws, the profession must search for more objective and accurate methods for rating teachers.

The evaluation of teaching is being carried on in several different ways. While only school administrators or supervisors evaluate teachers in some school districts, parents and students also rate the teachers in other districts. In some instances, teachers evaluate themselves. One of the newer and more promising practices involves a cooperative manner of evaluation between administrators and teachers. Taking into consideration two of the most important reasons for rating teachers, this method of evaluation attempts to determine the tenure status of the teacher, and to improve instruction.

The Cupertino School District, Cupertino, California, has been perfecting a teacher evaluation procedure during the past several years. The school district first used a plan on a try-out basis before it was revised by a committee of teachers and administrators. Slight revisions have been made each year as need for change was determined by the teaching and administrative personnel. Containing most of the basic elements needed for the objective rating of teachers, this unique plan provides for the principals and teachers to evolve mutual ratings, and for teachers to offer a written evaluation of district services. This section of the rating form gives the district administration insight into the attitudes teachers have concerning possible improvements that may be made in important aspects of the administrative and supervisory programs. Although programs such as the one found in the Cupertino School District show improvement in the rating procedure, there is need for continuing study and effort in the majority of school districts as attempts are made to find more efficient and satisfactory ways of evaluating teaching.

PROMOTIONS, TRANSFERS, AND TERMINATION OF CONTRACTS

PROMOTION POLICIES

Only in a small number of instances does one find incorporated into the school policies handbook a plan for promotion of certificated personnel within a school system. This may be one of the reasons that far too many personnel problems arise from misunderstanding or lack of understanding of the professional course of action one should take if he wishes to be promoted within a school system. The question frequently arises whether applicants from outside the school district will be or should be considered for vacant administrative or supervisory positions. Boards of education should adopt policies in regard to promotion if they wish to avoid tedious and disturbing morale problems. An example of such a policy statement is found in the Personnel Handbook of the Palo Alto, California, Unified School District.

Promotion in the Palo Alto Schools.

> Candidates within the District seeking promotion may apply to the Director of Personnel. They must possess the proper credential for the position vacant, and hold a Master's degree or the equivalent.
>
> When all qualifications, including training, experience, and personal fitness for the position are generally equal, persons applying from within the District will receive preference over those applying from outside the District. However, if candidates from outside the District have superior qualifications in training, experience, and personal fitness, they may be selected.
>
> The superintendent will recommend to the board his nomination for the position to be filled. He will base his recommendation upon all the factors previously mentioned; namely, training, experience, demonstrated ability, personal fitness, written examination, and the recommendation of the oral interview committee.[9]

TRANSFERS

Not enough attention has been given in school board policy to the transfer of personnel within a school system. A lack of policy often causes uneasy feeling among teachers. They know that transfers are

[9] Palo Alto Unified School District, *Personnel Handbook* (Palo Alto, California: Board of Education, 1959), p. 3.

Form for
EVALUATION OF TEACHING PERFORMANCE

Cupertino School District
Cupertino, California

Name ____________________ Grade _____ School ____________ Date _____

Use the following in indicating the quality of the teacher's performance.

1. *Outstanding Performance.* Denotes that performance is of superior quality.
2. *Commendable Performance.* Denotes that performance is of commendable quality.
3. *Acceptable Performance.* Denotes that performance is of acceptable quality, existing problems are correctable, and teacher is making needed corrections.
4. *Performance Doubtful.* Denotes performance includes critical problems which require more effective attention. (Possibly acceptable for first year teachers but not for second or third year teachers.)
5. *Performance below District standards.* Denotes performance includes serious deficiency. (Usually used only after evaluation of "4" above and after extensive cooperative effort toward improvement has been made.)

ELEMENTS OF TEACHING PERFORMANCE	Ratings					
Date						
I. *Instructional Procedure*						
A. Makes Effective Daily Preparation.						
B. Individualizes Instruction.						
C. Skill in Developing Interest.						
D. Shows Skill in Classroom Organization and Procedure.						
E. Shows Skill in Developing Study Habits.						
F. Skill in Presenting Subject Matter.						
G. Creates Physical Environment Favorable to Learning.						
H. Trains Pupils in Effective School Routines.						
II. *Teacher Pupil Relations*						
A. Is Regarded as a Leader by Pupils.						
B. Has and Applies Knowledge of Pupil Problems.						
C. Maintains an Effective Balance of Freedom and Security in Classroom.						
III. *Teacher-Staff Relations*						
A. Performs Assigned Duties Well.						
B. Is Prompt and Accurate in Making and Keeping Records.						
C. Utilizes Supervisory Helps.						
D. Works Effectively with Other Members of Staff.						

ELEMENTS OF TEACHING PROCEDURE Date	Ratings
IV. *Teacher-Parent-Community*	
A. Achieves Parent Understanding and Cooperation.	___ ___ ___ ___ ___ ___
B. Interprets School Program.	___ ___ ___ ___ ___ ___
C. Conducts Parent Conferences Satisfactorily.	___ ___ ___ ___ ___ ___
D. Takes Part in Civic and Cultural Life in the Community.	___ ___ ___ ___ ___ ___
V. *Personal Characteristics*	
A. Appearance	___ ___ ___ ___ ___ ___
B. Health—Physical and Mental	___ ___ ___ ___ ___ ___
C. Shows Enthusiasm	___ ___ ___ ___ ___ ___
D. Voice	___ ___ ___ ___ ___ ___
E. Personal Habits and Mannerisms	___ ___ ___ ___ ___ ___
F. Judgment	___ ___ ___ ___ ___ ___
G. Punctuality	___ ___ ___ ___ ___ ___
VI. *Professional Attitude*	
A. Maintains Favorable Attitude Toward Total Assignment.	___ ___ ___ ___ ___ ___
B. Shows Professional Growth.	___ ___ ___ ___ ___ ___
C. Willing to Participate in Professional Organizations.	___ ___ ___ ___ ___ ___

VII. *Extra Curricular Activities*

A. Athletics ....

B. Social Activities ....

C. Musical Activities ....

D. Publications ....

E. Dramatics ....

F. Clubs ....

G. Assemblies ....

H. Membership and Participation in School Service Organizations .....

....

I. Any other Service to the School ....

FIRST YEAR

Comments by Principal*		Comments by Principal*	
______	______________	______	______________
Date	Principal's Signature	Date	Principal's Signature
Comments by Teacher*		Comments by Teacher*	
______	______________	______	______________
Date	Teacher's Signature	Date	Teacher's Signature

SECOND YEAR

Comments by Principal*		Comments by Principal*	
______	______________	______	______________
Date	Principal's Signature	Date	Principal's Signature
Comments by Teacher*		Comments by Teacher*	
______	______________	______	______________
Date	Teacher's Signature	Date	Teacher's Signature

THIRD YEAR

Comments by Principal*		Comments by Principal*	
______	______________	______	______________
Date	Principal's Signature	Date	Principal's Signature
Comments by Teacher*		Comments by Teacher*	
______	______________	______	______________
Date	Teacher's Signature	Date	Teacher's Signature

Recommended Rehire___ Not Recommended___ Date_____ Principal__________

Recommended Rehire___ Not Recommended___ Date_____ Principal__________

Recommended Rehire___ Not Recommended___ Date_____ Principal__________

Recommended: Grant Tenure Yes___ No___ Principal______________________

* If desired, space on reverse may be used for summary of conclusions reached during conference.

VIII. *Teacher Evaluation of District Services**

TYPE OF SERVICE	HOW MIGHT SERVICE BE MADE MORE HELPFUL?
Supplies and Equipment	
Help Given By Curriculum Consultants through Conferences and Workshops.	
Help Given by Special Services, i.e., Testing, A–R Teachers, School Nurse, and Speech Correction Teachers.	
Help Given by Principal and Vice-Principal.	
Teacher Evaluation Procedure	

* This section of the form enables the teacher to evaluate the District's services that affect the conditions of teaching. Opposite each of the items, please indicate ways in which you believe the service might be made more helpful.

made, but they do not always understand why they are made. There have been examples of school administrators transferring personnel in an autocratic manner. This kind of action tends to lessen morale.

An examination of policy statements shows that a growing number of school districts are now including statements in regard to transfer. Two such statements are included below to serve as examples of the way in which such policies may be written.

Transfer of personnel—Albuquerque, New Mexico.[10]

> Teachers desiring new experiences for professional growth will be transferred whenever practicable and in the best interest of the system, at their own request. When a request is made, it is desirable, in most cases, for all parties concerned to arrive at a common understanding. However, the person asking for a transfer may make the request directly to the Personnel Department.
>
> The Superintendent may transfer teachers who are occupying positions for which they are not suited or when such transfers appear to be in the best interest of the system.

It is necessary, in the large city school system, to include a considerably more detailed statement than the one quoted above. It is not possible to cover all instances and cases without a rather detailed statement. The San Francisco public schools, by direction of the board of education, have developed a policy on transfer which could serve as a guide for other large city school systems.

Transfer and appointment distinction—San Francisco, California.[11]

1. A "transfer" is the movement of a teacher within the same instructional division, from one school to another.
2. A "transfer-and-appointment" is the movement of a teacher from one instructional division to another.
3. Original appointment to the San Francisco public schools is by instructional division, such divisions being: elementary, junior high, senior high, junior college, adult, vocational, and child welfare areas.
4. Since original appointment is by division, in the case of "transfer-and-appointment" the teacher enters upon a probationary period in the new division unless he already has tenure there because of previous service.
5. In the case of "transfer-and-appointment," the teacher retains his

---

[10] Albuquerque Public Schools, *Handbook of Policies and Procedures* (Albuquerque, New Mexico: Board of Education, 1958), pp. 12–13.

[11] San Francisco Public Schools, *San Francisco Public Schools Bulletin,* Vol. 29 (San Francisco, California: Board of Education, February 10, 1958).

tenure in the division from which he moves, if he has passed probation. Once he passes probation in the second division, he then officially chooses between the two.

Reasons for transfer. Common reasons for transfer within a division or to another division are:

1. Consolidation of classes.
2. To increase the teacher's background of educational experience.
3. To give the teacher a chance to succeed in a new situation after a period of service which has not been wholly satisfactory.
4. To solve problems of personal relationships.
5. To assist teachers whose present assignments constitute an unreasonable hardship.
6. To provide stimulation by change of assignment.

The school situation is best served when teachers are assigned in accordance with their preparation and abilities and to positions in which they are able to make a successful personal and professional adjustment.

Initiation of transfer proceedings. Transfer may be requested by the teacher, the principal, or the head of the instructional division.

Teacher initiated requests. Duplicate requests shall be submitted to the Personnel Office on forms provided by that office. One is filed there and the other with the head of the instructional divisions concerned. A conference with the latter is recommended.

If it is a transfer-appointment from one division to another, cards should be filed in the offices of both divisions.

Such requests may be submitted at any time, but those filed before May 1 and December 1 will receive prior consideration for the following semester. Requests which have not yet been approved will be kept on file in pending status unless withdrawn by the written request of the teacher.

Teacher transfers requested by principals. When a principal concludes that the transfer of a teacher is required, he shall submit a written request for the teacher's transfer to the head of the instructional division concerned.

If the services of the teacher have been unsatisfactory, the request shall take the form of an evaluation of teaching services which will set forth the nature of the unsatisfactory services, and such report shall be discussed with, and signed by, the teacher in question.

If the services of the teacher have been satisfactory, this request shall be made in writing and a copy of the letter shall be furnished the teacher, setting forth the reason for transfer.

Teacher transfers initiated by instructional division heads. When such transfers are made, the teacher shall be notified by the principal or the instructional division head, in writing or in conference, concerning the reason for the transfer, except when the transfer takes effect during a period when a teacher is on leave of absence.

Teachers on leave of absence whose positions have been transferred during their absence, shall be notified by the Personnel Division of the transfer and may request, in writing, re-transfer to positions in the school to which assigned at the time the leave was granted. Such requests will be approved whenever possible.

Transfers within schools. Transfers of teachers to other subjects or grades may be made by the principal of the school, with the approval of the appropriate instructional division head. Certification regulations must be respected in all cases.

Probationary teachers in the junior or senior high schools are required to serve at least 50 per cent of their assignments in the subject field(s) in which they were originally appointed. Upon completion of the probationary period, they may be reassigned in accordance with certification and the administrator's discretion.

Transfers should be initiated as far in advance as possible, in order that the transferee may prepare adequately for the new assignment. Transfers during the school semester are recognized as necessary on occasion, but should not be effected except in cases of emergency or when necessary in the interests of the children, the teacher, or the school district.

Transfers Between Divisions.

1. Teachers may qualify for transfer between instructional divisions by placement on an appropriate eligibility list.
2. When no eligibility list exists, a transfer may be effected by recommendation of the head of the division to which transfer is desired.
3. Not more than 2 per cent of the teachers in any instructional division, nor more than three teachers in any subject field, may be transferred and appointed to any one other division on the eligibility list without agreement by the heads of the two divisions concerned.
4. The applicant can always present his case to the personnel coordinator for assistance. It is the responsibility of that office to coordinate the effort of transfer either within a division or from one division to another.
5 If the head of the instructional division to which transfer and appointment is desired approves the qualifications of the teacher desiring the change, he must recommend, prior to June 1 or Decem-

ber 1, the transfer-and-appointment of the teacher, notifying the head of the instructional division from which transfer is being recommended, of his action.

EMPLOYEE BENEFITS AND SERVICES

School districts should give more attention to the areas of employee benefits and services. Only a limited number of district personnel policy statements examined recently gave detailed treatment to such matters as: group insurance, health services available to school personnel, travel expenses, legal aid, pensions, sick leave, leaves of absence, sabbatical leave, and other benefits which may be termed "fringe benefits."

The need for more attention to the problems of employee benefits and services for classified employees was forcibly stated in a recent study made by Edgar Egly. He studied 109 public school districts in cities of 100,000 or more population. Some of his more important findings were as follows:

1. The range and amount of fringe benefits provided by school districts tend to increase proportionally with the size of the city in which the school district is located.
2. School systems in the western part of the nation provide more extensive fringe benefits than do schools located in other sections of the country.
3. Office employees in business and industry have a broader benefit program for retirement plans, life insurance, hospitalization, medical and surgical insurance than do the classified employees of school districts.
4. Fringe benefits should not be granted at the expense of adequate wages and salaries.[12]

A more extensive treatment of the area of employee benefits and services is to be found in Chapter XVI.

CONCLUSION

The administration of personnel policy in schools can no longer be disregarded in the belief that personnel problems will be met and solved regardless of whether or not the school system has perfected a sound policy. There is now adequate research, implemented by examples of sad experience, to conclude that the hopes, desires, and human

[12] Edgar Carl Egly, *Fringe Benefits for Classified Employees of Large City School Districts* (Unpublished Doctoral dissertation, University of Southern California, 1959).

needs of school employees must be of top concern to an effective school administration. The school principal has become a key person in the school's attempt to meet and solve these problems. He is now in a trusted position, serving as a leader in organizing the efforts of teachers, other administrators, and noncertificated employees as they plan policy. If he successfully fulfills his leadership role, the modern elementary school principal must be aware of the research and proved practices in the field of personnel administration.

Short Case 1

Transfer Policy

In the New Town school system there was no written board of education policy in regard to transfer of certificated school personnel. The superintendent of schools has been making some transfers each year. Some of the transfers are made at the request of the teachers involved, and in other instances the transfers are made because the superintendent believes such action to be in the best interests of the instructional program of the schools.

During the past three years there has been a growing interest on the part of some of the members of the board of education in regard to the importance of transferring school personnel. At a board of education meeting, two board members expressed strong opinions in regard to transfer of school personnel. They expressed the opinion that teachers and principals should not be allowed to remain in a school until they become "entrenched." The press reported the statements of the board members.

Problem: The superintendent of schools began to hear rumblings of discontent from teachers and administrators as a result of the statements made by board members in regard to transferring school personnel. The superintendent realized that there was need for something to be done to alleviate the fear and discontent that had arisen among the staff.

Assume that you have been requested by the superintendent to prepare a memorandum proposing a course of action which the district should follow in the matter of transfer of school personnel. What are your recommendations?

Short Case 2

Merit-Rating in Schools

You have accepted a principalship in the New Town school system. This system is in a state that is hundreds of miles from your last location of employment. You did not find out many details of the salary schedule in this school system where you were to assume the principalship. After you got on the job, you discovered that the school system has a merit-rating plan involved in the district's tenure and salary policy. You have a strong conviction against merit-rating as a method of paying school personnel and granting tenure. It is quite evident that you will have to rate each of your teachers by the end of the school term.

Problem: What is your plan of action? Do you expect to resign? Formulate a clear statement of the steps you plan to take in this predicament.

Chapter Sixteen

Administrative Leadership in Building Staff Morale

BUILDING AND KEEPING STAFF MORALE

When we talk about employee morale as it relates to personnel in a school system, we are describing two possible conditions. The first is one in which morale is high among the teachers and other school employees, as shown in happy work situations where few criticisms and dissatisfactions are present. The second possibility is one in which morale is low among teachers and other school employees, and is exemplified by an unhappy work atmosphere accented with criticism and dissatisfaction.

The business and industrial world has been increasingly aware of the importance of building and maintaining a high morale among its workers. Steckle has estimated that human attitudes, feelings, and general unhappiness cost American industry over three billion dollars each year.[1] Recognition of this has caused industry to spend millions of dollars annually in attempts to bring about better employee morale. In contrast to industry, however, we cannot estimate in dollars the damage that may be done in the teaching profession if school personnel have poor attitudes, or are generally unhappy. Teachers are

[1] Lynde C. Steckle, *The Man in Management* (New York: Harper and Brothers, 1958), p. 4.

dealing with the minds of children, youth, and adults. No monetary equation can assess the loss that accrues in the teaching-learning process when a teacher does less than he is capable of doing.

The people responsible for management in schools must realize the tremendous potential for gain to education if they can find ways of attaining high staff morale in school systems. More effort and money must be allocated to the task of helping teachers find satisfaction and pleasure in their jobs.

FACTORS RELATING TO MORALE IN A SCHOOL SYSTEM

If it were clearly understood why school employees act as they do, it would be much easier to perfect plans that would cause more of them to be content and effective in their jobs. Some attempts have been made to discover the elements involved in job satisfaction as they relate to teachers. Augnot compared the job expectations of 1,248 Connecticut teachers with the beliefs of what 120 school superintendents in that state thought the job expectations were for the teachers.[2] The superintendents thought that the teachers placed more stress on the following aspects of employment than was actually the case:

1. Salary credit for military and previous teaching experience.
2. Opportunity to meet eligible persons of the opposite sex.
3. Availability and cost of rooms, board, and houses or apartments for rent.
4. General cost of living in the town.
5. College or university training.

The teachers actually placed more importance than the superintendents on the following conditions of employment:

1. Kind and frequency of reports to parents, principals, superintendents, and other school officials.
2. Pupils' records to be kept.
3. Provisions for participating in the establishment of policies which concern the teacher, and participating in the selection of school supplies.
4. Organization of the school system.
5. Whether or not the board has written policies, and whether they are available to teachers.
6. Philosophy of education in the school system.

There were no significant differences between the reactions of married and single teachers.

[2] Stephen Augnot, "Comparison of Connecticut Superintendents' Beliefs Concerning Job Expectations of Experienced Teachers with Reported Expectations of the Same Teachers" (Unpublished Doctoral dissertation, University of Connecticut, 1958).

Redefer studied twenty-four school systems involving 5,000 teachers in an attempt to discover the factors that relate to morale in teaching.[3] Among his more important generalizations are these:

1. Marital status, sex, or age are not the determining factors of morale status.
2. Salary or salary schedules do not determine the morale status of the individual teacher or the faculty group.
3. The socio-economic status of the school community does not determine the morale status of the faculty.
4. There is a significant correlation between the morale score of teachers and their superiority in teaching.

Among the positive morale factors that seemed to create job satisfaction were these:

1. A belief that the board is interested in improving the educational program.
2. The relationship of the central administration and principal does not interfere with the educational improvements of the faculty.
3. Requests for transfer are handled in a satisfactory manner.
4. Immediate superiors do what they can to make working conditions satisfactory.
5. Superiors are competent in their jobs.
6. Teacher committee work operates well.
7. Supervisors and principals make reasonable allowances for each teacher's personal limitations and problems.
8. The parents appreciate the work teachers are doing, and the parents do not interfere with the work of the teachers.[4]

Many studies indicate that social factors are the most important determinants of success and productivity in human enterprises. This has caused business, industry, and education to become aware of the significance of human factors as they relate to the general objective of attaining high morale. Probably the most important task of any organization is that of creating and continuing a favorable social and emotional climate that will capitalize on the potentials of workers and provide the basic satisfactions that people want. This is just as true in the operation of a school system as it is in a business organization. High employee morale is not always easy to attain, because workers tend to respond within the framework of their beliefs and feeling, not in accordance with actual working conditions.

---

[3] Frederick L. Redefer, "Factors That Affect Teacher Morale," *Nation's Schools,* LXIII (February, 1959), p. 59.

[4] *Ibid.,* p. 60.

THE ADMINISTRATOR AND SCHOOL MORALE

A recent study by Frederick Bewley attempted to identify successful school superintendents, and to determine why they were successful.[5] Bewley made an intensive study of the personal and professional characteristics of twelve superintendents recognized as being successful administrators. Among the outstanding characteristics which seemed to contribute to their success were:

1. They had recognized individual differences among employees.
2. They had insisted that their school districts operate on staff-developed, board adopted, written policies.
3. They had created channels of authority that were clearly defined and followed.
4. They recognized employees' accomplishments, and acknowledged them publicly.
5. They followed democratic administrative procedures.
6. They used administrative advisory groups.
7. They were good listeners.
8. They tolerated those whose opinions disagreed with theirs.
9. They kept the channels of communication open.
10. They loyally supported staff members.

Bernstein studied the role-perception and role-expectation patterns of 282 teachers in a unified school system.[6] Her findings indicated that:

1. The teachers appreciated the "administrative" obligations of the administrators, but they stressed the importance of the personalized, human relations aspect of administration.
2. There was a strong positive relationship between teachers' perceptions of the principal and their morale status.
3. The elementary teachers tended to think of their principals in a more personal way than did the junior high school and senior high school teachers.

Silverman devised a list of 81 items that were designed to sample teacher opinion in the area of morale as it is affected by the actions of principals.[7] These items were checked by 452 teachers. The 15 items of greatest importance to teachers indicated that a principal directly influences teacher morale positively if he:

---

[5] Frederick Winslow Bewley, "The Characteristics of Successful School Superintendents" (Unpublished Doctoral dissertation, University of Southern California, 1960).

[6] Mildred Ruth Henrich Bernstein, "A Study of Teachers' Role-Expectations and Role-Perceptions of a Principal, Superintendent, and Board of Education, and the Relationship Between Convergence and Divergence of Role-Expectation and Role-Perception and Teacher Morale" (Unpublished Doctoral dissertation, New York University, 1959).

[7] Martin Silverman, "Principals—What Are You Doing to Teacher Morale?" *Educational Administration and Supervision,* XLIII (April, 1957), p. 205.

1. Backs up his teachers in conflicts with parents.
2. Has a good knowledge of current elementary school methods and materials.
3. Gives praise and credit where due.
4. Does not hesitate to assume responsibilities or to take a stand; shows initiative.
5. Pays special attention to his teachers' physical comfort. (Furniture for the teachers' room; a minimum of interruptions or conferences during the lunch period; coverage for a teacher who is suddenly indisposed, and the like.)
6. Works for the good of the school and the children rather than for his own personal glory.
7. Follows up disciplinary cases referred to the office.

On the other hand, a principal's actions were shown to have a negative effect on teacher morale if he:

1. Criticizes a teacher in front of others; makes her lose face.
2. Does not seem to trust his teachers; is always snooping around.
3. Is sneaky; hypocritical.
4. Allows after-school conferences to drag on until unreasonable hours.
5. Is petty; emphasizes trivia.
6. Plays favorites among his teachers.
7. Is stubborn; won't budge from his point of view.
8. Is a gossip monger.

Merton V. Campbell, in a study conducted with 15 principals and 284 teachers, attempted to ascertain the reasons why the "highly satisfied" teachers like their principals.[8] These teachers consistently referred to certain attributes of their principals, such as his scholarly attitude, general competency, respect for the teachers' worth, his ability to guide without interfering, his effort to make it easy for teachers to teach, his maintenance of good discipline, his patience, understanding, fine personality, and courteous manner. Just as consistently the "highly dissatisfied" teachers failed to mention the principal, but they listed several annoyances, such as being given sections of slow learners, shortage of equipment, and extra-curricular activities.

It seems abundantly clear that the principal is a key person in any attempt to formulate plans and procedures for attaining and keeping morale high in a school system. The principal of a school must himself have high morale, or he cannot develop it in his associates.

MEASURING AND APPRAISING MORALE IN A SCHOOL SYSTEM

The one important deterrent to measuring morale in a school system is the current lack of enough effective instruments and other

---

[8] Merton V. Campbell, "Self-Role Conflict Among Teachers and Its Relationship to Satisfaction, Effectiveness, and Confidence in Leadership" (Unpublished Doctoral dissertation, University of Chicago, 1958).

means for such measurement. Not enough research has been done in exploring better ways of measuring morale with that particular group of workers, the school employees. At this point, business and industry provide most of the examples of practices which, with modification, can be of use in working with school personnel.

There are a few objective instruments available for use in attempting to evaluate teacher morale. *The Rating Scale of Hostile Behavior* asks the teacher to respond to thirty items. (A sample item: The principal blames the same faculty member when things go wrong.) Another scale, *The Faculty Morale Rating Scale,* was developed by the Personnel Research Board of the Ohio State University. This scale consists of eighteen declarative statements about specific characteristics of the faculty. (A sample item: Certain members of the staff are considered uncooperative.) A test titled: *A Study of Group Morale,* published by Psychometric Affiliates, provides an assessment of satisfaction of interpersonal relations, homogeneity of attitude, and satisfaction with leadership.

If a school system is making an attempt to determine the attitudes of the teachers toward their general job and working conditions, the school system would probably want to examine the *SRA Employee Inventory,* published by Science Research Associates. It can be answered in about twenty minutes, and yields fourteen profile category scores, in areas such as Job Demands, Pay, Confidence in Management, and Adequacy of Communication.

Industry places much reliance on oral surveys in determining attitudes of workers. School systems can make use of that technique if the central office staff, the principals, and supervisors are skilled in its use.

The importance of learning the attitudes of employees lies in the use that is made of such information. There is little need for collecting information from employees unless it is used as a basis for action.

STAFF PARTICIPATION IN DECISION-MAKING

The philosophy expressed in this book stresses the importance of school employees having the privilege of contributing their ideas to the formation of general policy structure of the school's operation. Considerable evidence has been presented to show that morale is likely to be better when teachers and other school employees have a part in the process of decision-making.

Briggs has stated the philosophy in this manner:

> Acceptance of a common goal by all of a staff, especially if they have given public expression of a whole-hearted approval, results in a sense of group solidarity and of mutual confidence. It encourages co-operation, the seeking of help from comrades who are trusted, and the generous giving of help when it is sought. There is no suspicion

> of sabotage, either active or the result of lagging effort. There is team play over which pride glows. Morale generates morale.[9]

When the process of decision-making is discussed, it is well to be explicit on what is meant; because confusion may result when there is lack of understanding concerning who should make policy and who should execute policy. The philosophy quoted below is sound:

> In a democratic school organization everyone concerned should have opportunity to voice his beliefs on policy questions, but the execution of policy is the responsibility of the status officials or persons to whom executive tasks are assigned. When groups try to carry out executive functions they may thwart organizational effectiveness and may reduce the freedom of members of the group in so doing. Implementation of policy decisions is primarily an executive responsibility.[10]

A plan of organization for employee participation in decision-making has been presented in chart form in Chapter XIV, page 321. This chart illustrates the centrally coordinated approach to policy and decision-making, and provides opportunity for all of the employees of the school system to be represented and have a part in decision-making. An adaptation of this organization may be used to solve morale problems in a school system.

LIMITATIONS TO STAFF PARTICIPATION

Caution needs to be exercised, however, to prevent the decision-making machinery from becoming cumbersome and time-consuming. The executive officers of the school system should implement policy once it is made. Hebeisen describes what can and does happen when this practice is not followed:

> Too often the superintendent of schools may fall victim to the extreme viewpoint where committees run rampant and everybody does everything and the simplest decision becomes a matter of group debate. Here, neither efficiency nor group morale is adequately served.[11]

EFFECTIVE COMMUNICATION—THE KEY TO GOOD STAFF MORALE

THE ELEMENTS OF GOOD COMMUNICATION

In practically every recent study of the characteristics of the successful school administrator, evidence is found that he is an effective

---

[9] Thomas H. Briggs, "Morale," *The Educational Forum,* XXII (January, 1958), p. 148.

[10] Roald F. Campbell and Russell T. Gregg, *Administrative Behavior in Education* (New York: Harper & Brothers Publishers, 1957), p. 278.

[11] Alfred B. Hebeisen, "A Look at Employee Morale," *Education,* LXXVI (November, 1955), p. 171.

communicator. The studies also show that the successful administrator is a member of a team in an educational organization that attempts to serve the aims of public education.

The educational team is composed of all the employees in the school system. If the team is to function effectively, ways must be found to pass along information and instruction. There is need for cooperation in solving problems, and all the members of the team will need to learn from the accomplishments and mistakes of each other. A workable system or plan of communication is necessary if these goals are to be reached.

Communication may be defined for purposes of this discussion as the transmission of factual information and values from one person to another or one group to another. The channel of communication is the complicated structure of personal relationships, including the desires, hopes, and aspirations of all of the people who work on the team. One of the most difficult of all tasks is that of attempting to convey meaning accurately from one mind to another; this, in essence, is what communication attempts.

DEVELOPING THE PROGRAM

The school administration is responsible for the initial concern about the effectiveness of communication within a school system. All of the people in decision-making roles are vitally involved in the process by which directions, information, ideas, and explanations are transmitted from person to person. The classroom teachers and non-certificated workers are equally important to the successful operation of communication procedures. It is necessary that means are provided for all of these people to receive and send messages via the communication channels. This means that representatives of all the elements of the working force in the school need to be involved in the development of a planned communication procedure.

When the central office administration in a system becomes sufficiently aware of the need for better communication, time, money, and effort should be spent in studying, planning for and perfecting an effective program.

The planning process will involve a study of these essential questions as they relate to communication:

1. Is there a clear understanding of the objectives of the school program?
2. Has the school system developed a clear statement of personnel policy that has been approved by the board of education?
3. What are the most effective ways to insure that communication is a three-way process—from the central offices down; from the

teacher to the principal to the superintendent in an upward direction; horizontally in such a manner that teachers at the same grade level may share information and custodians may communicate with other custodians?

4. What are the specific communication responsibilities of the central office staff members, the principals, and the supervisory staff?
5. What are the specific communication needs and responsibilities of the teachers and the non-certificated employees?
6. What media are available, and what needed, for effective communication?
7. What are the current attitudes of the school employees toward the general operation of the school system?
8. What means of evaluation may be used to test the effectiveness of any program of communication within the school system?

After the planning group has completed their research based on the questions mentioned above, they are ready to draw specific plans for improving communications within their school systems.

PERSONALIZING THE PROGRAM

There is no tailor-made plan of communication that can be adopted to fit all schools. Each school system is unique. Each employee in the school system should be encouraged to believe that he has a part in any success or failure the schools may experience. When all employees understand and accept that philosophy, there is good reason to hope for success.

COORDINATION OF THE PROGRAM

The program of communications may be coordinated in the same way that a school system coordinates curriculum practices. It is reasonable to suggest that in many districts a specific person should be designated to spend time in coordinating such a program. Some school systems assign this function to the Director of Personnel. The person coordinating the program will need the help of a committee that represents all segments of the employee group. This committee should have the same status, and operate in the same way, as other important committees in a school system.

CONSTANT REVISION OF COMMUNICATION MATERIALS AND METHODS

The committee responsible for coordinating communication should be constantly evaluating the effectiveness of each aspect of the program.

This evaluation will include the use of attitude or morale surveys and other objective means of determining what needs to be changed or improved. Checks should be made frequently to find out if the written materials, such as handbooks, are easily read and understood, and if they attract the interest of the readers.

THE PURPOSES AND CONTENT OF COMMUNICATION IN SCHOOLS

There must be a means of communicating both downward and upward in the school system. Communication is not sufficient if personnel merely get the word from the superintendent and the central office staff. Ways must be found to communicate the thoughts and reactions of all the members of the school team. Teachers do not expect the administrator to offer solutions to all their personal problems, but they do prefer the administrator who plans, organizes, and communicates in ways that keep them informed. They want to be informed and consulted when changes affecting them are anticipated. There is often wide disparity between what the principal says he expects of teachers, and what the teachers say the principal expects of them.

The purposes of communication in schools include the following:

1. To enable all employees to understand the objectives of the school program.
2. To provide means for receiving and understanding employee attitudes and ideas that relate to what happens in the schools.
3. To break down the status relationships that often exist in a school system. Such relationships tend to inhibit the free flow of information.
4. To provide means for motivating the school employees to give their best efforts.
5. To bridge the gap between the policy-making and policy-enforcement function of school management.
6. To provide school employees with specific ways they may contribute to the successful operation of the schools, and to assure them of the benefits they may receive as a result of their efforts.

MEDIA AND DEVICES OF COMMUNICATION

It is important that the philosophy of communication upon which this text is based be understood before the media and means of communication are discussed. Effective communication does not consist of systems, media, or facts; but rather of understanding, awareness, and mutual confidence. Emphasis must be placed upon people, and not on machines or gimmicks; communication is a tool for working harmoniously and effectively with people.

In attempting to increase the understanding, confidence, and aspirations of school employees, the administration must find ways to transmit and receive messages accurately. It is at this point that the devices and media of communication become important.

One of the most important immediate objectives of communication is that of reaching as many people as possible in the most efficient and economical way. To transmit messages to the largest number of receivers requires the use of all proven media. These include: conversation, interviews, discussions, speeches, newspapers, letters, posters, memos, information sheets, audio-visual materials, orientation materials, printed statements of policies, handbooks, manuals, bulletin boards, annual reports, pay checks and inserts, suggestion systems, attitude and morale studies, television, radio, and telephones.

McCloskey recently presented an adaptation of Wilbur Schramm's *Model of the Communication Process*.[12] Any school system attempting to evaluate or improve the communication process could profitably study the McCloskey Model presented below.

A Source	"Encodes" A Message	And Tries to "Transmit" It	To "Receivers" Who Try to Decode It	and Respond
You have facts or ideas you want others to understand	You select words, gestures or pictures to prepare a "message" you hope others will notice and understand	You try to convey your "message" by means of conversations, letters, bulletins, newspapers, magazines, television, radio	Those who notice your message interpret it in a framework of their interests, attitudes, and group relationships	They may decide to think about your message, to discuss it with you, to support your idea, to oppose it, or to do nothing about it

There are essentially two media for transmitting communication—speech and writing. The typical school system approach depends too much on writing. More thought and effort should be given to interpersonal communication. Some business executives estimate that they spend two-thirds of their time in direct consultation with other people. Research does not indicate clearly the amount of time the average

[12] Gordon McCloskey, "Principles of Communication for Principals," *The Bulletin of the National Association of Secondary-School Principals,* XL (September, 1960), p. 18.

principal or supervisor spends in this way, but it is safe to say that it is not enough. School systems should explore avenues for the opportunity of giving and getting information where small groups of school employees are involved. The performance of principals and supervisors is highly important in this aspect of communication.

The gossip, rumor, grapevine method. The school administrator often overlooks the importance of the "grapevine" in the mysterious circuit of the communication channel. Much of the process of communication is carried on in schools in ways that are not included in the framework of a planned system or program. Any superintendent or principal will testify to that fact if he has earned some "service stripes" in the profession. Coffee breaks in the teachers' room, discussions over bridge, gossip at evening affairs, the word passed along by the girls in the front office—these and many other examples can be offered to explain why the grapevine is, and will continue to be, a channel of communication among school personnel.

The school administration has only one effective means of combating any bad effects of the grapevine, and that is by making full information available as soon as possible. By this means, the grapevine can be used to help circulate accurate information, and help insure its acceptance.

THE MISTAKES OFTEN MADE IN COMMUNICATION

Many of the mistakes made in the attempt to communicate with others are made because the communicator does not realize the importance of words. He forgets that words are only symbols for things and that they may have far different meanings to different individuals. The word "transfer" will have a different meaning to a teacher who has experienced an autocratic demand by some administrator that he be transferred to another school, as contrasted with a teacher who has not had that experience. Different social backgrounds account for different interpretations of words. These varied interpretations of words make for sabotage in the communication lines.

The school administrator or supervisor often does not realize that the image he has created may be a deterrent to his communication with teachers. His image may be that of a pompous dictator with the power of promotion or dismissal, or he may be seen as a kind, generous person. The image he creates in the minds of others is a determinant of the success he has in communicating. Many administrators are so idealistic that they do not understand the importance of planning for the practical situation where they are seen in both the role of the dictator and of the benevolent friend. The problem is to be able to find ways of communicating with those who see him as a dictator, as well as with those who see him as a friend and helper.

MACHINERY FOR SETTLING GRIEVANCES

There is little likelihood that a school system can operate for very long before employees have questions and complaints. The complaints may be termed "grievances," and they must be settled quickly or low efficiency and low morale may follow. The problem of settling grievances has been one of the blind spots in school administration. The majority of school faculties have not been unionized, and it is relatively easy to make the mistake of depending upon the supposed inherent benevolence of the administrator to offer the correct solution to complaints. The school administrator cannot solve all grievances simply and easily. Well-conceived policies are often unfair as they are applied to individuals.

A school system should not delay in setting up machinery for settling grievances. The policy-making phase of creating grievance procedures should involve representatives from all segments of the school system, thus insuring a higher degree of employee understanding and cooperation once the policy is made.

Robert E. Sibson has suggested a basic set of requirements for any employer who is thinking of setting up a grievance system or evaluating an existing system. His requirements apply to the handling of grievances in school systems, as well as to business organizations.

The requirements are as follows:

1. The company must have definite and fair personnel polices, and these must be effectively communicated to all employees and all members of management.
2. Management at all levels must sincerely believe in the importance of solving grievances, and they must vigorously support the grievance system.
3. The system must expressly and formally handle all questions and complaints which may arise.
4. Employees must have complete confidence in the sincerity of management and the effectiveness of the grievance procedure.
5. The system must recognize in a straight-forward manner that management is always the final arbiter of grievances in a non-union shop.
6. The grievance procedure should be a positive tool in human relations.[13]

In school systems where grievance machinery has been set up for several years, it has been found that the administrators and supervisors

---

[13] Robert E. Sibson, "Handling Grievances Where There Is No Union," *Personnel Journal,* XXXV (June, 1956), p. 56.

should waste no time in handling problems as they arise. Experience shows that disciplinary action against an employee should never be taken because of his seeking help through the established grievance settling machinery. The history of the use of grievance machinery in schools indicates that confidence in its effectiveness will gradually develop, if it is soundly conceived and administered wisely.

WORKABLE PLANS FOR SETTLING GRIEVANCES IN SCHOOL SYSTEMS

A small fraction of the school systems in our country have established firm policies which spell out procedure for handling grievances and complaints. There is a definite trend in the direction of forming such policy. This trend will increase as more administrators and teachers understand the great need for such policy and procedure.

Some selected plans for settling grievances and complaints are presented here, in order that the philosophy and procedures of some school systems may be known.

Detroit, Michigan, is representative of a large city school system where grievance-settling machinery has been in operation for several years. The Detroit Plan is presented here:

When Problems Arise

> This article has been written mainly for teacher reassurance, because it should not be necessary to explain to a teacher that grievances ought to be discussed through channels whenever possible.
>
> In matters requiring communication between a teacher and the Administrative and Supervisory-Instructional Aids Staff, the principal is usually the person with whom the problem should be discussed.
>
> Most grievances result from misunderstandings or mistakes. There should be no hesitation about reporting an apparent error in pay or classification, or an inappropriate assignment, to one's principal, who will help the employee to adjust the matter with the proper department. And in most cases when a teacher feels unfairly treated, a frank discussion with the person believed at fault will usually produce good results and prevent ill feelings.
>
> If a complaint to one's principal does not produce satisfaction, the matter may be taken to the chief of one's administrative division. Or if, for special reasons, one prefers to keep the inquiry confidential for the time being, he may discuss it with his supervisor or with the Personnel Department.
>
> An appeal may always be made to the Superintendent, or, as a last resort, to the Board of Education. But a thoughtful teacher will realize that such an appeal, although it certainly would create no

> prejudice, should be undertaken only as a final resort if the best interests of the school system are to be considered.[14]

Small and middle-size city school districts are now beginning to establish policy providing for grievance-settling procedures. The Cupertino Union School District, Cupertino, California, currently enrolls approximately 12,000 students. This district placed a grievance procedure into board policy in 1959.

> *Grievances*
>
> Grievances should be settled by those immediately concerned, if possible. In the event a grievance cannot be settled between an employee and his principal or supervisor, either party may present the grievance in writing to the Superintendent or his authorized representative who will transfer the employee, reassign duties, issue reprimands, or take other action in conformance with good personnel practice.
>
> Requests, suggestions, or complaints of employees should be made through proper channels and using proper procedures as outlined below:
>
> 1. Immediate Supervisor
> 2. Head of Department
> 3. Superintendent
> 4. Board
>
> The Superintendent and his assistants recognize that most matters should be cleared first with the principal, supervisor, or department head before discussing them with the Superintendent or his assistants. Principals, supervisors, and department heads, however, understand that channels should be kept open for district personnel to discuss personal matters as well as matters relating to the job with the Superintendent or his assistants.
>
> Personnel may utilize the services offered by the Cupertino Union School District Personnel Committee.[15]

INCENTIVES, BENEFITS, AND SERVICES AS THEY RELATE TO TEACHER MORALE

THE TEACHING PROFESSION DISPLAYS A GROWING INTEREST IN "FRINGE BENEFITS"

No discussion of teacher morale would be complete without reference to numerous benefits and services that should accompany the payment

---

[14] Detroit Public Schools, *Detroit Public Schools Teachers' Bulletin,* No. 2 (Detroit, Michigan: The Board of Education of the City of Detroit, 1958), pp. 34–35.

[15] Cupertino Public Schools, *Handbook, Classified Personnel* (Cupertino, California: Cupertino Union School District Board of Trustees, 1959), p. 38.

of a good salary schedule. In today's usage, employee benefits and services are called "fringe benefits." In many areas of industry, the workers are receiving benefits equal to twenty per cent of their average hourly wage. The school employee has generally not been receiving benefits comparable with those of workers engaged in industrial employment.

"Fringe benefits" for teachers might include such items as: housing for teachers, credit unions, legal aid, food services, insurance plans, sick leave plans, holidays, coffee breaks, sabbatical leaves, retirement plans, social security benefits, health services, and periodic medical examinations. It does not seem necessary now for the profession to be campaigning for unemployment benefits, guaranteed employment plans, or severance allowances. These last mentioned benefits may become important at some future time if employment conditions change in teaching.

The teaching profession is definitely turning attention to the importance of securing more benefits and services for school employees. A recent study in California points out that the granting of non-wage benefits generally rests with local boards of education. This study also indicates that professional educators have been conservative in their approach to which non-wage benefits are professionally desirable, and when these benefits should be recommended.

Ferguson recommended that California professional educators should begin now to press for the following benefits and services for school employees:

1. Health (medical), catastrophe, and physical examinations at regular intervals.
2. Time off without loss of pay, with expense for attendance at professional meetings.
3. Time off without loss of pay while performing necessary duties as an officer or committee member of a local, state, or national professional organization.
4. Sabbatical leave.
5. Free parking on private or commercial lot while at work.[16]

There is substantial evidence to indicate that teachers regard non-wage benefits of enough importance that it affects their tenure in particular school systems. In a study made of the reasons why 2,500 teachers withdrew from their positions in one state, it was found that school systems granting cumulative sick leave, maternity leave, paid leaves for certain absences other than illness, and providing social

[16] Wayne Sander Ferguson, "Non-Wage Benefits for Teachers in the State of California" (Unpublished Doctoral dissertation, University of Southern California, 1960).

security and credit unions had only half the rate of turnover as those systems which did not have these benefits.[17]

A NEED FOR ACTION PROGRAMS BY BOARDS OF EDUCATION

The time has come for school boards and school administrators to place much more emphasis on extended programs of non-wage benefits for school employees. Considerable progress has been made in recent years toward providing better sick leave plans, insurance plans, and retirement plans. At the present time, a relatively small percentage of our school systems have framed into board policy plans to offer the following benefits:

1. Sabbatical leave
2. Legal aid to school employees
3. Credit union services
4. Periodic medical examinations

If school systems are really concerned about building and keeping high morale among employees, they will start now to formulate and implement benefits and services for school employees.

THE PRINCIPAL AND STAFF MORALE

Attention has been given in this chapter to the duties and responsibilities of the central school administration in formulating policies and plans for effective personnel administration. The principal has a dual role to perform in personnel administration. He is not only a part of the central administration with a share in the policy-making responsibility, but also the administrator of a specific school. This places the principal in a uniquely important position of being able to determine, to a large degree, the success of any program of morale building. Effective communication depends on attitudes, needs, and desires of the people in the school he administers.

There is a current need for school systems to organize workshops or other types of in-service training programs in aspects of personnel administration. Specialists from business, industry, and school administration should be brought in to work with the principal as he studies the problems for which he has specific responsibility. Particular attention should be given to such topics as: Effective Methods of Measuring Staff Morale; Communication as It Relates to Staff Morale; Workable Communication Programs in Schools; Practical Plans for Settling Grievances; and Incentives and Benefits as They Relate to Staff Morale.

---

[17] Darold Raymond Beckman, "Teacher Turnover and Personnel Administration in Georgia Elementary Schools" (Unpublished Doctoral dissertation, New York University, 1960).

Training programs for principals generally are in need of more instruction in the areas enumerated in the preceding paragraph. Research points out the need for better training, and there is a recent encouraging trend in some outstanding colleges and universities to organize more course work in personnel administration.

CONCLUSION

The modern school system cannot disregard the importance of employee morale if it is to operate at the efficient level expected by the general public. There is sufficient evidence, supported by research, to establish the need for school district concern over matters that pertain to the working conditions of school employees. Written policy, formulated from representative opinion of school employees, is the base from which the school administration may build confidence and mutual respect among all school personnel.

The elementary school principal has a significant obligation and opportunity in the personnel administration of a school and a school system. He is involved in the basic policy planning, and in the day-by-day implementation of the program. It is the principal, in his interpersonal communication with teachers, who has the opportunity to help find swift and amicable solutions to problems arising at the school level. The well trained, efficient principal of the present and future will be alert to the importance of attaining and keeping high morale in the school he administers. He will approach the solution to personnel problems with research designs which will eventually permit him to go beyond the present knowledge in this field.

Short Case 1

Assessment of Attitudes of School Employees

There is considerable evidence that school employee morale may not be at a very high level in the New Town School System. The custodial staff, the maintenance men, and the secretarial workers have begun to talk about the need for some type of organization to protect their "rights," and to help them get the "benefits" they believe should be theirs.

The "grapevine" among the teaching staff often carries stories about the school system being top-heavy with supervisors and administrators. Evidently, quite a number of the teachers do not believe that the school administration and the school board are vitally concerned with the problems of the classroom teacher. The rate of turnover among the teaching staff seems to be increasing.

Problem: The superintendent of schools has become aware of some of the discontent among school employees. He wants to begin some type of effort which may lead to an objective assessment of the attitudes the school employees have toward their work and toward the school administration. You are principal of one of the large elementary schools. You have developed very good rapport with your teaching staff. The superintendent has great confidence in your ability as a school administrator. The superintendent has requested you to outline a course of action for making a careful and objective study of employee attitudes in the school district. What is the plan you are going to present to the superintendent?

Short Case 2

Settling Employee Grievances

The New Valley School System has grown at a rapid rate. The system now employs 350 certificated and 100 non-certificated employees. The school administration has been very effective in being able to build schools and employ staff members to keep pace with the rapid growth. For a time, so much emphasis had to be placed on getting enough buildings and teachers, that some other aspects of school administration were neglected. Every year there have been a few instances where school employees had real grievances that did not get settled in a smooth, satisfactory manner. These cases have resulted in damage to employee morale. The school board does not have clear-cut policy established for handling grievances. School employees are not sure what they should do when they cannot reach a satisfactory solution to their problems with building principals. Several of the principals seem to regard it as unprofessional for an employee to go beyond the principal's office in attempting to find a solution to a personal problem.

Problem: It has become evident that an effective means of settling grievances must be found if employee morale is to be improved. The superintendent of schools has appointed you to propose a plan for settling grievances within the school system. You are an elementary principal. You have worked in this school system for eight years. The superintendent has told you that you may suggest whatever means you think necessary to solve the problem. He hopes that your plan will be sound enough that it could be presented to the Board of Education for implementation into school policy. What is the plan you wish to propose?

Chapter Seventeen

The Elementary School of the Future

Prediction of things to come is hazardous at any time. In the midst of cataclysmic change it becomes especially risky. It is essentially true, however, that the past is but a prologue to the future, and certainly recent events do provide a reasonable basis for anticipating some major developments in the elementary school of the future.

It is apparent that the elementary school of 1980 will bear little resemblance to the elementary school of 1962. As education at all levels responds to the increased and urgent demands of the space age, the elementary school will inevitably expand its programs and improve the quality and excellence of its services. Mastery of the Three R's will continue to be an essential purpose of the elementary school. Increased curricular attention will, however, be given to science, mathematics, and social studies. Art, music, and dramatics will be included as essential and integral phases of the total instructional program. The function of the elementary school of the future will be seen in larger perspective. The school will be expected to provide a broad general education as the foundation upon which increasingly specialized educational experiences are developed. It is safe to predict that the elementary school student of 1980 will acquire considerably more knowledge and greater competency than either his father or grandfather did when they attended school.

Within recent years, continuing efforts have been made to achieve greater flexibility in grouping and promotion practices in the elementary schools. Experiments with ungraded primary programs, dual progress arrangements, and special programs of enrichment for gifted students have been described. All of these innovations are designed to provide a flexible school organization within which each student can progress in accordance with his own individual rate of growth and development. Conventional practices of grade placement with annual or semi-annual promotions were originally developed for administrative convenience; as schools continue their efforts to make more effective provisions for the individual needs and differences of pupils, grouping and promotion practices will become more flexible. It is most probable that conventional practices of grouping and promotion will have been largely abandoned in the elementary schools of 1980.

The achievement of maximum flexibility in the organization and administration of the elementary school will require increased provisions for the study and guidance of individual students. Appropriate instructional programs designed to meet individual needs will require extensive information about each student. The services of psychologists and guidance counsellors will be required to secure vital information concerning the intellectual, social, and emotional development of students. Doctors, nurses, and dentists will be sources of significant information concerning the health and physical needs of pupils. The services of trained social workers will be required to provide assistance for those students whose difficulties stem from home and family sources. These special services, effectively organized for the study and guidance of students, will be recognized as indispensable resources in the elementary schools of the future.

Educational leaders throughout the country are currently concerned with the urgent need for curriculum revision and improvement. "What knowledge is of most worth?" has always been a matter of deep interest and serious study by philosophers, scholars, and educators. With the rapid and dramatic explosions of new knowledge, the question of what to teach in the schools has assumed new and strategic dimensions. It is evident that continuing evaluation and revision of curriculum programs will be a central concern of teachers and school administrators for many years to come.

As the educational leader of his school and community, the elementary principal of the future will become increasingly responsible for the continuous improvement of instructional programs. In the exercise of his educational leadership, the principal will seek to secure the active cooperation and participation of teachers, experts representing the various subject-matter fields, and lay citizens. As the elementary school principal assumes greater responsibility for the improvement of instruction, the position he occupies will achieve increased prestige and become an increasingly attractive and rewarding career for creative and dedicated men and women.

Developments designed to improve the pre-service and in-service professional education of teachers and administrators have been described in previous chapters. Present trends suggest that requirements for the certification of teachers and administrators will be increased substantially during the next decade. As efforts to improve the professional preparation of teachers continue, increased attention will be given to the more effective utilization of teaching skills and competencies. Recent studies and experiments indicate that a considerable portion of the teacher's time is devoted to essentially clerical and routine activities. In several secondary schools throughout the country, teachers of English have been relieved of many clerical responsibilities by the employment of non-professional aides. These non-professional, but essentially competent, individuals assume responsibility for the reading and correction of students' written assignments, thus freeing the teacher for the more creative aspects of his teaching responsibility.

At the elementary school level, similar efforts to relieve the teacher of clerical responsibilities have been made through the employment of instructional secretaries. Under this plan several classroom teachers, usually six in number, are assigned a secretary. The secretary assumes responsibility for the preparation of routine reports, the maintenance of records, and the requisition and service of instructional supplies and equipment. The results of the experiments with instructional secretaries suggest that it is an inexpensive means of more effectively utilizing the competencies of professional teachers.

Team-teaching arrangements are rapidly being organized in elementary schools as another means of utilizing the competencies of teachers more effectively. These arrangements make it possible for teachers with varied interests, competencies, and experience to plan cooperatively a program of instructional services in which each member of the team can make his most distinctive contribution. The larger number of students involved in the team-teaching arrangement also provides for greater flexibility in the grouping of students, and achievement of a more appropriate balance between large group and small group instruction.

The beginnings that have been made toward achieving a more effective utilization of teachers' competencies are most promising. It is an area in which far-reaching changes and improvements can be expected in the future.

Competent observers have noted that the schools of the nation are involved in an instructional revolution. The impact of new technological developments is beginning to effect significant changes in the organization and operation of instructional programs at both the elementary and secondary school levels. Throughout the country experiments are being conducted with teaching machines. Based upon the psychological principle of reinforcement in learning, there is considerable evidence to suggest that these machines can be utilized effectively to improve instruction for some children. The learning materials used in the machines are presented in sequential steps. They are self-instructive and self-corrective, thus permitting each student to progress at his own individual rate. Research evidence indicates that, for most students, the teaching machine makes possible the achievement of more learning in considerably less time than is possible with conventional methods and materials.

Programmed instruction is another innovation intended to serve the same purposes as the teaching machine. Learning materials are prepared in book form with built-in techniques which make them both self-instructive and self-corrective.

At the present time, there is considerable discussion and controversy among educators concerning the value of teaching machines and programmed instruction, and the extent to which they should be utilized in the classroom. Certainly the principle of reinforcement in learning is a valid concept, with many implications for the improvement of instruction. The need for improved methods of individualizing instruction is great, and programmed learning has significant implications for such improvement. It can safely be predicted that experimentation with these innovations will continue, and that the results of such experimentation will be reflected in the instructional practices of the elementary school of the future.

The use of television in the schools can scarcely be considered an innovation or a new educational development. Television instruction has been widely used in a number of school systems throughout the United States during the past decade. The Midwest Project in Airborne Television Instruction, launched in the autumn of 1961 with a substantial financial grant from the Ford Foundation, has stimulated renewed interest and created increased opportunities for the use of television in the schools. The project involves the broadcasting of instructional programs from an airplane. The programs cover a variety of subjects at both the elementary and secondary school levels, and are available to schools in six midwestern states.

The Midwest Project has created unprecedented opportunities for the expanded use of television instruction in the future. The high cost of installing broadcasting facilities and the preparation of programs has, until recently, limited the use of television to large cities and centers of dense population. The experience with the Midwest Project in Airborne Television Instruction clearly suggests that television instruction can be made widely available through regional, and perhaps national, arrangement. Some enthusiastic proponents of educational television are confidently predicting that through the use of a satellite, educational television will achieve national and hemispheric coverage within the foreseeable future. Certainly, educational television has progressed well beyond the experimental stage. It seems certain to become as indispensable a part of the instructional program of the elementary school of the future as the textbook has been in the past.

In recent years, language laboratories have been installed in large numbers of secondary schools, and used to teach foreign languages to high school students. The results achieved with these laboratories have been highly satisfactory for some purposes. As the demand continues for extension of foreign language instruction to the elementary schools, it is evident that language laboratories will be extensively utilized. The mobile classroom is a promising development in the use of these laboratories. Auto trailers are equipped to serve 20 or more student stations, and the laboratory is driven from school to school to provide instruction. The mobile laboratory makes instruction available to small school systems that could not afford the installation of permanent equipment.

The instructional revolution resulting from the utilization of new technological developments will necessitate far-reaching changes in school organization and operation. School buildings will need to be designed to provide far greater flexibility than in the past. Spaces will be provided with movable partitions, in order that they may be readily adjusted for both large group and small group instructional purposes. In the construction of buildings, provisions will need to be made for the installation and operation of a variety of mechanical and electronic equipment. There is already need in all schools for resource centers and libraries to accommodate the increased instructional supplies, materials, and equipment that are available for the enrichment of instruction.

There will be need for a thoughtful re-examination of the role of the teacher in the changing classrooms of the future. It is unthinkable to assume that the teacher can be replaced by a television screen, a teaching machine, or a language laboratory. The challenge of the future for educational leadership is to plan educational programs so that all of these newer devices are utilized to enrich instruction, and to free the teacher for those creative contributions which will always be essential to effective teaching and learning.

Current trends indicate that the length of the school year will be increased in the years that lie immediately ahead. The conventional school year of nine or ten months was established when life was much simpler, and when considerably less was expected of young people in their preparation for the responsibilities of citizenship. Studies reveal that learning opportunities and expectations have been increased more than two-fold in recent years, with little or no change in the length of the school day or the school year.

In many places throughout the country, planned summer sessions are being added to the educational program to serve the needs of students at both the elementary and secondary school levels. Thus far, attendance in most of these summer programs is voluntary, and many of them are self-supporting through the assessment of tuition fees. The authors predict that within the next decade the length of the school year at both elementary and secondary levels will have been increased to eleven months, with full tax support of the extended program.

The authors are confident that the promising practices described here and the changes predicted for the future will greatly enhance the quality of elementary school education. However, change for the sake of change itself has little or no merit. Innovations in the organization and operation of schools can be accepted only to the extent that newer practices clearly represent improved means of achieving the historic purposes of a democratic society.

Since the beginnings of our national life, education has been interpreted as the means of achieving and improving the ideals and aspirations of a free people. Throughout the years, programs and practices in the schools have been continuously improved to meet the changing needs and conditions of a dynamic society. The record of the schools in responding to the changing and increased demands of the nation is a magnificent one. Education has certainly been the most important means of achieving more fully the promises of the American dream. The changes that are now being made and that will continue to be made in the nation's schools will be valid only if they continue to make effective contributions to accepted national purposes and goals. The challenge to educational leadership in the future will be to evaluate newer programs and practices in terms of their effectiveness in the achievement of fundamental and essentially unchanging democratic purposes and values.

Respect for the intrinsic worth and dignity of human personality is the ideal which most sharply distinguishes democracy from totalitarian forms of government. As efforts are made in the schools to identify and more effectively meet the individual needs of students, this ideal will be increasingly fulfilled. As attempts are made to give greater attention to the individual, it will be necessary to make sure that such efforts do not result in the designation of some students as inferior to or less important than others. Classification and grouping practices should be made for specific instructional purposes, and should not result in labelling students as low, average, or superior.

It is certainly time that the importance of varying the content and methods of instruction was recognized, in order to accommodate the differences in the interests, aptitudes, and abilities of students. It is to be hoped, however, that such adjustment will never be interpreted to mean that any student will be denied the opportunity to acquire those basic skills, knowledges, and competencies that are essential for the success of all future citizens.

Comprehensive methods of evaluation will be an essential means of safeguarding and enhancing respect for the worth and dignity of human personality. The results of standardized tests will not be considered the only evidence of successful individual achievement. Evaluation will include appraisal of attitudes, habits, and interests. Significance will be attached to such personality traits as independence, creativeness, responsibility, cooperation, and the like. The individual student will participate in the evaluation of his own progress; he will be motivated to improve his own achievement, rather than to compete with some mythical average or norm.

In a free society, it is completely essential that citizens be able to think for themselves and to make judgements based upon reason. In an age increasingly characterized by the impact of mass media of communication, the responsibility of the schools to teach students to think independently, creatively, and critically assumes increased importance. Contrast this with the schools of a totalitarian society, where students are not permitted to think for themselves, but are told what to think and how to think.

Schools in the United States have made considerable progress in the use of the problem-solving method of instruction. Under this method, students acquire skill in the identification and analysis of problems, and in the utilization of pertinent evidence as the means of arriving at independent and creative solutions. A continuing responsibility of teachers and administrators will be to evaluate any future changes in educational programs and practices to make abundantly sure that learning is always a meaningful, thoughtful, and reflective process. No greater injustice could be inflicted upon the youth of the nation than to utilize in their education methods that are designed for the education of robots and slaves.

In a democracy, the individual is entitled to respect only to the extent that he maintains and practices respect for others. In an age of jet propulsion and space exploration, the world has become small and the peoples of the world interdependent. The hope of lasting peace in the world depends almost entirely upon the ability of people everywhere to accept their common humanity, and to live and work together as members of the human race.

Many of the developing practices in the elementary schools have been designed to increase the efficiency of administration and operation. They seek to provide more effective learning experiences, and to prepare students more appropriately for the changing and unpredictable world in which they live. These are realistic and worthy purposes. Educational leadership also has the inescapable responsibility, however, of evaluating current and future changes in the elementary schools in terms of their moral and spiritual implications. Unless the elementary schools of the future can produce better human beings, intelligently dedicated to the service of all mankind, the changes that are made may carry the seeds of their own destruction.

Bibliography of Selected Reading

CHAPTER II. TRAINING PROGRAMS FOR ELEMENTARY ADMINISTRATORS

American Association of School Administrators, *Professional Administrators for America's Schools,* Thirty-eighth Yearbook (Washington, D.C.: the Association, 1960).

American Association of School Administrators, *Something to Steer By* (Washington, D.C.: the Association, 1958).

An Appraisal of the Internship in Educational Administration (New York: Bureau of Publications, Teachers College, Columbia University, 1958).

Campbell, Roald F., *Administrative Theory as a Guide to Action* (Chicago: Midwest Administration Center, University of Chicago, 1960).

———, and John E. Corbally, Jr., and John A. Ramseyer, *Introduction to Educational Administration* (Boston: Allyn and Bacon, Inc., 1958).

Chandler, B. J., and E. T. McSwain, "Professional Programs for School Administrators," *Phi Delta Kappan,* XLI (November, 1959), p. 61.

Graff, Orin B., and Ralph B. Kimbrough, "What We Have Learned About Selection," *Phi Delta Kappan,* XXXVII (April, 1956), pp. 294–296.

Moore, Hollis A., Jr., *Studies in School Administration* (Washington, D.C.: American Association of School Administrators, 1957).

Southern States Cooperative Program in Educational Administration, *Better Teaching in School Administration* (Nashville: McQuiddy Printing Co., 1955).

CHAPTER III. NEW PROGRAMS FOR THE TRAINING OF TEACHERS

Cottrell, Donald L. (ed.), *Teacher Education for a Free People* (Oneonta, N.Y.: The American Association of Colleges for Teacher Education, 1956).

DeYoung, Chris. A., *Introduction to American Public Education,* 3rd Edition (New York: McGraw-Hill Book Co., 1955).

Hill, Henry H., "Wanted: Professional Teachers," *The Atlantic Monthly,* CCV (May, 1960), pp. 37–40.

Hillway, Tyrus, *Education in American Society* (Boston: Houghton Mifflin Company, 1961).

Hughes, James M., *Education in America* (Evanston, Ill.: Row, Peterson and Company, 1960).

Mason, Barbara T., "The Principal's Role in In-Service Education," *The National Elementary Principal,* XLI, No. 5 (February, 1962), pp. 21–23.

Myers, Edward D., *Education in the Perspective of History* (New York: Harper and Brothers, 1960).

National Society for the Study of Education, *Inservice Education,* Fifty-sixth Yearbook (Chicago: University of Chicago Press, 1957).

Ryans, David G., *Characteristics of Teachers* (Washington, D.C.: American Council on Education, 1960).

Thayer, Vivian T., *The Role of the School in American Society* (New York: Dodd, Mead and Company, 1960).

Thelen, Herbert A., *Education and the Human Quest* (New York: Haıper and Brothers, 1960).

The University Council for Educational Administration, *Simulation in Administrative Training* (Columbus, Ohio: the Council, 1960).

Thomas, Lawrence G., Lucien B. Kinney, Arthur P. Coladarci and Helen A. Fielstra, *Perspective on Teaching* (Englewood Cliffs, N.J.: Prentice-Hall, Inc., 1961), Chapter 15.

Unruh, Adolph, "What's Needed in Teacher Education?" *Phi Delta Kappan,* XXXVII (March, 1956), pp. 258–261.

Woodring, Paul, *New Directions in Teacher Education* (New York: Fund for the Advancement of Education, 1957).

CHAPTER IV. NEW PLANS OF ORGANIZATION FOR INSTRUCTION

Anderson, Robert H., "Three Examples of Team Teaching in Action," *The Nation's Schools,* LXV (May, 1960), pp. 62–65.

———, "Team Teaching in an Elementary School," *School Review,* LXVI, No. 1 (Spring, 1960), pp. 71–84.

Carbone, R. F., "The Nongraded School: An Appraisal," *Administrator's Notebook,* X, No. 1 (September, 1961).

Cross, A. J. Foy, and Irene F. Cypher, *Audio-Visual Education* (New York: Thomas Y. Crowell Co.).

Fritz, John O., "Educational Technology: A Way to Its Assessment," *Administrator's Notebook,* IX, No. 6 (February, 1961).

Fry, Edward B., et al, "Teaching Machines: An Annotated Bibliography," *Audio-Visual Communication Review,* Supp. 1, Vol. 8, No. 2 (Washington, D.C.: National Education Association Department of Audio-Visual Instruction, 1960).

Galanter, Eugene (ed.), *Automatic Teaching: the State of the Art* (New York: John Wiley and Sons, Inc., 1959).

Goodlad, John I., and Robert H. Anderson, *The Non-Graded Elementary School* (New York: Harcourt, Brace, 1959).

Hahner, John M., "Grouping Within a School," *Childhood Education,* XXXVI (April, 1960), pp. 354–356.

Holland, James G., "Teaching Machines: An Application of Principles from the Laboratory," *Journal of Experimental Analysis of Behavior,* III, No. 4 (October, 1960), pp. 275–287.

———, and B. F. Skinner, *The Analysis of Behavior* (New York: McGraw-Hill Book Co., 1961).

Lacy, Don, *Freedom and Communications* (Urbana, Ill.: University of Illinois Press, 1961).

Lumsdaine, A. A., and Robert Glaser (eds.), *Teaching Machines and Programmed Learning: A Source Book* (Washington, D.C.: National Education Association, 1960).

Morse, Arthur D., *Schools of Tomorrow—Today!* (Garden City, N.Y.: Doubleday and Company, 1960).

National Education Association Research Division, "Studies of Utilization of Staff, Buildings, and Audio-Visual Aids in the Public Schools," *Research Report* 1959–R17 (October, 1959), pp. 9–24.

Ohm, Robert E., "Toward a Rationale for Team Teaching," *Administrator's Notebook,* IX, No. 7 (March, 1961).

Schramm, Wilbur (ed.), *The Impact of Educational Television* (Urbana, Ill.: University of Illinois Press, 1961).

Tarbet, Donald G., *Television and Our Schools* (New York: The Ronald Press Co., 1961).

The Ford Foundation, *Time, Talent, and Teachers* (New York: The Foundation, 1960).

Trump, J. Lloyd, and Dorsey Baynham, *Focus on Change* (Chicago: Rand McNally and Company, 1961).

Ward, J. O., "Another Plan for Co-Ordinate Teaching," *American School Board Journal,* CXXXX (February, 1960), p. 10.

CHAPTER V. MOTIVATION: A CREATIVE APPROACH

Abelson, Herbert I., *Persuasion: New Opinions and Attitudes Are Changed* (New York: Springer Publishing Company, 1959).

Arnold, Magda B., "Motivation and the Desire to Know," *Education,* LXXVII (December, 1956), pp. 220–26.

Association for Supervision and Curriculum Development, *Learning and the Teacher,* 1959 Yearbook (Washington, D.C.: the Association, 1959).

———, *New Insights and the Curriculum* (Washington, D.C.: the Association, 1963).

Bindra, Dalbir, *Motivation: A Systematic Reinterpretation* (New York: The Ronald Press Co., 1959).

Culbertson, Jack A., et al, *Administrative Relationships* (Englewood Cliffs, N.J.: Prentice-Hall, Inc., 1960).

Gagne, Robert M., *Psychology and Human Performance* (New York: Holt, Winston, and Rinehart, Inc., 1959).

Griffiths, Daniel E., *Human Relations in School Administration* (New York: Appleton-Century-Crofts, Inc., 1956).

Hughes, Arthur G., *Learning and Teaching* (London: Longmans, Green and Company, 1959).

Hullfish, H. Gordon, and Philip G. Smith, *Reflective Thinking* (New York: Dodd, Mead and Company, 1961).

Lawson, Philippe R., *Learning and Behavior* (New York: The Macmillan Company, 1960).

Lazarus, Richard S., *Adjustment and Personality* (New York: McGraw-Hill Book Co., 1961).

Lindzey, Gardner (ed.), *Assessment of Human Motives* (New York: Holt, Winston, and Rinehart, Inc., 1958).

Loree, M. Ray (ed.), *Educational Psychology* (New York: The Ronald Press Co., 1959).

March, Leland S., "Motivation, the Key to Good Teaching," *Education Digest,* XXV (January, 1960), pp. 24–26.

Mayer, Frederick, *Education for Creative Living* (New York: Whittier Books, 1959).

"Motivation in the Elementary School," *National Education Association Journal,* XLVIII (January, 1959), pp. 12–13.

Mouly, George J., *Psychology for Effective Teaching* (New York: Holt, Winston, and Rinehart, Inc., 1960).

Pressey, Sidney L., et al, *Psychology in Education* (New York: Harper and Brothers, 1959).

Shane, Harold G., Mary E. Reddin, and Margaret C. Gillespie, *Beginning Language Arts Instruction With Children* (Columbus, Ohio: Charles E. Merrill Books, Inc., 1961).

Skinner, Charles E. (ed.), *Educational Psychology* (Englewood Cliffs, N.J.: Prentice-Hall, Inc., 1959).

Waetjen, Walter B. (ed.), *New Dimensions in Learning* (Washington, D.C.: Association for Supervision and Curriculum Development, N.E.A., 1962).

CHAPTER VI. PUPIL ACTIVITIES IN THE ELEMENTARY SCHOOL

Belsito, Petrina, "Organizing the Elementary School Newspaper," *Instructor,* LXV (January, 1956), p. 66.

Bureau of Educational Research and Service, *School Camping* (Laramie, Wyo.: University of Wyoming Press, 1951).

Butler, Barbara, "School Clubs in the Elementary Grades," *School Activities,* XXXII (November, 1960), pp. 82–83.

McKown, Harry C., *Extracurricular Activities* (New York: The Macmillan Company, 1952).

Middleton, W. E., "Basic Principles of Extra-Curricular Activities," *School Activities,* XXXI (April, 1960), p. 127.

Miller, Franklin A., James H. Moyer, and Robert D. Patrick, *Planning Student Activities* (Englewood Cliffs, N.J.: Prentice-Hall, Inc., 1956).

Santa Clara County (California) Department of Education, "Science and Conservation Program Under Way at Camp Campbell," *Superintendent's Bulletin,* XIV (April, 1960), p. 4.

Smith, Julian W., *Outdoor Education for American Youth* (Washington, D.C.: American Association for Health, Physical Education, and Recreation, 1957).

Sterner, William S., "What is the Role of the Principal and the Sponsor in the Student Council?" *School Activities,* XXXII (October, 1960), pp. 47–49.

CHAPTER VII. EVALUATING THE INSTRUCTIONAL PROGRAM IN THE ELEMENTARY SCHOOL

American Association of School Administrators and National School Boards Association, *Judging Schools With Wisdom* (Washington, D.C.: The Association, 1959).

———, *Quest for Quality* (The Association, 1960).

Baron, Denis, *Evaluation Techniques for Classroom Teachers* (New York: McGraw-Hill Book Co., 1958).

California State Department of Education, *Evaluating Pupil Progress* (Sacramento: California State Department of Education, 1960).

Heyl, H. H., "Standards for Instruction in the Elementary School," *National Elementary Principal,* XXXVIII (May, 1959), pp. 48–52.

Jacobi, F. H., "Changing Pupils in a Changing School," *Educational Leadership, XVII* (February, 1960), pp. 283–287.

National Education Association, "Ten Criticisms of Public Education," *Research Bulletin,* XXXV (December, 1957), p. 4.

———, *How Good Are Your Schools?* (Washington, D.C.: National Education Association, 1958).

Reinhardt, E., and E. K. Lawson, "Experienced Teachers View Their Schools," *Educational Administration and Supervision,* XLV (May, 1959), pp. 147–152.

Shane, Harold G., *Evaluation and the Elementary Curriculum* (New York: Henry Holt and Company, 1958).

Stafford, C., and Dwight Shafer, "Public Relations and Test Results," *The Clearing House,* XXXV (January, 1961), pp. 270–272.

CHAPTER VIII. IMPROVING INSTRUCTION THROUGH SUPERVISION

Bradfield, Luther E., "Elementary School Teachers: Their Problems and Supervisory Assistance," *Educational Administration and Supervision,* XLV (March, 1959), p. 102.

Burton, William H., and Leo J. Brueckner, *Supervision,* 3rd Edition (New York: Appleton-Century-Crofts, Inc., 1955).

Cappa, Dan, and Margaret VanMeter, "Opinions of Teachers Concerning the Most Helpful Supervisory Procedures," *Educational Administration and Supervision,* XLIII (April, 1957), pp. 217–222.

Chapman, Gail N., "Beginning Teacher and the Supervisor," *Clearing House,* XXXII (November, 1959), pp. 163–164.

Cramer, Roscoe V., and Otto E. Domian, *Administration and Supervision in the Elementary School* (New York: Harper and Brothers, 1960).

Crosby, Muriel E., *Supervision as Cooperative Action* (New York: Appleton-Century-Crofts, Inc., 1957).

Ellsbree, Willard S., and Harold J. McNally, *Elementary School Administration and Supervision,* 2nd Edition (New York: American Book Company, 1959).
Everett, J. Bernard, Mary Downing, and Howard Leavitt, *Case Studies in School Supervision* (New York: Holt, Winston, and Rinehart, Inc., 1960).
Hicks, Hanne, *Educational Supervision in Principle and Practice* (New York: The Ronald Press Co., 1960).
Lewis, Claudia, and Charlotte B. Winson, "Supervising the Beginning Teacher," *Educational Leadership,* XVII (December, 1959), pp. 137–141.
Moore, Walter J. (compiler), "Selected References on Elementary School Instruction: Evaluation and Supervision," *Elementary School Journal,* LX (October, 1959), pp. 51–54.
National Education Association Department of Elementary School Principals, *Elementary Principalship.* Thirty-seventh Yearbook (Washington, D.C.: the Department, 1958), Chapter II, pp. 13–35.
National Society for the Study of Education, *Inservice Education.* Fifty-sixth Yearbook, Part I (Chicago: the Society, 1957).
St. Mary, Maurice E., "Team Approach in Supervision," *Educational Administration and Supervision,* XLV (September, 1959), pp. 300–304.
Wiles, Kimball, *Supervision for Better Schools,* 2nd Edition (Englewood Cliffs, N.J.: Prentice-Hall, Inc., 1955).

CHAPTER IX. PROVIDING FOR THE MENTALLY SUPERIOR

Abraham, Willard, *Common Sense about Gifted Children* (New York: Harper and Brothers, 1958).
Association for Supervision and Curriculum Development, *Perceiving, Behaving, Becoming* (Washington, D.C.: the Association, 1962).
Barbe, Walter B., "Homogeneous Grouping for Gifted Children," *Educational Leadership,* XIII (January, 1956), pp. 225–229.
California Elementary School Administrators Association, *The Gifted Child: Another Look.* Monograph Number 10 (Palo Alto: National Press, 1958).
Cutts, Norma E., Nicholas Moseley, et al, *Providing for Individual Differences in the Elementary School* (Englewood Cliffs, N.J.: Prentice-Hall, Inc., 1960).
———, and Nicholas Moseley, *Teaching the Bright and Gifted* (Englewood Cliffs, N.J.: Prentice-Hall, Inc., 1957).
Getzels, Jacob W., and Philip W. Jackson, *Creativity and Intelligence* (New York: John Wiley and Sons, Inc., 1962).
Gibbs, Elsie Frances, "The Gifted Need Administrative Leadership," *American School Board Journal,* CXXXVI (March, 1958), pp. 22–25.
Havinghurst, R. J., E. Stivers, and R. F. DeHaan, *A Survey of Education of Gifted Children* (Chicago: University of Chicago Press, 1955).
Kough, Jack, *Practical Programs for the Gifted* (Chicago: Science Research Associates, 1960).
Maclean, Malcolm S., "Should the Gifted Be Segregated?" *Educational Leadership,* XIII (January, 1956), pp. 215–220.

Otto, Henry J., *Curriculum Enrichment for Gifted Elementary School Children in Regular Classes* (Austin, Tex.: University of Texas Press, 1957).

Paschal, Elizabeth, *Encouraging the Excellent* (New York: Fund for the Advancement of Education, 1960).

Strang, Ruth M., *Helping Your Gifted Child* (New York: Dutton Company, 1960).

Sumption, Merle R., and Evelyn M. Luecking, *Education of the Gifted* (New York: The Ronald Press Co., 1960).

United States Department of Health, Education, and Welfare Office of Education, *The Gifted Student,* Cooperative Monograph Number 2 (Washington, D.C.: Government Printing Office, 1960).

CHAPTER X. PUPILS WITH PROBLEMS: THE MALADJUSTED AND HANDICAPPED

Cook, Walter W., "The Gifted and the Retarded in Historical Perspective," *The National Elementary Principal,* XXXVIII (December, 1958), pp. 14–21.

Cutts, Norma E., and Nicholas Moseley (eds.), *Providing for Individual Differences in the Elementary School* (Englewood Cliffs, N.J.: Prentice-Hall, Inc., 1960).

Garrison, Karl C., and Dewey G. Force, Jr., *The Psychology of Exceptional Children,* 3rd Edition (New York: The Ronald Press Co., 1959).

Ingram, Christine P., *Education of the Slow-Learning Child,* 3rd Edition (New York: The Ronald Press Co., 1960).

Magary, James F., *The Exceptional Child* (New York: Holt, Winston, and Rinehart, Inc., 1960).

Magnifico, Leonard X., "Social Promotion and Special Education," *School and Society,* LXXXVI (May 10, 1958), pp. 216–218.

CHAPTER XI. GUIDANCE: THE "COMING" AREA IN THE ELEMENTARY SCHOOL

Barr, John, *Guidance and the Elementary Teacher* (New York: Holt, Winston, and Rinehart, Inc., 1958).

California State Department of Education, "Good Guidance Practices in the Elementary School," *Bulletin,* XXIV, No. 6 (August, 1955).

Cottingham, Harold F., *Guidance in Elementary Schools* (Bloomington, Ill.: McKnight and McKnight, 1956).

Crow, Lester D., *An Introduction to Guidance* (New York: American Book Company, 1960).

Foster, Charles, *Guidance for Today's Schools* (Boston: Ginn and Company, 1957).

Jennings, Helen H., *Sociometry in Group Relations* (Washington, D.C.: American Council on Education, 1959).

Johnston, Edgar Grant, *The Role of the Teacher in Guidance* (Englewood Cliffs, N.J.: Prentice-Hall, Inc., 1959).

Knapp, Robert, *Guidance in the Elementary School* (Boston: Allyn and Bacon, Inc., 1959).

Langford, Louise M., *Guidance of the Young Child* (New York: John Wiley and Sons, Inc., 1960).

Martinson, Ruth A., and Harry Smallenburg, *Guidance in Elementary Schools* (Englewood Cliffs, N.J.: Prentice-Hall, Inc., 1958).

Peters, Herman J., *Guidance, A Developmental Approach* (Chicago: Rand McNally and Company, 1959).

Rosecrance, Francis, *School Guidance and Personnel Services* (Boston: Allyn and Bacon, Inc., 1960).

Willey, Roy D., *Guidance in Elementary Education* (New York: Harper and Brothers, 1960).

CHAPTER XII. ACCOUNTING FOR OUR POTENTIAL PRODUCTS

Anderson, Paul S., "Group for Better Reading," *Grade Teacher,* LXXIII (March, 1956), p. 19.

Bremer, Neville, "First Grade Achievement Under Different Plans of Grouping," *Elementary English,* XXXV (May, 1958), pp. 324–326.

Brown, Edwin John and Arthur Thomas Phelps, *Managing the Classroom,* 2nd Edition (New York: The Ronald Press Co., 1961).

Dallmann, Martha, "Mexico," *Grade Teacher,* LXXIII (April, 1956), p. 54.

Gallagher, Catherine, "Homogeneous Grouping," *New York State Education,* XLIV (May, 1957), p. 538.

Greco, Anthony J., "Group Methods in Primary Grades," *The Arithmetic Teacher,* IV (February, 1957), pp. 28–29.

Grieder, Calvin, Truman M. Pierce, and William Everett Rosenstengel, *Public School Administration,* 2nd Edition (New York: The Ronald Press Co., 1961).

Hansford, Byron W., *Guidebook for School Principals* (New York: The Ronald Press Co., 1961).

Heffernan, Helen, et al, "Facing the Problem of Grouping for Instruction," *California Journal of Elementary Education,* XXVII (November, 1958), p. 71.

Heyl, Helen May, "Grouping Children for Instruction," *The National Elementary Principal,* XXXVIII (December, 1958), pp. 6–9.

Netzley, Harold W., "Meeting Individual Differences," *American School Board Journal,* CXXXVII (November, 1958), p. 36.

Stoops, Emery, and Max L. Rafferty, Jr., *Practices and Trends in School Administration* (Boston: Ginn and Company, 1961), Chapter 12.

Vernon, Philip E., "Education and the Psychology of Individual Differences," *Harvard Educational Review,* XXVIII (Spring, 1958), pp. 91–104.

Witzler, Wilson F., "Reporting Pupil Progress," *The Grade Teacher,* LXXVI (April, 1959), pp. 20–21.

CHAPTER XIII. PUPIL SERVICES AT THE ELEMENTARY LEVEL

Cromwell, Gertrude E., "School Nurse Is Part of School Program," *The Nation's Schools,* LIX (February, 1957), pp. 63–64.

Fauble, Ed, "A Functional School Office," *The National Elementary Principal,* XL (October, 1960), pp. 20–21.

Hicks, William V., and Marshall C. Jameson, *The Elementary School Principal at Work* (Englewood Cliffs, N.J.: Prentice-Hall, Inc., 1957).

Langton, Clair V., Ross L. Allen, and Philip Wexler, *School Health—Organization and Services* (New York: The Ronald Press Co., 1961).

Pilson, Lois McAlister, "Cooperation Developed an Elementary School Library," Instructor, LX (November, 1958), p. 79.

Shuster, Albert H., and Wilson F. Wetzler, *Leadership in Elementary School Administration and Supervision* (Boston: Houghton Mifflin Company, 1958).

Spain, Charles R., Harold D. Drummond, and John I. Goodlad, *Educational Leadership and the Elementary School Principal* (New York: Holt, Winston and Rinehart, Inc., 1956).

CHAPTER XIV. ORGANIZING FOR EFFECTIVE PERSONNEL ADMINISTRATION

American Association of School Administrators, *Staff Relations in School Administration*. Thirty-third Yearbook (Washington, D.C.: the Association, 1955).

Campbell, Roald F., and Russell T. Gregg, *Administrative Behavior in Education* (New York: Harper and Brothers, 1957).

Chandler, B. J., and Paul V. Petty, *Personnel Management in School Administration* (New York: World Book Company, 1955).

Department of Elementary School Principals, *Elementary School Principalship*. Thirty-seventh Yearbook (Washington, D.C.: National Education Association, 1958).

Grieder, Calvin, Truman M. Pierce, and William Everett Rosenstengel, *Public School Administration* (New York: The Ronald Press Co., 1961).

Lemke, B. C., and James Don Edwards, *Administrative Control and Executive Action* (Columbus, Ohio: Charles E. Merrill Books, Inc., 1961).

Saunders, J., "Job Analysis, Junior High School Principals," *National Association of Secondary Principals Bulletin,* XLIII (December, 1959), pp. 46–55.

Stoops, Emery, and M. L. Rafferty, Jr., *Practices and Trends in School Administration* (New York: Ginn and Company, 1961).

Weber, Clarence A., *Personnel Problems of School Administration* (New York: McGraw-Hill Book Co., 1954).

CHAPTER XV. POLICIES, RULES AND REGULATIONS IN SCHOOL PERSONNEL ADMINISTRATION

National Commission on Teacher Education and Professional Standards, *The Education of New Teachers* (Washington, D.C.: National Education Association, 1958).

National Education Association, Research Division, "NEA and Teacher's Welfare: Sick Leave," *National Education Association Journal,* XLV (March, 1956), pp. 170–171.

National Education Association, Research Division, "Why Few School Systems Use Merit Ratings," *Research Bulletin,* XXXIX (May, 1961), pp. 61–63.

Schinnerer, M. C., "Merit Rating," *Nation's Schools,* LIX (June, 1957), pp. 47–48.

Shuster, Albert H., and Wilson F. Wetzler, *Leadership in Elementary School Administration and Supervision* (Boston: Houghton Mifflin Company, 1958).

Staehle, John, *Administrative Handbooks,* U.S. Office of Education Bulletin No. 13 (Washington, D.C.: Government Printing Office, 1960).

Utah School Merit Study Committee, "Report and Recommendations," *Utah School Merit Study* (Salt Lake City: The Committee, November, 1958).

Weber, Clarence A., *Personnel Problems of School Administration* (New York: McGraw-Hill Book Co., 1954).

CHAPTER XVI. ADMINISTRATIVE LEADERSHIP IN BUILDING STAFF MORALE

Bewley, Frederick W., "The Characteristics of Successful School Superintendents" (Unpublished Doctoral dissertation, University of Southern California, 1960).

Clarke, David L., and Arvid J. Burke, "Economic, Legal, and Social Status of Teachers," *Review of Educational Research,* XXV (June, 1955), pp. 239–251.

Cornell, Frances G., "When Should Teachers Share in Making Administrative Decisions?" *Nation's Schools,* LIII (May, 1954), pp. 43–45.

Harap, H., "Many Factors Affect Teacher Morale," *Nation's Schools,* LXIII (June, 1959), pp. 55–57.

Hunter, Elwood C., "Attitudes and Professional Relationships of Teachers: A Study of Teacher Morale," *Journal of Experimental Education,* XXIII (June, 1955), pp. 345–352.

Mathis, C., "Relationship Between Salary Policies and Teacher Morale," *Journal of Educational Psychology,* L (December, 1959), pp. 275–279.

Medsker, Leland L., "The Job of the Elementary School Principal as Viewed by Teachers" (Unpublished Doctoral dissertation, Stanford University, 1954).

Moore, Harold E., and Newell B. Walters, *Personnel Administration in Education* (New York: Harper and Brothers, 1955).

Redefer, Frederick L., "Factors That Affect Teacher Morale," *Nation's Schools,* LXIII (February, 1959), p. 59.

Silverman, Martin, "Principals—What Are You Doing to Teacher Morale?" *Educational Administration and Supervision,* XLIII (April, 1957), p. 205.

Index